DÜRER

By Wilhelm Waetzoldt

PHAIDON

DÜRER'S SELF-PORTRAIT. 1498. Detail from Plate 8.

DÜRER
AND HIS TIMES

BY WILHELM WAETZOLDT

LONDON: PHAIDON PRESS LTD

TRANSLATED FROM THE GERMAN
BY R. H. BOOTHROYD

MADE IN GREAT BRITAIN
TEXT PRINTED BY TONBRIDGE PRINTERS LTD · TONBRIDGE
COLOUR PLATES PRINTED BY HENRY STONE & SON LTD · BANBURY
PHOTOGRAVURE PLATES PRINTED BY CLARKE & SHERWELL LTD · NORTHAMPTON
BOUND BY KEY & WHITING LTD · LONDON

CONTENTS

THE PLATES

DÜRER AND HIS TIMES

Numbers in the margin refer to the plates following the text. Figures in the text preceded by the letter 'L' refer to Lippmann's edition of Dürer's drawings (Berlin 1883 ff., seven volumes).

CHAPTER ONE

ORIGIN AND STATUS

THE earth in which Dürer was laid to rest was not the soil from which his family sprang. In the autumn of his days, when he was over fifty, Dürer studied the origin of his family and, with that delight in self-revelation which was peculiar to him, recorded all that he knew of his father and forefathers. But for this document, which has come down to us in copies, it is unlikely that anyone would have questioned his Franconian origin. Nevertheless, Germany was only the second home of the Dürer family. Dürer's birth, life, work and death connect him with Nuremberg and Franconia, but the history of his forefathers leads us back to Hungary.

The original home of the Dürer family was in the no longer existing village of Eytas (Aytòs), near the town of Gyula, about forty miles from Grosswardein (Nagy Varad). The name Dürer is derived from the name of the village—Eytas means 'door' ('Tür'). Dürer's father signed himself 'Türer'; his coat-of-arms and his son's travelling seal show an open door. But although the Dürers came from Hungary, it does not follow that they were of Magyar blood. Scholars like Georg Habich and Ferdinand Laban have described the long-haired head of the wooden model for Hans Schwarz' Dürer medal (Brunswick) as a type inexplicable without a strain of Magyar blood, but one cannot help asking whether they would really have detected in this head the 'unmistakable' features of a herdsman from the steppes, if they had known nothing of the Hungarian provenance of the Dürer family. Carefully tended long hair and beards were not an exclusive perquisite of the Hungarians, they were an ordinary and fashionable feature of Late Gothic personal adornment. Dürer's marked, but harmless, masculine vanity and his meticulous care for his external appearance could have invented this personal style of coiffure and beard without any 'strain' of Hungarian blood.

The assumption that the Dürer family were of Magyar peasant descent is contradicted by the typically Germanic countenance of the artist's father, as shown by the loving and reverently accurate portraits made by the son. It is difficult to believe that the grandfather's features were those of another racial type. It is more probable that Dürer's forebears were descended from the German colonists whom King Bela IV summoned to devastated Hungary after the Mongolian invasion (1241). There they would have worked in the ore mines or as cattle-breeders, for how many generations we cannot tell, but in any case until the grandfather, Antony Dürer, came as a boy from the village of Aytòs to Gyula and set up as a goldsmith (1410). For three generations the family was transplanted from the wide-open steppes to the confined surroundings of the workshop. Its members exchanged the warm hides of horses for the cool smoothness of precious metals, they learned the use of the saddler's awl and the cleric's pen. Of the three sons of the goldsmith Antony and his wife Elizabeth, Albrecht, born in 1427, followed his father's trade, Laszlo, the second son, became a bridle-maker, and

Hungarian Origin Name, Coat-of-arms

Ill. facing p. 8

Albrecht Dürer the Elder

the third a priest in Grosswardein. After serving his apprenticeship in the little Hungarian town, Albrecht, the goldsmith, felt the desire to travel. After visiting the Netherlands, ruled at that time by splendour-loving Burgundian princes, he brought his family to Germany in 1455. There he was joined by his nephew Niklas, son of the bridle-maker Laszlo, who entered his uncle's house and goldsmith's workshop as an apprentice and therefore lived side by side with his cousin, the young Albrecht Dürer. In view of his family's origin, Niklas took the surname of Unger, and he became a master goldsmith, first in Nuremberg and afterwards in Cologne, where Dürer visited him on his journey to the Netherlands.

The Move to Nuremberg

That Albrecht Dürer the Elder should have chosen to settle in Nuremberg, may have been partly due to the fact that he had stayed there during the youthful days of his apprenticeship and as a militiaman had even taken part in the somewhat inglorious expedition of the Nurembergers against the robber knights of Waldenfels in Veste Lichtenberg. These facts were discovered by Gümbel in the city archives, but sober economic considerations must have played a greater part in his decision than these purely personal motives.

Zenith of the Goldsmith's Art

The imperial cities of Southern and Western Germany had the same significance as the princely cities of the Netherlands. They were centres in which the craftsmen of precious metals flourished, for the prosperity and mode of life of the ruling classes assured them a constant demand for objects in gold and silver. During his stay in Germany, the Italian Enea Silvio Piccolomini was astounded at the abundance of gold and silver ware in German houses. The goldsmiths of Strasbourg, Cologne, Nuremberg and Augsburg were not only highly respected craftsmen, whose fame was carried far beyond the walls of their cities, but, as their numbers steadily increased, they also formed a powerful and perfectly organized guild. A goldsmith's workshop was by no means the worst cradle for artistic talent, especially if it were situated in an important commercial city like Nuremberg. Since 1420 the Nurembergers had been complete masters of their own town, to which even the castle belonged, the Burgrave Frederick VI having sold it to the city when he became ruler of Mark Brandenburg.

When Dürer the Elder came to Nuremberg, the 'families' were just celebrating the marriage of one of their members—Philipp Pirckheimer, whose nephew Willibald was to become Albrecht Dürer's closest friend. It was to a house belonging to Willibald Pirckheimer's father Johann that the elder Dürer moved when in 1467, at the age of forty, he married his master's daughter, Barbara Holper, who was then only fifteen years old. He had 'served' the old goldsmith Hieronymus Holper for twelve years, 'a long time', as Dürer the Younger notes in his family chronicle in 1524.

Birth of Albrecht Dürer

On 21st May, 1471 a son, Albrecht, was born to the Dürer couple—the third of their eighteen children. This was perhaps the first time in the intellectual history of the country that a German family from abroad had given birth to a genius who brought glory to the family name in the original home of the race. It is worth recording that about a hundred years after Dürer's father, the forebears of Johann Sebastian Bach also migrated from Hungary to Germany, in their case to Thuringia.

None of the gold and silver ware created by the diligent hands of Dürer the
Elder has been identified, though it is possible that much of it has been preserved.
In a letter written from Linz to his wife in 1492, the master mentions some work
for the Emperor Frederick III. It may have been a goblet commissioned by the
Nuremberg Council. Documents have come to light concerning drinking vessels
which Bishop Uriel of Posen ordered in 1486. In 1489 Dürer made two mon-
strances for the Hospital of the Holy Ghost in Nuremberg; one of them was to
hold a thorn from Christ's Crown of Thorns, the other a knot from the rope with
which He was scourged. Then there are the little silver shields which the master
made for the town musicians—and that is all. Dürer's father was appointed to
positions of trust in the guild and in local government. From 1482 to 1488 he
was a 'juror' of the guild, in 1482 he was appointed 'street captain' (Gassenhaupt-
mann), and he also held honorary appointments in the goldsmiths' office of
inspection and as assayer to the mint. From 1480 on he sold his gold and silver
ware in a shop at the Rathaus.

In 1475 Dürer the Elder bought a house of his own, 'Unter der Vesten', for
200 guilders. It lay in what may be termed the 'Latin Quarter' of old Nuremberg.
Quite close to it were the houses of the painter Wolgemut, the physician and
chronicler Hartmann Schedel, the publisher Koberger and the calligrapher
Neudörfer. Albrecht Dürer's words and portraits confirm what documents tell us
of his father—he was a clever master of his craft, a clean-living, experienced man,
taciturn and god-fearing, a conscientious and understanding father. It was with no
light heart that he allowed his son to become a painter, when he could no longer keep
him in his workshop; the thrifty and cautious man regretted the time his son had
'lost', working, embossing, enchasing, enamelling and engraving precious metals.

When the fifteen-year-old Dürer drew his father (L. 589, Vienna), he had in
front of him in his working clothes a careworn, thin-lipped, prematurely aged
man, from beneath whose cap sprouted grey hair, whose eyes were slightly
drawn as are those of all engaged in fine precision work. The youthful draughtsman has had difficulty with the folds and his father's left hand has disappeared, but
neck and face are modelled with the sharpness and firmness of line of a copperplate
engraving. There is no inscription to attest this drawing and some scholars think
that it is either a self-portrait by Dürer the Elder, or else by an unknown Nuremberg master. The attribution to the younger Dürer is, in our opinion, confirmed
by a comparison with the youthful self-portrait of 1484. That the sitter is, in any
case, Dürer's father is proved by a glance at the portrait of the old Dürer which
his son painted in 1490 (Florence, Uffizi). Between the two portraits lie the years
during which the goldsmith's apprentice was transformed into a youthful journeyman painter. In 1486 Dürer drew his father with a small ornamental figure in his
hand, as a symbol of the goldsmith's craft which the son had just renounced; in
1490, when Dürer left Wolgemut's studio to begin his Wanderjahre, he applied
his newly acquired and already so well mastered art in order to paint his father
and perhaps his mother as well. This time he put into his father's hands, which he
had now learned how to draw, the rosary of a devout worshipper; his father is no

longer in working clothes, but in his Sunday attire. The alert tension of his father's head in 1486 has been transformed into thoughtful seriousness. Dürer took with him during the years of his apprenticeship and wanderings the impression of this head, modelled by the hardships of life, but not striving against destiny. The back of the panel bears the double coat-of-arms: the door of the Dürers and the leaping goat of the Holpers. Very probably it is one half of a diptych, of which the other, lost half, showed the likeness of Dürer's mother.

2

Seven years later Dürer painted his father again (copy or original? London, National Gallery). There is nothing to denote the sitter's profession and no symbolical accessory to indicate the mood of the time. The body is built up into the picture with blocklike weight and breadth and we are struck by the severe glance of the eyes inured to care and pain. According to an old inventory, the picture was a pendant to a self-portrait of Dürer which the Nuremberg City Council presented to King Charles I of England. The solemn mien justifies its choice as a gift for a king, who in these two portraits would receive from an official source two examples of the best type of man that Germany could produce. Dürer had learned during his sojourn in Italy to see himself and others in this grandiose and monumental manner. Is it illusion, or has the human warmth, which made the earlier portrait of his father so pleasing, given way to the cool breath of the impressions received from the paintings of Northern Italy?

Portrait of his Mother

13

We are compensated for the absence of a painted likeness of Dürer's mother by the monumental charcoal drawing which he made in 1514, two months before her death (L. 40, Berlin). 'A pretty, upright maid'—to quote Dürer's own words—when at the age of fifteen she married the goldsmith Dürer, this woman brought eighteen children into the world, 'often had the pestilence and many other severe diseases, suffered great poverty, derision, insults, mocking words, terrors and great afflictions, yet she never became vindictive.' These words written by the son about his mother lead us to conclude that Dürer's parents led lives full of care. The mother must have experienced the cruelty of her fellow-creatures, the dangers of life in a mediaeval town repeatedly afflicted by epidemics, famine and economic crises. Dürer's wife, too, must have had her fill of derision, insults and mocking words when she sat in the fair-booth, selling her husband's woodcuts and copperplate engravings. Even Dürer's best friend Willibald Pirckheimer, when the master had hardly closed his eyes, did not shrink from letting his widow feel the arrogance of his class. Two years after his father's death—in 1504—Dürer took his 'pious' mother into his own house. She was poor—the old goldsmith had left her nothing. From then on the widow sat in her room, thinking only of the spiritual welfare of her children. When Albrecht went in and out of her room, 'her words were always: "May Christ be with you!" ' Dürer's mother lived a narrow life and thus became narrow-minded. Fear of what the next day would bring forth and the struggle to meet the next need left furrows of care and apprehension on her face. The rest was the result of old age, which, as Dürer says in his Treatise on Proportion, is 'uneven, gnarled, wrinkled' and 'consumes the flesh'.

For nine long years Dürer's mother gradually declined, until her last illness overcame her so suddenly that one morning her relatives had to break down her door. After another year's grievous suffering she closed her eyes—those unusually large eyes which in Dürer's drawing seem still to belong completely to life. Of her death Dürer writes: 'I saw how Death gave her two great stabs in the heart and how she closed her mouth and eyes and passed away in the midst of her pain.' But Death made her head seem younger and nobler: 'in death she looked more beautiful than she had done in life'.

Death of Dürer's Mother

At the time of his mother's death, Dürer had been living for twenty years in childless wedlock with his wife Agnes, daughter of Hans Frey. The children whom Providence denied to Dürer flutter and glide as little angels throughout his pictorial work. His marriage was arranged in the sensible, realistic manner of earlier times by the elder Dürer and Frey, and accepted willingly by Albrecht and Agnes. For the Dürers this wedding meant relationship with a prosperous family of higher social standing than their own. Hans Frey was a kind of universal genius, originally a coppersmith, but with a peculiar gift for all the mechanical arts, and also a musician. From his workshop there went forth figures for all kinds of fountains, so popular throughout the Middle Ages and down to the beginning of the eighteenth century, for instance small portable fountains for banqueting tables. About three years after his marriage Dürer drew a table centrepiece with fountains (L. 223, London).

Dürer's Marriage

The Father-in-law

Dürer's father-in-law thus belonged to that great school of Nuremberg masters of metal-work, which produced the makers of guns and armour, the inventors of musical boxes and of the pocket watches known to the world as 'Nuremberg eggs', the precision-mechanics who turned out astronomical instruments, compasses and dividers. It was to visit the compass-makers that the celebrated astronomer Regiomontanus came to Nuremberg in 1471. These trades required just as much skill and ability as gold- and silversmith's work—mastery of the most delicate technical processes, the utmost conscientiousness of the craftsman, and Nuremberg 'wit'. Dürer stood in close relationship to this world of thought and work, as is proved by his devices for perspective drawing and for sighting, his admirable drawings of instruments, e.g. the scales and the compasses in his 'Melancolia'. That Dürer, who sprang from a goldsmith's workshop, whose father and two grandfathers had followed the same trade, whose brother and cousin became goldsmiths, should have taken an expert interest and share in his father-in-law's work, by making designs for such metal instruments, is highly probable. Hans Frey was related by marriage to members of the Council, and was not only a craftsman, but also a municipal official. Until 1486 he held the office of municipal measurer of honey and nuts, after 1487 he was steward ('Hauswirt') of the Rathaus. He provided food and drink for the convivial councillors and was custodian of the Council's silver. There were many curious offices in this circle of municipal functionaries to which Dürer's father and his mother's father Holper also belonged; such were the city measurers of coal, grain, salt, fruit and hops, all forming part of the organization of wholesale trade, which compelled both

The Art of making Measuring Instruments

103

buyers and sellers to make use of the city weighing-machines and to pay fees to the weighers and measurers.

Hans Frey was able to give his daughter a dowry of 200 guilders—about £500 according to modern values. The marriage was therefore arranged by the parents before Dürer returned to Nuremberg from his wanderings in 1494. A great deal has been written about Dürer's married life, precisely because so little is known about it. It was probably as remote from the romanticism of an artist's marriage as it was from the depths of despair which Pirckheimer endeavours to impute to it. As docile students of ancient authors, the humanists thought that a certain misogynism was becoming. In his days of rancour, personal sorrow and general animosity, Dürer's friend accused the artist's wife of being 'nagging, jealous, shrewish' and reproached her for her sulky piety and petty avarice. Gustav Pauli has tried to deduce these unpleasant characteristics from her features. Dürer remained silent about his marriage. As a young bridegroom he called his wife 'my Agnes', but he never spoke of her with the same warmth as he did of his father and mother. The uncouth jest in one of his letters to Pirckheimer must be attributed more to the completely unsentimental relationship between man and wife in earlier times than to any personal feeling on Dürer's part. We are repeatedly surprised by the lack of sentiment and feeling in the conjugal life of Albrecht and Agnes—in so far as we know anything about it. On his journeys to Italy Dürer left his wife at home; he took her with him to the Low Countries, but Agnes did not play a very brilliant rôle by the side of her celebrated husband. Dürer agreed with his host in Antwerp that he himself should eat with the master of the house, Planckvelt, but that Agnes and Susanne, the maid who had accompanied her from Nuremberg, should take their meals 'upstairs in the kitchen'. Usually Dürer did eat with his host, but he used to sit in the guest-room 'alone with myself'. Often he was invited by patrons and great noblemen, or went to eat in other inns. On the occasion of the great banquet in Dürer's honour, the artists of Antwerp invited Agnes and Susanne as well. The amiable Italian Bombelli also saw the two women in his house. Perhaps Frau Dürer felt more comfortable alone with Susanne, with whom she could speak in Nuremberg dialect, than she did in the company of the arrogant and elegant wives of the Antwerp merchants.

The simple, modest head of Frau Dürer, neither beautiful nor ugly, solid, but becoming sharp and hard with age, makes one or two appearances in her husband's works, but we possess no authenticated painting of her. Of the five attested drawings of Dürer's wife, the most pleasing is the pen-drawing of 1495 (L. 457, Vienna), in which she appears as a young bride, with a schoolgirl's 'pigtail'. Her not-too-easy life by Dürer's side has already given her a firmly closed mouth and fixed gaze, and girlish insouciance is soon replaced by a feminine energy (silver-point drawing of 1504, half-destroyed, L. 133, Breslau). Her head, with the imprint of the dignity of a hardworking married life, appears twice in the sketch-books of the journey to the Netherlands. This mature woman in her forties, in Flemish costume, was drawn by Dürer in Antwerp, 'because we have been joined

Dürer's Married Life

Frau Agnes

Portraits of Agnes Dürer

6

14

together in wedlock for 26½ years' (L. 64, Berlin). The second sketch (L. 424, Vienna) bears the inscription: 'On the Rhine—my wife near Boppard'. 38

The understandable human desire to discover more portraits of Frau Dürer has led to a number of alleged identifications: Meder, Dodgson and Pauli claim to recognize Frau Dürer in a half-length of 1497 (L. 113, Bremen). Pauli also claims 7 as portraits of Agnes the painted head of a woman with hair let down (1497, Paris, Bibliothèque Nationale) and the Berlin charcoal drawing of 1503 (L. 5), 25 showing a woman with a coif. The desire to endow Dürer with a beautiful wife has even led to the inclusion among the likenesses of Agnes of the portrait of a woman painted during the journey to Venice in 1506 (Berlin, Deutsches Museum), 29 because the embroidery of the Italian dress reveals the letters A. D.

It is wrong to conclude from Dürer's complaints about his 'poverty' that his *Dürer's* day-to-day life was constantly overshadowed by financial worries. He was not a *Financial* Bohemian, and still less was he an academic professor; we must try to think of *Circumstances* him as a man of his times and his profession. In money matters Dürer, like many artists, was meticulous and reckless at the same time. He entered every Pfennig in his notebook, turned every florin over three times before he spent it, but at the same time gave away his prints like a rich man. He was glad to be able to save the cost of two midday and two evening meals when his wife and her maid were invited out, but he brought back from the Netherlands twelve pairs of gloves as presents for ladies of Nuremberg. Goethe, the worldly-wise son of a prosperous family, shook his head over Dürer: 'The poor man! The way he miscalculated in Venice and made an agreement with the priests, whereby he wasted weeks and months! And on the Netherlands journey, the way he exchanged his beautiful works, with which he had hoped to make a fortune, for parrots, and, in order to save tips, painted the portraits of domestics who brought him a plate of fruit! I find a poor fool of an artist like that really touching . . .' Nevertheless, on the whole the poor fool did not calculate so badly. When it came to important deals, he was a good salesman and he had the thrifty nature of a craftsman. Compared with the takings of contemporary Italian painters, the fees he received were modest, but they were big enough to raise Dürer to bourgeois prosperity, to allow him to indulge his expensive taste for collecting and to leave his widow the not inconsiderable legacy of 6,848 Guilders, 7 Pfund, 4 Pfennigs.

Agnes Frey's dowry of 200 guilders must have been the foundation of Dürer's economic independence. When he had become a master and burgher of Nuremberg, he set up in 1497 his own workshop, with a printing press and journeymen. Before that he had worked for his godfather, the printer and publisher Anton Koberger. In 1470 the latter had founded a printing press and bookshop in *Anton* Nuremberg, which he developed with time into an important publishing and *Koberger's* printing business. He employed more than a hundred journeymen, compositors, *Press* correctors, printers, binders, illuminators and woodcutters. During the heyday of his business Koberger had his own printing works in Lyons and depots for the products of his firm in sixteen towns. For Hartmann Schedel's Chronicle of the World, printed in 1495, he employed Nuremberg artists, such as Dürer's teacher

Wolgemut and Wilhelm Pleydenwurff, to draw the woodcut illustrations. It was therefore a bold step on Dürer's part when, in 1498, he had his first great work, the set of woodcuts of the Apocalypse, printed by Koberger, but published by his own publishing firm, thus freeing himself from the big firm and from the patronage of his important godfather.

Sales Organization

For the sale of his graphic works, Dürer also made use of the women of his family. His mother—when illness did not confine her to the house—sat in the market booth at the Heiltumsfest in Nuremberg, at the great fairs in Augsburg, Frankfurt and Ingolstadt, and sold Dürer's works. The wagons of friendly Nuremberg merchant families such as the Tuchers and the Imhoffs carried parcels of Dürer's prints throughout the land. The robber knight Kunz Schott once seized a package of Dürer's works—and was probably disappointed with his booty! Colporteurs like Jacob Arnolt distributed the prints, and unwelcome advertisement was given to Dürer's works by the copying of his engravings by skilful artists of the Netherlands (Israel von Meckenem, Wenzel von Olmütz) and Italy (Marcantonio). Dürer had continually to think of his market and the possibility of extending it. Even in Germany his works were copied; for example, his Apocalypse series was reprinted in 1502 by Hieronymus Greff in Strasbourg. The only protection against this was a so-called 'privilegium', such as Dürer sought to obtain from the Emperor and which his widow received in 1528 from Charles V for the four books of his Treatise on Human Proportions. The Council of Nuremberg had continually to protect Dürer against dealers who forged his monogram, and the plan for his second journey to Venice may have been connected with matters of this sort. In any case, during his journey to the Netherlands the sale of woodcuts and engravings, which was in the careful hands of Frau Agnes, played an important rôle. The years between 1497 and 1504 must have been busy times for Dürer's workshop, although we have no information as to the sums of money received for his altar-pieces and portraits.

Copies

Dürer's Fees

Dürer's numerous commissions (e.g. for the Elector Frederick the Wise, for the Tuchers, the Paumgärtners and the Krells) did not, however, bring in sufficient money to finance a journey to Italy, and for this he had to resort to a loan from his friend Pirckheimer. This debt had to be paid off, not only by carrying out the numerous commissions which Pirckheimer asked Dürer to undertake for him during his stay in Venice, but also guilder by guilder after Dürer's return home. Dürer took with him to Italy five of his pictures, which he sold for 100 guilders, and the commission for the 'Feast of the Rose-garlands' brought him another 110 guilders. We do not know what fees he drew from members of the German colony for portraits of these wealthy merchants and their wives. In any case, Dürer was in flourishing circumstances after his journey to Italy. He first spent 100 guilders on purchasing the best Nuremberg colours; in 1507 he freed his father's house, 'Unter der Vesten', from the mortgage upon it by a single payment of 116 guilders, and in 1509 he purchased a very fine house at the Tiergärtner Tor. Dürer paid over half of the purchase price, which amounted to 275 Rhenish guilders, in cash, and the remainder by redeeming a mortgage and other small

Purchase of a House

DÜRER MEDALLIONS. Berlin, Münzkabinett.
Above: Medal by Mathis Gebel, 1527—Below: Medal by Hans Schwarz, 1520.

IMITATOR OF DAUCHER (?): DUEL BETWEEN DÜRER AND LAZARUS SPENGLER.
Relief on Solnhofen slate. Berlin, Deutsches Museum.

charges on the house. In addition, he bought for 90 Rhenish guilders in 1512 a garden in the Bamberger Strasse. When one remembers that in those days it was possible to live on 50 guilders a year and that the highest salary paid to a Nuremberg official, the imperial magistrate (Schultheiss), was 600 guilders a year, one can gain an idea of the relative value of Dürer's receipts and expenses. One can also understand how attractive must have been the offer from the City of Venice, which wanted to take Dürer into its service at a fixed salary of 200 ducats a year.

If Dürer, and more particularly his wife, were, in spite of this, in financial difficulties, this must be partly attributed to Dürer's mania for collecting, which led him to purchase works of art, curiosities, weapons, costly clothing, furs and jewellery, but it was also partly due to his kindness. He says that he suffered heavy losses, 'because I lent, and received nothing in return, and the same with journeymen who could not pay. One of them once died in Rome, with loss of my property'. Such conditions explain the painful correspondence between Dürer and his rich patron Jacob Heller in Frankfurt am Main concerning the raising of the stipulated fee for the altar-piece of the Assumption of the Virgin; Dürer was able to get the fee raised from 130 to 200 guilders. Throughout his life Dürer bitterly resented the fact that his native city only twice gave him commissions. For the portraits of the Emperors Charles and Sigismund as decorations for the Chamber of Reliquaries, he received in 1512 a fee of 85 florins, 1 Pfund, 9 Pfennigs and 10 shillings. For his 'Visierung' (i.e. his designs) for the hall of the Rathaus in 1522, he received 100 guilders.

In Nuremberg—and in Germany as a whole—there was a lack of those splendid and luxurious surroundings in which the pampered artists of the Italian Renaissance were accustomed to live and work. Despite the Tuchers and the Imhoffs, the Fuggers and the Welsers, there were no patrons of the stature of the Medici. It is true that the Emperor Maximilian kept many an artist busy with his commissions, but he was a poor emperor. When it came to payment, His Majesty wished to honour his debt at the expense of the Nuremberg Council, to whom he gave instructions in 1512 to exempt the artist from all taxes, imposts and dues— a proposal which Dürer regretfully declined. The annual pension of 100 guilders, granted to Dürer by the Emperor in 1515, had to be paid by Nuremberg out of the taxes due to the Kaiser. In 1518 the sum of 200 guilders was allotted to Dürer for his work in connection with the Triumphal Car, but this, too, was to be paid on St. Martin's Day 1519 out of the city taxes; Maximilian died at the beginning of 1519 and the city raised difficulties. In vain Dürer offered his house as surety, in case the new Emperor should refuse to honour his predecessor's obligation. Like Sebastian Brant of Strasbourg, he had to make up his mind to present in person a written confirmation of Maximilian's bequest to the court of the newly elected ruler of Germany, Charles V. This involved a journey to the Low Countries. In 1520 Dürer at last received the 'confirmacia', i.e. the ratification of his annual pension—but nothing more. The imperial account-books show payments to Dürer of 300 and 200 guilders in 1519 and 100 guilders in 1520, but we do not

*Money
Worries*

64

*Dürer's
Pension*

B

know for what works these were, nor whether they were in settlement of promises made by Maximilian.

Homage from the Netherlands

The journey to the Netherlands brought Dürer great moral successes. Like the Venetian Republic at an earlier date, the city of Antwerp offered him an annual salary of 300 'philips' if he would remain in the Netherlands. But Dürer once more resisted the temptation. Germany did not lose him to the Netherlands, as Switzerland later lost her son Hans Holbein the Younger to England. From the artistic standpoint this journey was profitable to Dürer, but when he came to reckon up the financial result of the journey—and he entered the smallest items in his notebook—he found that he had not made, but lost money.

Last Years

In the last years of his life Dürer prospered. After the Netherlands journey commissions for portraits flowed in to his workshop. In 1524 he owned two houses in the town and a capital of 1,000 guilders, which he lent to the city of Nuremberg at 5% interest. He was in a position to be able to present his painting of the 'Four Apostles' to the City, which, however, spontaneously paid him a fee of 114 Rhenish guilders. The Nuremberg Council knew what Dürer and his fame signified for the city. Every possible favour was shown to the artist. By causing certain work to be done on his house Dürer in some way violated the building regulations and was therefore condemned to pay a fine. He appealed against this and in 1527 received the answer that 'one is well disposed towards him, but as regards his secret compartment (presumably a closet), he cannot be treated differently from others; nevertheless, as soon as he has paid the fine, it will be refunded to him'.

Dürer's Status as a Burgher

By residence, profession and marriage Albrecht Dürer became a burgher of Nuremberg. The father had migrated from Hungary, the son became an ardent Franconian, a headstrong Southern German, wilful to the point of obstinacy, endowed with an imagination which bordered on dreaming. The Dürer family sprang from the peasantry, or at least from the professional classes of a country district, but his father's migration and his own marriage raised Dürer to the class of the city bourgeoisie. His life fell in a time in which the Late Gothic artisans were developing into a freer, socially higher community of artists. By his habits and his attitude towards the essential questions of life Dürer belonged to the sound, often narrow-minded, but at other times heroic citizenry of the German towns. This middle class was circumscribed by the aristocracy of the Council families, who ruled it, and by the intellectual aristocracy of the scholars and artists who sprang from its own ranks. The resulting tension intensified Dürer's life, but also added complications to it. The bourgeoisie in the days of Dürer, Hans Sachs and Luther were the leaders of the community, the most living section of the German nation, the foundation of its art and culture, the pillars of its religious, political and intellectual future. The burghers were not satisfied, comfortably dozing petty bourgeois, they were an aspiring, ambitious section of the nation. Piety and integrity were their watchwords. Their highest law was that conscientiousness by which every achievement was measured, a moral virtue for which Dürer used the word 'diligence' ('Fleiss').

Many of Dürer's joys and sorrows can be understood only if we consider his life from the standpoint of the social conditions and opinions of his time. In Lomazzo's 'Idea' we read that Dürer was so unassuming that he wore his painter's smock in the street—rather like Bramantino, who used to go out with his brush behind his ear. Dürer's father and brothers were artisans, his friends were patricians, his father-in-law belonged to that group of craftsmen who had a share in the administration of the city. In 1509 Dürer entered the Grand Council as a 'nominee' ('Genannter'). Each class had its own pride, its own sense of superiority. How characteristic it is that at the very time when Dürer was at the height of his fame Melanchthon expressed his surprise that an 'ordinary painter' should have fared so well in a wordy battle with the highly respected scholar Pirckheimer. There is an echo of this arrogance of the patricians vis-à-vis the artists in the Dürer anecdote related by Quadt von Kinckelbach in his book, 'Teutscher Nation Herrlichkeit' (1609). The incident took place during Dürer's journey to the Netherlands. During his stay in Cologne the members of the City Council showed the already famous Nuremberg painter Stephan Lochner's painting in the cathedral. ' "This man", they said, "died here in the poorhouse", giving Dürer a nudge, as if to ask what these poor dreamers were thinking about with their art, when they had to live such wretched lives. "Aye", answered Dürer, who had felt the scorn. "You may well brag about that; a fine honour it will be for you that you speak so scornfully of a man through whom you might have gained fame".'

Dürer appreciated all the external marks of his growing fame. For example, the *Marks of Fame* visit of the Doge and the Patriarch to his workshop in Venice, and the homage shown to him in Bologna in 1506, when—as the eyewitness Christian Scheuerl relates—the Italian painters, with true humanistic courtesy, assured him that they were now more ready to die since their longstanding wish to see Albrecht Dürer had been fulfilled. Finally there were the tributes received on the journey to the Netherlands, such as the banquet given to him by the Antwerp artists, when the populace stood on either side 'as if a great man were being brought there', and all bowed with great deference to Dürer. He was proud when the King of Denmark sent for him to have his portrait painted and invited him to table, and it was with full consciousness of his rank as an artist that he took part in the State banquet which the Danish King gave in Brussels for the Emperor, the Regent and the Queen of Spain. The granting of armorial bearings and of a pension by the imperial house thus signified for Dürer not only a great economic success, but also the recognition of his status as an artist and the confirmation of his social position.

Dürer had his share of burgher virtues, but he also had some of the defects of his class. He had the self-consciousness and the demeanour of a man who had risen by his own efforts to the highest level in his profession. He loved order in both big and small matters; he made no secret of his reverence for God-ordained authority, on whose side he placed himself with his painting of the Apostles. He had a consciousness of 'high' and 'low', of a natural division of mankind into classes, a feeling which was deeply instilled in the mind of the Middle Ages, though it was far removed from objectionable class prejudice or mean servility. Similar feelings influenced Luther's political activities.

The Master   Albrecht Dürer thus stands before us as the German 'master', possessing all the qualities which we associate with the term 'master'. Although the painters of Nuremberg were not organized into a guild until 1596, Dürer was not, socially speaking, an artisan, despite the fact that the customs and sense of honour of an artisan were natural to him. To these belong also his conscientiousness in his choice of panels or canvases, his use of the best colours, the careful technical execution, in order that the painting might, as Dürer wrote of the altar-piece commissioned by Jacob Heller, 'remain clean and fresh for 500 years', and finally, if this was stipulated in the contract, the execution by his own hand or the supervision of his assistants. Dürer was a man who, by character and achievement, had authority in his house and his workshop and who felt himself responsible not only for his family, but also for his 'painter boys'. After the death of his father, he took

Hans Dürer into his workshop the youngest of his three brothers christened Hans. 'I would gladly have taken him with me to Venice,' writes Dürer to Pirckheimer in 1506. 'It would have been of advantage both to me and to him, and he would have learned the language.' But the pious old mother at home feared that 'the Heavens would fall on him' and for this reason Dürer asked Pirckheimer to persuade the mother to let Hans enter the workshop of Wolgemut—or any other master— until Dürer's return from Italy. He also asked Pirckheimer to keep an eye on Hans: 'He loses his head over women. Persuade the boy, as well as you can, to study and behave himself until I come back, and not to be a burden to his mother.'

Rules for Apprentices   The educational book which Dürer left unfinished, 'Die Speise der Malerknaben', contains not only instruction on matters pertaining to art, but also certain rules of conduct. Dürer knew from his own bitter experience what went on in workshops. His aim was a moral and spiritual training of the rising generation, an 'education' which should include not only practical workshop matters, but also the formation of character and the conduct of life. Inspired by the spirit of order, simplicity and wholesomeness which prevailed in his own house, Dürer— following Italian literary models —laid down certain rules for young artists: Fear of God, moderation, avoidance of vice, knowledge of Latin, good and purposeful living, sparingness, etc. Dürer was a true master, who could demand everything from others because he never thought of himself—he was a model of patience, devotion to work, integrity and accuracy. It seems a miracle, when we follow his career, how so much temerity could exist side-by-side with so much homeliness and how Dürer could have risen from the warm atmosphere of the workshop to the cool heights of genius.

Subsequent History of the Dürer Family   For the space of four generations the Dürer family emerges into the light of history from the darkness of the ages. Albrecht Dürer died childless. Most of his brothers and sisters soon disappeared. In 1507 one of the three Hans was received as a master into the Nuremberg tailors' guild; it is believed that the portrait of a young man with angular features—a typical sectarian's face (1500, Munich,

PORTRAIT OF AN UNKNOWN WOMAN. 1500–1506. Paris, Bibliothèque Nationale

DÜRER'S COAT OF ARMS

(1523)

22

Ältere Pinakothek)—represents this tailor Hans Dürer. In 1524 only three out of the eighteen brothers and sisters were still alive: Albrecht, his brother Hans, the painter, born in 1490, and Andreas, known as 'Endres', a goldsmith. The careers of these two brothers can be followed only for a short time. Five paintings are now attributed to Hans Dürer—all of them very disappointing. His destiny led him—as it did other Nuremberg artists, e.g. Veit Stoss and Hans Süss of Kulmbach —to Poland, where he lived as court painter in Cracow until his death in 1534. His brother Andreas seems to have inherited his property. In 1514, when this 'Endres' became a master goldsmith in Nuremberg, he was drawn by Albrecht

32

104

(L. 532 and 533, Vienna). This gaunt man appears once again in profile, with flattened nose, in Dürer's enigmatic etching on iron of 1516: 'Despair'. Andreas Dürer survived his brother Albrecht and inherited the old paternal house 'Unter der Vesten', which he sold in 1538. He prolonged the race of the Dürers for one more generation; he had a daughter Constantia, who married the goldsmith Kilian Proger (from Prague?).

Thus ends the brief family history of the Dürers. The end, like the beginning, is in a goldsmith's workshop, in the modest circumstances of an artisan family.

End of the Dürer Epoch

The artistic generation of the Dürer epoch, like the Dürer family, disappeared very soon after the master's death. By the middle of the sixteenth century many of the foremost painters and sculptors whom Providence had bestowed on Germany had died. Adam Krafft (died 1509), Bartholomäus Zeitblom (died after 1517) and Hans von Kulmbach (died 1522) had preceded Dürer to the tomb. In 1528, the year of his death, Peter Vischer the Younger and Matthias Grünewald (Mathis Neidhardt Gothardt) also died. Peter Vischer the Elder died in 1529; Riemenschneider and Burgkmair in 1531; Veit Stoss in 1533; Albrecht Altdorfer in 1538. The next decade saw the death of Hans Holbein the Younger (1543) and Hans Baldung Grien (1545). Hans Sebald Beham died in 1550. Hans Lautensack and Augustin Hirschvogel survived the middle of the century, as did Wolf Huber and Lucas Cranach the Elder, both of whom died in 1553. One other brilliant star of German painting was to arise and shine, but only for a few decades, until the dawn of the seventeenth century—Adam Elsheimer (1578–1610).

CHAPTER TWO

SELF-CHARACTERIZATION

THE lack of restraint in nineteenth-century biographies was a form of curiosity posing as scientific investigation. Proper appreciation of great men should be based on respect. We ought not to want to know the details of a great man's career merely for the sake of knowing them; we ought to study careers in order to find out of what stuff great men are made. That is the question we must ask ourselves when we approach Dürer, and we must hope to find the answer in the portraits of himself which he has given us in his art and in his writings.

Dürer's self-portraits, both painted and sketched, his diaries, letters, poems, autobiographical notes and scientific writings contain a characterization of himself such as we do not possess of any other German artist of the fifteenth and sixteenth centuries. The urge to examine the depths of one's being, to know oneself, is not peculiar to Dürer, or to artists in general, but the desire and the power to exercise lifelong self-control is an emotion inseparable from Dürer's character. It is to this that we owe the visible and legible achievements which are the cornerstones of any attempt to construct a general picture of Dürer's personality. If we peer into the depths of Dürer's soul, we find that the noblest and most essential element in his character was the religious urge. Without this Dürer's character would have dissolved into the impersonality of pure art; he would have remained within the narrow limits of the commonplace man. The religious urge is the unifying element in Dürer's being, from which his genius developed, just as the spreading branches of a tree develop from its earthbound roots. Only from this standpoint can we understand his troubles and his fears, his moments of happiness and of anxiety.

Love of Self-examination

The Religious Urge

This religious foundation is, however, tempered by Dürer's subjection to the spirit of his time, by the fact that he belonged to the closing period of the Middle Ages. The religious feeling which we find in the depths of his character, is not modern, but has a mediaeval hue.

The men of late mediaeval times considered the examination of conscience as one of their chief tasks. Spiritual anguish is one of their fundamental feelings, arising from the conflict between humility and the desire for self-perfection, from the staggering contrast between the weakness of their own efforts and the grandeur of the divine commandments. From this feeling spring the essential characteristics of monasticism. The brooding of the monk revolves around the certitude of his own salvation. Luther was a product of real monasticism, and the Christian man's examination of conscience, his sense of responsibility, are elements of his religion which undoubtedly go back to the monk's cell. For Dürer his workshop had the same significance—it was his haven of solitude, the field on which the battle of his struggling and tormented soul was fought, prison and impregnable stronghold at the same time. Throughout his working career Dürer was obsessed by the fear of not making good, of not being able to answer at the Last Judgement. He was

Monasticism

Art as a Calling

far removed from the contentedness of the artisan, who does what he has to do as well as he can and then goes off for the evening with a light conscience. Nor had Dürer anything in common with the spiritual homelessness of the modern artist, who is concerned only with atelier problems and knows only aesthetic griefs. On the contrary, Dürer considered his artistic activity as a calling to the service of God. All that is very mediaeval, but the fact that Dürer talked and wrote about it, that he brought his joys and fears into the light of consciousness and expressed them in his words and in his art, that is in accord with the spirit of the Renaissance and the Reformation period.

Autobiography and Self-portraiture

If the Renaissance, wherever it penetrated, discovered the 'individual', that means that it taught us not only how to find personality in our fellow-men, but also to base our analyses, our observations and our reflections on our own person-alities. This was the origin of autobiography and of the first self-portraits. The growth of this interest in oneself brought upon the stage of all the world the Renaissance conceptions of religion, politics, science and the arts, and upon the minor stage of bourgeois life the desire to represent family matters. The bourgeois love of order and family created a mode of literary expression which at first was of a very sober and modest kind. Family records, such as Dürer's father began and his son continued, contained not only business and monetary entries, but also notes on journeys, illnesses, births and deaths, mingled with confessions of a quite intimate character. From the family chronicle sprang the individual diary. Dürer's diary of his journey to the Netherlands is an example of this earliest form of autobiography. He was not alone in this respect, but did what in similar circumstances every good father of a family would have done. In Nuremberg the genre of family notebooks began with Ulmann Stromer's chronicle for the years 1360–1407. In 1468, a few weeks before his death, Nikolaus Muffel wrote a story of his life for his children. Similar stories were written by townsmen and merchants such as Muffel and Berthold Tucher, by knights such as Götz von Berlichingen and even by wandering scholars, as is proved by Johannes von Butzbach's record of his wanderings.

Family Chronicles

Lastly, Dürer's urge to self-expression is a product of that German national emotion—our tendency to self-absorption—which is one of our weaknesses, but also one of our sources of strength, to which we owe, from Dürer to Schiller, the profoundest self-revelations of the German mind.

Dürer's Self-Portraits

Dürer is the first Northern European artist of whom we possess 'independently' painted self-portraits. By the time (about 1510) the Dutchman Lukas van Leyden had painted his fine self-portrait (Brunswick), Dürer had already produced a whole series of paintings and sketches of himself. No artist has endeavoured to depict his own likeness at an earlier age than Dürer, who was thirteen years old at the time. Raphael was one year old and Sodoma seven, when the Nuremberg infant prodigy sat down in front of his mirror and studied his schoolboy counten-ance with such effect that his still uncertain hand was able to draw it (L. 448, Vienna, Albertina, 1484). At that time the boy was an apprentice in the paternal goldsmith's workshop. There he had to work cleanly and delicately with silver-

1

point, engraving with a steady hand line after line on the tough metal. The young Dürer had already learned this and it helped him when he came to draw his own long hair (the hair on the right side of the head is by a later, less skilled hand; originally the line of the cheek continued upwards). This boy with the delicate features, the pure, childish mouth and earnest young eyes, still has long, smooth hair. The contemporary love of decoration and ornament has not yet taken possession of his head and pleasure in his personal appearance will not be found until the youth has grown into a man. From the sleeve of the jacket emerges a slender hand with outstretched forefinger, like that of a diligent schoolboy who wishes to attract the attention of his teacher. It is that hand which Dürer painted so often and so willingly, the bodily instrument of genius, of which a contemporary, Joachim Camerarius, once said: 'There is nothing more delicate to be seen than his hand.' The drawing bears the inscription, added later: 'I drew myself from the mirror in the year 1484, when I was still a child. Albrecht Dürer.' In order to draw himself, Dürer looked in the mirror, but he had not yet the technical ability to draw himself full-face, and the eyes in this portrait look sideways, which Dürer could draw, but could not see in the mirror. It is not until the next two sketches of himself that the eyes look straight at the spectator.

The magnificent Erlangen sketch (L. 429) dates from 1492. The young man had already made two vital decisions. Two years after he drew himself as a boy, he went to his father and explained how his 'pleasure' drew him more to painting than to goldsmith's work. In 1486 Wolgemut took him into his workshop. There the young Dürer had to suffer much at the hands of the journeymen, for at all times and in every workshop in the world apprentices are teased by the journeymen and have to suffer every kind of insolence and trick. 'The Devil would like to be everything except an apprentice,' says a Swabian proverb. The mediocre always takes its revenge on what it feels to be superior and nothing is more easily wounded than a young heart, dully conscious of its higher status. When Dürer had 'served his time', he left his brush and palette and his paint-boxes and, in accordance with the customs of the guild, went on his 'Wanderjahre'. When he drew himself from the mirror again, with his head resting on his hand, he had been roving for two years through Franconia and Swabia, the Upper Rhineland and Alsace, free for the first time from the anxious exactitude of his father, from the direful piety of his mother, from the coarse jests of his workshop colleagues, from the patronage of his publisher-godfather. In Wolgemut's atelier he had learned everything necessary to enable him to work on those great altar-pieces which were the joint productions of a number of artists, but he was attracted by the quicker and freer work of drawing for woodcuts. Illustrations were needed by an age hungry for books and pictures, and the big publishers in Nuremberg, Basle, Strasbourg and Augsburg were happy if they could attract a number of young, inventive draughtsmen and skilled woodcutters.

To have entered one of these establishments connected with the publishing trade would have ensured Dürer his daily bread and a definite activity at an early age. Once more Dürer stood at the cross-roads. For the second time he chose the less certain path, the path to a goal which he did not yet know, but to which his daemon irresistibly urged him on. From this period of tension, self-examination and brooding, dates the Erlangen self-portrait—as personal and direct as a lyric poem by the youthful Goethe. The well-behaved child has become an awkward young man, more absorbed in himself than in the rest of the world. Historians— like Hubert Schrade—detect in this restless head the unrest of the late Middle Ages; for psychologists and teachers this sketch is a priceless document of the spiritual state of youth.

In the treatment of hair and eyes in his self-portraits the young Rembrandt found similar means of expressing the turmoil of such periods of crisis. In the restless Erlangen sketch and in the more tranquil self-portrait in Lwów (L. 613, 1493) we see Dürer for the first time full-face. An asymmetry of the face is clearly visible. Dürer noticed in himself and in others, and reproduced in his works, slight divergences of the line of sight. Either he wanted in this way to produce a special artistic effect, for instance (as Hugo Magnus believes), to show that diverging lines of sight occur in persons absorbed in thought, or else (as W. Reitsch assumes), he was using a stylistic symbol which can be found in Roman portraiture of the second and third centuries after Christ and also in the early Italian Renaissance. To conclude from the occurrence of diverging lines of sight in some of his portraits that Dürer suffered from a slight squint, is not convincing: side-by-side with a whole series of 'squinting' faces, e.g. the sketches of his mother, of Lukas van Leyden, Caspar Sturm, etc., we have others in which there is no trace of a squint, such as those of Oswolt Krell, Holzschuher, Muffel, etc. The diary of Dürer's journey to the Netherlands contains two entries concerning disbursements for 'eye-glasses', and it may be that in his later years Dürer had to wear spectacles for work at close range.

One year after the Erlangen 'student' portrait, Dürer completed his first painted self-portrait (1493), which after many vicissitudes found its way to the Louvre. This is the first self-portrait in Northern Europe in which—as Hans Jantzen points out—the artist has represented himself not as one of a community, but alone, with the intention of 'confessing'. Goethe saw a copy (now in the Grassi Museum, Leipzig) in the Beireis Collection at Helmstedt in 1805 and describes it with enthusiasm and in detail. The picture—Goethe calls it 'rich and innocent'—gives us the whole man in both the literal and the figurative sense. He stands before us in the rich, dandified attire of a young nobleman, the numerous trimmings giving him an almost effeminate air. The child's overall and the wandering apprentice's work-jacket have disappeared and we have a gentleman before us who attaches importance to his external appearance. The long hair falling to his shoulders does not yet show the exaggerated curls of the coiffure which Dürer later adopted in Nuremberg. The face is thin and expressive, the nose juts sharply from it, round the sensitive mouth the first beard is sprouting. The left hand— with the little finger stretched out with Gothic delicacy—is holding a species of thistle known as 'husband's fidelity'. There is some symbolic reference in this plant, which was known to the Middle Ages as an aphrodisiac, but we do not

3, 4

Asymmetry of Countenance

5

The Man

know what it is. That Dürer felt and painted himself as a bridegroom and therefore chose a symbol of fidelity, is a vain supposition and is contradicted by the fact that the story of his marriage did not begin until his return home in 1494. Women, too, were depicted holding an eryngium, e.g. the 'Serving-woman' at Lützschena near Leipzig (which, however, was not painted by Dürer) and the 'Little Fortune' (engraving, 1496–98). To the right of the date (1493) is the inscription: 'My sach die gat, als es oben schtat' ('My fortunes will go as it is written in the stars'). 'Oben', of course, means 'in the stars' and the saying is an illustration of that belief in the influence of the powers above which Dürer never lost. This first painted self-portrait of Dürer already reveals that characteristic which was to permeate all his later works, with their earnest self-examinations and maxims.

Flechsig has studied the linguistic aspect of the inscription and has made the noteworthy comment that the text is not Franconian, but Alemannic. In Franconian it would have read: 'Mein Sach die get, als es oben stet.' From this Flechsig draws the conclusion that the picture was painted during Dürer's wanderings on Alemannic soil—probably in Basle or Strasbourg.

Five years pass; Dürer has married and opened his own workshop. He has already received the first important commissions for portraits which will open the way to fame, among them the portrait of Frederick the Wise; he is on friendly terms with the wealthiest, most learned and most distinguished patrician of Nuremberg—Pirckheimer. He has been in Italy and has tasted the life of an Italian 'gentiluomo', has worn fine clothes and even learned to dance, and his first great *The* graphic work, the series of woodcuts of the Apocalypse, has been published at *'Gentiluomo'* his own risk. Once more Dürer has reached a decisive turning-point and once again a self-portrait reveals to us his physical and spiritual condition. In the Prado at Madrid hangs the self-portrait of 1498, with the inscription, added in later *8* years: 'This I painted after my image, I was six-and-twenty years old. Albrecht *cf. Frontispiece* Dürer.'

This time Dürer has 'pulled himself together' in front of the mirror even more thoroughly than in the Paris self-portrait from his 'Wanderjahre'. The fingers of his left hand are clasped firmly over the back of the right, just as one pulls oneself together at decisive moments, to avoid 'giving oneself away' by some incautious gesture. The right arm rests firmly on the breastwork, which, with the Gothic arch in the background, provides the architectonic framework into which the portrayed figure is inserted and to which it is adapted, this in accordance with Italian models. The view from the window over an anonymous mountain landscape may be a formal concession to what was then the modern style, but it may also be a memory of his journey through the Tyrolese mountains to the Adriatic Sea. Dürer is once more nobly attired in cap and gown, everything is so freshly washed and ironed that Frau Agnes herself could not have wished for a tidier image of her husband. From the face, now framed in curls and adorned with moustache and beard, the eyes look out kindly and rather sorrowfully, here too with a slight divergence in the line of sight and expression. The man has become much more sure of himself and he emphasizes by his upright attitude this inner feeling of assurance. This is the first of Dürer's self-portraits in which he adopts a formal pose, repressing the unconcerned self-revelation which lends such human interest to the drawings in Erlangen and Lwow and to the Paris self-portrait, in favour of a dignity which accords with his rank but forbids all intimacy.

Just as in the Madrid portrait the ideal picture is visible in the artist's rendering, so the most famous of Dürer's self-portraits, in Munich, is generally considered as a deliberately created allegory of Dürer and of all that is noble in the artistic world. In our opinion, this is wrong. The inscription, with the date 1500, runs: 'Albertus Durerus Noricus ipsum me propriis sic effingebam coloribus aetatis anno XXVIII', but was painted on subsequently over the original light-coloured inscription tablet, which, however, does not imply that the contents are false. Nevertheless, since Ludwig Justi in his important book, 'Konstruierte Köpfe und Figuren unter den Werken A. Dürers', claimed that this head is 'constructed', i.e. built up in accordance with certain laws of proportion, it has generally been regarded as the one self-portrait of Dürer which shows how he wanted to appear and how he wished to go down to posterity. If he really intended to convey this and accordingly gave to his head such noble and harmonious proportions, then he may be said to have succeeded, for the popular idea of Dürer's appearance and the erroneous conception of a Christlike Master, who may be reverently adored but with whom close human relationship is impossible, are derived from this picture.

Most Dürer scholars date the Munich portrait from the time of his second journey to Venice, i.e. about 1506, because they assume that his brush was guided by the influence of Italian classical art and by the Italian monumental conception of figures, in other words that Dürer wanted to paint an 'antique' picture. Against this supposition of the art historians we have, first of all, a fact, quite external, but to which Flechsig has rightly drawn attention, namely, that the picture is painted, not on Italian poplar, but on German lime-tree wood. Furthermore, in his letters from Venice, which give a faithful account of everything that happened in him and around him, Dürer makes no mention of a self-portrait painted in Italy, let alone of such a majestic rendering of his person. Lastly, the physiognomy gives no reason to suppose that the picture was not painted in 1500, when the artist was 28 years old. There is no problem more difficult than judging the age of a sitter from a portrait. Generally one thinks that the sitter is older than he really is, and the most common complaint of models to their painters is: 'You have made me look older than I am.' The Dürer of the 1498 portrait in Madrid looks older than he was at that time, yet nobody has dared to question the accuracy of the age given in the inscription. The Munich picture shows, for instance, the same transparent growth of beard as the Madrid portrait and—if one covers up the fur-clad body and the wig-like hair—the same countenance with its serious, but youthful eyes. We do not, therefore, need the Italian theory or the idea of construction to explain the peculiar manner which Dürer chose in order to create from the reflected image a self-portrait dominated by 'atmosphere'. He has merely gone to the end of the path which he first entered upon in the Madrid portrait; in other words he has achieved idealization of his head. For that he needed neither

SELF-PORTRAIT. 1498. Madrid, Prado

Italian-antique nor German-Gothic systems of proportion, he had only to correct the asymmetry of the face, turn the head to a strictly frontal position and make the lines of sight of the eyes run parallel. Stateliness is always a by-product of symmetry, as all painters know. The old Nordic prototype of the 'Salvator Mundi', with its frontality and symmetry, was, as Jantzen has shown, adapted by Dürer for this representation of himself, to which he wished to give a stately air.

That the head of the Munich self-portrait is not 'constructed' in the strictest sense of the word, but only 'equalized', or adapted to a design, is shown when the Hallervorden photographic process is applied to this picture. If we divide the face into two halves by means of a perpendicular line running down the nose and then unite the photograph of the left half of the face with its reflection as seen in the mirror (i.e. by drawing a proof from the back of the negative), so as to form a new head, and then do the same with the right side of the head and its reflected image, we obtain three completely different Dürers, because the formation of Dürer's left eye—despite all stylization—is fundamentally different from that of the right. The head constructed as seen by the eye and from its reflection is more expressive, more active. This, however, would not be the case if the head were the result of mere construction with the compasses. Just as Dürer did not 'construct' the measurements of his head, but merely corrected them in accordance with the idea of beauty he had in mind, so did he deal with the mane of hair—he heightened the effect of what was actually there and enhanced it by means of symmetry. Dürer's friends made fun of him on account of the care he bestowed on his hair and beard, and he was jokingly known as 'our barbatus'. The sharp-tongued Lorenz Beheim once asked Dürer whether he still sharpened and turned his beard. It says something for Dürer's shrewdness and sense of humour that he parried this jest by making fun of himself; in one of his doggerel rhymes he calls himself the 'hairy, bearded painter'.

Anybody who takes the trouble to verify the dates in Dürer's inscriptions, is confronted by the apparent contradiction that Dürer describes himself on the Madrid self-portrait as being 26 years old in 1498, whereas he was born in 1471 and must therefore have been 27, while in the Munich picture he describes himself as being 28 instead of 29. The explanation is that Dürer did not reckon by calendar years, but by the actual years of his age; thus he did not become 27 until 21st May, 1498, and became 29 on 21st May, 1500. From this Flechsig deduces that the Madrid picture must have been painted between 1st January and 20th May 1498 and the Munich picture between 1st January and 20th May, 1500. A Röntgen photograph tends to confirm the latter, for it shows that, although the date has been renewed, it has not been altered. *Dürer's Indications of his Age*

The three sketched and three painted self-portraits are followed by three self-portraits—still preserved—showing the artist among the so-called 'assistance' or bystanders. It was the Italians who introduced the custom whereby a painter drew attention to himself by inserting his own head and signature at some suitable point in the great religious or historical paintings—which is not only a sign of artists' growing consciousness of their importance, but is also the noblest form of *Self-portraits among Bystanders* trademark. Well-known instances of this are the head of Benozzo Gozzoli with an inscription on the cap (Procession of the Three Magi, 1463) and the self-portrait of Fra Lippo Lippi, painted in 1447, to whom an angel offers a scroll with an inscription stating that he was the creator of the work. Raphael and Sodoma appear later in their frescoes in full-length—thereby bearing personal witness to their artistic achievements. During his journey to Italy Dürer must have seen 'bystander self-portraits' of this kind, e.g. that of Gentile Bellini in the Procession on St. Mark's Square, or at all events he must have heard from Italian colleagues of this usage, which was quite in agreement with his own consciousness of his rank, his pleasure in self-portraiture and his accuracy in the matter of signatures and dates. He thus depicted his own likeness among the crowds of bystanders who fill three of his chief works: the 'Festival of the Rose-garlands', the 'Martyr-dom of the 10,000 Christians' and the 'Adoration of the Trinity'. Between 1506 and 1508, the busiest and most successful years of his life, Dürer thus makes three appearances on the pictorial scene. These bystander portraits have the disadvantage that they are small—within the framework of the action of the picture they are mere details—but they have the advantage that they show us Dürer in full-length. He was slightly above medium height, well-built and slender; Lorenz Beheim describes him as fragile. He really wore his hair long and in locks, and liked going about in a fur-mantle, which he would draw around him, as if feeling rather chilly. Even in these bystander portraits Dürer looks older than a man in his late thirties. Attitude and inscriptions are similar in all three cases, but nevertheless characteristically varied.

Festival of the
Rose-garlands

61

The 'Festival of the Rose-garlands' was the product of five months' tireless work in a Venetian workshop (1506). Distracted by a hundred and one things, by the foreign climate, the foreign language, strange lodgings, strange light, by the behaviour of his Italian colleagues, who despite all their southern politeness yet made the young German feel how unwelcome was his competition with their works, busy with all Pirckheimer's commissions which he could not ignore, disturbed by visitors, inquisitive Venetians, leaders of the German colony who had to be handled with tact, by visits to his atelier of the highest nobility and the Doge himself, and, lastly, absorbed by numerous artistic problems and obsessed by the desire to become a 'gentleman' and, with his fine clothing and exquisite manners, to be received in society as an equal and not to be regarded as a German 'barbarian'—such was Dürer's position and frame of mind while he was creating this masterly work. In the self-portrait which appears in this picture Dürer is wearing the French cloak and the brown coat which he mentions in one of his letters to Pirckheimer. The inscription, which the master, leaning against a tree, holds in his hand, proudly proclaims the short time which he took to paint it and the Nordic origin of the creator: 'Exegit quinquemestri spatio Albertus Dürer Germanus M.D.VI.' Even though the 'Festival of the Rose-garlands' is no longer in the Venetian church for which it was destined—San Bartolomeo, where members of the German colony were buried—it still bears witness in its present location (Prague, Museum) to the prowess of German art.

The 'Martyrdom of the 10,000 Christians' by order of King Shapur of Persia *Martyrdom of the 10,000 Christians* 68 was a terrible subject for a picture. Dürer did not choose it himself—he was commissioned to paint it for Wittenberg by the Elector Frederick the Wise, who, like many of his contemporaries, was an ardent collector of relics. (Nikolaus Muffel, for instance, told his children that he had increased the family collection of relics by almost as many pieces as there are days in a year.) Once again the master himself appears in the picture: he is watching the gruesome scene, which is a veritable compendium of the art of torture and methods of killing. But Dürer does not venture alone on this expedition amidst torture and blood; he is accompanied by his friend Pirckheimer. Did he have some share in the choice of subject *12* or did it occur to his learned mind that this slaughter of Christians by a legendary Persian king was the best means of satisfying the unusual pictorial desires of the princely patron? Or—as I am inclined to believe—is this pair of friends wandering through this hell of torture like Dante and Virgil through the horrors of the Inferno? Such a resuscitation of a sublime theme would certainly have appealed to the humanistic mind of Pirckheimer. Dürer is holding, as if it were a flag of truce or a gigantic safe-conduct, his official envoy's staff and a scroll, bearing the inscription: 'Iste faciebat anno domini 1508 Albertus Dürer alemanus' (Vienna, Kunsthistorisches Museum). In the 'Festival of the Rose-garlands' Dürer is standing to one side, like a stage-manager in the wings who has just given the order to ring up the curtain, but in the 'Martyrdom' this couple in dark attire cannot be overlooked, for they are traversing the middle of the picture.

When Dürer depicted himself among the bystanders for the third time, in the *Adoration of the Trinity* 'Adoration of the Trinity' (1511, Vienna, Kunsthistorisches Museum), he placed himself in the usual position for a signature—the right-hand bottom corner. *69-71* Wrapped in a long, fur-lined mantle, he stands solemnly there, his hand gently supporting the tablet bearing the inscription. The picture was destined for the chapel dedicated to All the Saints in the Zwölfbrüderhaus at Nuremberg. It was therefore unnecessary for Dürer to state that he was a 'Germanus' (Northerner) or an 'Alemanus' (South German), but he announced with justifiable pride that the painting was the work of a son of the city. The inscription runs:'Albertus Dürer Noricus faciebat anno a virginis partu 1511.'

The self-portraits mentioned above do not represent all the portraits he planned, and not even all those he carried out. Between 1511 and his death in 1527 he made a sketch of himself as a sick man. We also know that he planned a self-portrait *10* for a medallion, for which three designs (London, British Museum) have come down to us.

Dürer left us nothing to show how he looked at the time of the journey to the *Portraits of Dürer by other hands* Netherlands—or if he did, these self-portraits have disappeared. But other artists portrayed him—a proof of his spreading fame. In his little notebook, in which the great artist entered so meticulously every Pfennig he spent, Dürer mentions that in 1520 he sent to Augsburg two golden guilders for Hans Schwarz of Antwerp for his 'countenance'. This is the fee for the portrait sketch of Dürer which Schwarz made for his beautiful boxwood model for a medallion (Brunswick).

The painter and medallist Schwarz had been in Nuremberg, where he had lived in the house of the well-known prior of St. Sebald, Melchior Pfinzing; in March, 1520 he had—for some unknown reason—been expelled from the walls of Nuremberg. He must, therefore, have sketched Dürer about the beginning of that year. In July, Dürer, with wife and maid, began his great journey to the Netherlands and during it he received both the sketch and the artist's bill. This pure profile shows us Dürer's head with its locks and the short beard, with the prominent, humped nose and the fine, sloping forehead. It is the portrait of Dürer from which some scholars have tried to deduce his Magyar origin. The striking physiognomic feature of the aquiline nose is lacking in the more or less frontal self-portraits; only the Paris painting of the young Dürer shows it. The accuracy of Schwarz' conception of Dürer is confirmed by the portrait of Dürer painted in 1520 in the Netherlands by Raphael's Bolognese pupil, Tommaso Vincidor, which is known to us through Andreas Stock's engraving (1629).

Hans Schwarz' medallion of Dürer undoubtedly inspired the anonymous sculptor who—perhaps after a relief by Daucher (1522)—executed the little slate relief showing a duel between Dürer and an unknown adversary (Berlin, Deutsches Museum). The older Dürer literature tried to identify the vanquished adversary as the mutual friend of Dürer and Pirckheimer, the Nuremberg 'Ratschreiber' (clerk to the council) Lazarus Spengler. Ph. M. Halm and Fritz Fr. Schulz have rightly cast doubts upon this identification. It is true that Dürer had become involved in a poetical controversy, but it is difficult to believe that this culminated in a clash of blades in the best mediaeval tournament style, and, moreover, before the eyes of the Emperor Maximilian and his court!

In the third decade of the sixteenth century Dürer appears to have changed his coiffure once again. In any case, Mathes Gebel's medallion (1528) and the woodcut made from it, which is attributed to Erhard Schön, show him with sleek, well-combed hair and a comparatively short, well-trimmed beard and moustache. If the woodcut is true to life, the artisan's head with its German bluntness and integrity has triumphed once more over the idealized forms and hairdresser's skill of Dürer's cavalier years.

Self-portrait as a sick man

10

To what period must we then assign the Bremen drawing (L. 130) touched up with water-colour, which the sick Dürer sent to a physician with a request for advice by letter? One might call it a plastic parallel to those descriptions of illnesses which occupy so much space in the autobiographies of the late Middle Ages. The drawing bears the inscription: 'Where the yellow spot is and where my finger points, there is my pain.' The coiffure is not yet that of Dürer's last years, to which some have wished to assign this curious and most intimate of all self-portraits. Flechsig has studied the handwriting with all the enthusiasm of a graphologist and has compared it with specimens from various periods of Dürer's life. By these philological and psychological means he arrives at the surprising conclusion —contrary to the general view—that the sketch must be dated as far back as about 1509. If we compare Dürer's aspect with earlier self-portraits, we find that the sketch is nearest to the bystander self-portrait in the 'Adoration of the Trinity'

(1511)—we see the same man, here as a nude, and there draped in a mantle. That Dürer's illness—an affection of the spleen or of the digestive organs—developed slowly, seems certain. It is not impossible, however, that the origin of the disease— indigestion—dates from the second journey to Venice, when Dürer was warned against the dangers of eating and drinking with Italian painters. He himself thought there was a danger of his being poisoned by competitors—a rumour was even current that a jealous Italian scholar had 'liquidated' the Nuremberg astrono- mer Regiomontanus by means of poison in Rome. Perhaps, however, it was only that Germans in Venice who knew the country warned Dürer as a Northerner against excesses in eating and drinking in the unaccustomed climate. As early as 1507 Dürer complained that fever prevented him from working for weeks at a time. He was a connoisseur of wine and was not averse to drinking bouts with his friends. When he was in the Netherlands, he had to consume 'over-rich food'. In addition, the finest wines were sent to him as gifts in the hostels, or for his consumption during his journey. Then there was the physical fatigue of the journey and the bitter cold, and above all the adventurous winter excursion to Zeeland to see the whale which had been washed ashore—to sum up, all these factors caused a recurrence of Dürer's trouble. He described his symptoms as: 'A high fever with great faintness, lassitude and pains in the head'. He attributed his condition to the trip to Zeeland and described it as 'strange', because he had never heard of anything of the kind before.

Dürer's Illnesses

The diary notes the many 'stivers' which Dürer—no doubt with a heavy heart— had to spend on physicians, male and female apothecaries and all kinds of medicine. Among the latter he mentions 'French wood', i.e. the West Indian guava wood, which was commonly believed to be a cure for syphilis (Benvenuto Cellini hoped to cure himself by taking 'lignum vitae' and Ulrich von Hutten had a treatise published by Schöffer in Mainz, entitled: 'Of the wonderful physic called "Guaicum" wood and how it is said to heal the French disease or pox'). His Flemish friends were worried about their German guest's health and sent him, as suitable diet, preserved fruits and other delicacies, e.g. compote of quinces.

We know no details of Dürer's last illness and death. Sickness must have shattered him completely, if we are to believe Pirckheimer, who wrote after his death: 'He was withered like a bundle of straw and could never be a happy man or mingle with people.' The earthly vessel broke when its content, Dürer's mighty power of expression, was consumed.

Dürer's Death

The desire to see self-portraits of an artist, which the custodians of palaces and churches are so willing to gratify, is not foreign to eminent scholars. It is tempting to talk of an unknown self-portrait, when amongst the works of an artist there is some head with the same physical characteristics as the skull and countenance of the master. Leonardo warns us against the dangers of an excessive zeal for discoveries, when he tells us from his own experience that painters 'depict most of their faces in such a way that they are very like that of their master'. Friedländer recognizes Dürer in a youthful horseman in the drawing 'Two Horsemen' (Munich, Graphische Sammlungen); Bechthold sees him, disguised as a Turk, in

Supposed Self-portraits

C

the etching of the 'Great Cannon'; Friedrich Haack has identified the youthful
Dürer, disguised as a young man, among the bystanders of the 'Men's Bath'
(woodcut, about 1497–98); Kurt Gerstenberg claims that the man-at-arms in the
woodcut of the 'Bearing of the Cross' (Great Passion, about 1498) is a self-portrait

9

of Dürer, and Hugo Kehrer makes the same claim for the drummer in the Jabach
altar-piece; Roh suggests that Dürer's features may be recognized in the head of
Hercules in the painting of 'Hercules with the Birds of Stymphalis'. If we are to
believe Emmi Voigtländer, Dürer, with mysterious symbolism, depicted himself

16

in the chalk-drawing at Bremen of the nude 'Man of Sorrow' (L. 131), a study
for the 'Charity' in Schloss Weissenstein near Pommersfelden; from this presumed
identification the sentimental and misleading conclusion is then drawn: 'It was
not previously known that he posed to the world as a sufferer; it is now easy to
understand why Dürer in his later years painted no more pictures of himself.'

The problem is more difficult when we consider a second group of unconfirmed
self-portraits of Dürer. F. Roh has identified as a self-portrait the study of a nude

15

man in Weimar (about 1507?, L. 156). In favour of this assumption—once we
have overcome our aversion to the idea of a completely nude self-portrait—is the
resemblance of the features to those of the undoubted self-portraits, as well as the
pose of the upper body, as if leaning towards a mirror, and the staring gaze
characteristic of self-portraits. If we can believe that a German artist at the beginning of the sixteenth century would have drawn himself completely undraped,
then we can certainly believe it of Dürer, the conscientious and ruthlessly objective
student of nature. The Bremen self-portrait of the sick Dürer would then be, so
to speak, a 'topographical' counterpart to the physiognomic study in Weimar,
the Bremen sketch giving merely the definite location of the seat of the pain in a
more schematically drawn body. In Stettin a small oil-painting has been discovered,

*Self-portrait
as a boy?*

which F. Henry has identified as a self-portrait of Dürer as a boy. It bears the date
1484 (only traces of the second '4' are visible) and the inscription: 'in . . . 13 . . . year
I was . . .'. It probably depicts the thirteen-year-old Dürer in the same clothing as
the Albertina drawing. The coarseness of the childish face and the crude technique
point to its being a sixteenth-century copy and not by Dürer's own hand.

*Lost
Self-portraits*

A self-portrait of Dürer was lost when the Heller altar-piece was destroyed by
fire in 1729. It was similar to the self-portrait in the 'Adoration of the Trinity'
and there is a copy by Jobst Harrich in the Städtisches Museum at Frankfurt am

64

Main.

Among other lost self-portraits of Dürer (from the years 1492 and 1497?) is the
small portrait painted in water-colour on linen, which Dürer sent to Raphael in
1515, in return for the gift of a red-chalk sketch of two nudes. Vasari admired
this 'little canvas'; Giulio Romano inherited it from Raphael and Sandrardt saw
it in the Duke of Mantua's art gallery. Since then it has disappeared and the same
fate has overtaken a portrait of Dürer by Burgkmair, probably executed at
Augsburg in 1518.

It is easy to enter a little man in the Book of Life, for the place where he belongs
is quickly found. But for the great man many pages are needed. Are we to include

Dürer among the brilliant careers? Can he be excluded from the pages containing the records of dark impulses? The life of a great man is full of contrasts; that which is irreconcilable in the normal man, is combined in him to form an incontestable whole. Dürer was a man who accepted the world and yet shut himself away from it, he had delicate feelings and at the same time was an eccentric. Joy and despondency alternated in his soul. He could show a youthful wildness and he could free himself of all pathos. At a time when a Kunz von der Rosen was Maximilian's court jester and when the wearer of the crown could not bear to have the wearer of the cap and bells absent from his presence, in the century of gay mummery and coarse foolery, a boisterous tone was not out of place and was customary among Dürer's Nuremberg friends. Dürer's humour speaks in innumerable witty conceits in the marginal drawings for the Emperor Maximilian's Prayerbook, but only the discovery of Dürer's letters to Pirckheimer from Venice—in a walled-up niche in the house of the Imhoffs—has revealed to us the full extent of his wit. For instance, when Dürer asks Pirckheimer whether he has lost his sweetheart, he draws a rose upon the paper, the lady's name being Rosenthaler; when he draws a brush (Bürste), the answer to the riddle is Frau Pörstin. It is, however, well to remember that such jokes were not peculiar to Dürer, they were common usage among young men at that time. Lorenz Beheim, a friend of both Dürer and Pirckheimer, affected the same tone; in 1507 he cast the horoscope of Dürer's birth and pretended to have discovered that he was an 'ingeniosus amator', a coveter of women. Such a horoscope would have been far truer of himself and Pirckheimer.

Nevertheless the element of sorrow in Dürer's soul far outweighed the element of levity. Dürer, the engraver of the 'Melancolia', was, as his contemporaries realized, in the language of the Renaissance a 'melancholic'. Melanchthon speaks of Dürer's 'Melancholia generosissima'. This does not mean a man continually depressed and by nature gloomy; it indicates a state of soul commonly found in those engaged in intellectual work. Dürer himself, in the unpublished preface to his 'Instructions for Young Painters', gives an excellent definition of it: 'The constant use of our understanding consumes the most subtle and clearest part of the blood and evokes a melancholy state of mind.' Depression is the result of work and meditation—that is what Dürer concludes from his own experience—and mind and melancholy are thus connected with each other. This depressing influence, however—and Dürer experienced this consolation also—is compensated by the Grace of God. Echoing a sentiment expressed by Marsilius Ficinus in his 'De Vita Triplici' when he speaks of 'divinis influxibus ex alto', Dürer acknowledges that art comes from divine inspiration. The life of a soul is suspended between this inspiration and the 'great fears'. Dürer was akin to many men of genius in that the pendulum of his moods swung to and fro from the manic to the depressive pole.

If we seek a parallel to Dürer among the great German minds of later centuries, our choice will fall upon Schiller. Separated by space and time, spiritually worlds apart, there are yet many links between them. In both of them a moving humanity,

Dürer and Schiller

overshadowed by the threat of illness; both possessed that loftiness of spirit which was felt by all who came in contact with them. Both created their greatest works—Dürer his 'Apostles'; Schiller his 'Wallenstein'—in the atmosphere of an imminent world crisis; both possessed that idealism without which no one can inspire his fellow–countrymen. From the pictorial art of the Franconian, who was the contemporary of Luther, and from the poetical works of the Swabian whom Goethe called his friend, shine forth the same ingenuousness, the same grandeur and the same purity. And there was a fundamental trait of heroism in Dürer, just as there was in Schiller.

'KEEP MEASURE!'
(Detail from the Triumphal Arch of Emperor Maximilian, 1515)

CHAPTER THREE

APOCALYPSE

THE spiritual atmosphere on the eve of the Reformation was stormy. An Augsburg chronicler speaks of 'swiftly-moving, dangerous' times. The world at that time was not—as the Romanticists imagined—peaceful and safe; it was full of uncertainty and strife. Germany was not a country inhabited only by honest craftsmen singing over their work in the cities, by pious priests celebrating the Mass, by noble knights riding down from their castles into the valleys and by devout peasants tilling the soil; it was a land full of unrest and turbulence, of upheaval and ferment. In this atmosphere of internal and external disruption, there was a violent clash of religious, social and political ideas. The breath of revolution was in the air. The men of the dying Middle Ages were torn by spiritual doubts and fears. The most glaring contrasts were found in close juxtaposition: craven fear of the approaching Day of Judgement and dauntless heroism on the battlefields of Europe; anxious sheltering in the shadows of the Gothic cathedrals and bold excursions into heretical spheres of thought; pitiful suffering beneath the old scourge of the plague and the new calamity of the French disease, and elsewhere a resplendent joie-de-vivre, served and enhanced by all the arts. It was the time of the last knights and of the first great city merchants, of an awakening laity and an exhausted church, of mediaeval ardour and cultured humanistic arrogance. Inside the walls of the cities the proletariat was murmuring; outside, the peasants were showing signs of unrest. The power of the Emperor was declining; that of the city states and the sovereign princes was rising.

In the summer of 1475 a curious religious movement swept over Central Germany. The young, in particular, were smitten by a spiritual epidemic—the urge to go on a pilgrimage to the 'Holy Blood'. Processions of children, singing and waving flags, marched through the villages. The peasants abandoned their ploughs, housewives their kitchens, artisans ran from the smithies and grooms from the stables, to join the pilgrimage, many of them without knowing what it was all about, few aware of their destination—the three bleeding wafers at Wilsnack in the Altmark—but all feeling that they were 'driven'. 'If they were to be locked up,' says a chronicler, 'they would go mad. And when it came upon them, they began to weep, the great, the old and the small, and began to tremble as if they had the ague, so that they could not speak, and they wept until they ran out of their houses into the streets and tore themselves with violence from those who would stop them.'

Another seat of spiritual disease was in the Odenwald and Spessart, remote valleys in which not only robbers, but religious fanatics found a home. A herdsman and village musician, Hans Böheim, toured the countryside, telling of his visions, calling the Emperor and the Pope scoundrels who were enriching themselves at the expense of the 'poor devils', inciting the populace against the landed nobility and the priests and calling upon them to join the pilgrimage to the shrine at Niklashausen in the Taubertal. Böheim's visions were quite apocalyptic in character and his sermons were full of Communistic ideas. The forests, water, air, game, fish and birds, should all be communal property; even the great lords should be made to work for their daily bread, and all taxes and imposts should be abolished. The pilgrimage fever gripped the populace from the Neckar to the Main and as far away as Alsace. The former village musician burned his drum and became a soul-catcher. In their thousands, singing wild German songs, the country-folk followed in his wake, kneeling to receive the blessing of the 'holy lad', the women offering up their tresses, their kerchiefs and their shoes, and the men their playing-cards, which 'Hänselein', as his worshippers called him, burned on a pyre, as worldly trash.

General Unrest The Church recognized the danger of this rustic Savonarola sooner than did the nobility. He ended his life at the stake in Würzburg, singing German hymns until the smoke choked him. Although his ashes were scattered in the Main, the wind carried the seed of his seditious ideas far and wide. Individual movements might die out or be suffocated in blood, but the general unrest and discontent remained. The remark that in times of grave political tension no one can sit still and everyone runs out on to the street, is true of Germany at that time. The cities were well aware that their highly developed organizations and jealously guarded privileges would be threatened if this epidemic spread from the country districts to the towns. Nuremberg, for example, forbade all its citizens to take part in the pilgrimages to Niklashausen. But rumour scaled even the stoutest city walls.

War, Distress and Plagues During the last decades of the fifteenth century, the Horsemen of the Apocalypse —famine, war and plague—rode through the German lands. Bad harvests, and consequent famine, gave rise to the formation in Alsace of the 'Bundschuh', the first peasant conspiracy on a large scale. In 1499 the Swiss war devastated parts of Swabia and Tyrol. Willibald Pirckheimer, who took part in this campaign as a commander and chronicler, gave the peace-loving and complacent Nurembergers a vivid description of the misery it caused. In three years a virulent plague carried off half the inhabitants of the cities on the banks of the Rhine.

Syphilis, which is said to have spread from Auvergne via Spain to Italy, pene-trated along the trade routes from the South to the North and reached the Southern German cities, appearing first of all in Augsburg. In 1497 the first penitential sermons on syphilis (the 'malum francorum') were preached in Nuremberg. In 1505 the Imperial city of Nördlingen was unable to pay its contribution to the Swabian League, because the city's expenses for the care of the sick had been doubled owing to an outbreak of the 'morbus gallicus'. This disease was a scourge of God which, unlike those due to malnutrition, attacked the higher social categories more than it did the poor.

In 1506, when Dürer was in Venice, he wrote to Pirckheimer: 'I know nothing that I now fear more (than syphilis), for almost everyone has it. It eats some of them away to such an extent that they die of it.' It also consumed one of the leading Germans—Ulrich von Hutten. In his 'Febrisgesprächen', Hutten, with grim humour and the grotesque imagery of contemporary woodcuts, converses with the personified disease. He wills his disease upon the Italian priest Cajetan, Papal Legate to the Diet of Augsburg. He thanks it for having revealed to him the dissoluteness, immorality and evils of a priest's life.

In 1496 Dürer contributed to a prophecy of the physician Ulsenius of Friesland —whither the disease had already penetrated—a flyleaf showing a man afflicted with the French disease; above his head is the globe with the Signs of the Zodiac, showing the conjunction of Jupiter and Saturn in the sign of the Scorpion, an event which the astrological beliefs of the time held to be responsible for the appearance of this plague.

God left tormented humanity in no doubts about his wrath; He warned and terrified them by signs and wonders. Meteors fell from the skies, comets drew their gleaming tails across the firmament and the miracle of the crosses appeared on the clothing of men and women. The spread of this religious illusion can be followed from a village near Maastricht, where it originated at Easter 1501, through Liége and Utrecht, down the Nahe valley and up the Rhine, to the Tyrol in the South, to Poland in the East and to Denmark in the North. In 1503 the phenomenon was observed in Nuremberg and Dürer describes it with profound credulity. About the end of the century, there was an increase in tales of consecrated wafers exuding blood, of nuns receiving the Stigmata and of similar miraculous renewals of the symbols of Christ's Passion. Deep disappointment with social and political developments, anxiety for their daily bread and the general unrest of the time made the popular mind eager to receive these signs. The greatest and most widespread of them was the miracle of the Crosses, which appeared on the clothes of women. Pamphlets and woodcuts told of these miracles. The exhibition of the garments on which the Crosses had appeared gave rise to processions and pilgrimages. Pilgrims from the Netherlands set out to fight the Turks carrying a girl's shift covered with Crosses as their standard.

Signs and Wonders

To the religious movements were added social and political disturbances which took place in the cities. The fifteenth century, and especially its second half, brewed a ferment among the burghers which culminated in a long series of disorders. The causes and aims of these revolts differed from one town to another. Discontented artisans and small tradesmen gained a footing in the councils and thus had their share in municipal government (e.g. in the Hansa cities). Elsewhere the guilds were in conflict with the proletariat over questions of authority (e.g. in Aachen and Mainz). Sometimes the trouble was due to alleged misappropriation of the tax moneys by the 'families' (e.g. in Rothenburg-ob-der-Tauber) or to the refusal of the clergy to grant land for grazing (e.g. Osnabrück). With these political struggles to gain control of local government were mingled social disturbances arising from the gulf between rich and poor. Both motives were soon amalgamated in the general psychosis of disorder. An example is the so-called 'Bread and Cheese' war, which broke out in 1492 in North Holland and Friesland and soon developed from a peasant revolt into an uprising of the lower classes. The leaders of such movements exploited the general discontent. That Germany was a source of trouble of the first order, was known even beyond the

Political Unrest

Alps. The Roman church regarded the new art of book-printing as its most dangerous opponent. For this reason Pope Alexander VI Borgia decreed that German books should not be published without the consent of the diocesan bishops. Two years later, the great Italian instigator of unrest, Savonarola, was burned as a heretic in the Piazza della Signoria in Florence. Spiritual upheavals convulsed the South as well as the North.

Fear of the End of the World

Fears that the end of the world was at hand had spread among the Sectarians of Bohemia and also reached Southern Germany. Not only religious fanatics, true and false prophets, but even spiritual leaders such as Wolfgang Aytinger of Augsburg and Bishop Berthold of Chiemsee, raised their voices in lamentation for the sinfulness of mankind, prophesied its downfall in the storms of the Last Judgement and the subsequent dawn of the perfect age of eternal peace in the world. Visions of destruction and salvation threw tormented mankind from one frenzy into another. And the overheated fantasy of the Late Middle Ages enriched these apocalyptic and chiliastic visions with every imaginable kind of figurative imagery.

The Revelation of St. John

It was in the Revelation of St. John on Patmos, which a Christian Jew of Asia Minor, his mind haunted by feverish dreams, had written in the time of Nero in the form of an epistle, that anxious souls sought the answers to the questions which filled the minds of men at this time. This old book of riddles and magic had repeatedly attracted the attention of mankind during times of severe religious affliction and had provided consolation with its mysterious phrases, for example, at the end of the tenth century when it was thought that the end of the world was at hand, and during the twelfth and thirteenth centuries at the time of the mystic sects. For the Orthodox Russians, the Apocalypse has never lost its significance. Wilhelm Neuss has traced the origin of apocalyptical illustration from its roots on Spanish soil to its Southern German, Franconian and English ramifications. Mediaeval art had limited itself to the representation of certain scenes—down to the woodcuts of the Cologne Bible of 1480. Dürer was the first to present the subject-matter of the Apocalypse as a balanced series of pictures. When he published the Revelation of St. John as his first great work, he knew how great was the hunger for reading and illustrative matter among his contemporaries. Nobody commissioned him to do this work, and the form he chose was as much his own as the idea. The format, so much larger than usual, is another proof of Dürer's determination to produce something out of the ordinary.

Dürer's Apocalypse (1498)

In 1498 Dürer published two editions—one German and the other Latin—of the Apocalypse with fifteen woodcuts. The sixteenth woodcut—the title-page—was not added until 1511. He took the text from the so-called ninth German Bible, published by his godfather Koberger in 1483, and also used a type-face of Koberger's which had been cut for the printing of Schedel's Chronicle of the World. Dürer did not possess a printing press of his own, nor is he mentioned in the Nuremberg registers as a book-printer. By placing at the end of the series of woodcuts the words 'Printed in Nuremberg by Albrecht Dürer Painter', he was merely indicating the publisher and the address from which the book could be obtained. In the strict sense Dürer was not a printer, and for that matter he was not a woodcutter either. The terminology of the time drew a distinction between 'Reissen', i.e. the drawing on the block, and 'Schneiden', i.e. the actual cutting of the wood. For the cutting of the blocks Dürer employed various assistants, some of them known, others unknown. But what would they have become without him? The essence and power of Dürer's drawing, the firm lines, the vigorous hatching, the varying lights and deep shadows—all these brilliant features of the draughtsman's art pointed the way along which the art of woodcutting was to develop to unsuspected heights. The inexpressible achieved expression, the invisible became visible.

With this 'Apocalipsis cum figuris' Dürer gave his contemporaries a real picture-book—they could look at the pictures and read the words of the Evangelist on the back of the woodcuts. We have unfortunately become accustomed to considering woodcuts as a kind of modern accessory, apart from the text, which very few trouble to read while they look at the pictures. By doing this we deprive ourselves of the pleasure of comparing the illustrations with the written word, and, what is even worse, we contemplate the pictures from a purely formalistic point of view, thereby doing Dürer an injustice and failing to appreciate the fantastic content.

Illustration and Text

Before the story of St. John's Revelation unfolds itself, a first woodcut shows us the last scene in his earthly life—his martyrdom in a cauldron of boiling oil. Beneath an awning, in front of a beautiful Italian tapestry, sits the Emperor Domitian, magnificent in his manly aspect and in the costume of an Eastern prince. The martyr, a nude figure with long locks, is praying amidst the leaping flames in the cauldron. Amongst the spectators behind the balustrade we see official personages mingling with the inquisitive crowd which gathers to watch every accident or execution. From the artistic point of view this woodcut, rich in detail but clear, is a marvellous overture, rising through every grade of black-and-white, from velvety depths to the metallic gleam of the cauldron. From these depths of human cruelty and earthly suffering the second woodcut lifts us rapidly to the heavenly sphere and the realm of visions.

Martyrdom of St. John

The youthful figure of St. John, borne upon clouds, is kneeling amidst the seven golden lamps of fire—a fervent figure with folded hands, his head framed in locks and reverently bowed, his face turned away from us and towards Christ. The countenance of the Son of Man is beaming like the sun and from His lips emerges the two-edged sword. In His left hand he holds the book sealed with the seven seals, its pages fluttering in the storm of supernatural events, while His right hand is stretched out into space, out of whose incalculable depths the seven planets, abandoning their prescribed orbits as if drawn by magnetic force, come hurrying to attach themselves, glittering, to the hand of the Lord.

The Seven Lamps of Fire Ill. p. 36

God speaks, the mighty doors of Heaven swing open and St. John, seen in profile, kneels before the throne of God. Pressing close to God's right arm, the Lamb with seven horns and seven eyes is about to take the book from the knees of the Father. In the inner almond-shaped sphere are the four mysterious beasts

The Summons to Heaven Ill. p. 34

ST. JOHN RECEIVES THE SUMMONS TO HEAVEN
(Apocalypse, 1498)

having the heads of a lion, a calf, a man and an eagle. The outer sphere is filled by the four and twenty elders, a rainbow shining around them. Far beneath the heavenly scene, borne upon clouds, lies the earth; a German castle stands on the shore of a lake, with a wood and a town behind it—the kingdom of this world from which St. John has been snatched away.

Four Horsemen go galloping by, the Angel of God hovering above them with widespread wings like a bird presaging a storm. On the white horse sits the crowned man with a bow, on the red horse the man swinging the great sword. The black horse bears a beardless man, the pair of balances in his hand swinging like a whip. With these three mighty ones—War, Sickness and Want—the pale horse of the fourth horseman keeps pace, on his back the skin-covered skeleton of age-old Death, who needs neither stirrups nor bridle, and spurs on with blows from the trident his skinny nag, as it picks its way over the fallen bodies of men. Men and women flee before the apocalyptic onslaught; those who are not trampled beneath the hooves are, like the fallen bishop, swallowed up by the Dragon of Hell.

The Four Horsemen Ill. p. 38

The sixth seal has been opened and the end of the world is at hand. The kindly light of the sun and moon is obscured and from the angry fringe of clouds the stars of heaven fall to the earth, 'even as a fig tree casteth her untimely figs, when she is shaken of a mighty wind'. Emperor and Pope, Cardinal and monk flee to the recesses of the hills, followed by men, women and children, all stricken with the same panic. Before the wrath of God the mendicant friar is equal to the wearer of the Tiara, the half-naked child suffers the same fear as the Emperor in his mantle. Arms are raised to heaven, where the souls of those who have died for the name of God gather around the altar, crying out for vengeance. Angels cover their nakedness and take them gently by the hand. Beneath the feet of the blessed, the hell of destruction is raging.

The End of the World

The multitude of the 144,000 elect is kneeling, filled with pious thoughts, while their foreheads are being sealed by an angel. There is not a single crowned head among the just; plain, austere heads receive the seal of the living God. While this is happening, the four angels with their swords protect the tree of life and dispatch the four winds over mountains and seas to blow into space.

The Angels holding the Winds

Clothed in white raiment, with palm-branches in their hands, the elect flock into Heaven, singing the praises of God, while far beneath them lies a coast indented with bays and a ship floats upon the calm waters.

The Song of Praise

When the seventh seal is opened, the face of the sun is darkened, the moon becomes as blood. Ships capsize in the storm and screaming men leap from a boat. Like a falcon the Bird of Woe swoops down. Destruction rains down from Heaven. To seven angels trumpets have been given and another holds the golden censer, from which incense ascends up before God. The vessel of the offering becomes the weapon of destruction, and fire from the altar of God is poured upon the doomed earth, together with thunder, lightning and earthquake. After the first angel has sounded, there is a hail of blood and fire, and the trees and green grass are burned up. The second angel sounds, and as it were a mountain of fire

The Angels with the Trumpets

ST. JOHN BEHOLDS THE SEVEN LAMPS OF FIRE
(Apocalypse, 1498)

is cast into the sea, destroying all living things in and upon it. When the third angel sounds, a great star falls from heaven into the rivers and fountains of waters and the waters are made bitter as wormwood. At the sound of the fourth trumpet, the third part of the sun, the moon and the stars is darkened and eternal twilight descends. At the fifth sounding the Bottomless Pit is opened and the swarm of locusts comes forth.

To the angel holding the sixth trumpet a voice speaks from the four horns of the golden altar, saying: Loose the four angels. The angels are loosed and their swords mow down horse and rider, emperor and pope, and a third of mankind.

Battle of Angels Ill. p. 42

By the side of the sea which has once more become calm, St. John is sitting, a book and writing materials near him. He is devouring the book which the angel hands to him, like a starving man taking food. (This scene from the Apocalypse has been preserved in the popular phrase: to devour an exciting book.) The feet of the angel are pillars of fire, he is clothed with a cloud; he sets his right foot upon the sea and his left foot on the earth and a rainbow is about his Apollinic head.

St. John eats up the Book

The fantasy of mediaeval readers was able to follow the visions of St. John as far as this point, for they contain merely exaggerations of events which are none the less possible and are kept within the bounds of imagination, e.g. comets, meteors, eclipses of the sun and moon, fire, floods and high tides, the turmoil of battle, plague, famine, martyrdom and death. But after the sounding of the seventh trumpet the visions leave the realm of what can be imagined or pictured and pass into the domain of that which is perceptible, yet imperceptible, comprehensible, yet incomprehensible. At this point even Dürer's power of imagination and pencil begin to flag. The vision of the pregnant woman clothed with the sun and crowned with twelve stars, standing upon the sickle of the moon, the dragon with its seven crowned heads (symbolizing the seven hills of Rome), ready to devour her child as soon as it is born, while his thrashing tail draws the third part of the stars down from heaven—all this, in Dürer's rendering, lacks the overwhelming power of expression which we find in the Four Horsemen, in the Battle of Angels or in the picture of St. John eating up the book. The little figure of the woman clothed with the sun, the angels carrying away the child and the many-headed, many-crowned and many-horned monster belong rather to the realm of heraldry than to that of magic.

The Woman clothed with the Sun Ill. p. 44

Twice more Dürer had to depict symbolic monsters rising up out of the sea and the earth. The beast like a leopard with the feet of a bear and seven heads which blaspheme for forty and two months, and the two-horned beast of temptation, half lamb and half dragon, rise from the sea and the earth. The scarlet-coloured animal with the horrible head carries the Whore of Babylon through the wilderness. With a horsewoman's gesture she holds up her scarlet robe with her left hand, while her right raises aloft the cup full of the abominations and filthiness of her fornication, which, however, is so beautifully embossed that it might be a goblet from the goldsmith's workshop of Dürer's father. In both woodcuts the emissaries of the Bottomless Pit are confronted by representatives

The Beast with horns like a Lamb

The Whore of Babylon Ill. p. 40

THE FOUR HORSEMEN OF THE APOCALYPSE
(Apocalypse, 1498)

of doomed and misguided humanity, shown as groups from all classes of the clergy and laity, looking as if they had just emerged from the gates of Nuremberg to contemplate and worship these diabolical abortions. But from the heavenly heights the representatives of divine power, armed with scythe and sword, are hastening down to gather the grapes and cast them into the great wine-press of the wrath of God.

Amidst the superabundance of mystery and exaggerated symbolism of this chapter of the Revelation of St. John, one scene kindled Dürer's imagination: St. Michael's battle with the dragon. Once again he divides the scene into two tiers—an earthly landscape basking in the peace of summer and a fierce battle raging in the heavenly regions. Like a ferryman urging his craft forward by driving his pole deep into the river-bed, St. Michael thrusts his lance into the dragon's throat. Beneath the shadow of the heavenly horseman's wings, angels assist him with sword, bow and arrow. It is a magnificent confusion of rustling feathers, fluttering locks, buckling shields, dragon's heads, arms, legs, sharp points and sail-like folds, dominated by the white robe of St. Michael and the inexorable downward thrust of the lance. *St. Michael and the Dragon*

In the last woodcut all is quiet in heaven and on earth, while birds fly across the cloudless sky. The gate of the many-turreted town is guarded by an angel. From the summit of a hill another angel is pointing out the peaceful scene to the Evangelist, who approaches the New Jerusalem with the weary air of a man returning from a long and perilous journey. In the foreground an angel, of the sturdy race of the champions and guardians of Heaven, drives the dragon, a chain round its neck as if it were a savage dog, into the Bottomless Pit, which will be closed for a thousand years by the key in the angel's right hand. *The Key to the Bottomless Pit Ill. p. 46*

Dürer's Apocalypse, like all his graphic art, was not intended for the portfolios of a few connoisseurs or for the cabinets of print-rooms, but for the low rooms in the houses of German burghers, for the workshops of artisans and artists, and also, of course, for the eyes of great princes and their counsellors in the chancelleries, of art-loving patricians with carefully-tended hands, of German bankers and merchants at home and abroad. Very few of them knew anything of the life history of the 27-year-old Franconian who created these woodcuts; hardly one of those who looked at the fifteen great sheets can have known anything of their origin and significance in the history of art. The sources are known; for several of them the Strasbourg Bible of 1485 served as a model. H. Friedrich Schmidt has pointed out the similarity of conception in individual episodes, e.g. the fall of the stars, the Bird of Woe, the sinking ship, etc. But nowadays we need know nothing of all that in order to appreciate the strength and beauty of these woodcuts. Our appreciation will not be diminished, but heightened, if we look over the master's shoulder as he works. *Sources*

When a young man undertakes a great work, requiring all his strength and enthusiasm, he is tempted to put into it the whole harvest of his previous work. Youthful works, whether they pertain to poetry, science or the formative arts, generally tend towards a superabundance of motifs, of contradictory elements of form and content. Economy of strength, condensation and compactness are the *Superabundance of Motifs in Youthful Works*

THE WHORE OF BABYLON
(Apocalypse, 1498)

marks of the mature artist and not the virtues of those who still have to mature. For the gigantic task of illustrating his Apocalypse, Dürer not only searched the depths of his soul; he also took from his sketchbooks that which he believed could be fused with this glowing fantasy. With what expert joy did the goldsmith's son draw the seven lamps of fire for the second woodcut! Each lamp differs in its ornamentation from the others. They are placed as carefully on their cushions of clouds as a goldsmith would place his wares on velvet in his shop-window. But the eyes of those among Dürer's contemporaries who loved and collected beautiful objects saw in these lamps even more than that—they saw their modernity. Beautiful lamps appear in Martin Schongauer's Death of the Virgin, but they were the products of pure Gothic art, whereas Dürer's show the influence of a new style—that of the Italian Renaissance. We would like to think that Dürer possessed models for these colossal lamps, amidst which St. John sinks to his knees, In another instance we know that this was so.

From Venice Dürer brought home a drawing of a very elegant Venetian courtesan (L. 459, Vienna). Evidently he had not been content to contemplate the seductive ladies of the South only from a distance. When it came to choosing an appropriate figure for the 'Whore of Babylon', Dürer made use of this souvenir of Venice and let the lady nonchalantly mount the scarlet-coloured beast. There are other reminiscences of Italy in Dürer's Apocalypse; for instance, the two angels in the foreground of the woodcut depicting the holding of the winds, whose swords are certainly not mere ornaments to be worn with fancy dress, while beneath their angelic robes, most unsuitable for combat purposes, their shoulders and manly breasts appear to be covered with coats of mail. The artist who created these stalwart heavenly warriors must have seen the emotional appeal which the Italians gave to their figures and have let his eyes follow the long folds of draperies drawn by Mantegna. Wölfflin may be right in his supposition that Dürer had already drawn the chief angel before he thought of depicting this episode of the Apocalypse. The trained eye of the scholar may detect here and there in Dürer's woodcuts reminiscences of Venetian and Northern Italian art, for instance a cupola from St. Mark's or the column with the lion from the Piazzetta amidst the architectural backgrounds, but that does not alter the fundamental character of the work as a whole, which is non-Italian, or even anti-Italian.

The formal element is Italian, the informal element is German. From the South comes the quiet juxtaposition, from the North the vivacious welding together. Mantegna and Signorelli base their scenes of battle and destruction on plastically conceived figures, whereas with Dürer the emphasis is essentially on the abstract line. If we seek a derivation for Dürer's use of line and method of composition during this 'storm and stress' period of his life, we must think of the restless vehemence of the animals with which Germanic wood-carvers covered the prows and sides of ships and of the bronze surfaces of buckles and clasps. That does not mean that Dürer had examples of such figures before his eyes, as he had examples of Italian art; it means that, through the medium of Gothic art, age-old currents of Nordic sentiment were handed down to him, as they were to the stonemasons

135

Italian and German Influences

D

THE BATTLE OF THE ANGELS
(Apocalypse, 1498)

and wood-carvers, e.g. to Michael Pacher, who died in 1498. Dürer may even have seen Pacher's altar-piece of the Early Fathers in Bressanone. The devil holding the missal for St. Wolfgang is a notion which would have appealed to the young Dürer's heart.

In the Apocalypse we feel that Dürer's St. Michael is a figure after the style of Siegfried, distinguished only by his celestial garments from the Nordic slayers of dragons. That is more than a romantic parallel, there is an element of historical truth behind it which we would instinctively feel even if we knew nothing about it. These are actually transformations of German mythological concepts into the terms of Christian art. Saints' days in Germany were frequently made to coincide with old heathen festivals, and churches dedicated to St. Michael were built on the summits of hills previously sacred to Wotan. Similarly, the popular figures of the heroic legends and fairy-tales were brought back from the dark forests wreathed in mists whither the new doctrine had banished them, and presented again, completely transfigured, to the eyes of men. Wotan's wild riders become the Horsemen of the Apocalypse. The young Siegfried is transformed into St. George clad in a coat of mail. Wate, who carried his child through the waters of the Gröna-Sund, changes his name to Christopher, and now, leaning on his knotted stick, carries the Infant Saviour across the rushing stream. Wate was a popular figure, particularly in the country districts; he had red hair like Thor and protected houses against lightning and storms. His popularity remained after he had been transformed into a Christian mediator, and even in our own times he is honoured as their patron saint by those modern pilgrims, the motorists!

The Nordic Heritage

Wate and St. Christopher

Dürer, too, loved this giant saint, good-tempered, fond of children, and strong as a bear, trudging sturdily through the water. St. Christopher and the pious and learned St. Jerome were, in fact, his favourite saints. Since 1442 the over-lifesize figure of the Schlüsselfeld St. Christopher had looked down upon the Nurembergers from the walls of the church of St. Sebaldus, and Dürer must often have gazed fondly at it as a boy. About 1500–05 Dürer made his first woodcut of St. Christopher, who also appears, looking milder and older, almost like a Father Christmas, in a woodcut of Dürer's dating from 1511. In a third woodcut, solid and typically German, made in 1525, the Saint is shown after he has reached the bank.

75–80

If we are to see in the Apocalypse cycle an attempt by Dürer to free himself from the toils of Italian—which, in Dürer's case, means Northern Italian—artistic influences with a mighty heave of his German and Franconian arms, then his version of the Revelation of St. John cannot be considered as a polemic against the Roman Church. Scholars and writers have emphasized the rôles played by Emperor, Pope, Cardinals and monks in the scenes of destruction. It is true that the Dragon of Hell swallows a bishop, that Emperor and Pope have to flee to the deepest recesses of the mountains and that a wearer of the cowl is the first to kneel before the Whore of Babylon, but after all, that is not very much more than we see in the Dances of Death, in the chapbooks, or in the carnival plays and farces, in which satire at the expense of the clergy was customary. In such pictorial representations the fundamental idea is that, before the wrath and vengeance of

THE WOMAN CLOTHED WITH THE SUN AND THE DRAGON WITH SEVEN HEADS
(Apocalypse, 1498)

God, all sinners are equal and that Death's scythe mows down all alike, great and small, high and low. It is not until the woodcuts, copied from Dürer's, in the September edition of Luther's New Testament (1522) that we find deliberately polemical, anti-papal pictures. The unknown draughtsman—deviating from Dürer's version—clothes the hybrid monster, half ram and half pig, in a monk's cowl and places the papal crown on the head of the Whore of Babylon. Be that as it may, we do not believe that Dürer's woodcuts were intended as theses to be nailed to the portal of the Church of Rome. They do not indicate in symbolic form his conversion to the ideas of the Reformation, but are more probably an avowal of that revolution in art which all eyes could perceive. The sensitive nerves of art can always foretell the storm long before it breaks on political or religious ground, and these woodcuts, revolutionary in the artistic sense, are thus presages of the coming revolution of religious conscience. Dürer's 'Apocalypse' has been compared with 'Faust'. If we mean the original version of 'Faust', that may be true. But for that matter, Dürer's 'Faust' was not the 'Apocalypse', but his painting of the four Apostles.

Scenes from the Apocalypse were favourite subjects in German art, even after Dürer. The best-known in more recent times are the Horsemen of the Apocalypse by Peter Cornelius. Dürer was restricted to the size of a folio sheet, whereas *Cornelius* Cornelius had whole wall-spaces at his disposal, though it is doubtful whether this makes his version any more impressive. It is clearer and more suitable for modern eyes than Dürer's version, just as the figures of Raphael, which have left their trace in Cornelius' cartoons, are more agreeable to the eye than Gothic gargoyles. Cornelius himself said of his cartoons: 'There is a lot of Phidias in them.' In German graphic art there is only one work inspired with a spirit similar to Dürer's and rivalling the Apocalypse woodcuts in power of expression—Alfred Rethel's *Rethel* series of woodcuts entitled: 'Yet another Dance of Death', created in that year of revolutions, 1848. We might adapt Cornelius' remark and say that there is a lot of Dürer in them.

The contrast in form and content between Heaven and earth, between the realm of visions and the earthly abode of those who see them, is found throughout Dürer's woodcuts of the Apocalypse. Thirteen years later he used this kind of double stage for another great religious composition—the 'Adoration of the Trinity'. Here, too, the action taking place in the higher spheres has a visionary *69* character. Dürer himself, however, is standing below in the landscape, not because he considered himself excluded from the congregation of the faithful or from the act of adoring the Trinity, but because the scene in Heaven is his vision, just as the apocalyptic events are the revelations which were vouchsafed to St. John on Patmos.

Artistic creations such as Dürer's 'Apocalypse' are the product of inner crises, *The* like Goethe's 'Werther'. Surprising though this achievement may appear at a *Apocalyptic* *Mood* time when Dürer was on the borderline between youth and maturity, still full of storm and stress, but already on the threshold of restraint and prosperity, we

THE ANGEL WITH THE KEY OF THE BOTTOMLESS PIT
(Apocalypse, 1498)

are not altogether unprepared for this entry of Dürer into the world of visions. At home, and more especially during his travels in the South, Dürer had tasted the cup of life with the natural zest of a healthy young man, but he had also become familiar with the shadier sides of life. His mind was filled with pictures of death, with dreams, visions of devils and witches, images of disease, monstrosities and so on. Death was far more visible in the streets of mediaeval cities than it is in our own time. The agony of death could be witnessed by all at the numerous public executions and torturings. Deformed and mutilated beings begged piteously for alms in the streets and on the steps of churches. The great plagues, which from time to time brought terror and distress to Germany, together with the spectacle of the cruelty of man to man and of licentiousness given free rein on the threshold of the tomb, were things he could not easily forget. The plague in Basle (1439) gave rise to the mural paintings of the 'Dance of Death' in the cemetery of the Dominican monastery in that city, which Dürer probably saw during his wanderings. The plague which raged in Nuremberg in 1494 may, according to Eduard Flechsig, have been the cause of Dürer's first journey to Italy. Devils and witches were among the things which, according to mediaeval ideas, were not only believed to exist, but might actually be seen and experienced, and Dürer's ideas on the subject cannot have differed from those of Luther. If we add to this Dürer's unusually developed capacity for dreaming and remembering his dreams, then we have all the necessary premises to explain why it was that Dürer's imagination was so struck by the Revelation of St. John. In Dürer's writings, in his paintings, woodcuts, copperplates and sketches, we find, both before and after the appearance of his 'Apocalypse', ample proofs of his apocalyptic mood. Axel Romdahl has emphasized more strongly than German scholars the gloomy side of Dürer's character.

A magnificent composition by Dürer from the same period as his 'Apocalypse' —'The Three Horsemen and the Three Deaths'—has come down to us only in copies (L. 668, Stuttgart and Vienna), but the drawing L. 193 (Frankfurt) must be one of Dürer's studies for this work. Death swoops down from the sky upon the horseman, like a falcon upon a hare; the horseman falls from his rearing horse. The copperplate known as the 'Promenade' may be of even earlier date, perhaps 1496. Here Death has crept up behind an elegant young couple and hides behind a tree, the hour-glass balanced on his bald skull, like a pitcher on the head of a woman. We go our ways and forget all too willingly that one day we shall encounter Death.

In the 'Apocalypse', Death is shown on horseback. Gruesomely aged, withered as a mummy, he gallops on the right flank of the terrible horsemen, madness gleaming in his wide-open eyes. On the charcoal drawing (L. 91, 1505, London), which is his most vivid rendering of death, Dürer wrote the words: 'Memento mei'. The horseman, whose name is Death, wears a crown on his head, one skeleton hand grips the horse's mane, the other holds the scythe, while the passing-bell swings from his sorry nag's neck. Never has Death been depicted with bolder fancy or more expressive lines. It was thus that Death rode through the streets of German cities stricken by the Black Death. In 'The Knight, Death and the

Pictures of Death

101

100

125 Devil' (copperplate engraving, 1513), Death, in a repulsive state of semi-decomposition, his head wreathed with serpents, holds up the hour-glass before the eyes of the knight 'sans peur et sans reproche', while his horse sniffs at a skull lying on the ground. Rethel's 'Dance of Death' and Böcklin's 'Adventurer' (Bremen) contain echoes of Dürer's figures of Death.

Belief in Witches

The belief in witches and devils sprang from the darkest recesses of the agitated soul. It existed from the most remote times, in the Germanic, the Antique and the Christian world, but it was not until the late Middle Ages that pictorial representation of these evil beings was reduced to a system, when psychological and legal procedure for the proving of witchcraft and the persecution of witches was introduced.

In 1484 Pope Innocent VIII issued his bull dealing with witches, known from its opening words as the 'summis desiderantes affectibus' bull. It was as a result of this bull that trials for witchcraft were first instituted in Germany and it was issued in order to give authority to the Inquisitors, the Dominicans Jacob Sprenger, Johann Gremper and Heinrich Krämer, who had been sent to the Rhineland, in their dealings with the spiritual and secular powers. Three years later there appeared, first in Cologne, and in 1494 in Nuremberg also, the famous 'Witches' Hammer' ('Malleus maleficarum de lamiis et strigibus et sagis'). This work, compiled by the above-named Inquisitors, was intended to be the final codex for the convening, conduct and judgements of witchcraft tribunals. It therefore contains not only examples of the existence of witches culled from the Bible and the Early Fathers, and from the works of mediaeval jurists, philosophers and physicians, but also a kind of index of the magic arts, as well as the regulations governing the convening and conduct of secular trials. For instance, the third chapter is devoted to the witches' habit of travelling by air, which the 'Hammer' attempts to prove by recalling that the Devil took Christ up into an exceeding high mountain and on to a pinnacle of the temple, and that an angel took Habakkuk by the hair and transported him through the air from Judaea to Chaldaea. According to the theories of the Inquisition period, everything in the Kingdom of Satan was the reverse of the natural process, for which reason witches rode backwards on their forks, brooms and spindles. Thus Dürer's witch sits back to front on her goat

99 (copperplate, 1505?); the hailstorm behind her is taken from the 'Witches' Catechism', which makes witches responsible for hail. Witches are depicted naked and with streaming hair when they are 'on duty' (Allihn). The putti gambolling on the ground are an alchemistic symbol, denoting the 'magnum opus' which the children master in their play.

98 The two engravings known as 'Death' (1493–94) and 'The Four Witches' (1497) belong to the borderland between the realm of Death and the world of magic and witchcraft. In the former, the repulsive lover, looking like a depraved tramp, grabbing the girl with his clawlike hand, is, as Allihn rightly surmises, not Death, but an 'incubus', i.e. the devil in human shape seeking carnal intercourse. The cloven foot of the nude old man betrays his satanic origin. It may be that the scroll above the couple's head was to have been inscribed with an

explanatory text. Whereas this little copperplate 'Death' really belongs to the category of witchcraft pictures, on the other hand the engraving known as 'The Four Witches' belongs to the group of representations of death. No satisfactory interpretation of it has yet been given. Sofie Dostal suggests (in a letter) the following explanation: The young woman is hesitating between the door of Hell on the left and the door of Heaven on the right, in other words, between Profane and Sacred Love; the old woman behind her is the procuress. The meaning of the letters 'O.G.H.' on the sphere (which Wustmann believes to be the male fruit of the mandragora officinalis) is obscure. Sandrardt, who collected many an item of ancient lore, thought that they stood for 'O Gott, hüte!' ('God forbid!'). The fashionable headdress of the woman on the extreme left would seem to exclude her from the category of witches. The skull and bones amid the women's feet would seem to be a symbol of death, denoting that even this fair flesh is mortal. The Devil, peeping out from the midst of his flickering hellfire, is already relishing the prospect of these four plump victims, for (according to Hartlaub's interpretation) the women have been assigned to him as a penalty for having indulged in the forbidden practice of love-spells. We find in Dürer's graphic art a whole family of monsters from Limbo, to which belong the huge lizard on the masonry (Little Passion, copperplate) and the devil in the Great Passion (woodcut),   74 shooting out of his den like a demoniacal watchdog. The ancestors of this devilish brood can be traced back through the fantasies of Schongauer, Pacher etc. to the remote origins of mediaeval art.

Dürer's copperplate of 1497–99, known as 'The Dream' or 'The Doctor's   106 Dream', is a pictorial enigma which has not yet been satisfactorily solved. A winged devil with a pair of bellows is blowing into the ear of a man seated before a stove. But what is he urging him to do? Is the nude woman, whose little angel companion is trying to walk on stilts, trying to entice the man out of the warm comfort of his refuge into the adventurous paths of life and love? Or is it that the God of Love can no longer move except on stilts and the Goddess of Love can comfort the aged man only in dream form? Attempts have been made to identify the 'doctor' as Dürer's friend Pirckheimer and to interpret the engraving as a satire on Pirckheimer's manifold ills. In this case the title 'Dream of a Podagrist' would be apt, for Pirckheimer in his 'Lob der Podagra' sang the praises of gout with somewhat peevish self-derision. Another interpretation is less innocent—it sees in this scene a reference to Pirckheimer's syphilis. In support of this thesis Oskar Hagen cites a passage from a letter which L. Beheim wrote to Pirckheimer; in it he mentions a stove which was particularly economical in its consumption of wood, and goes on to say: 'If anyone thinks he is dying, then let God tempt me with a young girl, and I would soon drive away all melancholy.' Be that as it may, there is certainly something sinister about this Eve, roasting her apple on the hot tiles of the stove.

Though the dream-pictures of St. John on Patmos, with all their horrors, gradually receded from Dürer's mind, the apocalyptic mood, which was one of the fundamental experiences of his soul, reappears from time to time. In 1503, the year in which a comet appeared to the terrified eyes of men, Dürer witnessed what he describes as 'the greatest miracle'—the appearance of crosses on the clothes of many people, especially on those of children. One of these crosses fell on to the linen shift of Eyrer's maid, who was sitting at the back of Pirckheimer's house, 'whereat she was so afflicted that she began to weep and cry out loudly, for she feared that she would die of it'. Dürer also makes a direct reference to the Apocalypse in that well-known and often quoted passage in his diary of the journey to the Netherlands, when, believing that Luther was dead, he broke into a cry of woe and admonition: 'O ye Christian men! Pray to God for aid, for His Judgement is nigh and His Justice will be made manifest. Then shall we see how the innocent bleed, whom the Pope, the priests and the monks have judged and condemned. Apocalypse! These are the slain who lie before the altar of God and cry for vengeance, to whom the voice of God will answer: Wait till the number of the innocent slain is accomplished and then will I judge.' It is the vision of St. John of which Dürer is thinking here, that vision which he depicted in the Opening of the Sixth Seal. The stormwind of the Apocalypse is also blowing in the two scenes which Dürer etched on iron in 1515 and 1516—the 'Agony in the Garden' (1515) and the 'Sudarium held by an Angel' (1516). Like a sail, the Sudarium of St. Veronica carries the angel up to Heaven, his heavy robe rustling behind him.

Until the last years of his life Dürer was haunted by apparitions and dreams, which came to him from the depths of a soul torn by religious experience. He could not rid himself of the fears of the earthly creature, no matter how often he tried to free himself by giving form to his emotions.

In the drafts for the introduction to his projected book on painting, Dürer noted the following personal observation: 'How often do I see great art in my sleep, but waking cannot recall it; so soon as I awake, my memory forgets it.' He did, however, note down one of these visions and try to preserve it by means of a water-colour sketch (L. 423, Vienna). In 1525 there came from many sources prophecies of a repetition of the Flood. This prophecy was so definite in form and the belief in signs and wonders was so strong at that time, that many prudent people reserved lodgings on the top floors of houses, and an evacuation of the seats of government to the high mountains was even contemplated. Dürer's dream was obviously influenced by these prognoses of disaster. Wölfflin has rightly described it as a 'piece out of the Apocalypse'. Dürer's note runs: 'In the year 1525, at Whitsun, between the Wednesday and the Pentecost (7–8 June), during the night in my slumbers I saw this vision, how many great waters fell from Heaven. And the first fell to the earth about four leagues from me with much horror and with a great rushing and spouting and drowned the whole earth. And at this I was so mightily afraid that I awoke before the other waters fell. And the waters which fell were very great. And some fell at a distance and some fell near and they rose so high that they seemed to be falling with the same slowness. But when the first water which fell upon the earth, had all but reached me, the wind began to blow with such violence that I awoke and was afraid. And my whole body trembled and it was long ere I came to myself. And when I arose in the morning I painted here above what I had seen. And may God grant that all things may turn for the best.'

CHAPTER FOUR

EUROPEAN ART ABOUT THE YEAR 1500

THE year 1498 marks the real entry of Dürer into the world of European art. With his woodcuts of the Revelation of St. John and the first prints of his 'Great Passion' beneath his arm, Dürer thrust open the portals of fame and entered the inner circle of the bearers of great names.

Let us try to imagine for a moment what would have happened if some famous centre of commerce and the tourist industry, such as Venice, had invited the foremost artists of the time to send their works to an exhibition, held in order to celebrate the passage from the fifteenth to the sixteenth century. What works would have been seen at such an exhibition and what rôle would the 29-year-old Nuremberger, Albrecht Dürer, have played amongst the leading artists of Germany, Italy and the Netherlands? *An Exhibition of International Art*

Let us begin our tour of this imaginary exhibition by entering the Italian Room. Two great sculptors, whose works must have made a deep impression on Dürer, died before 1500—Donatello in 1466 and Verrocchio in 1481. Donatello's Gatta-melata in Padua—at the latest in 1506, on the occasion of his second visit to Italy—and Verrocchio's Colleoni in Venice must have opened the eyes of the young Dürer to the problems of movement and proportion in the representation of equestrian figures. Antonio Rizzo died in 1498 and his open-mouthed 'Adam' was present in Dürer's mind when he painted his own 'Adam' (Madrid, Prado). In his preparatory studies, many years later, for the engraving of the 'Knight, Death and the Devil', Dürer had frequent recourse to his memories of these works and of the bronze horses outside St. Mark's. The three leaders of the Italian Renais-sance—Leonardo da Vinci, Michelangelo and Raphael—might well have been represented at our exhibition. At the beginning of 1498 Leonardo finished his most famous and extensive work, the fresco of the Last Supper on the refectory wall of the convent of Santa Maria delle Grazie in Milan, and he might have exhibited some of his drawings for the Last Supper, such as the studies for the Apostle James or his sketch for St. Peter's sleeve (Windsor Castle). Dürer never saw the Last Supper, but he knew of it, as is proved by his own versions of the theme, e.g. in the 'Great Passion' woodcuts and in the single print of 1523. Echoes of Leonardo are found in many of Durer's works, e.g. of the so-called caricatures, his 'Knots', his studies in proportion, the cartoon for the 'Battle of Anghiari' etc. About the end of the century, Dürer used for his engraving of the 'Virgin and the Monkey' the motive of the Infant Jesus with the little bird in Leonardo's cartoon, 'The Holy Family' (London, Royal Academy), which must date from Leonardo's Milan period. In these years, which were among the most fruitful of Leonardo's life, he also busied himself with the problems of equestrian statues; he made numerous drawings and plastic studies for the equestrian monument of Francesco Sforza, of which the gigantic clay model was destroyed by Gascon bowmen after the fall of Lodovico Sforza il Moro. A second series of sketches

The Italians

111

Leonardo

was made by Leonardo for the equestrian statue of Trivulzio, Sforza's adversary. A third group, from which Leonardo might have shown at our exhibition the so-called 'Five Horsemen' print (about 1499, Windsor Castle), consisted of studies of antique costumes.

Raphael

Raphael could have been represented at an exhibition held in 1500 only by youthful works, but among these might have been two which would have excited Dürer's lively admiration—'The Vision of a Knight' (London, National Gallery) and 'The Three Graces' (Chantilly). Count Klaus von Baudissin has interpreted the London painting as follows: The female figure with book and sword is inciting the dreaming young hero to study and feats of arms; the other female figure offers him a flower as a symbol of the pleasures of life; the young knight has to choose between 'virtus' and 'amor', not, like Hercules, between 'virtus' and 'voluptas'. That favourite Renaissance subject, 'Hercules at the Crossroads', also attracted Dürer. His copperplate engraving of about 1500, the so-called 'Great Hercules', of which more will be said below, shows a Herculean man taking part, as the protector of Virtue, in the fight against Lust. Dürer's Hercules is a naked wild man of the woods, who has broken off a branch from the nearest tree. The meaning of Raphael's 'Three Graces', with the apples of the Hesperides in their hands, is clear. Antique gems may have provided inspiration for its artistic construction, or reliefs and Renaissance medallions. Comparison with medallions enables us to identify the three figures as Caritas, Amor and Pulchritudo. Between this little picture and Dürer there is a link, for the same subject, a group of nude female figures, the middle one with her back towards the spectator, had been treated by Dürer in his own way about three years earlier. Under the impressions received from Italian art, Dürer transformed his drawing of the 'Women's Bath'

117

(L. 101, Bremen), dating from 1496, into the celebrated copperplate of the four nude women (1497). Raphael gives us three Graces; Dürer, three witches and a burgher's wife. The Italian created a picture of gay youth, soft as a spring morning in Umbria; the German produced an image of dedication to Death, as uncanny as a scene in a haunted house.

Michelangelo

Michelangelo could have been represented at our exhibition by two famous works, those which Carl Justi describes as his 'most commonplace' and 'most devotional' works in marble—the 'Bacchus' and the 'Pietà'. Both were created between 1497 and 1500. Dürer would have loved the 'Bacchus' and bowed his head reverently before the 'Pietà'. A hard drinker, as became a German, and a man who also understood wine, Dürer has left us variations—not monumental, but of a light ornamental character—on the theme of bibulous exhilaration and the Bacchic mood in his marginal drawings for the Emperor Maximilian's Prayer-book (e.g. the Silenus on the wine-cask, p. 52, verso). Michelangelo's 'Pietà' was commissioned by a French Cardinal in 1497 for the chapel of St. Petronilla in the old Vatican basilica. It is a picture of grief, 'as reticent as Death itself' (Justi).

Dürer never created a 'Vesper picture', as representations of the Pietà were called in Germany in the fourteenth and fifteenth centuries. What was the reason

for this omission? Perhaps he thought that this motive of painful loneliness—
the Mother and her dead Son, nothing else in the world!—was indeed a subject
for sculpture with its possibilities of detachment, but not for painting, which is
essentially an art of combination. In the year of Dürer's birth, 1471, an unknown
Swabian master, with his own Hedelfingen 'Vesper picture' (Stuttgart, Museum
of Antiquities), created a German counterpart to Michelangelo's 'Pietà'. But it
was not until 1521, when he was a mature man in his fiftieth year, that fate led
Dürer to Notre-Dame in Bruges, where he saw the Madonna of Bruges. Michelangelo's 'Madonna' was finished in 1504, and the commission was given to him by
Flemings.

The young Dürer had a feeling that the birthplace of 'modern' art lay outside
the frontiers of Germany, which also remained untouched by the political life
of Europe, until, at the time of the Reformation, she took the lead in a European
question. Dürer never visited Florence or Rome, the actual home of the Italian neo-
classical revival—he himself calls the Renaissance a 'reawakening'. For him Italian
art meant Northern Italian art, and in particular Venetian painting. Dürer had
always had a great veneration for Giovanni Bellini, perhaps not only for the painter   *Giovanni*
of Madonnas, but also for the creator of thoughtful allegories (Venice, Accademia).   *Bellini*
In 1488 Giovanni Bellini completed his magnificent triptych of the Madonna
enthroned with four Saints for the church of the Frari in Venice. This 'santa
conversazione', bathed in the deep melodies of the Venetian atmosphere, gilded
by the sun of late afternoon, must have filled Dürer with rapture. How this
pleasing spectacle was transformed by the emotional atmosphere of the German
Reformation into the inexorable severity of Dürer's 'Four Apostles', is a subject   *82–84*
to which we shall return in a later chapter. Between 1490 and 1500 Bellini was
busy painting portraits and his great historical pictures for the Ducal Palace. He
would have had hardly any works in his atelier which could have been shown at
our exhibition in 1500, but paintings by other Venetian artists would certainly
have hung on the walls, for example, Gentile Bellini's scenes from the story of
the relics of the Holy Cross (Venice, Accademia). Dürer took note of one detail
from the painting of the Procession in Piazza San Marco—the two Turks with a
servant—which appears, transformed, in one of his drawings (L. 93, London).

Between 1490 and 1495, Vittore Carpaccio painted his scenes from the Legend   *Carpaccio*
of St. Ursula (Venice, Accademia), as charming as fairy-tales and interesting for
their details of customs and morals. The 'Vision of St. Ursula' would certainly
have been seen at our exhibition. This king's daughter, sound asleep in her room
in a Venetian palace and visited by pious dreams, is the Italian sister of Dürer's
'St. Jerome in his Study'. And Dürer could even have seen a St. Jerome by
Carpaccio, in the Scuola degli Schiavoni. Carpaccio's Prince of the Church, more
youthful than Dürer's Saint in the engraving of 1514, pauses in his work and casts
a quick glance at the window, while his raised hand holding the pen is about to
fall back on to the paper. In Carpaccio's picture, glance and gesture are fleeting,
but Dürer shows us St. Jerome completely absorbed in his work, deaf and blind
to the outside world.

During Dürer's first stay in Venice, the Muranese school was still flourishing under its leaders, the two Vivarini. Bartolomeo Vivarini died in 1499. One year earlier he painted his Resurrection for San Giovanni in Bragora, where Dürer must have seen it when he came to Venice for the second time. Our imaginary exhibition would have included only a youthful work by that noblest of all *Giorgione* Venetian painters, Giorgione, but nevertheless a magnificent one—'The Judgement of Solomon' (Florence, Uffizi). Dürer's letters make no mention of Giorgione, but he must have known of him. K. F. Suters makes the tempting suggestion that without Dürer's expert advice Giorgione would not have been entrusted with the execution of the paintings on the façade of the Fondaco dei Tedeschi in Venice. If there was really a link between the young Venetian and the young Nuremberg master, it would appear to be in their landscapes. In many of Dürer's landscape backgrounds we seem to recognize parts of the Venetian mainland, the Lower Alps and the Dolomites, such as Giorgione and Titian, both of whom were born there, loved to paint. Giorgione's 'Moses and the Burning Bush', his counterpart to the 'Judgement of Solomon', was not painted until the first years of the sixteenth century.

Mantegna In the Italian Room one wall would have been reserved for the works of Mantegna, that great power in the world of art who came from Padua to Venice to dispute for mastery with the school of Murano. Mantegna was the brother-in-law of Gentile and Giovanni Bellini, and one might say that by his marriage—like a reigning prince—he enlarged his domain. His paintings in the Eremitani chapel in Padua had opened new paths to Northern Italian painting. Engravings by Mantegna and his school found their way to Northern Europe at an early date and penetrated to the booksellers' shops and the artists' ateliers. Dürer's 'Apocalypse' woodcuts show, as has already been mentioned, traces of this contact between German and Italian art. Dürer had made his copies of a drawing of Orpheus by Mantegna and of the latter's engravings, 'The Battle of Tritons' and 'Bacchanal with the Tub', before his first journey to Italy. The middle panel of Dürer's altar-piece (Dresden), which Frederick the Wise commissioned him to paint for Wittenberg in 1496, has a Mantegnesque harshness and severity; it is like a foreign body amidst the works of Dürer. Between 1497 and 1500 Mantegna painted one of his finest works—the 'Parnassus' (Paris, Louvre), in which Apollo and the Muses are celebrating the triumph of Venus over Mars. In this painting idealized figures move their limbs, the latter having a harmony of proportion which is not the product of caprice or chance, but is derived from a study of the antique and from measurements made from Nature. It is easy to understand why Dürer, who heard of Mantegna towards the end of the century, wanted to go from Venice to Mantua in 1506 to visit the great master. But he had the same ill-fortune with Mantegna as he did with Martin Schongauer—he never saw him alive. Dürer was unable to visit Mantua on account of an outbreak of the plague, and Mantegna died in 1506 at the age of 75. Although Antonio Pollaiuolo's 'Rape of Dejanira' (New Haven, U.S.A., Art Museum) was painted as far back as 1480, it must not be omitted from this list of Italian works which influenced

Dürer. The latter's mythological painting of 'Hercules and the Birds of Stymphalis' (Nuremberg, Germanisches Nationalmuseum), which we shall see in the German room, is undoubtedly derived from Pollaiuolo's composition (cf. also Dürer's copy, made in 1505, of Pollaiuolo's 'Rape'; L. 347, Bayonne, Musée Bonnat). In 1500 appeared the view of Venice, almost five feet long and carved in wood, which Jacopo de' Barbari made for the Nuremberg merchant Anton Kolb. This Meister Jakob Walch (Wellisch = Italian), as the Nurembergers called Jacopo, acted as a liaison man between the North and the South and probably drew Dürer's attention to the leading figures in Italian art.

We will now leave the Italian Room and take a look at the cabinet reserved for artists of the Netherlands, where the arts and crafts developed along uniform lines during the fifteenth century. Flanders had become the home of realism and the starting-point of oil painting. This artistic development had furnished wandering artists with inspiration and encouragement, and through them—and also through other channels—had spread to Germany, France and Italy. Dürer's father must have told his son of the palmy days of the Netherlands under the Burgundian princes. The greatest master of Flemish painting, Jan van Eyck, had died before the middle of the century. On his journey to the Low Countries Dürer saw and admired in the abbey of St. Bavon in Ghent 'the panel of St. John', that 'most precious, so intelligent painting'. Rogier van der Weyden died in 1464; when Dürer saw some of his works in Brussels and Bruges, he spoke of 'Rüdiger' as a 'great old master'. In 1495 Hans Memling died. At the end of the fifteenth century the proud heritage of old Flemish art was in the hands of Gerard David and Quentin Matsys, whose magnificent house in Antwerp Dürer visited. *The Flemish School*

Quentin Matsys, the great master of Louvain, would probably have been represented at our exhibition by one of his youthful works, the St. Christopher (Antwerp, Museum), which is believed to have been painted about 1490. This rendering of St. Christopher is highly emotional. The agitated features, the open mouth and the furrowed brow reflect spiritual and physical tension and a sensation of almost fearful astonishment that so light a charge can prove to be so heavy a burden. Dürer's father was a goldsmith and his son had learned the same trade; Quentin Matsys' father was a blacksmith and his son spent his early days in the smithy, until he exchanged the anvil for the palette. Matsys did not produce his greatest works until after 1500—between 1507 and 1511. *Quentin Matsys*

In the art-loving city of Bruges Gerard David reigned supreme. For the hall of the magistrates in the Hôtel de Ville he painted between 1487 and 1498 a series of pictures, two of which—the sentencing of the corrupt judge Sisamnes by Cambyses and the flaying of Sisamnes—have been preserved (Bruges, Museum). We may well assume that the Judgement of Cambyses, dated 1498, might have appeared at our imaginary exhibition. In the oval relief (showing Marsyas, who was also flayed) behind the judicial seat of Cambyses, Italian spectators would have recognized a theme made familiar to them by antique gems and also by their own artists. In the diary of his journey to the Netherlands Dürer does not mention Gerard David, whose name was forgotten far more quickly than that of Quentin Matsys. *Gerard David*

*The German
Artists*

Let us now turn to the German artists. By 1500 many of the pioneers of fifteenth-century German art were already dead. First of all, Martin Schongauer (died 1488), whose engravings Dürer had studied in Wolgemut's atelier and whose widespread fame had been the magnet which drew the young Dürer to Alsace during his Wanderjahre. The works which Schongauer left in the city of Colmar had been Dürer's school of copperplate-engraving. In Colmar he had also seen the engravings of Schongauer's forerunner, the Master E. S., whose genre-pictures inspired him. In 1498 Michael Pacher, the German Mantegna, died. His sphere of influence, South Tyrol, had been traversed by Dürer on his first visit to Italy. Lastly, Stefan Lochner had been dead for nearly half a century, but his name still lived and every traveller to the Rhine who prided himself on his culture, when he came to Cologne Cathedral asked to see Meister Stefan's 'Tafel'. Dürer too did so on his journey to Flanders.

Wolgemut

About 1500 Wolgemut's atelier in Nuremberg was still prospering. One altar-piece after another was despatched to the surrounding territories of Franconia, Swabia and Saxony, to bear colourful witness to the devoutness and joyfulness of Late Gothic art and also to the religious fervour and proud sense of responsibility of pious and prosperous donors. Wilhelm Pleydenwurff, a close atelier collaborator of his stepfather Wolgemut and a friend of Dürer, died in 1494, one year after the publication of his and Wolgemut's great joint work, the illustrations to Schedel's Chronicle of the World. Of Wolgemut's pictures there could have been shown in 1500 his portrait of Hans Perkmeister (1496, Nuremberg, Germanisches Museum), the right wing of an altar-piece from the Dominican church, painted about 1490 and showing the representatives of the priesthood (Nuremberg, St. Lorenz), or the wings of the St. Martin altar-piece (Nuremberg, St. Jakob), likewise painted in 1490.

Lucas Cranach, born one year after Dürer, would not have been represented in any exhibition of German masters round about 1500, nor would the great Matthias Grünewald. Cranach's first woodcut of the Crucifixion dates from 1502, his first painting of the theme (Munich, Ältere Pinakothek) from 1503. Grünewald's first figure painting, the Mocking of Christ (Munich, Ältere Pinakothek), belongs to the same year. To the Nuremberg school we must add the masters of Augsburg and Ulm. North Germany would have been represented by artists from Hamburg and Lübeck, South Germany by a master from Salzburg. In 1499

*Hans Holbein
the Elder*

Hans Holbein the Elder painted in Augsburg his beautiful Virgin with Angels, now in Nuremberg (Germanisches Museum); traces of Flemish influence (Rogier van der Weyden?) cannot be missed. From Ulm would have come, like a last message of the Middle Ages and Swabian tranquillity, the Heerberg altar-piece

*Bartholomäus
Zeitblom*

*Hinrik
Bornemann*

Berndt Notke

of the Nativity by Bartholomäus Zeitblom (1497–98, Stuttgart, Museum). The Hansa cities of the North would have sent Hinrik Bornemann's Christ in the Garden of Emmaus—the right wing of the altar-piece of St. Luke, painted in 1499—from the Jakobikirche at Hamburg. Berndt Notke, born in Ratzeburg and active both in Lübeck and Scandinavia, created in 1489 the magnificent St. Jürgen group in Stockholm and in 1496 the painting of St. John on Patmos

THE HOUSE BY THE POND. Water-colour, 1495–97. London, British Museum

(Lübeck, Museum). It would be better not to hang his tranquil Baltic saints side-by-side with the works of the Franconian visionary Dürer. And from the remote parish church of Grossgmain there might have come another work, painted in 1499, just before that close of the century which was not merely a date in the calendar, but a turning-point in style and life—the Miracle of Pentecost by the Salzburg painter Rueland Frueauf, whose son, also named Rueland, worked with Dürer in Wolgemut's atelier.

Rueland
Frueauf

Such were the pictures which the worthy minds of the Old German Masters produced. Swabian love of ease, Franconian flexibility, Northern reverie and Saxon alertness sat at their easels. Conscientiousness guided their brushes and love for their pictures added the finishing touches. Only one element did they lack—genius! But that disquieting spirit of genius was present in the young Franconian painter Dürer, who had learned all that there was to be learned in Wolgemut's atelier and henceforth was to be his own teacher.

Dürer

Several works by Dürer might have hung in our imaginary exhibition, for instance his portrait of Oswolt Krell (1499, Munich, Ältere Pinakothek), with his eyes darting a glance charged with energy at us; his grandiose and solemn 'Lamentation' (1500, Munich, Ältere Pinakothek); the romantic picture of 'Hercules and the Birds of Stymphalis' (Nuremberg, Germanisches Nationalmuseum) and the 1498 self-portrait of the artist in ornate dress (Madrid, Prado).

17

8

In the glass cases, beside the woodcuts of Wolgemut and Pleydenwurff for Schedel's Chronicle of the World, would have lain the great prints of Dürer's 'Apocalypse', the first seven prints of his 'Great Passion' and those deeply poetical prints: the 'Prodigal Son', the 'Virgin with the Monkey', the 'Sea-monster' and the 'Great Hercules'. On the one side the products of local schools, on the other the youthful works of Dürer—two different worlds of art! Whence did he derive that power which is already visible in his first works? What is the link which binds him to the comrades of his wanderings and his first years as a master?

57, 86, 97

If we want to understand Dürer's 'Apocalypse', his 'Great Passion' and his graphic allegories, it is useless to approach him by way of the gentle slopes of German painting between 1480 and 1500—we must scale the steep cliffs of German altar sculpture. This heroic period of Late Gothic sculpture in Germany begins with three altars of approximately the same date—the altar of the Virgin in Cracow, by Veit Stoss; the St. Wolfgang altar by Michael Pacher in St. Wolfgang; and the Nördlingen altar by Simon Leinberger. These are three mighty works which already contain the germs of the passionate tempo, the fervour and the heroic agony which characterize Dürer's 'Apocalypse'. For example, the St. John of Veit Stoss' altar of the Virgin and Dürer's St. Michael in the 'Apocalypse' are of the same blood. To these warriors, who put body and soul into the fight and know how to conquer, must be added the St. Christopher carved by a great master of South-East Germany for the altar at Kefermarkt in Upper Austria.

Late Gothic
Altar
Sculpture

Veit Stoss

Michael Pacher

Simon
Leinberger

The Master
of Kefermarkt

If it had been possible to transport the great altars from Nördlingen and Kefermarkt to Venice—borne on the shoulders of strong men, 'wrapped in tapestry and much cotton', as was the case when Dürer's Festival of the Rose-garlands was

E

transported from Venice to Prague—and exhibit them by the side of the works of Michelangelo, Donatello and Verrocchio, they would have seemed to Italian spectators like a rustling wind from the forests of the North.

The stormy spirit of German sculpture in the 1470's and 1480's was lulled before the end of the fifteenth century. The forms, previously agitated, became more *Tilman* compact. The inner feeling, hitherto glowing, became softer. Tilman Riemen- *Riemen-* schneider brought the new tone and the new form from his native Harz mountains *schneider* to Southern Germany (Adam and Eve, on the south portal of the Marienkirche in Würzburg). In 1498 Hans Seyfer of Heilbronn executed his St. Kilian altar, in the Virgin of which Wilhelm Pinder has rightly perceived a temporal parallel with the youthful works of Michelangelo. This brings us once again to the Italian Room, and our imaginary wandering through European art about the year 1500 is finished.

Let us glance once more at Dürer, as he depicted himself in the self-portrait of *8* 1498 (Madrid, Prado). In these firm, yet delicate hands lay the future of German art; behind the sensitiveness mixed with obstinacy which the forehead reveals, there lay a force which was to dominate the minds of Europe—Dürer's fantasy.

CHAPTER FIVE

FANTASY

IF we judge by modern standards there seems to be throughout Dürer's work
a contradiction between those works which can be easily and generally understood and those which can be grasped only with the aid of explanation and
interpretation. This has led some critics to speak of an inner schism in Dürer's
work, or even to deplore his 'double-sidedness'.

Dürer, so these critics maintain, was in himself one of the most 'popular' of *Popular and*
artists, but under the influence of his cultured, or in some cases over-cultured *Erudite Art*
friends, he was led to produce works which could be understood only by a small
circle of refined intellectuals; in other words, Dürer's fantasy, that magic force
which had mastered even the inflexible and abstruse subject-matter of the Apocalypse, was led astray by the seductive voice of humanistic erudition.

There is a manifold error in such an assumption. To consider Dürer in this way,
is to misunderstand the man, the essence of his fantasy and his time. His indefatig-
able study of books, his travels, his own reflections, his intercourse with distinguished *Dürer's*
men in every walk of life, made Dürer one of the most cultured men of his time. *Education*
The scope of his knowledge was far greater than is generally supposed, though it
is true that the substance of this knowledge differed widely from that which forms
the foundation of modern culture. Dürer certainly had to absorb a mass of material
which has long vanished from the curricula of our schools. As a boy (1477–1483?)
he attended one of the public grammar-schools in Nuremberg before the advent
of educational reforms under humanistic influence (1485). In these schools the
boys were taught reading, writing, arithmetic and the elements of Latin grammar,
and they also read extracts from the Bible in Latin. As attendance at church formed
part of the school curriculum (serving at Mass, singing of Vespers etc.), the
children acquired a fair knowledge of the Latin tongue and were also fully *Knowledge of*
acquainted with the narrative material contained in the Bible and legends. If *Languages*
Dürer had needed any further knowledge of Latin, he would certainly have been
helped by his bosom-friend Pirckheimer, a Latinist of the first rank. For instance,
we learn from a letter written by Christoph Scheurl to Lucas Cranach in 1509
that it was Pirckheimer who advised Dürer to sign his works in Latin and in
doing so, to follow the example of Apelles and Polycletus, as recorded by Pliny,
and use the imperfect tense. Thus in the inscription on the 'Martyrdom of the
10,000 Christians' we find Dürer using the form 'faciebat' and on the Munich
self-portrait, 'effingebam'. At all events, Dürer knew sufficient Latin for his
artistic and scholarly purposes, though it is quite possible that he did not know
enough to enable him to read difficult Latin texts fluently. Thus in a letter to
Spalatin written in 1520, Dürer asks him to send him the latest works by Luther
'in German', and in 1524 he writes to Niklas Kratzer, asking whether he has
continued his work on a German edition of Euclid.

In the Netherlands Dürer was able to get along by speaking German, but in

Venice he had to learn Italian. Subsequently he often made use of Italian terms when he did not know the German equivalent. For instance, he uses the Venetian word 'fortuna', when referring to the high tide which washed the whale off the beach at Zierikzee before his arrival there.

In any case Dürer, as Erasmus noted with astonishment, was capable of holding his own in conversation with learned friends and was conversant with the religious, philosophical, mathematical and astrological literature of his time. Pirckheimer would certainly not have dedicated his Latin translation of the Characters of Theophrastes to a friend who knew nothing of philosophy. Dürer was an eager student of the ideas of Aristotle, Plato and Plotinus. He speaks of the 'inner ideas of which Plato wrote' and thinks that, if a painter once mastered them, he would always have something new to tell the world, even if he went on living for ever. His key to this classical learning was, however, his knowledge of Latin and that is why he insisted that all students of art should be 'brought up with the Latin tongue, that they may understand noble writing'.

Travels
The letters from Venice and the diary of the journey to the Netherlands also show how keen was Dürer's power of observation, how great was his desire to have intercourse with many people and how thoughtfully he observed the many sides of life. He wanted to see everything that was new, not only works of art in which he took a professional interest, but anything which might provide him with a fruitful source of inspiration. His heart rejoiced when he saw in Brussels that 'wonderful thing of art', i.e. the Mexican goldware, part of the booty brought back by Cortez, and he admired the 'subtle genius of men in foreign countries'.

In those days travel abroad meant, from the point of view of personal experience, far more than it does in our own times, and there was still a daring and thrilling element associated with the penetration of new worlds of thought. Dürer was as far removed from the complacency of the city-dweller as he was from the tranquillity of the life of a learned man. The 'Viking spirit' is how Wilhelm Pinder has described that conquering urge in the soul of Nordic man and it was this ancestral heritage which drove Dürer to seek new fields of intellectual knowledge, from which his fantasy brought back a rich booty. In Wolgemut's atelier Dürer had learned how to handle the traditional forms and the inexhaustible store of religious material, and he succeeded in mastering what were then the newest ideas and processes of the Italians—but still he was not satisfied. On his second journey to Venice he commented on the Venetian painters' poverty of invention; 'It is always one and the same thing', is what he writes to Pirckheimer. Dürer wanted to invent new subjects himself. He was the first Northern artist to create 'free' graphic art, i.e. single engravings which, without text and without forming part of a series, achieve, like paintings, an independent aesthetic existence. What to the prejudiced eye and the mind unschooled in art may appear to be a contradiction, is in reality an exercise of creative fantasy, when considered in relation to the spiritual constitution of a man of genius.

Creative Fantasy
The fantasy of a great artist permeates all the folds and recesses of his soul, from its darkest depths to its most sunlit heights, but it also comprises the spiritual goods

and chattels of a nation. Dürer was not a painter 'and a poet as well'. He was a painter who drew his inspiration from the same Castalian source as the poets. He was not a court painter or a religious painter or an illustrator of bourgeois customs and morals, nor was he the artistic propaganda director of one class or the mouthpiece of one profession—Dürer was there for all, and all were there for him. He was not therefore guilty of any contradiction when he created, side-by-side with 'popular' illustrative works, others of a more 'cultured' trend, when at times he spoke the language of the people and at other times addressed his words to narrower circles. For more 'aristocratic' subjects he used a finer technique—most of his allegories, and especially the profoundest, are engraved on copper, not cut in wood. Dürer knew perfectly well for whom his works were intended and he adapted tone and technique to his clientele. The greatest example of this is the painting of the 'Four Apostles', which, with its emphasis on the connection between picture and text, takes into consideration not only the place for which it was destined—the Hall of the Nuremberg Treasurers—but also the people who would see it, namely the rulers of the city, who were to interpret it as responsible politicians and not as aesthetic connoisseurs.

Knowledge of Men

The age in which Dürer lived demanded both qualities: a belief deeply rooted in the popular conscience and a fantasy soaring to philosophical heights, piety and free thought, Christian belief in salvation and echoes of ancient heathen wisdom. Proverbs, farces and folksongs, the mastersingers, mystery plays and romantic poetry, sermons, anthems and broadsheets—in a hundred forms did literature express the desires, the martial fervour, the meditations, the wit and the grief of the German nation. And the formative arts offered to the fantasy of artists of the time an equal number of outlets. The neat decorative fantasy of the goldsmiths adorned precious metals with flowers and foliage, with allegorical figures and unreal ornamentation. In broadsheets the inflamed fantasy of political adversaries found its outlet in the form of crude witticisms and wild allegations. In the loftier regions of painting and sculpture, German power of imagination invented a wealth of conceits. And Dürer, with his independent copper engravings, created a completely personal mode of expression.

Spirit of the Age

His contemporaries regarded Dürer's fantasy as one of his most outstanding characteristics. And it was the non-Germans in particular who recognized in the fullness and power of his imagination an incomparable and irresistible element. Johannes Cochlaeus states in 1512 that the woodcuts of Dürer's 'Passions' were purchased by merchants all over Europe, as models for the artists of their own countries. Erasmus of Rotterdam says that Dürer knew how to transfer even the inexpressible on to canvas and could express 'almost the language itself'. And the very engravings which have retained their fame the longest (e.g. down to Carducci and Gabriele d'Annunzio), are those which are richest in fantasy, in particular the 'Melancolia'. In 1515 Anton Tucher of Nuremberg bought three prints of Dürer's 'St. Jerome' and four of his 'Melancolia', as presents for friends in Rome. In his 'Ricordi' (Venice, 1560), Monsignore Sabba da Castiglione mentions the great numbers of Dürer woodcuts which had found their way from Germany to

Power of Imagination

Italy. Dürer knew what he was doing when he took with him on his journey to
the Netherlands not only his 'Apocalypse', 'Life of the Virgin' and 'Passions', but
also a supply of the single prints such as the 'Melancolia', 'Hercules', 'Nemesis',
the 'Sea-monster' and 'St. Jerome in his Study'. With the presents he made,
Dürer, consciously or unconsciously, was creating a very good advertisement for
his art. The foreign recipients of these presents took them to every country in
Europe: Kratzer of Munich, court astronomer to King Henry VIII, carried Dürer's
fame to England; the numerous Italians employed by the Netherlands Princes, or
Italian merchants such as the silk-merchant Bombelli in Antwerp, the Portuguese
commercial agents, Spaniards and Dalmatians, carried Dürer's engravings and
woodcuts to their southern homelands, and through the Danish King Christian II,
Dürer's finest prints were distributed as presents in the North. And at the same
time Frau Agnes, sitting in her booth on the German fairgrounds, was selling
both the 'popular' woodcuts and engravings and the choicer single prints. There
were buyers and lovers of both categories of Dürer's graphic works.

Allegories   Dürer's contemporaries knew no distinction between 'popular' art and 'cultured'
art in the modern sense. What for us is a picture-puzzle, was for the men of the
sixteenth century a perfectly clear allegory. It must not be forgotten that the
Middle Ages spoke to mankind through the great picture-books of mural paintings
and statuary and that the subjects of these portal sculptures, door reliefs, choirstall
carvings, gargoyles, illustrated manuscripts and calendars, altar-pieces, stained-
glass windows, block-books etc. were really understood and not just 'appreciated'
from the artistic point of view. The walls of the Palazzo della Ragione in Padua
are covered with the greatest popular astrological encyclopaedia in existence.
The Palazzo Schifanoia in Ferrara was decorated with Francesco Cossa's pictures
of the months, which represent in three tiers the daily life at the court of Borso
d'Este, the symbols of the fixed stars and the signs of the Zodiac, and on the top
tier the Gods of Olympus on a triumphal car. For Borso and his entourage this
combination of astrology and everyday life must have been as easy to read as a
written poem. About the same time, in the last decade of the fifteenth century,
Giovanni Bellini painted his five Allegories, which have cost German scholars,
and in particular the perspicacious G. Ludwig, great trouble to interpret. In Venice
Dürer may well have seen Bellini's 'Fortuna Inconstans', gliding away in the
bark of Fortune, or the 'Summa Virtus', that nude and winged female figure with
lion's claws, rolling away on spheres through a river landscape (Fortitudo,
Temperantia and Justitia combined in one person). Do paths, closed to our under-
102, 97   standing, lead from here to Dürer's 'Great Fortune', to his 'Sea-monster' and to
his other allegorical prints? The understanding of pictures is circumscribed by
the time factor, because the subject-matter of culture changes with time. The
biblical knowledge of the modern man—compared with that of his forefathers—
is already so slight that only the best-known biblical subjects can be generally
understood without the aid of inscriptions or explanatory texts. And how much
more rapidly has the allegorical subject-matter of the Renaissance sunk into
oblivion!

Dürer put his whole soul into everything he created. He would construct a sheet of some fantastic subject-matter with the same attention to detail, the same conscientiousness and fervour that he would use in a drawing for the 'Life of the Virgin'. Dürer did not want to create 'mood pictures', the contemplation of which would arouse a mixture of feelings and produce only a very general impression, he wanted to create precise images of ideas, probably comprehensible down to the last detail both to himself and to his public. There are two ways in which we can regard this fanciful art of Dürer's: either we can limit ourselves to accepting its general effect, because we feel that we cannot completely comprehend the whole picture, or else we can endeavour, by explaining every single component part, to elucidate the meaning of the whole. The solution of Dürer's picture-puzzles is a long and difficult business, involving knowledge of his sources, i.e. of the philosophical, poetical and astrological works which Dürer read and which filled his fantasy. The artistic mind has the undisputed right to dismiss with a gesture of the hand all the attempts at interpretation by scholars with the aid of philosophy and iconography and to extract from Dürer's immortal prints only that which makes a direct appeal to our feelings. But it is also the right and the duty of the historian to try, with the means which knowledge provides, to unravel the workings of Dürer's fantasy.

In the minds of Dürer and his contemporaries, many allegories were still alive. *Personification* This delight in allegory was related to the predilection of humanistic minds for *of Ideas* mythology. The whole manner of thinking of the time craved for allegorical representation. It was a favourite device to present discussions by means of the personification of ideas. For example, the sick Pirckheimer quarrels with the personified Podagra, who has caused him so much suffering. Ulrich von Hutten brought on to the stage of thought Febris and Fortuna, who engage in discussion. Such conceits, as common as the political slogans of our own time, were introduced into everyday life, and it was the mark of an educated and humanistically-minded man if he were able to invent them. In Dürer's circle they were a favourite pastime and their Latinized names suited them as well as their neo-classical robes. The Emperor Maximilian's Triumphal Car is drawn by 'Ratio', the reins are labelled *143* 'Nobilitas' and 'Potentia'. Among Dürer's sketches from the years 1496 and 1497 we find a 'Prudentia', a 'Justitia', a 'Speranza' and a 'Fede'. We are no longer capable of reading fluently the sign language of the Renaissance, interspersed with emblems, symbols, devices, armorial bearings, allegories and hieroglyphics; what appears to us as a riddle, was in all probability no riddle at all to the men of the sixteenth century.

In the diary of his journey to the Netherlands, Dürer mentions his copperplate *The 'Nemesis'* engraving 'Nemesis', which was probably created in 1503. As it would be wrong *102* without valid reason to alter an artist's own nomenclature of his works, this engraving has appeared under this title in all catalogues since the days of the connoisseurs Wagner and Passavant. Sandrardt called it the 'Great Fortune', in order to distinguish it from the 'Little Fortune' of the engraving of 1497(?) (B. 78). A number of other designations for this engraving have been based on the attributes of the female figure, which is considered, on account of the mighty pair of wings, to be, like the 'Melancolia', a personification and not a person. Thus Vasari, on account of the bridle, calls it a 'Temperantia', while others have concluded from the goblet that it is a 'Pandora'.

The older Dürer scholars sought to interpret his 'Nemesis' on the basis of family associations, while the more recent critics have found in it literary allusions. For example, Heller saw in the goblet a reference to the family's connection with the goldsmith's craft and in the bridle a reference to the bridle-maker Laszlo Dürer; Sandrardt identified the landscape as the village of Aytòs, the original home of the Dürer family, while Knorr recognized in the countenance of the Nemesis the features of Frau Agnes. Very little of these fanciful interpretations has stood the test of time. Haendtke was successful in proving that the landscape beneath the feet of the fabulous figure is the small town of Chiusa (Klausen) in South Tyrol and that Dürer modelled it after a sketch made during his first journey to Italy. The interpretation of the goblet and bridle as symbols of liberality and restraint put Giehlow on the right path. In 1498 a posthumous work by Angelo Poliziano, entitled 'Mano', was published in Venice. It is possible that Pirckheimer brought this book to Dürer's notice and that he used it as a source; but perhaps Poliziano's verses are only a somewhat surprising parallel to Dürer's pictorial representation, though it is true that the Italian poet represents Nemesis as a dispenser of fate borne by clouds and winds—she has the reins ready to restrain the rash, while the cup of joy in her hand is an encouragement to the victors in life.

Form and Fantasy

What did the Italians, who produced so many noble Fortunas, slender and smiling, think of the German master's 'Great Fortune'? They must have shaken their heads on beholding this heavy Franconian product, whose lines are as remote from the elegant elaborations of Gothic figures as they are from the pure plastic lines of Renaissance forms. What must have filled the Italians with boundless admiration, however, was the typically German combination of fidelity to nature and extravagant fantasy. Vasari admired with the eyes of an expert the great wings, strong as an eagle's, which would really have been capable of lifting the heavy female form. The Italian eye, schooled to a smooth linear construction, enjoyed the unaccustomed sensation of being led into a maze of forms and a labyrinth of lines. Behind the taut female figure there is a fluttering of feathers, the wind catches the flowing ends of the draperies and a thong of the bridle streams out in the breeze. The cushion of clouds yields beneath the weight of the rolling sphere, forming itself into folds and curls. The medallion-like clarity with which the figure stands out against the pure sky is contrasted with the earthly landscape, with its numerous trees and rocks, churches and little houses, the winding river and the stacks of wood in the meadows. What a wealth of experience, what a delight in symbolism, what a 'winged spirit' (as Dürer called fantasy), must have lain hidden in the bosom of the artist who created such works, worldly and spiritual at the same time, admirable and yet full of strangeness. A comparison between the figure of Nemesis and the Eve of the engraving made in 1504 will show us what fantasy meant to Dürer. There could be no greater contrast. The one breathes the spirit of the North, the other that of the South; in the one we find observation, in the other construction. And yet these are not contradictions, they are merely two opposite poles in the essence of Dürer's being.

At all periods of spiritual and social upheaval, of political revolution, the popular fantasy is easily excited and doubly susceptible to all the wonders of heaven and earth. In our own days popular fantasy has been caught by the problems of radiation and the so-called death-rays, by the stories of diviners and the predictions of astrologers. The development of stratospheric flight and rockets, the attempts to scale the Himalayas, the discovery of remains dating from the earliest periods of history—these are all questions which interest the entire world. *Excitability of Popular Fantasy*

Dürer lived in a period of great discoveries, inventions and revolutions which transformed the world. In the religious, political and social spheres, in the fields of intellectual study and natural science, old ideas died out, to be replaced by new. Although the men of the time could not judge the whole significance of what was going on around them, because they were caught up in the stream of events, they nevertheless felt the tension which was in the air and endeavoured to free themselves from their fears and apprehensions by means of the 'winged spirit' of fantasy. Fantasy took refuge in the wonders of nature and art, it was attracted by the adventurous, the exotic, the 'curious'. At the end of the Middle Ages natural history and geography were still full of fables and legends. The boundary-line between the realm of facts and the world of fairy-tales was still fluid. In 1492 Christopher Columbus discovered the islands of Guanahani, Cuba and Haiti, between 1492 and 1504 he reached the mainland of Central and South America. In 1498 Vasco da Gama discovered the sea route to the East Indies, between 1519 and 1521 Cortez conquered Mexico, while Magellan discovered the Marianas in the South Seas and sailed round the world. The early navigators brought back from the New World not only sea-chests full of shells, turtles, weapons, textiles, birds and ostrich-eggs, but also a fund of sailors' yarns about sea-monsters, wild men and animals. Popular fancy was caught by many of these peculiar products of nature. For example, narwhal's teeth were believed to be the horns of unicorns, already associated with the Virgin; ostriches were already known from the Bible; the so-called 'bezoars'—concretions found in the stomachs of camels—were believed to be a protection against poison. These curiosities found their way not only into the treasure-rooms of secular princes, but even into the churches, for they were held to encourage worshippers to meditation and to be signs of the wonders of God's creation. Even today one can see in the Capilla del Lagarte in Seville Cathedral a crocodile, an elephant's tusk and the bridle of the Cid's horse. In St. Stephen's Cathedral at Vienna, in the Johanniskirche at Lüneburg and elsewhere, 'giants' bones' (fossils) hang on the walls. In Antwerp Dürer carefully recorded in his sketchbook the upper thighbone and shoulder-blades (fossil bones) of the 'Antwerp giant'. The first collector on the grand scale, Duc Jean de Berry, brother of Charles the Bold, who died in 1416, collected not only beautifully illuminated books, relics and goldsmith's ware, but also ostrich-eggs, snakes' jaw-bones and the teeth of prehistoric animals and 'sea-monsters'. From these collections *The 'Winged Spirit'* of the Dukes of Burgundy came the dowry of Charles the Bold's daughter Mary, part of which was pawned by her husband Maximilian, who was never free from financial difficulties.

Dürer's letters, diary and prints show that he took a keen interest in such things. Turtles' shells, jawbones of asses, stags' antlers, golden chalices, harness, a unicorn, a pig with eight legs, a walrus and a rhinoceros, are all to be found in his work. We have already mentioned his admiration for the booty brought back from Mexico. But Dürer's diary is also indebted to the collection of the Regent Margaret of Malines, in which real works of art, as opposed to exotic and curious objects, took the foremost place. What Dürer could not bring to his workshop, he carried in his head, which was a veritable museum of curiosities, from which he produced first one piece and then another.

From about 1501 dates the copperplate engraving which has long been known as the 'Sea-monster' or the 'Sea-robbers'. Either of these titles indicates the essential factor: the ravishing of a woman by some creature of the sea. Dürer called the print the 'Sea-monster', but in the sixteenth century this word had a general sense of 'fantastic creature'—even nowadays it is often used jokingly and Hans Sachs addresses Melancolia as a 'grave sea-monster'. The many mythological interpretations date from times in which science was considered more important than superstition and scholars had forgotten that superstition was the earliest form of science. One of the first interpretations dates from the beginning of the nineteenth century and has been ventilated by scholars from Bartsch down to O. Lenz (1924). According to this interpretation the print represents the Rape of Amymone by Triton. But this does not seem to fit in with Lucian's story, according to which Amymone, while searching for water, was carried away by Triton and brought to his master Poseidon, for in Dürer's engraving one chief personage, the God of the Sea, is lacking. The same may be said of other suggestions, such as Glaucus and Scylla (W. von Seidlitz) and Nessus and Dejanira (Veit Valentin). H. Dollmeyr went from classical to old German mythology and drew attention to an old Merovingian legend, according to which Theodelinda, mother of Meroveus and wife of King Clodion, was ravished by a sea-monster, the result being the birth of the founder of the Merovingian dynasty. As Maximilian I was anxious to trace his origin back to the Merovingians, this strange episode is said to have had a romantic attraction for him. There are, however, certain discrepancies in this theory which cannot be overlooked. The same applies to a similar Lombard legend which Hans Sachs took from the Dresden 'Book of Heroes' (1472) and related in one of his songs. That Dürer knew this Merovingian legend in 1500, before he had begun to concern himself with Maximilian's ancestors in connection with the Triumphal Arch is, to say the least of it, doubtful. Hans Sachs' poem (1552) was not written until long after Dürer's death. E. Conrat-Tietze has sought to interpret the print by reference to the 37th story in Ovid's Metamorphoses, which relates the ravishing of Perimela by the river-god Achelous. In his wrath, Hippodamus, the father of Perimela, threw his daughter into the river, but Achelous carried her to the sea, where Neptune transformed her into an island. Achelous lost a horn in this encounter, and the broken antlers of Dürer's monster may be a reference to this. But however much we try to twist and turn this mythological motive, we can never quite reconcile the text with Dürer's picture. Certain figures in the engraving, such as the little Turk on the bank and the fleeing bathers, cannot be traced in any literary source; conversely, certain figures in the ancient legend are not to be found in Dürer's print.

Konrad Lange, who made a critical collation of the attempts at interpretation made before 1900, did not waste much time over Lombardic or Merovingian legends, and even treated the mythological explanations with reserve. He did, however, draw attention to the stories circulating in Dürer's time concerning the raping of women by sea-monsters. Poggio's 'Facetiae', for example, which by 1500 had run through twenty-six editions, contain many such seamen's yarns. Most of them seem to have originated along the coasts of the Adriatic and they might well have reached Dürer's ears in Venice without the agency of Poggio. Sea-monsters have always been popular and still are today! At that time people believed firmly in the existence of such monsters and illustrated books spread tidings of fabulous beings and abortions such as the eight-footed sow of Landser in the Sundgau (see Dürer's engraving of 1496, after an astrological-political broadsheet by Sebastian Brant).

Against Lange's interpretation has been urged the fact that a realistic artist of Dürer's stamp would have represented rape as rape—in the etching on iron of a woman being carried away on the back of a unicorn, he has given us a scene of violent feminine resistance (Rape of Proserpine?). But it is precisely the dreamy conception of the sea-monster that is so characteristic of Dürer. Suggest to an imaginative man the words 'Knight', 'Death', 'Devil'. If he has never seen Dürer's engraving, he will at once conjure up a scene of battle, or at all events of lively animation. But Dürer transforms these three concepts into a scene of ghostly silence, in which the aloofness of the knight is the decisive factor. He has remodelled the theme of a woman and a sea-monster along similar lines. That the women bathing by the river-bank have any inner connection with the monster's victim, that the ravished woman belongs in any way to the turbaned Turk with arms raised above his head—all that is mere supposition and not a fact which can be read from the picture. Who can say with certainty that the woman who has thrown herself down on the slope is the victim's mother? After all, the scene can be adequately explained by assuming that the inhabitants of the riverside town are saluting with Oriental gestures and shouting the passing of this miraculous double apparition and that the women flee to the bank like any bather would if the fin of a shark appeared above the water. But the two mysterious beings on their journey to the open sea come from another world. Unperturbed by all the excitement, they go floating on their way through the rippling water, the woman reposing peacefully as if in a seashell. For the formal construction of this engraving a study made by Dürer in 1501 (L. 466, Vienna) is important. Whence the impulse came to transform the formal idea of a recumbent nude and the subject-matter of a rape into the composition of the 'Sea-monster', whether it came from representations of battles between Nereids and Tritons by Italian artists—we need only think of Mantegna's groups of fighting Tritons (cf. the drawing by Dürer in the Albertina; L. 455, 1494)—are things we do not know.

How unreliable such interpretations are, however keen the perception of the interpreter, is shown if we take a glance at a modern work of art which is very close to Dürer's 'Sea-monster'—Böcklin's 'Elysian Fields' (Berlin, National-galerie). Here, too, we have a fabulous creature carrying a nude woman on his back through the water; here, too, we see female bathers sporting in the water and figures on the bank. This induced Guido Hauck to interpret the scene as a reference to the Second Part of Faust—'Charon and Helen . . . approaching Elysium, deaf to the allurements of the Sirens'. When Böcklin heard of this interpretation, he is said to have laughed and remarked that in actual fact both he and Goethe had the same thing in mind—the banks of the Arno. Perhaps Dürer would have said in answer to a question as to the meaning of his 'Sea-monster', that both he and Poggio had the same thing in mind—the shores of the Adriatic.

'Ercules'　In his diary of the journey to the Netherlands, Dürer mentions a print which he calls 'Ercules'. He means the engraving dating from about 1500, the so-called 'Great Hercules'. The first question we have to answer is the relationship between the four figures in this struggling group. Whom is the cudgel-swinging, draped woman attacking? The pair of lovers below on the left? Or the nude woman in the arms of the satyr? Or only the satyr reaching for the jawbone of an ass? And what is the nude man in the foreground doing? Is he preparing to join in the fray with the tree-branch which he grips with the gesture of a ballet-dancer? Or is he defending the pair of lovers against the assault of the woman swinging the cudgel? The engraving has been interpreted in a variety of ways, some allegorical, some mythological. It has, for example, been described as representing 'Jealousy' or 'The Cuckold'. It has been suggested that three of the participants are Hercules, Nessus and Dejanira; this involves converting the centaur Nessus into a satyr and leaving the aggressive woman nameless. If, as Veit Valentin has suggested, we call the picture 'Jupiter and Antiope', then the woman with the cudgel must be Juno and the man in the foreground must be Mercury, fulfilling his rôle of witness. In 1924, O. Lenz, with better reasons, suggested another interpretation. According to him the satyr is the centaur Eurytion, the nude woman is Hippodamia, the man with the branch in his hands Hercules, and the woman with the cudgel one of the Lapithae. Boccaccio included this story in his 'Genealogia Deorum'. This book was much read by cultured Humanists and the scandal in celestial circles of the punishment of Eurytion by Hercules frequently formed a subject for illustration, e.g. by Aldegrever and Franz Floris. There is still one more chapter, however, in the history of the interpretations of this engraving. After Heinrich Wölfflin had described it as a struggle between Chastity personified by Diana and Unchastity, Panofsky in his book 'Herkules am Scheide-wege' made a new suggestion, based on literary grounds, according to which the engraving, retaining its original name, represents Hercules as paladin of Virtue in her struggle with Lust. Thus the draped female figure becomes Virtue, who has hurried down from her stronghold; the nude figure is Voluptas, who lies in the arms of a satyr personifying Vice. We thus have before us in the form of an engraving a late mediaeval 'morality', its edifying action filled with reminiscences of ancient mythology.

The story of the construction of the picture is just as involved as that of its subject-matter. The recumbent female nude is derived from a drawing by Dürer after an engraving by Mantegna (Battle of Tritons, L. 455, Vienna, 1494); the woman with the cudgel, the undergrowth and the fleeing putto are adapted from Dürer's drawing of Orpheus and the Bacchantes in Hamburg (L. 159, 1494), which in turn is derived from an engraving by Mantegna. For the upper part of the body and the left arm of the standing male nude, Dürer used a copy which he made in 1495 of a 'Rape' by Antonio Pollaiuolo (L. 347, Bayonne).

A few years before the 'Hercules' engraving, Dürer made the woodcut known *'The Fighters'* as 'The Fighters', which bears the word 'Ercules' in a scroll on the top border. H. Kleiber maintained that this represents the fight between Hercules and Eurytos. Eurytos offered his daughter Iole to him who shot a bow better than himself. Hercules was successful, but Eurytos then refused to give him his daughter, whereupon Hercules killed Eurytos and his sons, destroyed his town and carried off the damsel. Panofsky, on the other hand, interprets the woodcut as the punishment of Cacus by Hercules. Cacus stole the cows which Hercules had carried away from Geryon and hid them in a cave. Caca betrayed her brother, Hercules discovered the hiding-place and overcame the robber, and the Eumenides then revenged themselves on Caca for her complicity in the murder of her brother. According to the legend Cacus had three heads and Panofsky interprets the fact that in Dürer's drawing a double man in armour is lying on the ground, as being due to 'triplex' having been mistaken for 'duplex', or as a pictorial rendering of the conception 'half-wild'.

We must get out of our minds the idea that Dürer was the head boy in a class *Dürer's* for the art of illustration. On the contrary he was fond of digressions, and that is *Method of* what makes the interpretation of his works so difficult for scholars with the *Work* minds of schoolmasters. We can reconstruct the genesis of the 'Hercules' prints more or less as follows: Dürer took from his folders drawings he had made from Italian models, he altered them here and there, because he was interested in questions of form, and particularly in the nude; and perhaps some learned and well-read friend looked over his shoulder, and, on seeing an athletic-looking nude, exclaimed: 'Hercules!'

And how about the choice of a title? An artist christens one of his works in *Choice of* order that his child may have a name; he keeps the name to distinguish that *Titles* particular work from others; he then elaborates a new idea, for which the already christened work can be used either in toto or in part, and then transfers the name to the new work, thereby creating difficulties of interpretation! We are always inclined to make the mistake of imagining that the artist's method coincides with the mental processes of those who look at his pictures.

The three engravings—'The Knight, Death and the Devil', 'Melancolia' and 'St. Jerome in his Study' are referred to by scholars under the collective name of 'master-engravings'. As regards date, they are very close to each other. The 'Knight' dates from 1513, the 'Melancolia' and the 'St. Jerome' from 1514. The format is almost identical. The 'Knight' measures $9\frac{7}{8}$ x $7\frac{1}{2}$ inches; the 'Melancolia' $9\frac{7}{16}$ x $6\frac{5}{8}$ and the 'St. Jerome' $9\frac{3}{4}$ x $7\frac{3}{8}$ inches. As these engravings, by the significance of the subject-matter, the perfection of their technical execution and their purely artistic beauty, also form a class to themselves within Dürer's graphic work, repeated attempts have been made to prove that they were the three parts of one programme. There is, however, no external indication of this. We find the figure '1' behind the word 'Melencolia', but no '2' on the 'St. Jerome', and in any case the 'Knight', as the first in date, ought to have been 'No. 1'. The 'S' before the date 1513 on the 'Knight' should not be interpreted as the first letter of the word 'Sanguinicus' (let alone of 'Secundus') but as an abbreviation, frequently used by Dürer elsewhere, of 'Salus'—'S 1513' thus means 'anno salutis 1513'.

If we are to exclude the theory that the inner relationship between the three engravings consists in the fact that they represent three of the four 'temperaments' —which still would not explain why the choleric temperament was omitted— the next question is whether the common factor can be found in the intellectual tendencies of Dürer's time. Writing in 1892, Konrad Lange tried to explain the spiritual background against which Dürer's fantasy saw the three figures of the Knight, Melancolia and St. Jerome, as being one of humanistic erudition, unflinching faith and scientific meditation—'The century of Erasmus, Copernicus and Luther has been immortalized in these three masterpieces.' But we cannot let this theory of Lange's go unchallenged. St. Jerome as representative of Humanism, Melancolia as female symbol of the Copernican theory, the Knight as symbol of religious faith—the internal and external contradictions are such that the idea cannot be reconciled with the pictorial representation.

Wustmann tried to group the three master-engravings on a basis of biographical reasons. The 'Knight' appeared in the year 1513, the year in which sickness forced Dürer's mother to take to her bed. The engraving is therefore a kind of religious consolation, intended 'primarily for his mother', but also, of course, for Dürer himself. Would it not have been natural for Dürer, asks Wustmann, 'to compare his brave mother, who was nigh unto death and a prey to vexations, with an old knight who rides on his way, certain of his goal, the Heavenly Jerusalem, which, as a lofty fortress, beckons to him from not too far away . . .?' The 'Melancolia', on the other hand, which dates from 1514, the year of the mother's death, is a symbol of mourning and grief, 'the nocturnal rainbow being a symbol of his mother's death'. And lastly, if we follow Wustmann's train of thought, in the clear ecstasy of the 'St. Jerome' Dürer found the way back to everyday life, 'as the grief for his mother's death subsided'. Such are the errors into which imagination can lead the interpreters of works of art!

Friedrich Lippmann expressed the opinion that the division, expounded by Gregor Reisch in his 'Margarita Philosophica' published in 1503, of the cardinal virtues into intellectual, moral and theological virtues, might unite Dürer's three engravings into one spiritual group. At first sight, this seems quite tenable, but unfortunately it is impossible to find in Dürer's life any confirmation of the theory that he himself regarded these three works as a group. When selling, exchanging or presenting his prints, Dürer occasionally combined the two engravings of 1514 ('Melancolia' and 'St. Jerome'), but not the three together.

We are therefore left with the fact that each of the three engravings is an independent work. Nevertheless, they are members of a family—Dürer's art of expression, in which his mind is as vividly expressed as it was in the 'Apocalypse' woodcuts and the painting of the 'Four Apostles'. There is, however, one factor which lifts the three master-engravings out of the mass of Dürer's work—they are personal confessions. Dürer's piety and belief in God enabled him to see in St. Jerome a kindred spirit, his moral code found in the 'Knight' an admirable parallel and the 'Melancolia' bears witness to the joys and sorrows, the successes and disappointments of a creative thinker. *Personal Confession*

Let us give precedence to the Prince of the Church. He has some right to this privilege, for he is one of the most popular and beloved of the Saints. Scenes from the legend of St. Jerome made a constant appeal to the fantasy of mediaeval artists and were reproduced by every kind of technique and in all degrees of artistic perfection. The learned translator of the Old Testament extracting the thorn from the lion's foot and thereby converting the monarch of the wilderness into a faithful companion, the Saint sitting and writing in his cave which also served him as a study, beating his breast with stones in moments of repentance, or drawing strength and peace from his solitude—all these were excellent themes for painters and poets. Dürer himself loved St. Jerome and Frau Agnes must also have had a regard for him, on account of the ease with which she was able to sell pictures of St. Jerome in the market-places, at church and during processions. From 1492 to 1521 pictures of St. Jerome constitute a whole group within Dürer's work. His first authenticated woodcut is a St. Jerome (1492), who interrupts his work of translation in order to free the lion of the thorn (cut as title-page for a Latin edition of the Saint's works published by Niklas Kessler of Basle). The engraving, dating from 1496–97, shows us the Saint doing penance; the figure is stifled by the landscape. The spiritual element first becomes visible in the woodcuts of 1511 and 1512, which illustrate two phases of the Saint's work in two different situations. In the 1511 woodcut, the old man is quietly writing in his study and the lion, blinking and half asleep, has his tail tidily tucked between his forepaws; in the 1512 picture, the hermit and translator looks up from the abstruse original text, as if seeking help and salvation from the image of the Crucified Christ, while the lion, sensing the atmosphere of tension, moves around with restless eyes. In the same year 1512 Dürer also created another 'St. Jerome', which, both technically and spiritually, represents a new departure. This work, engraved with the dry point, depicts the rocky forest landscape with an almost Rembrandtesque wealth of variations of light and shade. The Saint, behind a writing-table consisting of a

St. Jerome in his Study

Dürer and St. Jerome

rough board, is imposing in the dignity, tranquillity and absorption of his attitude of prayer.

76–80

An isolated version of St. Jerome is that which Dürer painted in 1521 (now in Lisbon), during his journey to the Netherlands, for the Portuguese agent in Antwerp, Rodrigo d'Almeda. He employed a 93-year-old model for the head, which, with its rolling eyeballs, is the head of an old melancholic.

75

The 1514 engraving of 'St. Jerome in his Study' is chronologically approximately in the middle of the group, but it shows the deepest penetration of the subject. The Saint has ceased to be a legendary figure and has become the symbol of erudite existence and felicity. The cell, which in previous versions was always more or less cave-like, cold and drear, has now become a warm, comfortable, Late Gothic study; the lion is now really a household pet, blinking peacefully, with a dog asleep at his side. The landscape element is restricted to the morning sun shining in at the window and intimated by the great gourd, transformed into a household plant. Even this harmless gourd has not escaped the attention of the learned seekers after hidden meanings. Wustmann disinterred the 'Book of Nature' by Konrad von Meggenberg, published in 1500, and with its aid explained the gourd as a 'mellow, ideal fruit; the struggles of its period of bloom are forgotten and it is the symbol of the Saint who has renounced the world'. The skull, that traditional 'memento mori', has been relegated to the window-sill, where it has no more importance than the books or the cushions. The slippers, pushed carelessly aside, give a pleasing suggestion of bachelor habits to the otherwise tidy room. The cardinal's hat hangs on the wall and the grey head of the silent writer is encircled with a halo. Everything breathes peace—even the little tablet bearing Dürer's monogram and the date is not standing upright, but is lying on the floor. When we think of Italian renderings of the same theme, for example of Antonello da Messina's St. Jerome in his draughty arched hall, Dürer's engraving seems to exhale the spirit of the North. In it he has expressed something, or rather the promise of something, which only Rembrandt fulfilled a hundred years later—the atmosphere of an interior room, of the four walls within which a Northern European feels at home, cosily confined but at the same time free. Not the least important element is the light, which, playing over the window-recesses, the ceiling and floor, gives life to the room. It is, in fact, the room which, as regards the impression conveyed, is almost more important than the figure, for it is the room that tells us what the absorbed face of St. Jerome, bent over his work, does not reveal. From the historical point of view it is interesting to note that the 'Master W. S.' (Wolf Stiber?), in his copy of Dürer's engraving, transformed the Bible translator Jerome into the Bible translator Luther, and Lucas Cranach the Elder in one of his pictures (1525, now in Darmstadt) represented Cardinal Albrecht of Brandenburg as St. Jerome. Dürer's engraving is in perfect accord with the taste of the time. In 1519, in the little engraving of St. Anthony, he employed once again this mood of absorption in intellectual work, so appropriate to the age which invented the art of book-printing and witnessed the first triumph of the printed word. The Saint is revelling in the joy of reading. He

YOUNG HARE. Water-colour, 1502. Vienna, Albertina

clutches his beloved book and, absorbed in his eager reading, forgets everything else around him, even the beautiful picture of the mountain town, beneath which he has settled down with his breviary.

Those who are not artists generally imagine the genesis and development of a picture to be a much more simple and methodical process than is usually the case. Artistic conception may depend on a number of fortuitous circumstances. We know something of Arnold Böcklin's methods, how widely different elements and chance impressions of landscapes, men, poetry and music would crystallize in his mind into the idea of a picture. One must therefore proceed with great caution when drawing from finished works conclusions concerning the spiritual and intellectual processes which gave birth to them.

Artistic Conception

The idea that all the component parts of a work of art are invented ad hoc, that they are brought with one stroke out of the secret recesses of fantasy into the broad daylight of the world, is by no means always true. It is no detriment to a work of art if it has a history made up out of all kinds of fancies and studies. We are too often inclined to forget the familiar intercourse between the artist and his accumulation of sketches. In their desire not to waste anything, even the greatest artists often search through their sketchbooks and folders, to see whether any item in store may be used for this or for that. Dürer, for example, brings out a sketch of a Venetian lady and turns her into the Whore of Babylon of the Apocalypse. While resting on his journey to Italy he sketched the little town of Chiusa in South Tyrol; he remembered it when he wanted a landscape for his 'Nemesis' and the sketch was promptly incorporated in that fantastic composition.

The famous engraving generally known as 'The Knight, Death and the Devil' (1513), abbreviated by Dürer to 'The Knight', had just such an origin. First of all there were Dürer's studies of the laws of equine proportions. As is proved by his constructional drawings and his engravings dated 1505 of the 'Little Horse', Dürer took a keen and conscientious interest in the proportions of the horse, probably influenced by Leonardesque models. The modelling of a horse as pure relief and the rigid intersection of its curves by the straight diagonal of a lance are found again in the 1513 engraving, whereas the construction and movement of the horse have undergone transformations which must be due to other influences. A counterpart to the 'Little Horse' under the neo-classical archway is provided by the engraving of the 'Great Horse', dating from the same year, this mighty Percheron being viewed obliquely from behind its massive crupper. Thausing interprets the engraving as Hercules carrying off the mares of Diomedes. It may well be that this portrait of a Nuremberg drayhorse was identified as a 'Hercules' owing to the presence of that 'tedious stableboy in grotesque would-be antique armour' (Robert Vischer) and the pillar with the fragment of a statue, and it may have been sold under this title.

The Knight, Death and the Devil

125

Secondly, we have the horse, looking as if it were cut out of a zoological diagram, which occupies the centre of the engraving known as 'St. Eustace', created between 1500 and 1503. This is an accurately drawn horse in the company of normal greyhounds and a normal stag, the latter losing nothing of its illustrative

124

F

effect through the appearance of a crucifix between its horns. It is significant that
the dogs in this engraving were, on account of their lifelikeness, used by Gessner
in his 'Historia Animalium' (1531).

A third source of 'The Knight, Death and the Devil' is to be found among the
drawings which Dürer made in his endeavours to solve the problem of a horse's
movements. St. Eustace kneels before his horse as it stands still, and both the 'Little
Horse' and the 'Great Horse' are motionless, but in a constructional drawing made
by Dürer (Nuremberg, Stadtbibliothek) the idealized horse is moving at a walk,
i.e. the fore and hind feet on the same side are raised, as Dürer could have seen
when he studied the bronze horses of St. Mark's and Verrocchio's Colleoni in
Venice and Donatello's Gattamelata in Padua. The pace of the bronze horses is a
walk, not the amble of mediaeval ladies' palfreys. Otto Grossmann has shown that
about 1505 trotting horses were also depicted by Italian artists. A trotting horse
places its right hindfoot and its left forefoot simultaneously on the ground, and
vice versa; in other words, it moves its limbs diagonally. This movement, which
to the painter's eye is contraposed, was also adapted from the Italians by Dürer,
who must have seen or heard of Leonardo's studies of horses (e.g. the silverpoint
drawing at Windsor Castle). For purely artistic reasons of form Dürer uses the
trotting posture even in cases where the horse would obviously have been proceeding at a walk, e.g. in 'The Knight'. Since that time trot and walk have frequently
been confused in the representation of horses.

The 'Knight' has a shorter pedigree than his steed. In 1498 Dürer sketched the
stable-lad of the Paumgärtner brothers on horseback, purely as a costume study—
'that was the armour in Germany at the time' (L. 461, Vienna). At first, therefore,
there was no knight, no death, no devil. The armour-clad stable-lad and his horse
then had the honour of posing for the St. George in the engraving of 1505. This
represents a kind of intermediate stage in the series of equestrian figures which
culminated in 'The Knight, Death and the Devil'. The costume study was transformed into St. George by the addition of the vanquished dragon and into the
'Knight' by the addition of the demoniacal companion. The combination of such
contrasting elements as the statuesque pose of the horseman and the wild forms of
the apparitions at his side and behind him gives to the rider, who in the 1498
drawing was a lifeless costume study, an emotional value—he now becomes the
symbol of the hero. This glimpse of Dürer's workshop methods is very instructive,
for it shows that in itself a figure need have no significance, it is the manner in
which it is fitted into its spiritual environment which gives it its decisive stamp.
The creative achievement of Dürer's fantasy was not the drawing of a horseman
looking calmly straight in front of him, but the idea of making this calm the
symbol of indifference to the contrasting subordinate figures which were added
to the scene.

Interpretations   A network of interpretations has been woven round 'The Knight, Death and
the Devil'. Dürer himself lends no support to any of these suppositions. The
fundamental meaning of the engraving is generally accepted as being in harmony
with that line of Luther's: 'And if the world were full of devils . . .', but one

solitary critic, who in my opinion has been overlooked, holds a different view. Writing in 1878, Heinrich Merz advances the original thesis that Dürer's engraving represents a robber knight, 'to whom Death calls, "Thy hour has come", and whom the Devil, to whom he belongs, is grasping with his talons, so that he becomes mute and rigid with the inner consciousness of his approaching judgement'. In making this bold interpretation, Merz is thinking of the historical conflict between the knighthood and the bourgeoisie at Dürer's time, when the knights were in a state of social decline and economic decay. The last knights regarded the traders and financiers of the cities with a bitter hatred, which was reciprocated. The 'shopkeepers' who ruled the towns avenged themselves for the raids on their convoys of merchandise by hanging the knights, when they could lay hands on them, or by burning down their strongholds. Dürer himself, as has already been mentioned, once lost some of his works as a result of an attack on a merchant's waggon. Merz' hypothesis of a robber knight is nevertheless untenable, because it is contradicted by the expression and because Dürer never indulged in religious or political propaganda. The polemical trait was absent from his character.

We must therefore accept the general opinion that the engraving does not represent Death triumphing over the Knight, but the Hero gaining a moral victory over Death. Long before Hermann Grimm emphasized the connection between Dürer's engraving and the precepts of the Christian knight, as expounded in Erasmus of Rotterdam's little book on the 'Christian Soldier' (Enchiridion Militis Christiani), writers of the Romantic school, on beholding Dürer's 'Knight', had been instinctively reminded of the figures of Ulrich von Hutten and Franz von Sickingen. They thought of Hutten's assertion that he still found pleasure in living, even though pestilence were creeping up behind his horse and Death stood before his eyes. Friedrich Schlegel called the engraving: 'Sickingen riding through the Forest'. Under the perfectly correct impression that the ethos which inspired Dürer's engraving is the same force which drove Luther to appear before Kaiser and Reich in Worms, those who see 'The Knight, Death and the Devil' are inevitably reminded of Luther's 'Feste Burg', although it was written after Dürer's death.

As Erasmus' book was not translated into German until 1520, it is possible that Dürer took the idea of the knight who is victorious over the powers of Evil, not from the various Latin editions which appeared from 1504 on, but from older German traditions. The conception of the 'Christian soldier' embodies an ideal of manly virtue which the traditional instincts of the Germanic race, German mysticism and Northern versions of Renaissance ideas all contributed to form. The Christian knight is an embodiment of Siegfried. Death and the Devil were familiar figures in poetry and the formative arts and above all in the mediaeval theatre. The fact that a beautiful setter is running by the side of the horse completes the picture of the Christian man as known to the Late Middle Ages—the man who, armed with faith and accompanied by religious zeal, symbolized by the faithful hound, goes on his way along the narrow path of earthly life menaced by Death and the Devil (Hubert Schrade).

'Miles Christianus'

It is a tribute to Dürer's greatness that the eternal human element, which needs no explanation, triumphs over all that is bound up with a definite epoch or technique. 'The Knight, Death and the Devil' remains for us the pictorial essence of the soldierly man, full of chivalrous courage and martial ardour, the man who rides on his way, with steely glance and open visor, deaf to the voice of cowardice and blind to the appeal of vileness. 'The Knight, Death and the Devil' was Nietzsche's favourite engraving.

'Melancolia' 103

Around the Second Part of Goethe's 'Faust' and Dürer's 'Melancolia' more interpretations and explanations have accumulated than round any other German work of literature or art. And yet these incredibly glorious works have retained the freshness of the days in which they were created!

Dürer himself christened his engraving; it bears the inscription 'Melencolia'. Dürer himself also interpreted two of the attributes of the seated female figure; he noted down on one occasion: 'The key means power; the purse means wealth.' Dürer has also told us quite clearly what he understood by melancholy. And we also know something about his spiritual condition at the time when he made this engraving—in May, 1514, after a painful illness, his mother died.

Conflict of Opinions

But right here, at the very start, the difficulties begin. The word 'Melencolia' is on the wings of a bat, that creature of the twilight; the bat thereby becomes vocal, like the Bird of Woe in the 'Apocalypse' (cf. the woodcut of the 'Seven Angels with the Trumpets'). But what is the meaning of the figure '1' after the word 'Melencolia'? Did Dürer plan a series of engravings? Was there to have been a second 'Melancolia'? Or was this engraving—as was mooted at the time—the first of a series of engravings, each of which was to be dedicated to one of the four temperaments? Those who could not or would not answer these questions, have denied that the '1' is a '1'. According to Passavant, it is a small 'i', that is to say, the imperative of the Latin verb 'ire', so that the meaning would be: 'Begone, Melancholy!' Others go even further and maintain that it is neither a number nor a letter, but merely a stroke to fill up the space after the word 'Melencolia'. We will refrain for the moment from answering these questions, because a probable solution can be found by interpreting the engraving as a whole.

Wustmann attempted to prove that the death of Dürer's mother, which made a deep impression on the artist, gave rise to the conception of this engraving. Wustmann also believed that he had found a direct, though mysteriously veiled reference to the mother's death. According to this theory, the figures of the two middle rows in the magic square above the head of Melancolia give the date of the mother's death: in the top row, the month ($3 + 2 = 5 =$ May); in the centre, reading diagonally, what Dürer wrongly presumed to have been the day ($10 + 7$, $11 + 6 = 17$; actually his mother died on the 16th); at the bottom the year 1514. Winterstein even ventured to give a psycho-analytical interpretation of the engraving, namely, that the composition shows the reawakening of a feeling of guilt towards his father, dating from early childhood.

Conception of Melancholy

Dürer's conception of melancholy is alleged to be connected with a passage in the educational work which he wrote for his 'painter-boys', in which he warns

WATER-COLOUR STUDY FOR 'THE KNIGHT, DEATH AND THE DEVIL' (Plate 125).
1498. Vienna, Albertina

them against the danger of too intensive thinking, which may lead to the mind being overcast and the melancholy spirit taking the upper hand. But Dürer's engraving does not show us a 'painter-boy' whom continual study has reduced to a state of depression; it shows us a burly female figure. Nor is there any sign of an artist's equipment, the accessories with which she is surrounded belonging rather to the technical side of scientific work. The figure of Melancolia has wings, and is therefore not a representation of a melancholic being, but the personification of the conception Melancholy. This already proves that we cannot explain the picture by reference to Dürer's psychological condition alone—or rather that we can gauge the significance of this condition only if we return to it after subjecting the engraving to a thorough analysis.

A peregrination through the history of the various interpretations of this engraving will not lead us straight to our goal, but will take us up blind alleys and back again, by detours back to the main road and thence past numerous viewpoints more or less to our starting-point, though on a somewhat higher plane. At first it will seem to us that we can no longer perceive the pure outlines of a work of art through all the dust of book-learning. One is often tempted to think that art historians copy the methods of detectives, with such sleuth-like persistence do they try to arrive at a solution of Dürer's 'deed'. Every nook and cranny of the engraving has been thoroughly searched, the woman herself, her clothing, her keys, her purse, her face, her garland, her compasses, her book, all the implements of medicine, science and artisanry lying scattered around her, the building, the bell, the sandglass and the sundial, the scales and the ladder, the block of stone and the sphere, the dog and the bat, the saucepan and the steps, the landscape with its sea, its coastline, rainbows, comets, etc., etc. Somewhere, so it was believed, the key to the understanding of the whole must be hidden; somehow it must be possible to make inanimate objects speak! It would be wrong and foolish just to shrug one's shoulders at all these enthusiastic efforts. We owe to this expenditure of learning an abundance of information on the spiritual background of Dürer's time and an exact knowledge of the materials with which his fantasy worked. The process of artistic creation will, however, always remain a secret, because it is enacted on a spiritual level which even the most detailed analysis of contents cannot penetrate.

Until the beginning of the eighteenth century the understanding of the 'Melancolia' seems to have presented no difficulties. One of the earliest admirers of this engraving—and of Dürer's graphic art in general—was Giorgio Vasari. Among the prints 'which will set the whole world in astonishment' he includes the ' "Melancolia" with all the instruments which make a man, and whoever uses them, a melancholic'. Vasari thus found it quite natural that familiarity with the technical apparatus strewn around the figure should make not only her, but anyone melancholy, for the doctrine of melancholy as a typical pathological consequence and symptom of intellectual work had already been formulated by the learned Italian physician Marsilius Ficinus. Joachim von Sandrardt, in his 'Teutsche Akademie' (1675), eschews the mood of melancholy and merely mentions

History of the Interpretations

Vasari on the 'Melancolia'

Sandrardt

the many 'oddities', secrets and 'profundities' to be found in the engraving, e.g. the square in which the figures, whichever way they are read, always add up to the same sum.

During the first century of research into Dürer's work, which opens with H. C. Arend's 'Gedächtnis der Ehren Dürers' in 1728 and closes in 1827 with Heller's 'Dürer', there was general agreement as to the interpretation of the chief figure in the engraving, though opinions differed as to the attribution of the various objects to certain categories of knowledge. Arend thought that, even without the inscription, anyone with a knowledge of art could have seen that the figure was meant to be Melancolia. The disorder of her hair was 'perhaps meant as an indication of a corresponding inner confusion'. Her eyes he finds 'staring and fearful', while he interprets the instruments on the ground not as the cause of her absorption, but as the subject of her meditations. Heller attributes the woman's 'despairing' mood to the closed book lying in her lap.

In the second half of the nineteenth century we find the first attempts to deny the gloomy character of the 'Melancolia'. Von Eye (1860) maintains that pessimism and melancholy were moods unknown to the healthy and vigorous world of the early sixteenth century, and will only admit the thoughtful and speculative element. Allihn (1871) goes still further in his neutral estimation of the female figure, in which he sees only a thoughtful attitude, a pensive expression and a contemplative tranquillity; 'nowhere is there a trace of despair or pessimism'. Eye and Allihn are certainly right in assuming that Dürer knew nothing of pessimism ('Weltschmerz') in the sense which the Romantics gave to the term, but both these scholars err in denying in their interpretation of the engraving the existence of the depressive element. No impartial spectator can be in any doubts as to the restless, almost uncanny general atmosphere. Dürer had other forms of expression to denote mere thoughtfulness, meditation and intellectual work, as is proved by his 'St. Jerome'. He combines inner equilibrium with external tidiness, such as reigns in St. Jerome's study. Nevertheless, Allihn's refusal to accept an interpretation of the 'Melancolia' based on the conception of an elegiac mood, led him on to very promising ground, namely, the mediaeval doctrine of the four temperaments or complexions. In this respect he was the first writer to pass from the question whether the figure of 'Melancolia' is 'melancholy' or not, to the other question of how Dürer came to choose the idea of personifying the melancholy temperament and the value which Dürer's age attached to the four types of men classified according to their temperament.

In their interpretation of the 'Melancolia' engraving, the two famous biographers of Dürer, Thausing (1876) and Springer (1892), lag a long way behind Allihn's gifted and farseeing studies. They both deviate from a firm basis of historical formulation to an interpretation imbued with colourless modern spirituality. Thausing has no doubts whatsoever that the woman sunk in gloomy meditation is human reason, in despair because she has reached the limit of achievement! She is the restless, dissatisfied spirit who brings Faust to the point of confessing that we know nothing. Springer, too, is satisfied with the explanation that intellectual striving consumes the peace of the soul and results in deep depression. Richard Wustmann's interpretation, written in 1905, of 'a mighty thinker who has reached the limit of her powers', depicted by Dürer as the first in 'a series of mournful engravings', also tends towards the despairing mood of Goethe's Faust, who has stormed his way through four faculties, through the great and the petty world. Quite rightly Wölfflin has described the abandonment of the worldly search for knowledge as a most un-Dürer-like conception. Nobody had a greater respect for knowledge or was more anxious to acquire it than the German contemporary of the Italian universal genius, Leonardo da Vinci.

In his 'Beiträge zur Weltanschauung Dürers' (1900), Paul Weber thought that he could define the 'Weltschmerz' of the 'Melancolia' in such a way as to bring it into harmony with the times. He considers the engraving from the viewpoint of the eve of the Reformation and as Dürer's confession of faith. The 'Melancolia' —Weber thinks—is grieved because the old theology is still making brutal use of its power, but the visible reason of her grief is that all the arts and accomplishments have failed to satisfy her and bring her happiness. This can only be achieved through faith. Dürer dedicated his engraving of St. Jerome to the glory of faith; the 'Melancolia' and the 'St. Jerome' are therefore counterparts to each other, like light and shade, peace and unrest, knowledge of God and worldly wisdom.

The value of Weber's contribution to the study of Dürer does not lie in the interpretation of the figure of 'Melancolia', but in the fact that he was the first to make a systematic attempt to explain, by examining the trend of scholastic thought in Dürer's time, the accessories of the 'Melancolia' as attributes of the seven free and seven mechanical arts. The little boy, sitting on a millstone and scribbling on a tablet, represents Grammar, the most elementary of the seven arts; in mediaeval representations Grammatica is usually accompanied by a learner of the alphabet. The scales can be explained as an attribute of Rhetoric, the source of advice in matters of law; Rhetoric is therefore in the service of Justice, who holds the scales. The square of figures is a reference to Arithmetic, the sphere denotes Astronomy, the compasses Geometry, etc. Weber identifies the flowers in the garland encircling the head of 'Melancolia' as a type of nightshade, which, according to the conception of the Late Middle Ages, symbolized a propensity to solitude.

The Attributes of the Seven Arts

In the course of a search for literary and philosophical sources which Dürer might have used for his engravings of 'Melancolia' and 'St. Jerome', J. A. Endres (1913) came across the philosophy of Cardinal Nicolaus Cusanos. The Paris edition of the Cardinal's works appeared in 1514 and was not unknown to Nuremberg humanistic circles. Endres tries to derive from the main lines of this philosophy not only the idea of the counterparts 'Melancolia' and 'Jerome', but also their construction, even including details of the accessories and the lighting. According to Endres, 'Melancolia' is the human spirit in its striving for truth and thereby for happiness. Dürer has represented the human spirit on the highest level to which it can attain by accurate research and by means of mathematical symbols —the intuition of the infinite. The personification of the human spirit is surrounded by its own creations—the free arts with their symbols, the mechanical arts with their symbols and, lastly, the magic means which make it possible for the spirit to rise from the visible to the infinite, e.g. the gyroscope and the square of figures. The ruler, the millstone and the polyhedron, on the other hand, are allusions to Nicolaus Cusanos' mathematical symbols—line, circle and polygon. In all these deductions Endres is following the path which Weber had trod so successfully. But he goes further than Weber in his interpretation of the connection between the 'Melancolia' and the 'St. Jerome'. 'Melancolia', according to Endres, is, in the scholastic sense, the 'second' theology, i.e. science, which, borne on the wings of reason, soars upwards to God, dwells in the middle regions of light and rules the mathematical and metaphysical sphere. In opposition to this second and 'natural' theology is the symbol of the 'first' theology, the doctrine of revelation and faith, which teaches in silence and in mystic contemplation rises to immeasurable heights. Its representative is St. Jerome, the learned Prince of the Church. Endres departs from Weber's hypotheses in that he rejects all allusion in Dürer's 'Melancolia' to the spiritual state of mankind at the beginning of the Reformation and also the connection with the doctrine of the four temperaments. 'The fundamental idea of Dürer's engravings is derived . . . from the despised doctrines of scholasticism.' Endres is unable to produce any proof that Dürer was acquainted with the main ideas of the philosophy of Nicolaus Cusanos, and this weakens the whole structure of his hypotheses.

Dürer's Source

In 1903, ten years before Endres, Giehlow had discovered Dürer's real source in the writings of Marsilius Ficinus and had shown that, with brilliant generalization which sprang from the depths of personal experience, Dürer had combined in one composition the two spiritual phenomena which in his time were most closely associated with the melancholy temperament—the highest form of occult intellectual activity and sorrowful meditation. Marsilius Ficinus' book on the triple life (De Vita Triplici) was published in Latin in 1500 and in German in 1505. The deep impression it made, especially on learned or artistic readers, was due to the fact that, in contrast to the traditional mediaeval doctrine that melancholy was the basest complex, it returned to the Aristotelian conception that 'all men who have excelled in a great art, have been melancholics'. That Dürer endorsed this old view, which at that time became once again modern, is clear, for it is the starting-point of his educational book for young painters. The prevalence of the opinion that melancholy was a typical spiritual phenomenon in the creative man is also illustrated by the remark of the Farnese legate Paulucci (1519) that Raphael was a man with a propensity to melancholy, 'like all men of such outstanding significance'.

Astrological Ideas

Giehlow's investigations also brought to light the close relationship between medical and astrological ideas. Each of the temperaments was assigned to a certain planet and the 'humor melancolicus' was under the influence of Saturn. In Dürer's own words, 'Melancolia' is a woman 'from whose eyes Saturn looks out'. The influence of this planet can be either good or evil. Saturn strengthens the melancholic in the pursuit of great things, but also makes him sad and fearful. The dangerous side of the melancholy propensity can be prevented from gaining the upper hand by medical and dietetical means, e.g. music, fresh air, regulation of the digestion, etc., and similarly the harmful influence of Saturn can be neutralized with the aid of magic antidotes, e.g. the counter-influence of Jupiter. The garland which Dürer's 'Melancolia' is wearing is thus one of these anti-melancholic remedies, a medicament consisting of damp roots. Warburg (1918), in amplification of Giehlow's theory, showed that the square of figures is also one of these magic remedies. It is the 'jovial' sign, the symbol of the planet Jupiter. It hangs above the head of 'Melancolia' like an ex-voto—'a thankoffering for the services of the kindly, victorious star-god'. Warburg thus sees in Dürer's 'Melancolia' not a warning against the evil consequences of the melancholic propensity, and not even a diagram to assist in the diagnosis of melancholy, but a consolation for 'the thinking worker'.

In 1923 Panofsky and Saxl, in the course of an investigation into sources and prototypes, continued and extended the researches of Giehlow and Warburg. The whole inventory of the 'Melancolia' engraving was gone through again, this time with a view to discovering possible astrological sources. This revealed that even Dürer's own interpretation: 'The key means power; the purse means wealth', might well be derived from astrology. Saturn, the planet of the melancholics, is the dispenser and protector of riches, he gives his children money and power over men. To him belong the ocean and those who venture upon it—which explains the seascape in the background of the engraving. But also the other objects strewn about the picture denote professions and spheres of activity which are subject to Saturn, e.g. architects, masons and workers in wood. Theirs are the building artisans' attributes, the tools and symbols of the builders' guilds. When Dürer visited Padua he may have seen the frescoes in the Salone, in which the activities and attributes of the children of all the planets are shown, among them those of the children of Saturn—the sick, melancholy man, the scholar, the carpenter, the treasure-digger, the stonemason, the knife-grinder, the gardener and the hermit. The instruments for measuring space and time—compasses, scales and sand-glass— also belong to Saturn. He also rules the various branches of geometry, including perspective, the symbol of which is the great polyhedron. But why did Dürer choose from among the numerous saturnian professions and activities those connected with the art of measuring? Because measurements, numbers and weights were the cornerstones of his own scientific work, because mathematics appeared to him (and not to him alone!) to be the most important of the sciences. Dürer personifies 'Melancolia', but in the form which was closest to his heart—as a typical predisposition of the creative mathematical man. That is his subjective contribution to the doctrine of Ficinus.

There are, as Sigrid Strauss-Klobe has convincingly shown, other allusions to the help given to men by the planets, as exemplified by Jupiter's square of numbers. For example, the scales. 'Saturn, according to astrological tradition, is exalted in the sign of Venus, the Scales, and in this sign unfolds his formative powers.' The dog is the animal of Mercury, who is here in the service of Saturn. These astrological attempts at interpretation have been supplemented by G. F. Hartlaub's studies of the alchemistic aspect. In the dog, the child and the scales Hartlaub recognizes hermetical alchemistic symbols.

Let us return for a moment to the smallest and most insignificant-looking item in this great picture-puzzle—the figure '1' after the word 'Melencolia'. Borinski and Wölfflin have given us what is probably the right interpretation. 'Melancolia 1' represents the mild form of melancholy, which attacks those engaged in intellectual work in the form of acute depression. But Ficinus describes a second, malignant and chronic form of melancholy, which deprives men of their senses and causes the body to waste away. It may be that a 'Melancolia 2' by Dürer's hand was to have depicted this hopeless malady of the soul and all its accompanying symptoms.

What remains out of all these learned attempts to solve the riddle of this engraving? First of all, the certitude that Dürer chose a subject which for him as a creative man and for the men of his time was a burning question—the dispute as to whether the melancholic temperament was of noble or ignoble character—and represented it with the aid of a pictorial language, the individual symbols of which are no longer comprehensible to us at the present day. We have also seen that we can easily forget all that scholarship has contributed towards the interpretation of the 'Melancolia' and still have before us a living work of art, which makes an intimate appeal and can be grasped without difficulty. We do not need profound and poetical interpretations such as Gabriele d'Annunzio has given and Waldmann has accepted, telling us of the 'sleepless genius, crowned with patience, which has devised all things known to man, which is never extinguished, but, like the eternal flame, penetrates the darkness and the depths of its own soul and triumphs over inanimate material'.

We will be content with a more humdrum, more human conclusion. Melancholy is the demon of the dead hour in the life of a creative man. There is no productive being, whether he be an artist, a scholar, a poet, a philosopher or a statesman, who does not know those dead hours, when everything comes to a standstill and nothing will go forward, when a man is filled with revulsion for those very things which normally make up the content and happiness of his life, when the tempter approaches and whispers in his ear that he should cast all that rubbish to the four winds and resign himself to the apathy or the good fortune of not knowing and to the peace of intellectual mediocrity. The external symptom of such a mood is what is commonly known as 'brooding'. When Michelangelo painted on the ceiling of the Sistine Chapel his Jeremiah, cast down by grief, he gave to this great melancholic an attitude similar to that of Dürer's 'Melancolia'. Once before—in the period of inner strife and questioning—Melancholy had looked over Dürer's shoulder, in that restless hour when he drew his own countenance as a young man (Erlangen, L. 429). Now Dürer, in his maturity, undergoes the same experience. His 'Melancolia' is the moving confession of a man of genius that he, too, knows the pangs of self-distrust. Therein lies the significance of the engraving for the understanding of Dürer's personality, but therein, too, lies its timeless value, its eternal pre-eminence.

If the engraving of the 'Melancolia' bore only Dürer s monogram and the date, without the word 'Melencolia', well-meaning biographers would nevertheless have succeeded in denying the tragic elements and in construing the 'obvious' disharmony as the expression of a harmonious mood. We may be thankful that the artist himself made it impossible for his admirers to impute to Dürer the satisfied complacence of a country parson. In other prints Dürer went a step further in the direction of the demoniacal, from a representation of doubt to one of despair. A remarkable etching on iron, dating from 1516, which still lacks satisfactory interpretation, is known as 'The Despairing Man' because its central figure is a nude man on his knees, running his hands through the locks on his bent head. Round about him are the most strange figures. On the left, seen in profile, is the half-figure of a clothed man with a broken nose. It has been established that this figure was derived from a portrait-sketch which Dürer made of his brother Andreas in 1514 (L. 532, Vienna). Georg Gronau and E. Popp have noticed that Dürer transformed the gaunt, bony face of his brother into a head resembling that of Michelangelo. Starting from this discovery, E. Popp has endeavoured to prove that the remaining figures—the man with the jug, the grey-haired man with mad eyes and the torso of the woman who looks as if she were groaning under pressure of a nightmare—are taken from works by Michelangelo. The whole picture would thus be a dream-like paraphrase of Michelangelesque moods. In actual fact, Dürer came far nearer to the essence of Michelangelo and his art with his 'Melancolia', which is the sister of the 'Night' in the Medici Chapel. It would appear futile to look for any deeper inner relationship between the five figures of this etching; one must accept them rather as separate conceptions which were combined on one plate. In any case, Dürer has subjected the theme of hopeless spiritual bewilderment to a fourfold transformation: from tormented sleep to conscious but disconsolate stupor, from the numbed eyes of a masculine Medusa to the senseless gesture of despair. This etching dates from the same year as that other etching, filled with the mood of the Apocalypse, of the angel brandishing the sudarium of St. Veronica. But this brings us into a greater domain of Dürer's fantasy, to the consideration of the religious side of his work.

'The Despairing Man'
104

32

CHAPTER SIX

THE RELIGIOUS SIDE OF DÜRER'S ART

FAR more misleading than the attribution to Dürer of works which are not by his hand, far worse than errors of dating, is the creation of a false impression of his personality by softening and debilitating the essence of his character, an impression for which the Romantics are largely responsible. Dürer was not a canting hypocrite, but, as he said of Luther, a 'God-minded' man. He was not soft, but rigid, not lukewarm, but fervent. He created works of art, not for the benefit of schoolgirls and bigots, but for mature men and women. The world in which Dürer lived was not an old German idyll of peaceful and comfortable bourgeois existence behind bull's-eye glass windows and Renaissance balconies. The age of Dürer was full of uncertainties; it mercilessly destroyed all those who were not able to fight for their bodily and spiritual existence.

The art, too, of this century of the German Reformation, sprang not from the peace of the soul, but from its very restlessness. Dürer was not a dreamy illustrator of the Bible; with his burin and paint-brush he was—despite his 'Life of the Virgin'—a soldier of God, and that at a time when religion and religious strife had a very different meaning from that which they have today. The religious impulse,

the relationship between God and man, was in the forefront of every activity. Religion was not a business for the professional savers of souls; every man looked after his own soul. Religion was not the food and consolation of the weary and oppressed; it was the salt of life for all. This saturation of the whole of existence by the religious impulse gave to religious writings and pictorial representations a peculiar pathos, the symptom of an inner strength which attained its goal in the face of all resistance and of a lasting solidity which remained when all around was dissolved into wavering forms.

Unlike the humanistic subjects, religious themes were alive and comprehensible to all. The painter or sketcher who sought and found the form of artistic expression for Christ's Passion, for the Life of the Virgin Mary or for the deeds and martyrdom of the saints, was expressing what the populace felt and what it became more and more willing to absorb amidst the growing religious fervour. In the course of history the task of expounding the feelings of the nation passed from one art to another. The mission which was the task of Dürer and Holbein in the fifteenth and sixteenth centuries was fulfilled by Schütz, Handel and Bach in the seventeenth and eighteenth. Then it was the turn of poetry to become the mouthpiece of the nation.

Dürer's religious art lies between two worlds—it closes the old world of mediaeval religiosity and opens the new era of the individual attitude towards faith. The church which Dürer found was no longer the impregnable church of the Middle Ages. By the beginning of the fifteenth century the first cracks had

begun to appear in the proud edifice which mediaeval faith had erected throughout the world. The Hussite storm shook it to its foundations. Underground, and fed

THE NATIVITY. About 1500. Munich, Aeltere Pinakothek

from various sources, there began that revolt of the German people against the oppression of secular, and particularly of national life by the Roman Church.

Two events of the greatest significance occurred in the early years of the sixteenth century—in 1516 work on the building of Cologne Cathedral was suspended; in 1517 Luther nailed his theses to the door of the Schlosskirche in Wittenberg. From the security offered by the mantle of the old church, Luther issued his challenge to his fellow-men and brought them face to face with God. With deep understanding for the weakness of men, the mediaeval church had provided them, in their relationship to God, with a whole succession of con-secrated mediators, equipped with special means of grace. Through the intervention of the saints, by means of donations, confession and repentance, the Church helped sinners to allay their fears. Luther's Reform fought against this hierarchy of mediators, it transferred the whole responsibility to the individual man, deprived him of all assurances and consolations and left him alone with his belief in God's mercy. Personal emotion, personal belief became the source of religious experi- *Luther's* ence. By making men themselves turn to God, by confining the decisive religious *Achievement* processes to their own breasts, Luther was returning to the beliefs of German mysticism, from whose depths of feeling the figure of the Christian Knight arose once more.

Dürer's religious art was the art of the Reformation period, but it was not Protestant art; it was born in the spirit of a new piety, but still bound up with old ideas and forms. It arose in a period of religious renewal, fulfilled amidst pain and strife, but it was not the servant of any particular creed. The link between this art and Luther's achievement is not the community of intention, it is a community of fundamental spiritual experience. To the end of his life Dürer remained a faithful son of the old Catholic Church. In Luther he saw a cleanser, a renewer of that church; in Luther he honoured the liberator of souls, the prophet of the pure word of God, not the destroyer of the old ideas or the founder of a new church. Moreover, most of Dürer's religious works were created before the rise of Luther and were still dominated by the ideas of the mediaeval church, e.g. the cult of the Virgin and the mediaeval world-order under the two swords which Pope and Emperor held in their hands. That Dürer's art satisfied to the full the chief *Old Forms—* requirement of the time—the need for spiritual edification, the longing for a *New Humanity* spiritual renewal of Christianity, the grief over the decay of religious life—was due not to his invention of new subjects, not to any deliberate departure from tradi-tional forms, but to Dürer's deep humanity, which filled every subject with warmth and with passion. Every one of Dürer's religious works is a personal confession—the youthful flame of the 'Apocalypse', the vivid preaching of the 'Passions', the warmth of narrative in the 'Life of the Virgin', the combination of courage and wisdom in the painting of the 'Four Apostles'.

That was the new, the individual aspect, the new subjective régime in Dürer's art, which by a slow and painful process freed itself from the metaphysical system of the mediaeval church and the arbitrary laws of the 'ars sacra'. It is of almost symbolic significance that Dürer's most profound declaration of his attitude

THE LAST SUPPER
(1523)

towards religious questions, the painting of the 'Apostles', was not destined for a church, but for a secular building, and that its urgent warning was meant for the 'worldly Regents'.

Despite this great achievement of the painting of the 'Apostles', the religious side of Dürer's art consists of prints rather than of paintings. His European fame and his popularity in Germany rest on his prints, though it is true that some of his greatest and most mature designs for paintings were never executed and remained at the stage of studies or sketches. External circumstances may have contributed to this. Commissions for paintings were rarely given, the execution of large religious paintings involved great expenditure of time, money and labour, and also, as the story of the Heller altar-piece proves, sometimes resulted in vexations of all kinds. Woodcuts and copperplate engravings, on the other hand, could be created on the artist's own initiative, quickly and cheaply, without the interference of patrons. But the decisive factor in the success of Dürer's graphic art was the spiritual mood of the age. For the men of the time, who realized that the religious struggles were transforming the whole national life, art was more than an aesthetic matter; it became the mouthpiece of the most intimate aspirations of mankind. The Reformation period therefore turned to those categories of pictures which had a universal appeal, which could be understood by all, i.e. the various forms of illustration. Book-printing spread throughout the world the highest forms of intellectual thought, and the printing of pictures propagated the profoundest artistic ideas.

Dürer's Graphic Art

Dürer's popularity in his own time was not due to that element in his work which appeals to us today. We are able to approach Dürer through many works which made no appeal to earlier generations, and conversely we reject much in his work which went to the hearts of the men of the sixteenth century. This does not detract from Dürer's greatness. We take with one hand and give with the other, and the fundamental human element in Dürer's work will retain its value for all time and will be unaffected by changes of taste.

Let us give one or two examples of this change in popular appeal and effect. In Dürer's 'Passions' and his 'Life of the Virgin' his contemporaries recognized many figures familiar to them from the Passion Plays, which had been given in Nuremberg in front of the Frauenkirche during Holy Week ever since the time of the plague, e.g. the grotesque masked figures of the executioners and myrmidons of the Lord. After the tragic figure of Christ, it must have been a relief to see the 'chocolate soldier' who pours out the water for Pilate ('Little Passion', 1512). Purchasers of the prints of the 'Great Passion' knew what it looked like when fettered men were dragged or pushed by hangman's assistants to the place of execution, through a crowd palpitating with morbid curiosity, horror, scorn and compassion. Such scenes could be recognized in the woodcut of the Betrayal of Christ ('Great Passion'). And who could refrain from a gasp of joy when St. Peter, abandoning his attitude of mildness, hews off the ear of the cudgel-wielding Malchus with a masterly stroke of his broad blade? Dürer took his figures from the scenes of daily life, and that is why they still seem to live. For example, a

Change in Popular Appeal

THE LAST SUPPER
(Great Passion, 1510)

drawing has been preserved of a carpenter's apprentice boring a hole in a beam (Bayonne, Musée Bonnat), and this harmless carpenter is converted by Dürer, in the 'Martyrdom of the 10,000 Christians', into a torturer performing his grim task on one of the martyrs (woodcut, about 1495–97). We note the realism of such figures, as we note that of Shakespeare's rogues and bullies, but we regard them with the eelfeings of a different age. The same applies to the many buildings in Dürer's religious pictures. His own generation stared with naive admiration at the wonderful engraving in the background of the scene of Christ taking leave of his mother, at the many fanciful of German castles and the fanciful adaptations Italian Renaissance, at churches, pillars, staircases and vaults, to build which which were separated by centuries, were for the men of that time symbols of the splendour of foreign countries, and he knew that his journeyings among them had given him great trouble, and that many of them took some of the motives from Italy. It is possible, too, that we are worried today by the indifference of the subordinate figures, by the largeness of the figures and by the amount of space occupied in the picture by architecture. But in making such criticisms we forget the traditional role played by the factors act by subordinate figures, which stand in the same relation to the chief figure as the congregation to the officiating priests; we confuse the ideal of beauty expressed in forms from the Italian Renaissance with the ideal of nature and power to give expression, and we are no longer capable of deducing from the folds of draperies the mood and essence of the figures which they cover.

Let us now turn to the other side—the immortal beauties, the unforgettable inventions of Dürer. The Virgin—in the Flight into Egypt ('Life of the Virgin')—motherly, sturdy, sitting firmly in the saddle, her hands busy spinning, her foot gently rocking the cradle of the Holy Child; the playful and eager activity of the little angels, those heavenly imps, sweeping up the shavings left by Father Joseph's carpentry work and packing them into the basket. Then the 'Christ as Gardener' (woodcut, 'Little Passion'); how tender is Dürer's touch, how tender his glance, how still it is in this southern garden on a summer's evening! It seems but a short step from this to Rembrandt, more than a hundred years later. The striking woodcut of 'The Penitent' (1510) touches upon those enigmatic acts of spiritual and bodily self-torture, by which the religious man seeks to free himself from his misery. But the same masterly hand, which here, as it were, plays a 'Miserere' on the organ, could sketch the lines, gentle as the words of a folksong, of 'The Virgin sitting beneath a Tree', with its view of a town in the distance (L. 443, Berlin).

The complete list of Dürer's works in Flechsig's book (1931) comprises 1312 items. Hundreds of paintings, engravings, woodcuts and drawings deal with religious subjects. If we wish to give an idea of Dürer's religious art and to speak of it to the wide circles of art-lovers, we must choose with care and limit ourselves to relatively few works. There are also many ways in which this material can be sub-divided. Heidrich, for example, in his book on Dürer's representation of the Virgin, wrote the story of a motive. Wölfflin has given us a masterly analysis of

Immortal Beauties

72

Subdivision of Dürer's Religious Works

G

Epitome in Divae Parthenices Mari
ae Historiam ab Alberto Dürero
Norico per Figvras Diges
tam Cvm Versibvs Anne
xis Chelidonii

Quisquis fortunæ correptus turbine.persers
Quam tibi iacturam fata sinistra ferunt.
Aut animæ delicta gemis.Phlegethontis & ignes
Anxius æternos corde tremente paùes.
Quisquis & vrgeris iam iam decedere vita
Alterius:migrans:nescius hospitij.
Huc ades:auxilium:pete:continuoꝗ rogabo
Pro te:quem paui lacte:tuliꝗ sinu.
Ille deus rerum mihisubdidit astra:deosꝗ.
Flectitur ille meis O homo suppliciis.

TITLE-PAGE TO THE LIFE OF THE VIRGIN
(1511)

stylistic differences in the representation of the same scene at various periods of Dürer's artistic development. Not a single print, not even the most casual sketch, has escaped the attention of the critics. The scope of Dürer's subject-matter is not so great as the number of religious works would lead one to expect. He had favourite themes, to which he returned time after time, with ever renewed strength and with changes of conception and form; there is also, however—and the fact is no less instructive—a whole series of biblical scenes which Dürer's fantasy never touched at all, e.g. he has given us hardly anything from the Old Testament. It is true that his representations of Adam and Eve (paintings, engravings, woodcuts and drawings) are of great importance to the study of his work, not, however, considered as religious subjects, but as contributions to the problem of the 'perfect' human form, one of the cardinal points in Dürer's scientific thought. Except for this, we have from the Old Testament only the 'Samson slaying the lion' (woodcut, about 1497), 'Cain killing Abel' (woodcut, 1511), 'The Mocking of Job' (about 1500, Frankfurt am Main) and a few drawings for the Samson motive. There is a complete absence of scenes of blessing and pardoning, such as Rembrandt's humanity loved to clothe in oriental dress, and also of the visionary episodes of Tobit, Daniel, Manoah, etc.

Absence of Old Testament Subjects

107–114

Dürer, a son of the fifteenth and sixteenth centuries, was guided in his choice of subjects by that Christian mythology which centuries had contributed to form. But on the eve of the collapse of the mediaeval world-order, he gave perfection to these conventional subjects, possessing as he did a hitherto unknown sincerity of feeling for nature, a propensity, peculiar to him, towards confession, and a great depth of humanity. Dürer was attracted only by the person of Christ and the story of His Passion. Rembrandt's religiosity flourished in a spiritually different age, and on different soil—in the spiritual atmosphere of seventeenth-century Dutch Protestantism.

The New Testament, too, appeared to Dürer in a different light from that in which it appeared to his Italian contemporaries or to the great painters of the Netherlands a century later. The Last Supper had been a favourite subject with Italian painters, until in 1498 Leonardo gave it its most perfect southern conception —the dramatic tension between the Master, His Disciples and the Betrayer, the culminating point of the tragedy at that supreme moment when word and gesture tear away the veil of uncertainty. Dürer's Last Supper in the 'Great Passion' (1510) shows us eleven Disciples crowded together behind the table, leaving the foreground free for the betrayer Judas and for the thirteenth participant, the master of the house, who, spiritually aloof, is waiting on the others (cf. St. Matthew 26, 18, and St. Mark 14, 13). In 1521 Martin Schaffner painted an imitation of Leonardo's Last Supper, the predella of the altar-piece in Ulm Cathedral. It was not until 1523, in the single completed woodcut of the projected 'Passion' series in wide format, that Dürer found the expressions and the degrees of spiritual agitation among the Disciples which the gravity of the moment demands (cf. the Last Supper in the 'Little Passion', 1509–11). Only once, in the 'Little Passion' woodcut, did Dürer depict that second mystical supper, when Christ appeared to His Disciples at

The New Testament

Ill. p. 88

Ill. p. 86

THE BIRTH OF THE VIRGIN
(Life of the Virgin. About 1502–5)

Emmaus, a subject of which the poetical and symbolical significance repeatedly attracted Rembrandt. In Dürer's work there is no echo of the miracles and parables of Christ, and the conception of the 'Man of Sorrow' takes precedence over the acts of the Saviour. On the other hand, Dürer was the discoverer and the profoundest interpreter of the Agony in the Garden. Those who seek in Dürer the exuberant and supernatural element, the fiery outbursts and the overwhelming flame, will find it in the 'Apocalypse' woodcuts of his youth. In his maturer years Dürer restrained his feelings within definite limits, even when he was depicting Golgotha or the Resurrection.

Lastly, there is one other thing which must not be forgotten. Much of the freshness, much of the direct appeal of Dürer's prints has been lost owing to the other hands which transferred his drawings to the woodblocks, and even his own hand and fantasy encountered innumerable technical difficulites while cutting with the burin on the copperplate. Many apparent contradictions can be explained in this way. For example, whereas at one moment we are surprised by Dürer's unwonted adherence to traditional forms of representation, in the next moment a new world of sensations is revealed; at one moment our eyes have to follow laboriously the theme of a print, at another we are able to take in at a glance the clear structure of a drawing.

If we are not concerned with the chronological evolution of Dürer's religious work, but wish only to extract the essence of his religious feeling and his manner of expressing it, then we must follow the example of the older Dürer scholars and start from the subject-matter. Dürer himself would approve this course, for his procedure started from the subject and then passed to form, and this was also the path which his fantasy was wont to follow. For Dürer the initial problem was not linear construction or harmony of colour or a phenomenon of chiaroscuro, but the narration of an episode, the description of a sensation in the language of a painter or an illustrator.

From Subject to Form

Worship is one of the fundamental religious experiences. In it the soul of man is in direct communion with God. The occasions which bring men into the presence of the supernatural powers are many and varied, and just as varied are the degrees of worship and the external gestures by which it is expressed. Worship comprises a whole series of spiritual emotions, ranging from the pole of religious contemplation to that of ecstasy—silent adoration, agonized appeal, timid supplication, fervent thanksgiving and frank confession. The gestures expressive of worship vary according to the depth of spiritual feeling: the raising of the arms above the head—the ancient gesture of worship—kneeling in humility, oriental prostrations, standing rigid and upright in the presence of God, the folded hands of a Christian in prayer, the outstretched arms of the supplicant and of the passionate yearner, the protective gestures of the saintly mediators between lowly mankind and the majesty of God. There is hardly one of these sensations or gestures which cannot be found in Dürer's devotional works.

Devotional Scenes

Let us enter the cathedral of Dürer's religious art and contemplate some of the figures absorbed in worship. St. John the Evangelist, kneeling on clouds amidst

THE FLIGHT INTO EGYPT
(Life of the Virgin. About 1502–5)

the seven lamps of fire, with bent head receives the divine inspiration—he is the vessel for what Dürer calls the 'influxes from above', he resembles a medium in a trance who is in the service of the supernatural powers ('Apocalypse', 1498). In contrast to this state of rapture is the agonized appeal to God, from the midst of his earthly misery, of the Prodigal Son (L. 222, London, and copperplate engraving, 1498). His prayer rises from the pigs' trough to the throne of God. St. John thrusts out his two hands as if they were bound by an unseen cord, his youthful locks falling over his averted head. The Prodigal Son wrings his hands, his eye wanders over the dilapidated roofs—he implores forgiveness from above. Another devotional picture is the engraving of the Nativity (1504), which Dürer himself called 'Christmas', but here the spiritual element is subordinated to the moral, the religious element to the profane. The atmosphere of this pleasing bourgeois idyll requires only a mitigated degree of devotion, for which reason the praying old man is relegated to the background, while Joseph in the foreground is busily engaged in filling a jug with water from a bucket—an everyday biblical scene such as Ludwig Richter used to produce in the nineteenth century for the delectation of simple souls! But Dürer again soars to a high level of conception in the figures of Apostles destined for the Heller altar-piece. There is a spiritual grandeur, the expression of which brings a new tone into German art, and a noble emotion in the drawing of the head of an Apostle, looking devoutly upwards (Vienna, 1508). Such were the men who, in Dürer's fantasy, embodied the victory of faith. Last in the series is the figure of the weeping St. John (L. 582, Vienna, 1523), a study for one of his unfinished devotional pictures. Full of devout seriousness, conscious of the greatness of his task, this youth belongs to the great family of Dürer's 'Four Apostles'. The prayer of an Apostle is in itself a supernatural thing, but humble worship is no less pleasing to the Lord, for example, the adoration of the knight, who—a solitary worshipper in the midst of an aristocratic crowd—stands among the spectators during the ceremony of the distribution of the rose-garlands (Festival of the Rose-garlands, 1506, Prague).

The religious figure belongs to another category in Dürer's work. Throughout his work Christ and the Virgin appear again and again. His religious art was not, like the devotional pictures of the Middle Ages, a mere intimation of a spiritual theme; it aimed at giving reality to the traditional spiritual theme. Dürer's artistic appeal no longer relied on symbols, but employed the language of reality. It was this proximity to life which enabled Dürer to narrate the Passion and the Life of the Virgin, and to enlarge upon them, in a way which at that time was just as new, and consequently just as popular, as Luther's translation of the Bible. Luther said: 'One must not ask the letters of the Latin languages how to speak German . . . one must ask the mother in her home, the children in the streets, the common man in the market-place, and see from their mouths how they speak and then interpret it; in this way they will understand and notice that one is talking German to them.' Dürer did the same; he, too, asked the mother in her home, when he wanted to transform the 'Santa Maria' into a picture of a 'worthy mother'. Dürer translated the Madonna of the Italians into the Maria of the Germans, and to do

57

61-63

The Religious Figure

ECCE HOMO
(Great Passion. About 1498)

that he sought inspiration not from the forms of Latin pictures, but from the children in the streets and the common man on the market-place, the very people whom Luther had in mind when he wanted to change the latinized German version of the greeting of the Angel of the Annunciation: 'Gegrüssest seist du, Maria voll Gnaden. Der Herr sei mit dir!' ('May you be greeted, Maria full of Grace. The Lord be with you.') into the really German form: 'Gott grüsse dich, du liebe Maria!' ('God greet you, dear Maria.') 'For that is what the angel wanted to say and how he would have spoken, if he had wanted to greet her in German.'

This new conception of the Virgin was not a gift which was bestowed on Dürer, it was the product of years of unremitting work and inner evolution. The history of Dürer's representation of the Virgin shows that he started from the traditional form, that his desire to create a solemn devotional picture with many figures remained with him from the time of his first journey to Italy until his journey to Livonia, and that he did not regard his own particular version of the figure of the Virgin as a revolutionary achievement. The earliest drawing by Dürer which has come down to us, made when he was a boy of thirteen, is a picture of the Virgin— the Madonna enthroned with two angel musicians (L. 1, Berlin, 1485). The story of his representation of the Virgin runs from this childhood work to the mature man's designs for great devotional paintings of the Virgin with eight or even ten Saints, dating from 1521–22 (L. 362, 363 and 364, Bayonne). He begins with hesitating restraint and ends with impressive monumentality. The 'dear little Virgin', who hardly dares to open her eyes, although only two angel musicians are looking at her, becomes the proud Mother of God and Queen of Heaven, surrounded by her heavenly court. The earliest drawing is, technically speaking, only a timid pen-drawing; the late versions of the theme are brilliant improvisations born from the emotion of the creative hour. They are forerunners of projected, or perhaps executed, pictures of numerous saints surrounding the Virgin, after the style of the Italian 'Santa Conversazione'. It is probable that during his journey to the Netherlands Dürer was commissioned to paint a picture by Wilmar Mey, prebendary of Riga Cathedral, and that on his return to Nuremberg he did paint such a picture, which was intended for the altar of the Virgin in the church of St. Peter at Riga, and was presumably destroyed during the iconoclastic disturbances in 1524. Five designs for the whole picture and fourteen individual studies still bear witness to the inner grandeur of the conception (e.g. the half-lengths of St. Barbara, L. 326, Paris, and St. Apollonia, L. 65, Berlin).

Between the early and the late extreme lie the various grades and types of Dürer's representations of the Virgin, in drawings, woodcuts, copper engravings and paintings. Three basic forms can be distinguished, which do not follow upon one another chronologically, but exist side by side during whole decades. These are: the Virgin enthroned and adoring the Child, the Virgin with the Holy Family, and the Virgin and Child alone. The impressions Dürer received during his journeys to Italy and the Netherlands, the personal experience of his mother's death and his childless marriage all contributed to his evolution of the theme. During his journeys and his years of maturity Dürer achieved complete mastery

*Dürer's
Representation
of the Virgin*

81

*Three
Basic Forms*

of the whole formal structure of a large picture, e.g. the arrangement of principal
and subordinate figures, the linking of the figures among themselves and with the
central figure, the balancing of closed and open portions of the picture, the calculation of relative positions, etc. He lost in this process the warmth, the simplicity
and the popular appeal which characterize his youthful works. The Paumgärtner
altar-piece in Munich, the 'Adoration of the Magi' in Florence, the Heller altar-
piece and the 'Festival of the Rose-garlands' were all pictures intended for public
worship in a consecrated building, not for individual delectation in the home,
created for solemn church services, not for intimate colloquies between the devout
and God.

The second category comprises the representations of the Virgin with the Holy
Family, i.e. Mother, Child and Joseph. The earliest version of this motive dates from
1492 (L. 430, Erlangen) and still shows clear traces of the influence of Schongauer.
But Dürer sounds a note of his own only a few years later in the 'Virgin with the
Locust' (copperplate engraving, about 1495). The heavenly throne has become a
grassy seat, no crown adorns the head of the Divine Mother, no angels make music.
Mary is alone with her firstborn. Joseph is relegated to one side; he is plunged in
deep sleep, his face showing the marks of care and toil. The woodcut of the 'Holy
Family with Three Hares' dates from 1497, the same period as Dürer's 'Apocalypse'. It is remarkable for its mixture of old-fashioned notions—the Gothic pose
of the Virgin's head and the enclosed garden (the symbol of virginity)—and new
conceits—the Child fingering the pages of the book, the quaint family idyll of the
hares. Above this gentle female gardener hovers, like a heavenly emblem, the
crown borne by angels. At the zenith of his graphic style in 1511, Dürer produced
two woodcuts of the Holy Family. One of them (B. 96) is fresh; the other (B. 97),
insipid; the first shows freedom from convention in the charming conception of
the Child struggling to get from his mother's lap into his grandmother's arms, the
second is a barren semicircle of relatives surrounding the Holy Women.

*The German
Maria*

86
The third category gives us the German conception of Maria—the Mother and
Child alone. It is a long series from which, as from the other two groups, only a
few examples can be taken. The 'Virgin with the monkey' (copperplate engraving,
about 1497–99) also has a place in the history of Dürer's landscape, because one
half of the background of this picture of a 'belle jardinière' is a reversal as seen in
the mirror of the water-colour showing the 'House by the Pond', this time
executed with the greater exactitude of the burin. The 'Virgin and Child with
Animals' (L. 460, Vienna) shows the Virgin dreaming joyfully of her Child, life,
the landscape and everything which creeps and flies in this animals' Garden of
Eden. This magnificent pen-drawing heightened with water-colour appears to
date from about 1503, for it was from this zoological garden that Dürer took the
various animals for his 'Life of the Virgin' and other engravings executed at this
time. The owl appears again on one of the arches spanning the 'Marriage of the
Virgin', where it has become mere ornamentation, the terrier will be found snuffing
in the foreground of the 'Visitation'. The little bird watches the Virgin suckling the
Child in the engraving of 1503, and the parrot appears again swinging on the

branch from which hangs Dürer's signature tablet in the Adam and Eve engraving 110 of 1504. If we are to judge according to moods, two subdivisions can be made, the categories of gay and sorrowful Virgins. Waldmann remarks at one point that Dürer created the type of 'melancholy' Virgin. But the same Dürer who in his letters from Venice to Pirckheimer made the coarsest jokes about his own wife, also created the sublime female figure of the 'Melancolia'. In the engraving of 1520 the Virgin sits beaming like a well-to-do peasant girl in her Sunday best. Her neatly combed hair—which must surely have been blonde!—is blown aside by the morning breeze, she has a cushion beneath her, so that her best dress shall not be crumpled by the rough wooden bench. On another occasion the Virgin is so cheerfully shy, and smiling so bashfully beneath the crown borne by two angels, that one might think it was the bridal garland they were bringing (engraving of 1518). Other prints display an elegiac mood, e.g. the 'Virgin with the Pear' (engraving, 1511); the Child is not attracted by the beautiful fruit and the Mother is lost in thought. In the 'Virgin beneath a Tree' (engraving of 1513), the Mother clasps the Child to her as if fearful that he will be snatched away.

Dürer's pictures of the Virgin soon became known and found their way across the Alps to the classic home of Madonnas. What did the Italians think of these German Virgins? Lodovico Dolce, in his treatise 'L'Aretino', finds fault with Dürer for drawing the Mother of God in German clothes and showing the Jews with German faces and German coiffures; he says that the nationality of the persons represented, their customs and the period must be taken into consideration. The historical sense of the theoreticians of the Italian Renaissance held that Dürer's popular representations of the Virgin were anachronisms. They must have had more or less the same effect on the Italians as Fritz von Uhde's pictures of Christ had upon our fathers, who were accustomed to an idealized version of biblical subjects. But what the Italians could not understand, what they avoided seeing in the picture because they could see it in front of their doors and on the steps of their churches, was the Virgin suckling her Child, in which Dürer recognized and often depicted the epitome of intimacy, the perfect symbol of the link between Mother and Child.

Italian and German Conceptions

A kind of legendary prelude to this group of pictures of the Virgin is the copperplate engraving entitled 'The Penitence of St. Chrysostom' (about 1497), which probably was inspired by the 'Passionale' printed by Koberger in 1488. Sitting naked on a rocky ledge, the Emperor's daughter whom Chrysostom seduced is suckling the fruit of her sin. This human material is raised to a sacred level in the print of the Virgin in the corner of the garden (copperplate engraving, 1503). The woman is sitting low down, as so to be able to hold the child comfortably on her lap and against her breast, her gaze is concentrated on the little head. It is a theme of pure motherhood, for the child still belongs entirely to the mother; it has not yet been designated by Fate and raised to its mother's level or—a little king dispensing grace—to a level even higher than hers. This version is the most beautiful of the 'quiet' category; it was modified by Dürer several times and used by him in 1511 for the title-page of the 'Life of the Virgin'. The Mother of Ill. p. 90

Jesus is sitting on the mystic sickle of the moon, amidst a garland of rays, beneath a hovering crown of stars. The intimacy of the scene is decorative, the motherly element has become heraldic. And lastly, if we compare any of the graphic versions of the Virgin with similar painted works by Dürer, the balance is invariably tipped in favour of the drawings and prints. With all its motherliness, the 'Madonna with the Goldfinch' (Berlin, 1506) is yet far behind the engraving of the 'Virgin with the Monkey'. Compared with the free drawing of the Virgin suckling the Child (L. 525, Vienna, 1512), the painting of the Virgin in Vienna (1512) seems artificial and stilted.

In the set of woodcuts for the 'Life of the Virgin', Dürer combined all that he had learned between 1497 and 1510 from his versions of the theme of the Virgin—the gay and sorrowful impulses, the idyllic and pathetic scenes, the whole gamut of the conceptions: Virgin—Mother—Queen—Goddess. This epic of illustration is not without traces of artistic tension. Drawings from the year 1510 have found their way into this series, of which the majority of the drawings date from 1502–1505, and demonstrate the formal and spiritual change which the artist underwent during these five years. They introduce a somewhat cooler tone, but at the same time a perfecting of composition. The earliest of these woodcuts, among them the Nativity of the Virgin, soon became famous. As early as 1506, copies were made by Marcantonio. Dürer published the 'Life of the Virgin' in 1511 as a book of woodcuts—like his 'Apocalypse' and his 'Passions'. The series consists of twenty woodcuts, with the title-page, which was probably executed after all the others, and of Latin (!) verses, which, like those for the 'Great' and 'Little Passion', were composed by Dürer's friend Benedikt Schwalber (Chelidonius), abbot of the Scottish monastery in Vienna. The cycle not only combines a number of woodcuts illustrating one story under one title, but was also carefully put together by Dürer and was intended not for those who just glance at pictures, but for those who peruse the text as well and grasp the entity of the work as a whole. The vignette of the Virgin with the Child at her breast strikes the keynote, the next three woodcuts tell the story of Joachim and Anna and serve as a prelude; then follow fourteen woodcuts, each depicting an episode in the Virgin's life, from her birth to her death. Two more woodcuts form the conclusion—the Assumption of the Virgin and her transfigured existence in heaven.

Thematically the 'Life of the Virgin' forms with the 'Apocalypse' and the 'Great Passion' a wonderful trilogy. In the 'Apocalypse' an impersonal, supernatural power is the dominant figure, in the 'Great Passion' it is Christ, who suffers and yet is victorious, while the 'Life of the Virgin' is the human story of a woman. Mariolatry, as successor to mysticism, had absorbed its warmth and fervour, it was filled with reminiscences of the Minnesingers' fanciful cult of women, and in it we find, on a higher plane, the purest traits of German family life. The cult of the Virgin as practised by the Church, the exaggerations of which already at that time constituted a challenge, served Dürer as a pretext for depicting the joys and sorrows of a mother on an epic scale, for translating an old and venerable biblical subject into the language of everyday life, at the same time transfiguring it by

[margin notes:]
73

'Life of the Virgin'
Ill. pp. 92, 94

Mariolatry

means of poetry. In this respect, too, Dürer shared the feelings of Luther, who loved the idea of talking with the personalities of the Sacred Story in a frank and childlike way, and preferred to think of the Saviour as a child, bringing Joseph his food at his work-bench, or being asked by his mother, if he has been away too long, where he has been all this time. The 'Life of the Virgin' is a popular book of woodcuts, containing in the form of drawings a number of folksongs, some of which have remained indelibly impressed on the fantasy of the German people, e.g. the cheery chorus of women in the room of the Nativity, one of whom is raising a Bavarian beer-tankard to her lips; the tender melody, like an organ prelude, of the scene of the marriage between Mary, a lady of Nuremberg, and the worthy Joseph; the pathetic duet between mother and daughter in the Visitation, set before a distant and grandiose landscape; the little lullaby which the mother sings to her Child during the pause on the Flight into Egypt; and, finally, the solemn lamentations and murmured prayers which fill the death-chamber of the Virgin, and the closing chorus of angels to the accompaniment of harps. If we call to mind the contrasts in mood between the 'Life of the Virgin' and Dürer's 'Passions', we are left in doubt as to which is better suited to Dürer's talent—the representation of that which is cogent and easily perceptible, or the telling of a dramatic story. To be at home in both these worlds, and invariably to fill a subject with the life appropriate to it, so that the spectator is led to suppose that only in this atmosphere can the artist work to his heart's content, is a real sign of genius.

Popular Tone

At an auction sale in 1638 Rembrandt bought Dürer's 'Great Passion' and nine sets of his 'Life of the Virgin'. He also owned a copy of 'The Art of Mensuration with Compasses and Ruler', a portion of which can still be seen today on Rembrandt's work-table in his house at Amsterdam. One would like to know which were the favourite prints of the great Dutch painter, who himself had drawn, painted and etched so often the Flight into Egypt, the Adoration of the Shepherds and the Presentation in the Temple. The figure of Christ swinging the scourge in Rembrandt's etching of the 'Purging of the Temple' is taken from Dürer's 'Little Passion', and Rembrandt's etching of the Visitation is inspired by Dürer's version of the theme in the 'Life of the Virgin'.

In the third decade of the sixteenth century, Dürer ceased to occupy himself with pictures of the Virgin. The main reasons for this were the change of dogmatic ideas, the absence of commissions from the Church and the general upheaval in spiritual life, where the talk was now of 'last things'. The moral earnestness of the Reformation period tended to repress both the warm sincerity of the cult of the Virgin and the spirit of humanistic culture. Mother and Child had to leave the field to men. It was not the Virgin, but Dürer's 'Apostles', who provided the answers to the questions which filled his last years.

In an often-quoted saying Dürer defined the tasks of painting as 'proclaiming' the Passion of Christ and preserving the likeness of a man long after his death. Dürer certainly never grew weary of depicting the Passion, for he busied himself with five versions of it. Three of these—two consisting of woodcuts and one of

The Passion of Christ

copperplate engravings—actually appeared; for the fourth, the so-called 'Green Passion', we have the designs drawn with his pen; for the fifth, which was again to have been a 'great' woodcut Passion, he produced one print—the Last Supper, which we have already mentioned. Three other scenes for the same series—the Bearing of the Cross, the Agony in the Garden and the Burial of Christ, exist in the form of drawings. There were, of course, extraneous reasons which led Dürer to return time after time to the story of the Passion. After the 'Life of the Virgin', which appealed primarily to women, the Passion was the most popular of all themes, for it showed to the eyes of all how God became Man and how, because He had become Man, He had to suffer, like the humblest of men. A more decisive factor for Dürer, however, was undoubtedly the realization that, by constantly returning to the story of Christ, His patience and restraint, His struggles and His victories, he was treading the right path. The 'Passions' were pictures for men. We cannot understand Dürer if we regard him only as a gifted illustrator of the New Testament. We must see in him, over and above the aesthetic values, a man possessed by God, who sought to free himself from the pangs of conscience and anguish of soul by placing his innermost visions before himself and before us, by 'expressing' himself in the language which God had vouchsafed to him, the language of pictures.

The 'Great Passion'
Ill. pp. 88, 96

The woodcuts of the 'Great Passion', which are accompanied by Latin verses, belong to two periods. The drawings for the following scenes date from the period of the 'Apocalypse' (1496–98): the Flagellation, Ecce Homo, the Bearing of the Cross, Crucifixion, Lamentation and Entombment. The following woodcuts, on the other hand, were executed after 1510: Christ in Limbo, Resurrection, Betrayal, Last Supper, and finally the 'Man of Sorrow' as title-page of the whole book (1511). If a poet begins his career by writing a tragedy, that does not mean that he will not finish by writing an epic. Youthful genius loves to handle the pathetic elements. His work on the inspiring scenes of the 'Apocalypse' trained Dürer's eye and hand to portray the dramatic elements of the Passion. A comparison between the prints dating from 1496–98 and those produced in 1510–11 shows us—as it did in the case of the 'Life of the Virgin'—how Dürer, as a result of the impressions received from Italian art, abandoned those earlier compositions overfilled with figures, but also filled with life. In the later prints a few, grandiosely conceived figures dominate the scene, and Christ Himself is transformed from the Gothic 'Man of Sorrow' into a 'hero' of the southern, athletic type.

The 'Green Passion'

The 'Green Passion' (pen-drawings on paper with a green ground, with the lights set off in white) still forms a subject of critical controversy. It is certain that the eight designs dating from 1504 are by Dürer's own hand. But is this true of the green sheets which have been worked over again? Meder, Pauli and Flechsig support the theory that they are by Dürer's own hand, whereas Springer, Wölfflin and Curlis believe that they are the work of pupils. The former group base their opinion on Dürer's monograms and dates, which are undoubtedly genuine; the others on the artistic sentiment. It cannot be denied that this 'Passion', with its miniature-like delicacy and formal clarity, is foreign to our conception of Dürer's work as a whole, but this does not necessarily imply that it is the work of another hand.

The 'Little' woodcut Passion of 1509–11 with its 37 prints is the most comprehensive, but the least dramatic of Dürer's 'Passions'. With great artistic discrimination Dürer has checked at several points the flow of the narrative, e.g. by the insertion of the Washing of Feet between the Last Supper and the Agony in the Garden, and of the Sudarium of St. Veronica between the Bearing of the Cross and the Crucifixion. The story of the Passion is preceded by an Old Testament prelude consisting of two prints: Adam and Eve and their expulsion from the Garden of Eden. After the end of the story there is a mystic epilogue consisting of eight prints, from the Resurrection to the Last Judgement; to this group belong the Appearances of Christ, the Ascension and the Descent of the Holy Ghost. *The 'Little' Woodcut Passion*

Ill. p. 107

The 'Little' copperplate Passion was created between 1507 and 1513, most of the engravings dating from after 1512. It consists of fifteen engravings, to which, probably to make up the sexto-decimo, a sixteenth engraving was added, the Healing of the Paralytic (or more correctly, of the Leper) by St. Peter and St. John. The narrative begins at the moment when Christ, in the Garden of Olives, resolves to take up the Cross, and ends with the Resurrection. Two other versions of the Agony in the Garden, dating from 1521 and 1524, are designs for the last of his 'Passions', which Dürer planned as a series of woodcuts in wide format. The print of the Adoration of the Magi (L. 584, Vienna), also intended for this series, was the last, maturest and most majestic version of this theme which Dürer treated so often. *The 'Little' Copperplate Passion*

74

Dürer's change of mood as regards the representation of the Virgin does not appear either in the version of the Madonna Enthroned or in that of the Virgin adoring the Child, but in the German conception of the Virgin suckling the Child. Dürer's achievement in the representation of Christ consists firstly of his own personal interpretation of the Agony in the Garden as the decisive moment in the whole story of the Passion; and secondly in the creation of a distinctive countenance of Christ, which since Dürer's days has dominated all German conceptions of it. Dürer's versions of the Sudarium of St. Veronica were the source of this German conception. *Dürer's New Mood*

It is not without some hesitation that we here give to a handful of prints a significance which is usually reserved for large altar-pieces. But an affirmation of this sort will surprise only those who seek to elucidate merely the formal evolution of church pictures, instead of studying the development of the religious idea in Dürer's art. The 'large pictures' have their own place and their own special significance. The 'Festival of the Rose-garlands' (1506) is the finest compliment which any German painter has paid to the glories of Italy, and at the same time it was the young Nuremberg artist's act of homage to the leader of the Venetian school, Giovanni Bellini. But by the time he painted his 'Adoration of the Trinity' (1511), Dürer had mastered the inner monumentality of Roman frescoes; he created the German counterpart—different in type, but equal in value—to Raphael's 'Disputa'. The painting of the distribution of the mystic rose-garlands *61–63*

69–71

by the Virgin and St. Dominic to the Emperor Maximilian and Pope Julius II, in the presence of numerous spectators, and the Adoration of the Trinity by the Emperor Charles, three kings, two Popes, knights, burghers and peasants and the holy men of the Old and New Testaments—these are both works which Dürer was commissioned to paint, according to stipulated programmes embracing even the smallest details. At the back of both of them are the intellectual structure of the Catholic Church and the traditional solemnity of its forms of representation. But Dürer's drawings and prints of the Agony in the Garden belong to a different world. Their essence—the moral decision which must be taken with full freedom of will—transports us to the world of the Reformation. It is significant that Dürer was working on his maturest versions of the scene in the Garden of Olives during the very years of his journey to the Netherlands, in which he was most deeply concerned with religious problems and was continually absorbed by them.

The Agony in the Garden

With the Agony in the Garden Christ enters upon the Way of the Cross. The conflict in His own breast is the prelude to His martyrdom at the hands of men. That hour in the Garden of Gethsemane is the hour of His greatest weakness, and at the same time of His greatest strength. Never, not even in His last hour on the Cross between the two thieves, was Christ so alone as He was in the Garden of Olives. While the disciples sleep, the Master watches and achieves the supreme victory, the victory over Himself.

The Evangelists differ in their versions of Christ's prayer in the Garden of Gethsemane, which was not a supplication, not an act of worship or thanksgiving, but a hard struggle with God. After the Last Supper Jesus went with His disciples (St. Luke speaks of eleven; St. Matthew and St. Mark mention only three—Peter, James and John) out of the city of Jerusalem into a garden at the foot of the Mount of Olives. The garden was called Gethsemane, which means 'oil-press'. St. Matthew (26, 39) describes how Jesus fell on His face and prayed, saying, O my Father, if it be possible, let this cup pass from me: nevertheless not as I will, but as Thou wilt. St. Mark (14) tells us how he began to be sore amazed and very heavy, and how he said to his disciples, My soul is exceeding sorrowful unto death. From St. Luke (22) we learn that Jesus kneeled down and prayed, and there appeared an angel unto him from heaven, strengthening him. And being in an agony, he prayed more earnestly, and his sweat was as it were great drops of blood falling down to the ground.

This scene, filled with the moving earnestness of a great tragic moment, made no appeal to the Late Antique world, and it is for this reason that the Agony in the Garden does not appear in representations of the Passion on sarcophagi. The spiritual profundity of the scene, i.e. as the representation of Christ struggling in prayer, was not understood or depicted in art until the second half of the sixth century.

Between 1498 and 1524 Dürer continually returned—in drawings, woodcuts and engravings—to this so human episode in the life of the Son of God, as if for him it were a symbol of the freedom, and at the same time the subjection of the Christian man. Dürer made use of both alternatives which the Evangelists offered

THE VIRGIN AND CHILD WITH ANIMALS. Water-colour, about 1505. Vienna, Albertina

to artists in their rendering of Christ's pose and movements—he has given us both the kneeling and the recumbent figure. The various versions of the kneeling figure represent an equal number of fundamentally different psychological interpretations of the situation by Dürer's own religious intuition.

Versions and Interpretations

The woodcut in the 'Great Passion', Dürer's earliest version of the Agony in the Garden, dating from the years of his 'Apocalypse', shows Jesus warding off the cup of sorrow with both hands. The flesh is weak, the fear is great. With the penetration typical of his earlier drawings, Dürer depicts in Christ's countenance His hesitation before the decision. This is found again in the corresponding engraving of the copperplate 'Passion', in which it is notably strengthened. The kneeling Jesus stretches out His arms in despair; passionately the tormented being appeals to God for help; the prayer becomes a cry. That is the Jesus whose sweat was like great drops of blood falling to the ground.

Completely different is the atmosphere in the woodcut of the 'Little Passion'. Jesus, here seen in vanishing profile, is the silent sufferer. The 'pathetic' fall of the locks, the hands raised to the level of the forehead and folded, tell us clearly that, rapt in silent prayer, He submits himself to God's will and is ready to accept the Cross which the angel is offering Him. This version, however, is not Dürer's last word. In 1515 he etched the Agony in the Garden on iron. In this the mood of the praying Christ is one of deep melancholy: 'My soul is exceeding sorrowful unto death'. The hands, on the point of being folded, hesitate, opened in a gesture of astonishment. And the eye of Christ perceives, as if with painful wonder, the fate which awaits Him. The figure itself is upright, but the branches of the olive tree in the background are twisted as if in agony and pain. The night wind blows across the beautiful landscape. In the two drawings in wide format which Dürer made for his uncompleted 'Passion', one (L. 200, Frankfurt) also shows Christ kneeling in prayer, but it is, despite the grandeur of the gesture of pathos, a constrained, heroic figure.

In the second group of representations of the Agony in the Garden, Christ is shown lying prostrate. As early as 1509 Dürer made a woodcut, intended for the 'Little Passion' but afterwards rejected, in which Christ is shown lying on the ground with outstretched arms, in the symbolical form of the Cross. This old formula, filled with new meaning, is found again in the beautiful drawing of the prostrate Jesus dating from 1521 (L. 199, Frankfurt). As in the etching on iron of the Agony, here, too, Nature is used to support the figures; the atmosphere of the landscape appears to be an echo of that which is taking place in the breast of the Man. Again Christ is shown lying with outstretched arms in the form of a Cross; but it is more than a mere pose, it is a clinging to the beloved mother earth, from which no man wishes to be torn away. Streaks of mist float through the trees and hover, grey and heavy as palls, above the prostrate figure.

What is the personal element in Dürer's interpretation and representation of the Agony in the Garden? In the Gospel story he saw a parallel to the truly heroic achievement of man, accepting suffering, scorn and derision, or even death, in order to accomplish the mission given to him by God. From this standpoint the

Dürer's Interpretation

H

whole Passion of Christ assumes a new and deeper meaning; it ceases to be a story of suffering and martyrdom, and becomes a tragedy of inner conflict. That springs from Dürer's conception of religion and of the ultimate aim of existence—including the artist's existence. Dürer could never satisfy himself, he could never rid himself of the feeling that he had been 'called', and that he would have to answer for his work before the throne of God. He would have agreed with Ibsen's words, that creation means keeping the Last Judgement before one's eyes.

The history of the religious element in Dürer's art is like a repetition of the evolution of the religious experience of mankind. The origin of all religion is man's fear of the elementary powers, and Dürer's first religious cycle, the 'Apocalypse', was born from the fear prevalent at that time of the end of the world and the imminence of the Last Judgement. But the cycle of Dürer's religious representations closes with the scenes on the Mount of Olives, symbols of the overcoming of human fears by the free decision to accomplish a heroic task, and—as Dürer's last word—the painting of the Four Apostles, his confession of faith. Between these two opposite poles of primitive religiosity dominated by visions and the free Lutheran certitude of faith lies the whole breadth and fullness of Dürer's religious feeling and his religious art.

The Countenance of Christ

By his many and varied representations of the 'Man of Sorrow' Dürer has earned a place in the history of the portrayal of the figure of Christ. But Dürer's conception of the 'Man of Sorrow' had no more influence on the German people's idea of Christ's countenance than his 'Madonna on the sickle of the Moon' had on its general conception of the Virgin. The conception of Christ's countenance originated from the 'Sudarium of St. Veronica'. Both the woodcut 'Passions' and the engravings of the 'Little Passion' give us (in the prints of the 'Bearing of the Cross') the background to the miracle of St. Veronica. It was the moment when Christ, bent beneath the burden of the Cross, turned his sweat-covered countenance towards St. Veronica, whose hands held ready the cloth which was to receive the miraculous imprint of His visage. In the 'Little' woodcut Passion, immediately after this episode,

Ill. p. 107

Dürer inserted a print showing St. Veronica, with the sudarium in her hands, standing between St. Peter and St. Paul (1510). In the 1516 etching on iron, the fluttering sudarium is borne up to heaven by an angel. During his journey to the Netherlands Dürer, as we learn from his diary, once more busied himself with the subject, for he writes: 'I have made a good countenance of Veronica in oil colour; it is better than the previous one.' By 'countenance of Veronica' he means in both cases the sudarium, for he also calls his celebrated engraving of 1513, known to the world as the 'Sudarium with two angels', a 'Veronica'. In this print Dürer has combined everything he had to say of the countenance of Christ. His is a Northern Christ, in contrast to the supreme example of the southern idea of Christ as shown in Leonardo's Last Supper. The Italian portrays a spiritualized sufferer, little more than a youth, whose hand says more than his mouth; the German gives us a man's head, from whose brow appear to shine forth the knightly virtues—'high courage', 'great feeling' and 'free soul', and whose glance, earnest and proud, is that of a king.

We will cast one more glance back over the religious work of Dürer. He *Dürer's Form*
possessed neither the serene balance of Raphael nor the sad sweetness of Leonardo.
Dürer's being was as remote from Michelangelo's 'terribilità' as it was from the
ecstasy of Grünewald. Dürer did not—like many Renaissance artists—sacrifice
soul to form, nor did he—like many Gothic artists—rend form asunder in order
to liberate the soul. Dürer's form is a soulful form, it is neither a gift from heaven
nor a form borrowed from Italy. Dürer's form is a fruit wrung from the northern
soil by dint of care and struggle—and it bears the imprint of the labour which it
cost.

ST. VERONICA WITH THE SUDARY
(Little Passion, 1510)

CHAPTER SEVEN

PORTRAITURE

'THE art of painting also preserves the figure of a man after his death.' Thus did Dürer, writing in 1512 in one of the drafts for his treatise on painting, define the task and the special achievement of the art of portraiture. To an ancient truism, to which all memorial sculpture of Antiquity and the Middle Ages owes its existence, Dürer gave a new form which reminds us of the words of the Italian theoretician Leon Battista Alberti: 'The figure of a man long since dead survives through painting for a long time.' Concern for their posthumous fame and delight in immortalizing individual appearance were characteristic of the men of the Renaissance. Like Pope Julius II, the Emperor Maximilian did not fail to make early provision for his own tomb, declaring that: 'He who makes no monument to himself during his lifetime, will have no monument after his death, and such a man will be forgotten as soon as his passing-bell has ceased to toll.' Painters and sculptors held the key to the portal of fame in their hands; they could erect a monument to a man, and they were well aware of it. Dürer had a very keen perception of this; proudly he wrote on his great woodcut portrait of his friend Ulrich Varnbüler (1522) that he wished to preserve for posterity the features of a man he loved.

Portraits satisfy a need of human nature which is always present, more urgent at certain periods, and at others subdued by aesthetic and ideal considerations. It is a branch of art which is really in the service of mankind. This was also Dürer's conception of portraiture, and he remained faithful to it throughout his life, for portrait commissions came to him as part of the needs of the time and formed a link between him and his fellow-men. Dürer made portraits of himself and of his friends, sometimes as a token of homage and affection, sometimes as a remembrance of men he had met, sometimes because he was interested in striking figures; he made portraits in return for a fee, as presents and as a return for favours shown, as psychological studies or as an artist's tribute. Commissions for portraits came to him through all the decades of his life. The earliest example of his art which has come down to us is a self-portrait, and portraits are among the finest works of his last years. At times, for instance during his journeys to Italy and the Netherlands, he created portrait after portrait in quick succession; at other times the flow of portraits is more restricted. In his youth Dürer's artistic ambition soared far beyond the limits of portraiture into the realm of grandiose dramatic narrative or profound pictorial poems. In his maturity he returned from these adventurous heights of fantasy to the sober but safer ground of portraiture, which binds the artist's genius down to one fragment of nature. About 1525 or 1526 Dürer must have discussed such matters with Melanchthon, of whom he created a delightful portrait at that time. In 1547 Melanchthon wrote to George of Anhalt: 'I remember how that man of rare spirit and virtue, the Master Albrecht Dürer, said to me that as a young man he had loved gay-coloured pictures with many figures, and that in contemplating

50

his own works he had admired in particular their diversity. But as an older man he had begun to contemplate Nature and to model it after its own image, and had recognized that this simplicity is the highest ornament of art.'

Dürer created hundreds of portraits. These were either drawn, 'gerissen' (i.e. sketched on the blocks and then cut by the woodcutters), etched on copperplates or painted. During his journey to the Netherlands alone (1520–21) he made about 120 'counterfeitings'. Some of these portraits were for private use, e.g. the self-portraits and family portraits, while some were destined for the houses of patrons and recipients, and were thus also intended for the eyes of few. But some of Dürer's finest portraits were designed from the outset for public exhibition. They appeared as prints, i.e. in a large number of originals, thus serving to spread the fame of the sitter. Portraits in the form of woodcuts or engravings naturally had the best chance of success at a time like the first decades of the sixteenth century, when a lively interest was taken in the leading figures in politics, religion, science and the arts. *Scope of Dürer's Portraiture*

Should the art historian now endeavour to follow the 'evolution' of Dürer as a portraitist? Should he draw attention to all the changes of conception and form to be seen in the portraits created by Dürer in the course of his life? It is, of course, obvious that Dürer did not remain stationary at the stage he had reached when he painted his own portrait at the age of thirteen. He grew up and matured as a portrayer of men, became wise and charitable in his judgement of them. And we feel that, just as Dürer matured, so did the whole of his generation mature with him amidst the stormy happenings of the time. Another race of men seems to gaze at us from the portraits of the mature Dürer, and yet they were the same men whom he had known in his earlier days. That which remains is more important than that which changes, and in the history of art the lasting elements in Dürer's portraiture are more important than changes of style.

Dürer's portraits of his fellow-Germans are affirmations of German character and form a group in the nation's gallery of ancestral portraits of which the German people may well be proud. In such an imaginary gallery we would find the Adam and the knight from Bamberg, the equestrian statue from Magdeburg, the figures of founders from Naumburg, Cranach's Luther and Holbein's Amerbach, heads by Dürer, Schlüter's Great Elector, Philipp Otto Runge's portrait of his parents, Rethel's portrait of his mother, Leibl's Baron Perfall, Menzel's Frederick the Great and Lenbach's Bismarck. *Men and Characters*

As regards the technique of his portraits, Dürer used every kind of tool and material. Silverpoint and pen, the brush for oil and water colours, charcoal, chalk, straight processes and mixed techniques, e.g. brush drawings with wash on coloured paper, heightened with white chalk. The type of technique, however, is no guide to the artistic merit of the work. A woodcut like the portrait of Varnbüler, an engraving like that of Melanchthon, a sketch like that of the Emperor Maximilian, are equal in quality to the painted likenesses. Many of the drawings are studies for paintings, whilst others are independent works in themselves. Some of them may be designs by Dürer for medallions, e.g. the silverpoint drawing of *Dürer's Technique*

35

52   the Imperial Statthalter Frederick II of the Palatinate (L. 293, London, 1522), and
the superb drawing, dating from 1527, of Ulrich Starck (L. 296, London).

Dürer has left us no theoretical expressions of opinion on the problems of
portrait-painting, but this lack is to a certain extent compensated by one of his most
curious, and at the same time least popular pictures—'The Young Jesus with the
58–60   Doctors' (1506, Rome, Galleria Barberini). Dürer himself had a very high opinion
of this painting, which dates from his second Venetian journey. He calls it a 'Quar'
(i.e. a 'quadro') 'the like of which I have never painted before', and—one might
well add—the like of which he never painted again. The picture is interesting, not
only because it was 'painted in five days', but also because it is the outcome of
Experiments   Dürer's study of physiognomy and gestures during his stay in Italy. It may have
in   been intended for Giovanni Bellini. In Northern Italy Dürer learned the language
Physiognomy   of hands, which the Italians use so expressively to supplement the language of the
mouth. He also appears to have had some knowledge of Leonardo's experiments
115   in physiognomy. Drawings by Dürer from the year 1513 have come down to us
(e.g. L. 34, Berlin, and L. 378, Paris), which show us in the one case ten, in the
other four male heads in left profile one behind the other. In each of these drawings
the artist appears to be striving, by means of modifications to the foreheads, noses
and chins, to convert normal heads into bestial or pathological abnormalities. The
expression 'caricatures' does not meet the case. These are linear experiments, essays
in mimicry and physiognomy.

In the third book of his Treatise on Proportion, Dürer returns once more to
physiognomical questions, maintaining that no one can know what produces a
good figure unless he already knows what is a 'misshapen' figure. He specifies,
for example, all possible shapes of noses, mouths and chins—'for some have great
hooked, long and overhanging noses. And again some have quite short noses,
turned up, thick, knotty, pressed deep in between the eyes, or high up on their
brows. And some have deep little eyes or high great round eyes. Some open their
eyes narrowly like a pig and raise the lower lid more than the upper lid. And there
are some who open their eyes wide in a circle, so that one can see into the whole
pupil. Then there are some who have the eyebrows raised high above the eyes, in
others they lie upon them or hang over them, and some have thin eyebrows and
116   others thick'. Dürer's Dresden sketchbook contains a number of such heads. The
aim of his Treatise on Proportion was to show how the experienced artist, by
'displacing' constructional lines, can change the physiognomy, and also how the
artistically possible forms lie between the artistically impossible extremes—'the
more the deformity is removed, the more the beautiful will remain'. The Doctors,
in the picture in Rome of 'Jesus with the Doctors', also look as if they were taken
from an album of character heads. But the focal point of the picture is the cluster
of four hands, the finger language of which excited the admiration of the Italians.
Titian's picture of the Tribute Money relies on the contrast between the 'coarse,
gnarled hand of the Pharisee and the delicate, answering hand of the Saviour'
(Thausing), like an echo of the physiognomical contrast in Dürer's youthful work.
59   How wonderful is Dürer's study for the hands of Jesus (L. 137, Brunswick). His

'Jesus with the Doctors' may be a clever trick of art rather than a great work of art, but it must not be forgotten that hardly any other work of the 'Italian-influenced' Dürer contains so much of the North as this interweaving of forms in the interests of a southern desire to achieve expression. Niccolò dei Barbari's 'Jesus and the Woman taken in adultery' (Venice, Palazzo Mocenigo) is an imitation of Dürer's picture.

The eyes and the hands are the two mirrors, in which the creator of a portrait sees the soul of his model. In Dürer's portraits the hands play a rôle of the first importance, with infinite variations in their pose and their contribution to the expression of the sitter's character. Dürer's hands retain traces of Late Gothic with their slender fingers and their 'delicate' poise, even when other portions of the picture have already been subjected to the Renaissance insistence on form. We thus find curious contrasts of style in one and the same picture, e.g. the solemn and tranquil full-face head and the pointed, mobile hand in the Munich self-portrait. Studies of hands played an important part in his preparatory work for his great altar-pieces, e.g. the 'Festival of the Rose-garlands'. Many of the hands in Dürer's portraits are holding something, e.g. a rosary (Portrait of his Father, 1490), a flower (Self-portrait, 1493), a sheet of paper (so-called Portrait of Barendt von Orley, 1524). Some of his hands are still, resting one upon the other (Frederick the Wise, 1495–1500; Self-portrait, 1498), others are grasping something, e.g. the lapel of a fur coat (Oswolt Krell, 1499; Self-portrait, 1500); while the hand of Erasmus of Rotterdam is shown writing. If Dürer, in three of the portraits painted during his sojourn in Flanders, partially absorbs the hands into the rest of the picture, that is probably due to the influence of the Flemish tradition in portraiture, just as it was an Italian custom to allow a glimpse of the landscape to one side of the head (Self-portrait, 1498; Oswolt Krell, 1499; portraits of Hans, Felicitas and Elsbeth Tucher, 1499).

Eyes and Hands
1, 3–5, 8, 11, 17, 51, 58–9, 62, 65, 78

8, 17–20

Dürer abandoned such methods of enriching and enlivening a picture when he had to portray a really expressive head, which he preferred to depict against a plain, neutral background, thus making it impossible for the spectator to escape the gaze of the sitter. Tranquillity of background and absence of accessories were in accord with Dürer's mode of spiritual expression. Whatever else he may have been, he was not an 'impressionist' of the art of portraiture. He did not wish to depict the momentary condition of the soul; no matter whether the countenance were bright or sad, tranquil or clouded with anger, his main concern was the construction of a character which would impress upon the spectator the lasting and decisive elements. Only in the 'private' portraits (the Erlangen self-portrait and his drawing of his sick mother) did he tear aside the veil concealing the deepest recesses of the soul—just as in his diary his true temperament suddenly bursts forth like an underground volcano. In portraits intended for other eyes he endowed his sitters with poise and restraint, emphasizing 'their substance and their manliness, their inner strength and permanence'. If we compare Dürer's portraits with Holbein's, Dürer's appear more full of soul, Holbein's more true to life. The soul which Dürer put into his portraits was his own soul; it is his energy which

Background and Accessories

inspires them, his purity of heart which looks forth from their eyes. Dürer gave more of his own blood than the scientific Holbein, who coolly recorded what his eyes saw. Therein lies the strength of Dürer's portraiture, but also one of its limitations.

Portraits are documentary evidence on men. It is for this reason that we are entitled, more so than is the case with other branches of art, to approach portraits from the human standpoint; in other words, to speak of those who sat for them and ordered them, commissioned them and received them.

Dürer's Sitters

A catalogue of Dürer's portraits shows us whom he frequented, how wide was the circle of his acquaintances and of what type they were, how Dürer at certain periods of his life was surrounded by interesting people, whereas at other times he lived for years in quiet and solitude. Dürer worked as a portrait-painter in three great cities—Nuremberg, Venice and Antwerp. Each of these was a centre of political, commercial, religious and artistic life. In Nuremberg—which, according to a malicious Venetian saying, was the only town in Germany which could see with one eye, the others being all blind—was to be found the old, indigenous German element with cosmopolitan views. Even today Nuremberg is a mirror of the complicated and many-sided history of Germany, and for centuries it has been the meeting-place of four of the best German racial strains—Franconian, Bavarian, Swabian and Saxon. The air of Flanders and Italy was wafted to the roofs of Nuremberg. Venice was the gateway to the Orient, through which the East streamed into the West, not only in the form of merchandise and men, but also as a current of art. Antwerp was the centre of the trade in silk and the spices of the East Indies. Italian agents, Portuguese factors, Burgundian statesmen, Flemish artists, Jews and Christians, all congregated here to form a motley society, to which Dürer, too, had the entry. He did not become the favourite portrait-painter of one particular class—for example, of the nobility or of the patricians; he found sitters everywhere, of all stations, professions and classes—from mine host to the German Emperor. And we do not find Germans alone among Dürer's portraits—we find Netherlanders, Portuguese, Italians and Englishmen, and even a negro and a negress.

Portraits in Dürer's Religious Pictures

53, 61–63, 66–67, 70–71, 77, 81, 82–83

The Festival of the Rose-garlands

We may find Dürer the portrait-painter also in his great religious works, which are full of portraits, especially the 'Festival of the Rose-garlands' and the 'Adoration of the Trinity'. The peculiarity of these 'bystander portraits' is that they are at the same time representative of classes and professions. They are mundane individuals to whom names can be assigned, depicted in the accomplishment of a supermundane task. In the 'Festival of the Rose-garlands' the whole of humanity, Pope and Emperor at the head, pays homage to the Divine Mother, the 'Rosa Coeli', to her Holy Child, and to the founder of the cult of the rosary, St. Dominic. From the hands of these three, the representatives of devout mankind receive the blessing of the rosary, in the symbolical form of rose-garlands. As a result of his studies of archives and iconography, Gümbel has, I believe, succeeded in identifying some of the participants. The three most distinguished are the Emperor Maximilian, whom the Virgin herself crowns with roses, Pope Julius II, whom the Child Jesus leans forward to crown, and Cardinal Grimani of Venice, who has received his rose-garland from the hand of St. Dominic. On either side of the Princes of the Church and of the Secular Power are figures portrayed from life. In the man in a violet gown and black skull-cap, standing in the centre of the group behind the kneeling Pope, Gümbel recognizes Jakob Fugger 'the Rich', head of the great Fugger family. He was the founder of the great firm of merchant-bankers in Augsburg and of the celebrated settlement known as the 'Fuggerei'; about 1520 Dürer painted him again, with deep furrows in his cold, clever countenance (Munich, Ältere Pinakothek; perhaps a copy of a lost original, a study for which is to be found in the Kupferstichkabinett in Berlin). Another member of the same family, Jakob's brother Ulrich the Elder, is kneeling on the opposite side of the picture, in a light-blue mantle and black cap, behind Maximilian. The woman by his side is believed to be his wife Veronika. The knight with the air of earnest and manly piety is also connected with the Fugger family, being the husband of Ursula, Ulrich's second daughter; his name was Ritter Philipp von Stein zu Jettingen. As leaders of the German colony in Venice, the Fuggers could, according to the custom of the time, lay claim to a prominent place in an altar-piece painted by a German artist for the church of the German colony. Already at that time the family had risen to a position of international importance, for it financed building plans, banking transactions and war loans, owned the most valuable trade monopolies and with its money was beginning to play a more and more important part in secular and religious politics. In 1514 Jakob Fugger advanced to Dürer's patron, Cardinal Albrecht of Brandenburg, the sum of 21,000 ducats, in order that he might become archbishop of Mainz. This was to be repaid by granting to the Fuggers a participation in the traffic in indulgences; an agent of the Fuggers accompanied Tetzel, the dealer in indulgences, and held the key to the indulgence-coffer. Without the vote-catching gold of the Fuggers, Charles V would never have been elected Emperor in preference to Francis I. Since 1505 the Fuggers had established an agency in Antwerp; Dürer frequented the society of the German agents in Antwerp during his journey to the Netherlands, and sketched members of the Stecher and Hamolt families.

One solitary representative of the intellectual world appears in the 'Festival of the Rose-garlands', standing modestly in the background by the side of the artist. He is the Augsburg humanist Konrad Peutinger, one of those gifted Renaissance personalities with universal interests. He had had commercial experience and sent reports on overseas matters from Italy to the Augsburg firms—he was related to the Welser family. Peutinger was a man of keen intellect, who translated the writings of Italian and Portuguese seafarers and, thanks to his extensive reading, was able to supply the Emperor Maximilian with the names of a hundred famous women, after whom Maximilian christened his guns. His knowledge of men and ability to handle them were put to the test when he had to mediate between the fanciful Emperor, the artists who illustrated the 'Weisskunig' and 'Teuerdank', and the printers of these works. Conscious that he had created a work which would worthily represent German workmanship and art on Italian soil, Dürer

61

added his own likeness to this festive gathering and paid a tribute to another
German artist by inserting—also among the laymen—the portrait of the Augsburg
63 architect Hieronymus, who had built the Fondaco dei Tedeschi for the German
colony in Venice. The brush drawing of Hieronymus, with white lights on blue
ground (L. 10, Berlin), is one of those portrait-drawings of Dürer's which are not
merely portraits of individuals, but are expressions of types of men. This Augsburg
architect with the set-square in his hand looks as if he had just been called away
from the drawing-table; his hair is rumpled, his eyes distracted because he is still
thinking of his work, and there is something almost troubled in his look. Never
again did Dürer succeed in giving such a vivid rendering of thoughtful absent-
mindedness and the 'anima candida' of an artistic man.

Adoration of the   In the 'Adoration of the Trinity' there is more justification than there was in the
Trinity   case of the 'Festival of the Rose-garlands' for the introduction of portraits of men
70–71   and women belonging to the great Nuremberg families, for to the uninitiated eye
they are mere representatives of the various social classes—knight and burgher,
peasant and monk, man and wife. Here, too, Gümbel has succeeded in interpreting
the contents of the picture. Both on the left and on the right are members of the
Landauer and Haller families. The donor of the picture, Matthäus Landauer,
approaches the Revelation of the Three in One humbly, hat in hand. The Cardinal,
more familiar with heavenly ceremonial, appears to be encouraging the aged
burgher to 'come nearer and rise to the higher spheres'. Landauer was not, as we
often read, an ordinary copper-founder; he was a 'Schmelzherr', that is to say,
the owner of a smelting works in Thuringia. In 1501, together with Erasmus
Schildkrot, he founded the 'Zwölfmännerhaus' in Nuremberg, an almshouse for
twelve old men, and in 1511 he commissioned Dürer to paint the altar-piece for
the chapel of this so-called 'Landauer monastery'. Behind Landauer we see—
dressed as a monk—his father Markus Landauer, who died in 1468, and on the
opposite side of the picture his knightly son-in-law, Wilhelm Haller. It is probably
correct to assume that the mother, sisters and nieces are among the women
portrayed. Such results of local research into pictures and family histories gratify
something more than mere curiosity and pride of origin. Trivial though the details
may appear, they yet serve to complete our knowledge of the network of human
relationships amidst which Dürer moved and in which he felt at home. For the
head of the old Landauer we have—as we had for the head of the architect
Hieronymus—a preliminary study in chalk (L. 75, Frankfurt am Main), and once
again the term 'study' is a misnomer. Just as, in the case of Hieronymus, the man
of art is portrayed at the moment of the conception of an idea, the old Landauer
becomes the very expression of devoutness. He is all eyes, his eyes 'see the heavens
opening'.

I. D. Ingres once said that every good portrait must have a touch of caricature
about it. What he meant to say was that the spiritually decisive features, which are
the vehicles of expression, must be emphasized and made visible even to the
untrained eye. Dürer's portraits possess this quality in the highest degree, and to
that is due the deep impression which they create. None of Holbein's heads has

achieved the same world-wide fame as Dürer's portrait of Holzschuher. As interpreter and portrayer of men, Dürer used no half-measures. If he has to depict an
energetic character, he overcharges it with energy until the tension becomes almost
unbearable; if the character of his sitter is introverted, he portrays him with a
reserve bordering on impenetrability. When portraying a man holding a prominent position in public life, Dürer endows him with so much dignity that we
forget to ask ourselves whether the grand attitude really denotes a great man. That
explains why we not only see in Dürer's portraits men of widely differing
temperaments, but believe that we are looking at representations of the temperaments themselves. The so-called 'choleric portraits' are not a series of pictures of
angry men, but portraits of men of character, to whose features their temperaments
lend an aspect of severity, tension and aggressiveness which is related to the
external symptoms of anger.

*Dürer as
Interpreter
of Men*

By bringing together the portraits of this kind, we can form a first great group
of Dürer portraits, full of enhanced spirituality, which is not the product of one
period in Dürer's life, but extends from 1499 to 1526, thus including both early
and late works. The two Weimar portraits of Hans and Felicitas Tucher (1499)
already display that atmosphere of tension and forthrightness so typical of Dürer
portraits. In the portrait of Oswolt Krell (Munich) this expression is dramatically
accentuated by the contrast between the angle of the body and the direction of
the glance. We feel that Dürer must have painted his sitter, not in an everyday mood, but at one of those fateful moments when every ounce of spiritual
strength is mobilized, when every nerve is strained, and also when every conventional pretence is dropped. This head of Oswolt Krell (1499), with the glance
of a falcon about to swoop on its prey, is the head of a man who is spiritually
akin to Dürer. Krell, too, belonged to the race of men consumed by an inner
fire. Heinz Braune has established that he was not a member of the well-known
Nuremberg family of that name, but came of Swabian stock, from Lindau
on the Lake of Constance. In Krell's hands lay great economic power and responsibility; he was a factor of the Ravensberger firm, which controlled a considerable
part of the trade between Italy and Western Germany.

18–19

17

Portrait drawings have more of the element of caricature than painted portraits,
in which the colours help to preserve equilibrium, for drawings reduce the sitters
to the simplest and most pregnant formulae of line. Between about 1505 and 1515
Dürer's pencil recorded a whole series of striking portrait aphorisms, e.g. the
fine chalk drawing of an ugly man in a cap (L. 74, London, 1505); the extravagant
head, with hawklike nose, of Konrad Verkell (L. 750, London, 1508)—an extraordinary example of inspired use of the charcoal line, showing a 'character' who
might have come straight out of a Shakespearean comedy. From the quiet and
reverent head of the old Landauer, this line of caricature-like sketches brings us
to the drawing of Dürer's mother, which he made in 1514.

*Portrait
Drawings*

There then comes the group of celebrated paintings, on which the fame of
Dürer as a portraitist has always rested. Firstly, the 1524 portrait in Madrid of an
unknown man, whose identity has been the subject of much conjecture. When it

*13
Painted
Portraits*

47

was still believed that this picture was painted in 1521, the sitter with small dark eyes and 'choleric' glance, holding a scroll in his hand, was identified as H. Imhoff the Elder or as Joos Planckvelt, Dürer's host in Antwerp. Glück, who was the first to establish that the picture was painted in 1524, believes that it portrays the treasurer Lorenz Starck. One of the oldest, and at the same time one of the most recent, identifications (originally advanced by Wustmann and recently revived by Winkler) claims that it is Pirckheimer. Dürer brought Pirckheimer from Flanders a 'great hat', and this fact, together with the scroll as attribute of a learned man and a certain similarity of features, is held to be sufficient ground for identifying this angry-looking man with the choleric Humanist of Nuremberg. I do not find these reasons quite convincing. Among other friends to whom Dürer also brought presents from Flanders were the two councillors Holzschuher and Muffel—to the former he gave a 'very large horn', to the latter 'a scarlet neck-cloth'. Their portraits, painted in 1526, are always mentioned together (they ultimately reached the same museum in Berlin) and the two sitters are generally held to be unsurpassed expressions of the types of men who helped to rule the ancient city of Nuremberg at the time of the Reformation. Nevertheless, typical temperamental contrasts are also discernible. That Dürer deliberately created a contrast is most unlikely, but he certainly achieved the limits of spiritual expression. Holzschuher looks alert, and darts a sharp glance from the corners of his eyes, as if ready to react at once; the hair hanging down in wisps over the wilful forehead is indicative of a 'fiery' temperament. More than any other portrait-painter Dürer relied on the hair to express the man. We have only to think of his head of Hieronymus in the 'Festival of the Rose-garlands', or of his own imposing mane in the Munich self-portrait. Compared with the hot-headed Holzschuher, Jakob Muffel seems frigid, a reserved nature, with sharply defined features, not altogether free from pettiness (e.g. the nose). From these tightly pinched lips we may expect only curt and cool answers. Muffel's father was the already-mentioned collector of relics and trafficker in indulgences, Nikolaus Muffel, whom the Council of Nuremberg caused to be hanged in 1469 for embezzlement of public monies, without regard for the fact that Muffel held the office of second treasurer. If Hieronymus Holzschuher might be given an honourable place as representing the choleric type in a series of the four temperaments, to describe Muffel as a phlegmatic would be an understatement—he was not phlegmatic, he was arrogantly reserved.

Dürer drained the spiritual resources of his sitters in his desire to ennoble their images. In his portrait of Pirckheimer's son-in-law Johann Kleberger (1526, Vienna), he made use of the methods of monumental sculpture in order to heighten the effect, and the secret desire to ape the Antique made him imitate the chisel with his brush, the head with its bare neck being framed in a circular orifice like a bust. Memories of Mantegna and of Northern Italian portrait busts may have been present in his mind.

And now for the man who was nearest to Dürer's heart, another member of the family of choleric men—Pirckheimer. Pirckheimer was what Goethe liked to call a problematic nature—the subject of controversy as a philologist (he translated Theophrastus, Lucian, Plato, Plutarch and Xenophon); as a statesman (he was one of Maximilian's Privy Councillors); as a military commander (he led the Nurembergers against the Swiss), and even as a man and a friend (he slandered Dürer's widow and his friend Lazarus Spengler). His lofty ideas aspired to far greater things than the petty environment of Nuremberg could supply, but his gifts and his depth of character were not on a par with his ambition. Life did not treat this pampered patrician too kindly. Pirckheimer was impressionable, but not willing to make sacrifices; stimulating and easy to stimulate, but without real affection and patience; he was a man of the world, but without charm— and at the end he was a sick man, lonely and embittered. We have three authenticated portraits of Pirckheimer by Dürer's hand—exemplifying the difference between lifelikeness and essentiality. The two drawings of 1503 (L. 142 in Brunswick, L. 376 in Berlin) are intellectual likenesses; they give us the man, with his faults   *27* and virtues, whom Dürer knew so well in his youthful days—the man of wealthy family, proud of his origin, his position and his intellect, and also of his external appearance; the lover of women who found it hard to say goodbye to youth, the elegant man of whose predilection for cosmetics Dürer made fun, writing in one of his letters that he could 'smell' him as far away as Venice. These two drawings, one of which (the Brunswick drawing, lightly written in with silverpoint) bears an obscene Greek inscription, which may have been added by Pirckheimer himself, suppress not a single detail in their adherence to truth, not even the broken nose. But when Dürer made his engraving for wider circulation in 1524,   *26* he extracted from Pirckheimer's head everything pertaining to the higher essence of the man—the vivacious, intelligent eyes, the prominent forehead, the eloquent vitality of the lips—not omitting the characteristic broken nose, but not empha- sizing it. The abundance and expressiveness of the hair are also unnaturally heightened in this engraving; the flabby epicure is endowed with the autocratic head of a lion. In a book of Ludovicus de Prussia, the 'Trilogium Animae', published by Koberger in 1498, Dörnhöffer has found a head which is a diagram of the position of the mental faculties. This 'caput phisicum' undoubtedly re- produces the features of Pirckheimer. The bulges in the brow to the left and right of the root of the nose are given as the locations of 'imaginatio' and 'fantasia'. A portrait of a man which has attracted far less attention (Rome, Galleria Borghese, about 1505) has also been claimed by Schleyer and Benesch as a likeness of Pirckheimer.

It is not true that the gentler aspects of men escaped Dürer's notice. Undoubtedly   *Learned Heads* he was more attracted by the 'active' natures, but he could also give a noble rendering of the contemplative tranquillity of learned heads and understand the still, but nevertheless deep waters of the soul as well as the more effervescent temperaments. It could hardly be otherwise, for Dürer was not only the dramatic artist of the 'Apocalypse', he was also the epic poet of the 'Life of the Virgin'. And as his life progressed, he, too, became calmer. It would be an inadmissible simplification of Dürer's art, if we were to seek the real Dürer only in the portraits

52

of Holzschuher and Oswolt Krell, and not in the late (1527) drawing of Ulrich Starck (L. 296, London) as well, and if we were to forget that there are also portraits of women by Dürer's hand, in addition to all his likenesses of men. And over and above all that, the painter of self-confident patricians was also the portraitist of German princes—which opens the door to the consideration of other groups of Dürer portraits.

Melanchthon

50

When Luther's most intimate confidant, Melanchthon, came to Nuremberg in the course of his duties as Praeceptor Germaniae, to reorganize the Nuremberg schools, Dürer made a sketch of this celebrated reformer, scholar, politician and educationist. This drawing (L. 869, Florence, 1526) served as a model for the copperplate engraving which Dürer made in the same year. If we compare the drawing, a document intended for private use, with the engraving, destined for public view, we find that the divergences not only illustrate the technical means by which an artist can heighten effects, but also bear witness to Dürer's sense of responsibility towards his sitter, for Melanchthon, the leader of German intellectual life, is, in the eyes of the German people, the man we see in Dürer's engraving. Dürer added nothing and suppressed nothing. In the drawing, as well as in the engraving, we see the same man—the scholarly head with its high, wilful forehead and dishevelled hair, the soulful eyes and the mouth of a man who is accustomed to much speaking. But there is not one of these characteristics that is not enhanced and emphasized in the engraving. The metallic technique of steel on copper has endowed the sitter with a kind of steely soul. The eye gleams from its beautifully modelled socket, the forehead curves like a hammered plate of metal. Thus fortified and 'steeled', Dürer's likeness of Melanchthon went on its way through Germany. The art of Dürer gave Melanchthon for all time a quality which he lacked in life—firmness.

Melanchthon, the man of moderation and appeasement, was close to Luther, the man who scorned compromise and half-measures. 'I must,' said Luther, 'root up the stumps and stems, hew away the thorns and hedges, fill in the swamps, and thus be a rough forester—but Philippus (Melanchthon) works cleanly and quietly, he tills and plants, sows and waters, doing all this gladly, for God has given him richly of his gifts.' It was Melanchthon's dream to conclude an alliance between the Reformation and Humanism. He was and remained a philologist—a lover of words—he saw in language, in writing, a rampart against the subjectivism of religion. For him religious politics meant educational politics. He was a real 'professor'—a believer, a searcher and a teacher.

Erasmus of Rotterdam

Melanchthon's spiritual next-of-kin is Erasmus of Rotterdam. He, too, was portrayed by Dürer, and also by Quentin Matsys and Hans Holbein the Younger. The opinion is current that in this portrait Dürer failed, that the head of this witty sceptic and complicated nature was too much for him. This idea is false, though it is certainly true that painter and sitter were disappointed in each other. Erasmus, the scholar of international fame, the leader of the Humanists, ex-monk and Burgundian Counsellor, ecclesiastical politician and ironical philosopher, was drawn twice by Dürer, in Antwerp and in Brussels in 1520. The Antwerp

drawing (L. 361, Paris) has been preserved and is a wonderful charcoal sketch,   37
showing the somewhat squat, frail form of the scholar, who is looking downwards
as if his unseen hand were writing, or as if he were reading an invisible book.
The corners of the narrow-lipped mouth reveal the mockery with which Erasmus
spared neither himself nor others. From the thin face of a man of indoor life juts
the curved nose with the long tip which is found so often in the physiognomies
of reformers, calm philosophers and dogmatic rulers of schools. Such was the
appearance of the 'little old man', of whom Dürer heard—perhaps during the
sittings—that he gave himself only two years in which he would still be capable
of doing something. When Erasmus made this doleful remark, he was fifty-three
years old, and God granted him, not two, but sixteen years more of life. If Dürer
saw and drew Erasmus in such a moment of spiritual frailty, he can hardly have
believed at that time that Erasmus would be the man to assume the heritage of
Luther, which is what Dürer calls upon him to do in that passage in his diary of
the journey to the Netherlands containing his outburst on receiving the false
news of the murder of Luther at Whitsuntide 1521. On that occasion Dürer
exclaims: 'O Erasmus of Rotterdam! Where art thou? Listen, thou Knight of Christ,
ride out with the Lord Christ, defend the truth and earn for thyself the martyr's
crown!' Here Dürer is referring to Erasmus' little book, the 'Knight of Christ', but
Erasmus was hardly the type of man to ride out by the side of the Lord. 'Let others,'   *Character of Erasmus*
he wrote in 1520, 'strive after martyrdom. I am not worthy of such an honour.'
Erasmus was no Luther, no Ignatius of Loyola, no Calvin. Luther, who, after
his final break with Erasmus, pursued this man, who in character and person was
the very opposite of himself, with an implacable hatred, described him as a
cunning and spiteful man, who mocked both God and religion. That former
Spanish knight and fanatical believer, Ignatius of Loyola, was disappointed with
Erasmus' writings, which appeared to him colourless and impotent. Erasmus was
a very refined man who lived in a very robust century, a smiling ironist in a time
of tragic earnestness, who wrote of the Soldier of Christ despite the fact that
everything to do with soldiering was completely foreign to his nature. If the
Devil himself had appeared before him, Erasmus would not have hurled the inkpot
at him, he would have conversed with him wittily and in the most elegant Latin!
  Nevertheless this clever man was vain enough to ask—through their mutual
friend Pirckheimer—to be portrayed by Dürer for the second, or rather for the
third time. This likeness, however, an engraving (1526) by the hand of the   51
greatest European master of the time, was, like the medallion of 1519, to carry
the fame of the great Dutchman to all lands. In 1525 Erasmus wrote to Pirckheimer: 'I would gladly be portrayed by Dürer, for who would not wish to be
portrayed by so great an artist? But how can this be done? In Brussels he began at
one time in charcoal, but I must long since have vanished from his memory.
If he can contrive something from memory and with the aid of the medallion,
then he may do with me what he did with you, whom he made rather too fat.'
Dürer complied with this request. He had not seen Erasmus for six years and he
therefore welcomed Quentin Matsys' medallion, from which he adopted the

Greek inscription: 'His writings will show you a better picture', a typically Erasmian inscription which disarms all criticism of the picture and at the same time advertises the sitter's books. As with the portraits of Pirckheimer and Melanchthon, Dürer was well aware of what he had to do, namely, to combine an imposing appearance with truthfulness to life. The engraving shows us Erasmus writing at a high desk, surrounded by his beloved books. For the counten-

37

ance Dürer doubtless referred to his charcoal drawing of 1520, but the lowered eyes of the sketch now have a meaning, for they are resting on a sheet of paper, probably one of those innumerable letters which the now somewhat aged right hand of Erasmus, creeping out of the broad sleeve, was wont to write. Erasmus was not altogether happy about this portrait. 'Dürer has portrayed me, but it is not at all like me,' he complained, but it may be that this criticism is the best proof of the portrait's lifelikeness. The physiognomist Lavater has maintained that the features of Erasmus reveal 'a refined, thoughtful, clever but timid man'. The presence of lilies-in-the-valley in the vase may be due to the fact that Erasmus, continually pursued by the fear of death, was particularly fond of these flowers, which in Germany have at all times been regarded as having the virtue of warding off death.

Eobanus Hesse
48

The third scholar to be portrayed by Dürer was Eobanus Hesse, author of the panegyric of Nuremberg: 'Norimberga illustrata', known to an age accustomed to superlatives as the 'Christian Ovid'. He was an assiduous poet and toper, the glory of Erfurt University, a 'character' whom Friedrich Paulsen has compared to Mr. Micawber. Dürer made a drawing of Eobanus Hesse in 1526 (L. 25, London). He carried a fine, intellectualized peasant's head on his shoulders and, like Celtis and other Humanists, came from a country district. This portrait, with the hands and the usual scroll added below, was coarsened by its translation in 1527 into the language of woodcuts, but it was not Dürer's hand which was to blame for this.

It has been maintained by some that Dürer, that most fervent admirer of intellect among German painters, was incapable of portraying men of intellect, and similarly, it has been said that he could not paint women. It is true that

Portraits of
Women

portraits of women constitute a minority in the whole complex of his work and that they are not represented at all in his prints, this because women at that time rarely became public figures, but in the sphere of private portraiture, e.g. his own relatives (wife and mother), wives of his patrons, and sometimes members of households which he frequented, we find a number of paintings and drawings by Dürer of stately and sometimes attractive women. Dürer was not without an eye and an understanding for female beauty. He was well aware of the seductive charms of the female body—we have only to think of the beautiful unknown who appears to the dreaming 'doctor', of the charming, bashful young lady who

106, 112

is crowned by the angels (engraving of 1518), of the Eve in the Prado (1507), whom others besides Adam must have found hard to resist, of the distinguished and cheerful Virgin in the Vienna drawing of 1512 (L. 525), and of many others.

In considering Dürer's male portraits, we left on one side the portraits of himself and his relatives, and we will therefore pass over those of his wife and

OSWALT KRELL. 1499. Munich, Aeltere Pinakothek

mother. To Dürer's immediate circle of acquaintances in Nuremberg also belongs
the young girl with the pigtail (L. 46, Berlin), whom he sketched in 1515. She is   *33*
a typical German 'Backfisch', a good girl, rather stupid, with the sleepy eyes of
adolescence, and the psychological significance of the drawing is on a par with
its artistic merit. As a portrait it is better than the paintings of the model, who
appears as St. Mary Magdalen in Frankfurt am Main. The ladies of Nuremberg
were by no means of delicate build, all of them having what are commonly
known as 'figures'. Dürer painted a magnificent female character head in water-
colour on canvas (Paris, Bibliothèque Nationale, about 1497?), which, however,   *25*
can hardly be that of Frau Agnes! The ladies of the Nuremberg patrician families
had rather hard features, with slightly protruding eyes which seem to look with
astonishment at life, e.g. Felicitas Tucher (Weimar) and Elsbeth Tucher (Kassel).   *19, 20*

One can imagine the pleasure with which Dürer painted the ladies of the
German colony in Venice, among whom were some particularly attractive and
radiant visages. On blue paper he drew with the brush a proud girl's head, with
broad, free planes, clear eyes and budding mouth (L. 501, Vienna), the same girl
whom he used in 1507 for the Eve in Madrid. How can we deny to Dürer a   *112*
feeling for female beauty when we see the two painted portraits in Berlin and
Vienna, both dating from the time of his second visit to Venice (1506-07)? We
know little of the identity either of the refined, cheerful girl of good family in
the Vienna portrait or of the mature, mild-looking lady in the Berlin portrait.   *21, 29*
The embroidery of the bodice in the Berlin portrait contains the letters 'A' and
'D', which led Bode to identify the subject as Agnes Dürer, but Gümbel is probably
right when he suggests that the woman is Anna Fugger, wife of Georg Thurzo,
also known as Jörg Dorssi or Jörg Dürze, in which case the letters would stand
for Anna Dorssin. The atmosphere of spiritual detachment and the construction
have been influenced to a certain extent by Giorgione's style of portraiture. The
curious portrait of a girl (1507, Berlin)—with its head half that of a girl, half
that of a boy—cannot be compared with these two portraits of German women
from Venice.

The diary of the journey to the Netherlands mentions quite a number of
female 'counterfeits'. Dürer often showed his gratitude for hospitality received
by sketching the wives and daughters, or even the maids, of his hosts. In this way
he drew the young girl (Gerardo Bombelli's betrothed) (L. 852, Frankfurt), a
woman of the household of Jan de Haas (L. 342, Chantilly) and even the factor
Brandan's negress Katharina (L. 851, Florence).   *41*

To close the series of female portraits—many may have been lost—we have
two princesses, both drawn in chalk in 1525. One of them, young, elegant,
wearing a big fashionable hat and carrying a little dog, may be Susanne, Margravine of Brandenburg-Anspach (L. 172, New York, Sachs), the other, a burly
woman of bourgeois aspect, is the Margravine Margarete, sister of Margrave
Kasimir of Brandenburg-Anspach (L. 868, London).

Court circles and the coterie of German and foreign merchants living in   *The Court and*
Flanders provided Dürer with an abundance of interesting subjects, among them   *the Merchant*
                                                                                  World

I

men who have made history. On his way from Germany Dürer stopped in
Aachen, where he made a drawing of the Imperial Herald, Caspar Sturm (L.
340, Chantilly)—the landscape background, showing Tiel on the Waal, was
added later. Sturm, who has a brutal face and one eye quite different from the
other, was the equivalent of a modern journalist, for as Imperial Herald he
distributed items of political news. In 1521 he was ordered to escort Luther to
the Diet of Worms and he is also said to have been the herald of the league of
princes who in 1523 brought to Franz von Sickingen the summons to surrender
his castle of Landstuhl. During his journey Dürer also portrayed, in half-length
and kneeling behind his coat of arms, another warrior of many talents, the one-
eyed Captain Felix Hungersberg, who was a lover of several of the arts, played
the lute 'exquisitely', bought prints from Dürer and allowed the latter to present
him with others, and sent a hundred oysters to the lodging of the Dürer couple
in return.

In addition to over a hundred portrait drawings in every kind of technique and
in varying stages of artistic completion, Dürer made in 1520 and 1521, according
to his own statements, five portraits in oils. The portrait of King Christian of
Denmark, the most eminent of his sitters in Flanders, has unfortunately been
lost, as has also the portrait of the wife of his host in Antwerp, Plankvelt. If Glück
is right in his assertion that the celebrated portrait of a man in Madrid was not
painted in 1521, but in 1524, this would invalidate the identification of the sitter
as Plankvelt and relegate it for the time being to the category of anonymous
portraits. In that case our knowledge of the features of Jobst Plankvelt would be
limited to the pen-sketch which Dürer made in 1520 (L. 196, Frankfurt am Main),
showing a 'tête carrée' with broad nose, prominent under-lip and a short neck.
I cannot accept Flechsig's claim that all the essential physiognomical characteristics
of this drawing coincide with those of the Madrid painting, for there is a fundamental difference in the type of glance. Chronologically earlier than the anonymous
Madrid painting, but also made in 1521, is the Dresden portrait, generally assumed
to represent Bernhard van Orley. The Christian name of the sitter was certainly
Bernhard, as it is possible to read on the piece of paper in his hand: 'dem Bernh . . .
zw . . .' but that is no proof that he was Bernhard van Orley. This theory was
first propounded by Ephrussi, but, except for a certain resemblance, there is
little support for it beyond the desire to think that this young man might be the
artist van Orley, whom Dürer knew. Flechsig, with the exactitude of a philologist
and his relentless pursuit of facts, suggests that the Dresden portrait should be
definitely considered as the 'counterfeit' mentioned by Dürer of Bernhard von
Resten, for which the sitter paid the painter eight guilders, at the same time
giving the maid Susanna a tip of one guilder and presenting 'one Cronen' to the
painter's wife. As to the third portrait in oils, in May 1521 Dürer notes in his
diary: 'I have "counterfeited" Treasurer Lorenz Sterck truly and diligently in oil
colours.' This is probably the man portrayed in the picture now in the Isabella
Stewart Gardner Museum in Boston. That he is a Netherlander is proved by the
turned-up front brim of the hat, which is found in many portrait-sketches made

by Dürer during his sojourn in Flanders. This earnest and noble man was the treasurer of the imperial domains, that is to say, he administered the revenues from Brabant and Antwerp. He came from the neighbourhood of Liége.

In addition to these paintings, we have a whole collection of portrait-drawings, of which only a part can be identified. They portray members of the Bombelli family, Portuguese factors, Southern German bankers and Flemish artists. The most prominent of these, and the closest to Dürer, was the secretary of the Portuguese agency, Rodrigo d'Almeda. Dürer reciprocated his many services and his unbounded hospitality by portraying him a number of times, and he finally presented him with his painting of St. Jerome (now in Lisbon). We can *76* form an idea of the appearance of the influential secretary of the Portuguese agencies, who on behalf of their king administered the pepper monopoly and dominated the European market in spices, from a brush drawing on greyish violet paper (L. 66, Berlin). It has not been possible to establish with certainty whether the drawing L. 53 (Berlin) represents the same person. Among the portraits of Germans, that of Hans Pfaffrod of Danzig (L. 178, Paris) is notable for the fine poise and treatment of the head.

Portraits of artists form a little group to themselves in the framework of *Portraits of* Dürer's portraiture. There are very few of them, if we consider how many fellow-*Artists* artists Dürer must have met in the course of his life. The only Nuremberg artist among them is Dürer's teacher Wolgemut, whom he painted in 1516 during his lifetime, adding the inscription after Wolgemut's death in 1519, which shows that the portrait was intended for Dürer's own house. Wolgemut does not look *34* his age (82) in this picture. He had been a second father to Dürer, who painted him with the same reverence and affectionate attention to detail with which he had painted his father in his youthful days. Wolgemut is the only representative of the Nuremberg artistic world and we seek in vain for portraits of Veit Stoss or Adam Krafft by Dürer's hand. Who can tell how many portraits may have been lost in artists' workshops! A self-portrait of Dürer which was once in Raphael's atelier must also be counted among the vanished masterpieces. At the meeting of the Diet in Augsburg in 1518, Dürer portrayed another well-known German artist—Hans Burgkmair—but this chalk sketch (L. 396, Oxford) is disappointing. The 'self-portrait' of Burgkmair, very similar to Dürer's sketch, in Vienna, has been proved to be an overpainting of a picture by Hufnagel in Burgkmair's style.

Rieffel put forward the bold suggestion that we possess a portrait of Grünewald by Dürer—the head of a young man (1500, Munich, Ältere Pinakothek) which is generally supposed to represent one of the three brothers of Dürer who were *22* christened Hans. It is undoubtedly a typically German face, modelled with unusual angularity—one of Dürer's real 'wood-carving' figures—but whether it is a portrait of Grünewald must remain a matter of doubt. We have no portrait-sketches by Dürer of Venetian painters, such as Giovanni Bellini, whom Dürer always held to be the greatest. Hieronymus, the architect whose portrait Dürer *63* introduced into the Festival of the Rose-garlands, was a native of Augsburg. Of

ULRICH VARNBÜLER (1522)

HIERONYMUS HOLZSCHUHER. 1526. Berlin, Deutsches Museum

the Flemish artists who feasted Dürer, and also imitated him—even before he visited them—only one is to be found among Dürer's portraits, if we are to reject the theory that the Dresden portrait represents Bernhard van Orley. Two drawings are generally supposed to represent Lucas van Leyden (L. 847 in Lille and L. 403 in London). The inscription 'Effigies Lucae Leidensis' and the 'L. 1525' on the London drawing were added in the eighteenth century. This 'little man', as Dürer calls him, looks less mournful in the Lille drawing (L. 847). A comparison with Lucas van Leyden's well-known self-portrait in Brunswick excludes all doubt as to the identification. Among the many anonymous portraits of young men which Dürer painted or drew, there may be several artists, e.g. the youth in the charcoal drawing of 1503 in Vienna (L. 426), who, according to the inscription, was eighteen years old at the time, and who Ephrussi has suggested might be Paumgärtner. Attempts have also been made to identify as Paumgärtner the young man, pleasant and well-groomed (L. 833, Dresden), who glances so warily at the spectator.

Dürer, as we have seen, was no stranger to the world of beautiful women, and among his sitters we also find male members of the aristocracy. In October 1523 he made a drawing of the English Ambassador Extraordinary, Henry Parker Lord Morley (L. 87, London), when he arrived in Nuremberg to deliver to the Archduke Ferdinand the insignia of the Order of St. George. The countenance of the English nobleman bears that expression of disinterestedness or momentary distraction which is not merely an individual or national characteristic, but part of the professional mask of the diplomat. The rigidity of the sitter's character is brought out in a characteristically English manner by the contrast with the calm poise and the nonchalant way in which the hand is tucked into the robe. Compared with the English diplomat, the high German official Ulrich Varnbüler looks sincere and warm-hearted (L. 578, Vienna, and woodcut of 1522 after this drawing). Varnbüler, a friend of Dürer's, was an Imperial Councillor and Proto-notary of the Supreme Court. The 1522 portrait illustrates once again what 'greatness' meant to Dürer in the closing years of his life and work. Accuracy in the sense of truthfulness to life was a fundamental principle in Dürer's portraiture at all stages of his career, but what he learned from life was how to express not only a man's outward appearance but also his inner being. This does not imply 'idealization' of the sitter, if by idealization we mean falsifying, beautifying, bloodlessness. The real meaning of idealization is the ability to read the intentions of Nature, whereby a portrait-painter follows the design of Nature up to a certain point, but also endows the sitter with that higher degree of lifelikeness which will remain throughout the centuries. In this sense Menzel's Frederick the Great is lifelike—so lifelike that the popular conception of Frederick's appearance is based on this portrait. Viewed from the same standpoint, Dürer's portrait of the Emperor Maximilian is also unimpeachably lifelike.

Dürer had none of the characteristics which usually go to make a court painter. The critical nature of his portraiture, which drew on his own experience and even transformed according to his own ideas, remained unchanged even when

30, 31

Nobles and Princes

Ill. p. 124

he was portraying the great ones of this world. Dürer's portraits of secular and spiritual princes combine the official with the private aspect, the personal with the Dürer element, thus forming a mixture which belongs to him alone and makes his portraits appear 'subjective' historical pictures in comparison with Holbein's 'objective' representations. It was through the Diets of Nuremberg and Augsburg that Dürer came into contact with the great, three of whom were particularly close to his heart—Frederick the Wise, Albrecht of Brandenburg and the Emperor Maximilian.

*Frederick
the Wise*
While Dürer was still fresh from the impressions of his first journey to Italy and the works of Mantegna he had seen there, he painted the first of his princely patrons, Frederick the Wise. Despite its restraint, there is something rather gloomy about this Berlin portrait, painted in April 1496. The face of the Elector has a mournful stare. As years went on, however, his head grew broader and acquired that expression of intelligent kindness which earned him the nickname of 'the Wise'. It is true that he founded the university of Wittenberg, but he was not 'wise' in the sense of 'learned'; in fact, 'irksome' books were not in his line, and he took more interest in arms, tournaments, horses and saddlery. But Frederick was wise in the way he used his common sense and his moderation for political purposes. Because, as their ruler, he felt himself responsible for his subjects, and because he knew the world, he obtained for the greatest of them, Martin Luther, an imperial safe-conduct when he went to Augsburg and gave him a safe refuge on the Wartburg. It was to the painters that the men of the time turned when they wanted to know something of the Elector's appearance, and it was Dürer who gave them the finest answer. Frederick of Saxony was a friend of artists, the patron of Lucas Cranach, Dürer, Burgkmair, Peter Vischer, Wolf Traut, Wolgemut, Conrad Meit etc. Like all princes of the Renaissance period he saw in art above all a 'useful' element, which was an embellishment of life and preserved the memory of men after death. But he was also—in this, a true son of his time—a collector of works of art and relics. Dürer put all his 'diligence' into his portrayal of the revered Elector, first in a silverpoint study for the engraving (L. 387, Paris, drawn in winter 1523-24) and then in the engraving itself, which is dated 1524, and was successful in reproducing the full strength of the commanding eyes, despite the intricacies of the fur mantle and the voluminous beard.

44
45

*Albrecht of
Brandenburg*
Albrecht of Brandenburg, Archbishop of Mainz, played an even more brilliant rôle as a German Maecenas than Frederick the Wise. He protected and encouraged Dürer, Cranach, Hans Baldung, Bachofen and Grünewald. He must not, however, be considered in the light of a modern connoisseur of art, guided purely by aesthetic principles. In his desire for fame, Albrecht rivalled the great Italian patrons of art. He knew that architecture provides the most conspicuous and lasting monuments to a man and to his time, and Halle became his favourite place of residence. He vied with the Elector of Saxony in collecting relics and calculated that his stock of these would ensure him indulgence for about one hundred thousand years. Dürer made a charcoal drawing of the Cardinal in 1518

43
(L. 547, Vienna) and two engravings of him on copper; the prints of these are

known respectively as 'The Little Cardinal' (1519) and 'The Great Cardinal' (1523), and the sitter purchased and himself distributed hundreds of copies of each. In the first of the two engravings Dürer gave a faithful reproduction—from his drawing—of the Cardinal's sensual and rather bloated face, but Albrecht does not appear to have raised any objection. Four years later, however, Dürer made many corrections, converting the face into a pure, medallion-like profile, thereby depriving it of some of its width and at the same time accentuating the really important features and suppressing the unimportant. Patrons expected medallions to reproduce with metallic sharpness the imperious expression of their princely countenances, and Dürer succeeded in doing this with both Frederick the Wise and the Cardinal, thanks to the manifold resources of his technique of portraiture.

42

When Dürer sketched the Emperor Maximilian on 28th June 1518 (L. 546, Vienna) at Augsburg, 'high up in his little room in the castle', he was not creating his first portrait of Maximilian, but his first portrait of the Emperor from life. For the Maximilian in the 'Festival of the Rose-garlands' he had used a drawing by another artist, probably Ambrogio de Predis (L. 17, Berlin). Now he had the opportunity of gazing into the haughty eyes of the Emperor and of making with quick strokes of the crayon, in the short time allowed for such a sitting, an image of this highly complicated character. Both as a human being and as an imperial politician, Maximilian was a man of extreme contrasts. His arrogance was unbounded, he was proud of his ancestry and ambitious for fame, but he was also subject to fits of depression during which he would complain that since the days of Jesus Christ no man had suffered as he had suffered, for he felt himself to be crucified and abandoned by all. In politics Maximilian wavered between a realistic domestic policy of the Austrian Habsburg type and the wildest fancies of the mediaeval emperors. When Pope Julius II, who appears in the 'Festival of the Rose-garlands' kneeling opposite Maximilian, fell ill, Maximilian conceived the idea of uniting the two offices—Emperor and Pope, the spiritual and the secular sword—in his own person. But the same man could associate with men in all ranks of life in the most amiable way and could be charming if he so desired. Maximilian always felt himself to be heir to the German rulers of the Holy Roman Empire and never forgot that to the great traditions belongs also the consciousness of that which Germany and the German people demand of their rulers. Charlemagne, that great Franconian, caused the old heroic poems of the Southern Germans to be collected and preserved, without which there would never have been any mediaeval poetry of chivalry. The most popular of the Habsburgs, Maximilian, by preserving the 'Ambraser Heldenbuch', saved the Middle High German epic; the 'Gudrunlied', for example, is found only in this manuscript. All these contradictory characteristics of Maximilian combined to endow him with an etherealized majesty, and Dürer, with a true instinct for the essentials, succeeded in reproducing this spirit of noblest chivalry. The woodcut of 1519 deprives the Emperor's head of some of its delicacy, but in return gives it terseness and weight and the decorative beauty of woodcut technique. Dürer used the Augsburg drawing on two subsequent occasions, for both the portraits

Emperor Maximilian

Ill. p. 128

Imperator Caelar Diuus Maximilianus
Pius Felix Augustus

THE EMPEROR MAXIMILIAN I (1519)

of the Emperor which he painted in 1519 (Nuremberg and Vienna) are derived   35
from it. Maximilian, by this time dead, is holding, not the imperial orb, but an
opened pomegranate, as a symbol of resurrection. Dürer took one of these two
portraits with him to Flanders, where he presented it to the Emperor's daughter,
the Regent Margaret of Savoy, in gratitude for her assistance in his endeavours
to obtain ratification of the pension granted to him by Maximilian from Margaret's
nephew, the new Emperor Charles V—and also in the hope that she would
reciprocate this gift by giving him the sketch-book of Jacopo de' Barbari which
he coveted. Dürer did not get the Italian drawings and his portrait of the Emperor
did not please Margaret, 'but', he writes in his diary, 'as she had such dislike for
it, I took it away again'. He did not bring this posthumous portrait of Maximilian
back to Germany, but persuaded the son-in-law of the Regent's paymaster,
Tommaso Bombelli, to accept it in exchange for a length of white English cloth.

Pictures, and portraits in particular, are the daily fare of modern times. In
the Middle Ages they spoke even to those who could not read, and nowadays
they have made it almost unnecessary for us to read. A consequence of this surfeit
of pictorial matter is that we no longer look at pictures in the same way. We have
learned how to look at snapshots, but we are liable to overlook portraits, which
contain more than a momentary impression, which give us the character of the
person portrayed. The men and women of Dürer's time sought eagerly for the
prints of his woodcuts and engravings, in which men not only looked as they
were, but expressed what they thought—and that was done with a penetration
which was due to the will and the spiritual strength of the man who created these
likenesses.

Dürer and the men and women he painted belonged to a generation which
transformed the aspect of Europe in more ways than one. At critical moments
in the life of a nation, forces which normally dwell apart, or even seem to exclude
one another, become the essential characteristics of one and the same personality.
Dürer, too, had more than one personality—the meticulous diligence of the
artisan and the 'winged spirit' of the gifted artist. The cool brains of investigators
and discoverers and the hot hearts of seekers and visionaries were fused in the
leading men of Dürer's time into an alloy which is peculiarly German. Time after
time, when in the course of our history this mixture of accuracy and temerity has
moved the spirits of great men, for example Bach, it has always appeared to
non-Germans as something uncanny, and in its essence incomprehensible.

CHAPTER EIGHT

LANDSCAPE

THE easiest approach to Dürer is through the gateway of his landscapes. No thorny problems of technique obstruct the path, no impenetrable obscurities of meaning lie between us and the beauty of the view; everything is clear and familiar—the village in the valley, the castle on the hill, the gliding river and the smooth mirror of the weir. We experience the joys of travel and accept with gratitude from Dürer's hand the water-colours and sketches, so full of the landscape beauties of his own country and of foreign lands. Dürer's landscapes are so vivid and real, that we are tempted to consider them as the really modern element in his art, the break with the past and the presage of the future. And we are both right and wrong in doing so.

Art without Epoch

We are right in one respect, for among Dürer's landscapes we find those celebrated water-colours which are really timeless, which had no precedent in his own work or in the art of his time and—more significant still—no sequel either in his own work or in the art of the sixteenth century. These are the admirable pictures which invite comparison with modern landscape-painters such as Cézanne, Dérain and Thoma, and are responsible for such erroneous statements as that Dürer was one of the discoverers of impressionistic landscape. Dürer himself would have countered such an assertion by saying that it was never his intention to place his landscape studies on a level, e.g. with his woodcuts of the Life of the Virgin or his mythological engravings, and that for him and for all his European contemporaries there was no such thing as a separate branch of art called landscape. These water-colours are just one group, which happens to be the most pleasing to our eyes, among the many landscapes which he painted and drew, for we must not forget the landscape backgrounds to his engravings, woodcuts and paintings, or the sketches which he made with silverpoint and pen.

Groups of Landscapes

If we were to assemble Dürer's landscapes and place them side by side, it would be possible to form a number of groups. We could classify them according to the nature of their origin or the purpose for which they were intended; we could group them chronologically or even geographically. Many of them originated as studies of nature, like drawings from the nude, studies of costumes and animals, portrait heads and hands, and in such cases it is easy to see that they had a definite purpose, that they formed part of his stock-in-trade, upon which he drew when he needed a landscape background. We shall find numbers of his woodcuts and engravings for which he used landscape studies that have been preserved to this day. But some of his landscapes—among them most of his water-colours—are independent works of art and were created as such; they are carefully finished, the drawing or painting is executed down to the last detail, and if they were given frames, they could be taken out of their portfolios and hung on the wall. When he painted his water-colours, Dürer may have been thinking of the possibility of sale or exchange, or of using them as gifts, though there is no authenticated case of this. It is, however, certain that Dürer himself would never have thought of framing any of these charming examples of colour. These 'independent' landscapes were painted during excursions in the environs of Nuremberg, during halts on his travels, while the horses were being changed or resting, or when he had reached the end of his day's journey. They were, in fact, Dürer's lyric poems, but, like all poetry, they include pure products of imagination, landscapes which no historian of art will ever be able to identify, which no camera will ever be able to photograph, simply because they came out of Dürer's head. We can therefore subdivide them into real and imaginary landscapes, and in each of these categories we shall find some which are 'independent' and some which are not.

So far the process of creation has been easy to follow, but now we come upon difficulties. Some of Dürer's landscapes were actually seen by him and can even be identified, others were invented; some reveal photographic objectivity and fidelity to topographical details, others are fantasies on landscape themes of great dæmonic and visionary power. But there are also—and herein lies the difficulty— *Hybrid Forms* landscapes by Dürer which are derived partly from nature and partly from his own fantasy—hybrids of truth and invention. The popular notion that an artist always starts from a single artistic idea and that the conception of a picture is one uniform process, is certainly not applicable to Dürer's methods. Dürer handled his materials very freely. If the fancy took him or if it were convenient, he would take two sketches and turn them into one; he would absorb a real landscape into one which he had never seen, or conversely he would introduce into an imaginary landscape details which he had sketched from Nature. In this, too, Dürer shows that he stood at the crossways between two styles. From the Middle Ages he inherited the conception of landscape as a useful element of the artist's stock-in-trade, but he was a child of the Renaissance in his free feeling for Nature and the world. Dürer, too, was one of those explorers and inventors who left their mark upon the age in which they lived. But he did not need to cross the ocean in order to discover a New World; he had merely to leave the gates of Nuremberg behind him.

In the eyes of his patrons and clients Dürer, in combining landscape motives of different origin—a realist as regards detail, an idealist as regards the whole— was a man of his own time, but behind the scenes, working alone in his atelier, he was far ahead of his age. His appreciation of the artistic value of every single thing, big or small, his recognition of every individual phenomenon, from a blade of grass to a thunderstorm—all that is modern. The graduation of the landscape ground and the piecing together of details actually seen are Late Gothic— the system adopted by Pacher and Witz. The distribution in breadth and the unfolding of the whole landscape background are derived from the Venetian school. We find both of these in Dürer, side by side or one after the other; the Gothic Germanic current and Italian Neo-classicism met in all Dürer's work, and in his landscapes, too. That the art of landscape, after a brief blossoming, withered even in Dürer himself, and that a hundred years were to elapse before a Rembrandt fulfilled what Dürer had promised, that too, is a consequence of this mingling of German and Italian currents.

When he cast Dürer's horoscope in 1507, Lorenz Beheim maintained that his desire to travel was foretold by the stars. Dürer was, indeed, a great traveller, if we take into consideration the difficulties of a financial, technical and hygienic nature with which travellers at the time of the Reformation had to contend. Despite all the obstacles, Dürer's contemporaries felt the urge to travel, and many of them, especially the patricians of Nuremberg and Augsburg, had travelled extensively. As merchants, law students, diplomats or pilgrims they went to Rome and Santiago de Compostela, and, if possible, to Jerusalem. For the great Hamburg and Bremen families overseas voyages were a tradition, and similarly, among the wealthy families of Nuremberg it became the fashion to make a pilgrimage to the Holy Sepulchre and to be dubbed knight in Jerusalem. Nevertheless, the motive for Dürer's frequent journeys was not educational, nor had it anything to do with his interests as an artist—it was, in fact, a much more mundane motive, namely, fear of the plague. The devastating epidemics which swept over Germany coincide fairly accurately with Dürer's journeys. He followed the example of many of his most esteemed fellow-townsmen, e.g. Pirckheimer and Sebald Schreyer, the warden of St. Sebaldus, and fled 'the horror and the fear', combining all kinds of professional business with the interests of his health.

Journeys Abroad Apart from his excursions in the neighbourhood of Nuremberg and his trips to Franconian and Swabian cities, Dürer made quite a number of longer journeys. At the beginning of his artistic career he spent four years wandering in Southern Germany, Switzerland and Alsace (1490–94). Then came his first journey to Venice via Tyrol (1494–95). Ten years later (1505–07) Dürer crossed the Alps again, visiting not only Venice, but also Bologna, the southernmost point he reached. That he went to Florence has never been established, despite the fact that Hermann Beenken has shown that he had contacts with Florentine artists, e.g. Masaccio, Fra Bartolomeo, etc. Dürer's desire to accompany the Emperor Maximilian to Rome in 1506 was not fulfilled. Oskar Hagen's attempt to conclude, from certain parallels in the development of motives, that Dürer had been in Rome, is not convincing. Nor did anything come of Dürer's plans, mentioned by Beheim, for journeys to England and Spain. In 1519 he visited Switzerland; in 1520 and 1521 he was in Flanders and in 1521–22 he made the last of his journeys, to Livonia, Riga being the northernmost point he reached. We possess landscape drawings from the neighbourhood of the Lake of Constance, and the backgrounds of some of his woodcuts and engravings appear to be derived from the same area. He painted water-colours of Alpine landscapes on both sides of the Brenner road, in the Adige valley. But Franconia was the great treasure-house from which Dürer, in the intervals between his journeys, drew his subjects for landscape drawings and paintings. From the deck of the vessels which carried him up and down the Rhine and from the windows of inns he also sketched the Lower German and Dutch towns and countryside.

It is generally supposed that Dürer visited Hungary, but proof of this is lacking.

Meaning of his journeys for Dürer For Dürer these journeys meant a broadening of his ideas and an opportunity of feasting his eyes on the achievements of foreign artists and at the same time of

LANDSCAPE. Detail from Plate 69. Vienna, Kunsthistorisches Museum

forming a comparative estimate of his own ability. He thoroughly enjoyed every moment—the accumulation of new impressions, the confirmation of his own position as an artist, the freedom from the restrictions of life at home and lastly the joy of returning. Dürer exploited his journeys far more intensively than would an artist of our own days. His pencil rarely left his fingers and he was always anxious to draw with his own hand everything there was to see, whether it were a lobster or a walrus, a mountain landscape or a Livonian woman's costume, a helmet or a lady's shoe, for one could never know whether it might not be possible to use all these things again.

This harvest of sketches Dürer stored in his granary; later, in the course of his work, he separated the wheat from the chaff. We are astonished—and sometimes even heave a sigh—at the number of sketches by Dürer which have been preserved, but what of all those which have been lost! It is certain that the 'corpus' of land- *Lost Sketches* scapes must at one time have been far greater. We know, for example, of lost sketches of Chiusa on the Isarco and of the town of Middelburg, which pleased Dürer so much, and we cannot refrain from hoping that one day these will come to light in some private collection. We must remember all these lost landscapes, when we think that we have discovered gaps, when we miss certain subjects and come across numerous examples of kindred themes. Much that the modern mind expects to find in the work of Dürer the landscape-painter, is missing altogether, e.g. the 'picturesque' aspect of old Nuremberg, with its crooked streets, balconies and gables, its courtyards and façades.

Dürer did, however, give us one old German town, dominated by its mighty castle, just as we expect and want a mediaeval town to be. This is the mountain town before whose walls St. Anthony, absorbed in his breviary, is resting during his pilgrimage, in the engraving of 1519. It is typical of the Romantics that this was their favourite print. Schnorr von Carolsfeld's drawing of Olevano (Dresden, Kupferstichkabinett) shows how close to Dürer, and yet how far removed from him, the 'Nazarenes' were.

In Wolgemut's atelier there was no 'landscape class', but his pupils learned *Preocular* the traditional lay-out for landscape backgrounds and foregrounds in figure *Representation of Landscape* pictures. In those days a winding street with gabled houses meant 'town'. In Dürer's earliest woodcut, the St. Jerome of 1492, we catch a glimpse of such a street through a Gothic window. For Wolgemut's atelier, 'country' signified drawing a few hills with globular trees, a clump of trees by the waterside in the foreground or a few half-timbered buildings in the middle plane. Conventional landscapes of this kind are to be found, for instance, in the illustrations to the 'Schatzbehalter oder Schrein der wahren Reichtümer des Heils und ewiger Seligkeit' (Treasury or Shrine of the true riches of Salvation and Eternal Bliss), published in Nuremberg by Koberger in 1491. They do not pretend to reproduce the form of Nature, but are formulae for representing Nature—'these are trees, those are rocks etc'. The mediaeval mind was content with such landscape-drawings, which in actual fact were merely symbols of landscape. No one in those days wanted to see a certain landscape or to recognize in the picture a spot he

LANDSCAPE. DETAIL FROM 'ST. JOHN RECEIVES THE SUMMONS TO HEAVEN'

knew; the conception of art was based on ideas and it was quite sufficient if the symbols of these ideas could be recognized.

Dürer was born to this preocular conception of landscape and had to educate himself out of it—which was what he achieved during his wander-years. It is true that we possess no definite proofs of this, i.e. signed and dated landscape sketches by Dürer from the years 1490–1494. But we can most certainly recognize in his early landscape backgrounds, in particular in the prints of his 'Apocalypse', echoes and after-effects of attempts to see and draw landscapes in his own way. We know pretty well where Dürer lived during these years, which were so decisive for his development as a man and as an artist—in Colmar, Basle and Strasbourg, in other words in the towns in which the great printers and publishers lived. We are not so sure as to how he earned his living, but presumably he did casual work as a draughtsman. During these apprentice days Dürer saw beautiful tracts of country in Southern and Western Germany, in Switzerland and in Alsace. Josef Meder conceived the clever idea of reconstructing Dürer's wanderings with the aid of a contemporary map, which was published in 1501 by the Nuremberg firm of Glockendon under the title: 'The high roads of the Roman Empire from one kingdom to another abutting on Germany, marked with points from mile to mile'. If we assume, which is very probable, that Dürer used the main roads shown on this map, then he would have travelled from Nuremberg to Nördlingen, Ulm, Ravensburg, across the Lake of Constance to Meersburg, Constance, Schaffhausen, Basle, Colmar and Strasbourg, and back to Nuremberg via Stuttgart and Nördlingen. In other words he would have traversed the country of the German castles and have seen Germany's greatest rivers, the Rhine and the Danube, and looking across the Lake of Constance, the great barrier of the Alps.

If we then look through the young Dürer's woodcuts, engravings and sketches, we really seem to recognize the banks of the Rhine and of the Lake of Constance. In the scene from the 'Apocalypse' showing St. John receiving the Summons to Heaven', we find a lakeside castle; the battle between St. Michael and the Dragon takes place high up in the skies, above a broad landscape with villages nestling in woods on the shore of a lake, and a mountain massif, in shape rather like the Santis, on the far shore. Similar lakeside landscapes are found in the prints of the 'Life of the Virgin', e.g. in 'Joachim and the Angel', and we find them again in the woodcuts of 'Ercules' and the 'Knight with Man-at-arms'. But the most beautiful of all these mountain, lake and castle landscapes is that of the 'Sea-monster' (1501). It must not be overlooked that Dürer's method tended to obscure the borderline between what he had actually seen and what he invented, and that he adapted his landscape grounds to the figure subject, just as the musician adapts the accompaniment to a song. His great sheets of water—whether we call them the Lake of Constance or not—his fantastic towns on the hilltops and his ranges of mountains, are all part of the ideological content of the picture, e.g. the contrast between a terrestrial landscape bathed in sunlight and the stormy regions of Heaven where an apocalyptical episode is taking place. Lightning and the fall

97

of stars, storms and earthquakes, were to the young Dürer what the sonorous iambic pentameters and the bloody climax to a tragedy mean to a young poet.

About the year 1494 we find ourselves on surer ground, in familiar surroundings, when we come to Dürer's really 'independent' landscapes, the first water-colours he painted of Nuremberg and its environs—the group of houses near the church of St. John and the wiredrawing-mill.

88, 89

The inscriptions and the monograms on Dürer's water-colours do not always coincide with the date of their creation. In 1501 and 1502 Dürer added inscriptions to those which were still in his possession, and the monograms were added later by an unknown hand. The water-colours are not dated, for which reason any attempt to arrange them in chronological order must be based solely on criteria of style. The latter are, however, in many cases so conclusive that they are the equivalent of an actual date. Dürer's 'independent' landscapes—water-colours and drawings—can be divided into a few groups, as to the exact dating of which scholars will continue to argue for a long time.

Nuremberg and Environs

The earliest landscape water-colour by Dürer which has come down to us shows the last destination of his earthly life—the cemetery of St. Johannis (Bremen, L. 104). Rembrandt, too, sketched the tower of the Wester Kerk—one of the few drawings he made of the centre of Amsterdam—without knowing that he would be laid to rest beneath it. In Dürer's early water-colours, there is a blending of landscape and figures in the foreground (walking or praying before a crucifix). Reminiscences of miniature-painting are still visible. A certain fondness for the chosen motive and an affectionate resolve to convert it into a small picture are the stylistic characteristics of these works. The wiredrawing-mill (Berlin, L. 4) also lacks uniformity in its artistic character. It shows the large and the small 'Weidenmühlen' (small wire factories) outside Nuremberg. The technique of wiredrawing was an invention of Nuremberg, that home of the metal industry. Dürer is still uncertain in his treatment of space—the superimposition of the landscape planes becomes rather confused in his hands trained in the Gothic school. He does not—as modern painters do—give us one visual impression, he piles one notion on top of another, thus leading the eye of the beholder to stray about the picture—a wayfarer is approaching the mill, a knight has ridden his horse into the pool, the miller is shooing his somewhat outsized hens out of the courtyard. Dürer is not very successful with his foreground, but this is more than compensated by the more distant parts of the picture, in which villages—Gostenhof, St. Leonhard, etc.—and towers (e.g. the Spittlertor) are set like jewels among the hills, meadows and woods. Dürer is accurate to the point of nervousness, neat to the point of meticulosity; one can rely on the topographical accuracy of his landscapes, but it is better not to examine too closely their arrangement according to the laws of optics.

It is certain that many works have been lost which could have been included in this first Nuremberg group; many of Dürer's engravings point to the existence of sketches. For example, Hans Seibold has detected in the lower group of buildings in the engraving of the 'Sea-monster' (1501), the inverted image of the castle of

89

88

INNSBRUCK. Water-colour, 1494. Vienna, Albertina

97

Nuremberg, before it was strengthened by the addition of the bastions (by Faguni, 1538–45), and Wilhelm Funk has proved that the background of the 'Virgin at the Wall' (engraving, 1514) shows the exact condition of the castle in that year, and believes that Dürer must have sketched it from a garret-window on the north side of his house at the Tiergärtnertor. Friedrich Frommann has recognized in the castle of the 'Knight, Death and the Devil', an inverted image of the castle of Nuremberg, combined with certain details from the water-colour of Innsbruck. Dürer never sketched the view from the castle over the town and the surrounding 'Hercynian' woods, but that arch-humanist Conrad Celtis has left us a description *Conrad Celtis* of it. In 1487 Celtis received his poet's crown in the castle from the hand of the Emperor. For his edition of the writings of the nun Roswitha of Gandersheim and his 'Quatuor Libri Amorum', Dürer made woodcuts in 1501 and 1502. In his celebrated panegyric on Nuremberg (on the model of Italian panegyrics), Celtis tells us of the gardens, from which 'even the slightest breath of air would waft the scent of the flowers into the sleeping-apartment and the inner rooms of the house'; of the jousting of the young men in the shady Hallerwiese and their walks to the Bleiche on fine summer evenings. And he omits neither the story of the good Emperor Frederick feeding the Nuremberg children under ten years of age with gingerbread cakes in the castle moat, nor the apocalyptical scenes when the starving and ragged peasants clamoured for alms at the doors of the churches during the famine of 1491. Of all that we find nothing in Dürer—only later, in the marginal drawings for the Emperor Maximilian's prayer-book, do we occasionally find some echo of Nuremberg—a burgher or a Franconian peasant round the corner.

In the late autumn of 1494 Dürer went to Italy. He brought a second group of *Landscapes* landscapes home with him—the Tyrolese group. In order to reconstruct Dürer's *from Tyrol* journey, Meder again had recourse to old maps. At the end of the fifteenth century a Nuremberg publishing house produced a map for the use of pilgrims and merchants proceeding to Rome—'This is the road to Rome, marked with points from mile to mile, from one city to the other, through the German land.' According to this map pilgrims followed the road through Donauwörth, Augsburg, Partenkirchen and Mittenwald to Innsbruck, the town where one bids hail and farewell to the South, and after that the Brenner road through Chiusa on the Isarco and Trento to Verona, where the road forks. Along this road Dürer culled a few landscape motives, using silverpoint for the fine preliminary drawing and the brush for the delicate delineation of a battlement or a building, or to indicate with a few quick, broad strokes the foreground. Some of these must have been hasty sketches made while sitting by the roadside and finished afterwards in his room at some Italian inn.

The question now arises whether any difference can be detected between the landscapes made on his outward and on his homeward journey. Between the two lay Venice and its art, a new world for Dürer's eye and a turning-point in his life *Echoes of* as an artist. In our opinion, the two views of the courtyard of a castle (L. 452 and *Venice* 453, Vienna) must be assigned to the outward journey. O. Mitius held that they represent the courtyard of the Hohenzollern castle of Cadolzburg near Fürth, as it was at that time, and the local knowledge and diligent investigations of Heinrich Thiersch have confirmed this. The 'Italian Castle' and the 'Castle by the Waterside' (L. 634 and L. 108) are Dürer's versions of the castle of Segonzano in Val Cembra, seen from the west and north. Dürer's pleasure in ornamental and calligraphic details, even in landscape, is exemplified in the fine linear rhythm of the wild-geese in flight and in the drawing of the stones on the river-bank, but becomes restrained as soon as he has to deal with the woodwork and masonry of the castle. Dürer's other Italian castle—the 'Welsch Pirg' (L. 392)—is neither the Welsberg (Monguelfo) in Val Pusteria, nor the Cornedo near Bolzano, but, as A. Rusconi and Theodor Honegger have proved beyond all doubt, the Dosso di Segonzano in Val Cembra. Both the castle and the mountain were sketched by Dürer in October 1494, i.e. on his way to Venice. During this journey he also painted from two different points the Brenner road and the bend of the Isarco near the Raben-stein (Escorial), and made his drawing of Chiusa on the Isarco, which he used

102

for his engraving of the 'Nemesis', where the landscape is inverted.

The characteristic which makes of these Tyrolese water-colours a uniform group and provides a link between them and the early Nuremberg landscapes, is the absence of sky. Dürer discovered sky as a necessary accompaniment or contrast to earth only in the course of his first journey to Italy, after he had seen pictures by Cima, Carpaccio, and Giovanni Bellini. Venetian landscape backgrounds also furnished him with a number of other motives, e.g. bushy slopes, rocky bridges, quarries, and the cubic conception of houses, all of which Dürer added to the storehouse of his fantasy.

Return from Venice

The water-colours which Dürer made during his return journey from Venice in the spring of 1495 bear witness to the training his eye had received, and we have the feeling that Dürer had more time to spare and could afford to make the digression to the Lake of Garda. The second Tyrolese group contains some very fine water-colours, including once more Trento and Innsbruck. The panorama of Trento (L. 109, Bremen) has been often reproduced and discussed. That it is really Trento and not some other town in the Trentino is certain as a result of Hans Eugen Pappenheim's investigations and is also confirmed by a fine water-colour which C. Ph. Fohr painted from almost the same spot. If we compare Dürer's panorama with the view of the castle and the Dosso di Trento, it is like comparing the essential with the fortuitous. The sector of landscape is clearly defined. The arbitrary perspective of the Nuremberg period with its exaggerated raising of the horizon and lowering of the foremost plane has been superseded. This landscape no longer 'stands', as the wiredrawing-mill does; it 'lies' in its valley between the mountains. The eye no longer has to dart here and there about the picture; it has to follow the guiding line of the river and is thus led gently to the town. A smiling blue sky looks down from above and is mirrored in the water beneath, and between the two is the essence of the picture—the town and its cornice of mountains. The same play of colour in sky and water justify the

87

mention at this point of the view of Innsbruck (L. 451, Vienna), despite the over-meticulous treatment of the architecture. The same exactitude in architectural details, and also a similar lack of form in less important parts of the picture, the same mixture of broad and thin strokes, can be seen in two other works by Dürer—the Castle of Trento (L. 90, London) and the 'Trintperg' (Hanover). The latter was recognized as a work of Dürer's by Dorner and the 'Trintperg' was identified by Winkler as the Dosso di Trento with the little church of Sant' Apollinare di Piedicastello.

In May 1495 Dürer went from Verona to the Lake of Garda and painted the 'Fenedier Klausen', that mountain crowned by a castle and covered with vines, olives and mulberry trees. The locality has been identified by Gerstenberg as Arco (L. 303, Paris). Those who, on seeing this 'farewell to the South' in the form of a castle bathed in sunlight, are tempted to quote Dürer's words: 'O wie wird mich nach der Sonne frieren' ('Oh, how I shall shiver for the sun'), will be disappointed to hear that Dürer was merely using a commonplace phrase, found in Hans Sachs' fables and anecdotes, the real meaning of which, whether in the North or in the South, is: 'How I shall long for the good old times!' Dürer, in fact, goes on to say: 'There I was a lord, at home I am a parasite.'

Dürer arrived in his home town with a trunk full of water-colours and his head full of unforgettable memories of southern landscape, art and life, many of which were to come to life again in the next few years. The Heavenly Jerusalem, which the angel is showing to St. John in the last woodcut of the 'Apocalypse', is built up from memories of Trento and Innsbruck. That curious drawing bearing the inscription 'Pupila Augusta' (L. 389, Windsor Castle), which was used again by Dürer for his engraving of St. Anthony and which, according to Pauli, represents the myth of the Lycaean Venus, also contains a mingling of architectural motives from towns on the Inn, the Adige and the Pegnitz. But Dürer's finest homage to Tyrol is the view through the window over a Dolomite landscape in the Madrid self-portrait of 1498. Dürer heard the voice of the mountains during his journey through the Alps and he was also not deaf to the appeal of the sea. Where could this Franconian landlubber have seen full-rigged galleons and many-oared galleys, if not on the Venetian lagoons and on the Adriatic Sea? Characteristic examples may be seen in the woodcut of the 'Seven Angels with the Trumpets' in the 'Apocalypse' series and in the engraving of the 'Sea-monster'. Nevertheless, it was not until the days of the seafaring Dutchmen of the seventeenth century that a genre of marine painting was created. Dürer did not bring back any sketches of the Adriatic Sea from the Lido, but only drew some of the monsters of the deep, e.g. the lobster and the common crab.

When Dürer, after his return from Italy, began once more to paint his native city and his native countryside, he had not forgotten how to see them through German eyes, but he had learned how to see them in the 'grand' manner. His mind had been opened to the possibilities of breadth and superimposition, which after all exist as well as height and abrupt projections. Dürer had learned how good it is to set off the void against the full and he now had an eye for fluctuating tones and a feeling for the use of colours in the construction of space. Without the

Memories of his Travels

96

95

97

In Nuremberg again

panorama of Trento we should never have had the view of Nuremberg from the
90   West (L. 103, Bremen)—from the Spittlertor, about where the Fürther Tor now
stands. In each case the focal point (the mountain peak in the panorama of Trento,
the top of the church spire in the Nuremberg picture) is gently emphasized. The
river as a guide for the eye is replaced by the broad road leading into the distance.
All subordinate figures are banished from this conception of space and the austere,
cool northern sky also plays a rôle. The change in Dürer's method of seeing can
also be detected in his rendering of the half-timbered houses of his native land.
The village houses of the 'Wiredrawing-mill' look as flimsy as the wood-and-
pasteboard buildings of an exhibition or a film studio, but those of the farmyard
57   in which the Prodigal Son kneels among the swine before a trough hollowed out
of a tree-trunk (drawing L. 222, London; engraving of about 1498), are as cubic
in shape and stand as firmly as those which can be seen today in any Alpine
valley.

If Dürer had been merely a 'talented' artist, he would now have done what
many of his biographers would have liked him to do—he would have gone on
painting water-colours of 'town and country views'. But, however inconvenient
this may be, Dürer was a genius, which means an adventurer, an incalculable
force. Scarcely had Dürer mastered the intricacies of local colours when he threw
himself into the adventure of pictorial construction based on groups of comple-
mentary colours. Hitherto his aim had been topographical accuracy, but now the
fantasy of a painter who started from colour and thought in terms of colour
began to assert its rights. But even that is an inadmissible simplification in Dürer's
case, for what we would like to designate 'stages of development'—first reality,
then the fairy-tale; first constraint, then freedom—are found side-by-side at the
same time in his work. We even come upon returns to stages which we thought
he had left behind, moments of hesitation and sudden deviations from the path of
progress. In short, we find innumerable multi-coloured threads which are gradually
woven into the mysterious pattern of the tapestry of life. Nevertheless, it can
hardly be the same hand which before 1499 created with the brush the chromatic
85   poem of the 'House by the Pond', that some two years later with pen and ruler drew
so pedantic a version of the footbridge by the little Hallertor in Nuremberg (L. 462,
Vienna). We can, however, group together without difficulty small batches of
works which have artistic affinity, e.g. the chromatic trio of the 'House by the
Pond', the 'Pond at Sunset' and the 'Castle by the Waterside'.

*The
Chromatic
Group*
The 'House by the Pond' (L. 220, London) is a picture in every sense of the
word. Everything combines to form a circle—the banks of the pond, the lines of
the boat. The little house is reflected, moistly transfigured, in the sheet of water
enframed by trees and bushes treated in the manner of still-life. The pathos of
the sunset lighting gives this idyll a dramatic undertone. The richness of Dürer's
palette, with its yellow, orange, blue, violet, red and green, has something almost
frightening. Dürer knew well what he had achieved with this water-colour. For
86   the engraving of the 'Virgin with the Monkey' he used the motive again—
reversed as in a mirror; in the print the branches of the pond to left and right of

the house are hidden by the figure of the Virgin or cut off by the edge of the paper, but on the other hand the pond is extended behind the figure to become an imaginary seascape. Italian engravers, always thirsting for subjects, who took whatever they could find, soon transplanted this little house, which can be found again, for example, in Giulio Campagnola's engraving, 'The Rape of Ganymede', and in Robetta's 'Adam and Eve with Cain and Abel'.

Dürer's method consisted of uniting, on one and the same canvas or print, impressions gathered direct from Nature, free inventions, reminiscences, hints culled from the work of other artists and motives of his own, and this shows once again how, when it comes to practical application, a genius scorns the dictates of reason and aesthetic theories. The landscape of the 'Sunset' (L. 219, London) represents the zenith of Dürer's fantasies in colour, with the reeds in the extreme foreground drawn so delicately that the hand of a Japanese artist might have guided the brush, and the vivid contrast between the wood of conifers on the one side and the five bare, unfinished tree-trunks on the other. The lighting, fantastically varied, is such that some believe it represents a sunrise, which may either mean that there is little difference between the chromatic phenomena of sunset and sunrise, or else that our eyes have become blind to Nature. The picture dates from the years of Dürer's 'Apocalypse', when he painted those flaming skies traversed by great banks of cloud.

In the backgrounds of the prints produced by Dürer between his first and second journeys to Italy we frequently find scenes from the environs of Nuremberg which Dürer drew either from Nature or from memory. For the tree-covered cliffs in the 1497 engraving of St. Jerome he used two motives (L. 106 and 107, Bremen) which he had sketched in the stone-quarries just outside Nuremberg. The beautiful landscape drawing in Berlin (L. 440), to which the figures of St. Anthony and St. Paul lend significance, has been identified by those who know Nuremberg as being in the neighbourhood of Schmausenbuck. *Landscape Backgrounds*

From autumn 1505 until January 1507 Dürer was again in Italy. This was the great journey during which he created in Venice the 'Festival of the Rose-garlands', the 'Jesus among the Doctors', 'the Virgin with the Goldfinch', the 'Virgin and Child' (Rohoncz Collection), portraits of men and women, and numerous studies in proportion. For the scenery through which he passed—for the second time—Dürer seems to have had no thought or no time, for with the exception of the little landscape with trees (L. 132, Brunswick), we can find nothing which appears to date from this time, unless the already mentioned 'Italian mountain' belongs to this period, which is a very debatable point. But after his return the whole glory of his native countryside was revealed to his eyes—the poetry of quiet retreats, the cosiness of the villages, the sombre mysteries of the German forests, the joy of spacious prospects over valleys and hills. The years between 1508 and 1518 are those in which he created his group of Franconian landscapes. In them Nature is harsh and austere—sandy soil and pine trees, ponds and pastures, stretches of heath and gorse, brown fields and green meadows surrounding the villages. The localities can all be identified by name. Mitius has *Franconian Landscapes* identified the drawing L. 355 in Bayonne as the village of Heroldsberg, about seven miles north of Nuremberg, and the silverpoint sketch L. 824 in Haarlem as Kirchehrenbach near Forchheim. The pen and water-colour drawing in Bremen (L. 105) is inscribed 'Kalchreut', while the silverpoint sketch in Bayonne (L. 349) again shows the wiredrawing-mill, seen from a rather lower viewpoint and further to the right than in the coloured version made some sixteen years before; the trees have grown and the buildings have altered, while the hills in the background, the roofs and towers, in contrast to the water-colour, no longer show that exaggerated height which is typical of Gothic art. The landscape of Heroldsberg, drawn very carefully from Nature, bears an inscription which, since Rapke's studies on perspective in Dürer's drawings, has been generally read as 'Hab acht auffs aug' ('take note of what you see'), which might be a hint by the artist to himself to pay attention to perspective construction. We learn from Pirckheimer that Dürer studied the theory of landscape-painting and made notes on the subject. Are we then to assume that he thought of a theory of proportion applicable to this, the freest of all branches of artistic reproduction, and of the possibility of approaching landscape with compasses and ruler and 'extracting' from the infinite variety of Nature the 'true', the perfect landscape governed by fixed laws? It is more probable that Dürer, like Leonardo in his book on painting, noted down his observations on wind and weather, light and colour. Be that as it may, the Heroldsberg drawing cannot be adduced as an example of a 'constructed' landscape, because it is not 'constructed', and the inscription was not written by Dürer, but is, as Flechsig has convincingly shown, a no longer decipherable part of a long inscription inserted by another hand.

About 1510 the series of Franconian landscapes is closed by two wonderful water-colours—'Kalchreut' and an unknown valley (L. 105, Bremen, and L. 14, Berlin; I am unable to accept Waldmann's dating—about 1501). Conrad Celtis compared the landscape round Nuremberg, with its sandy soil, its strata of sandstone and scattered trees, to a 'German saddle', with patches of woodland projecting and receding 'like inlets on a sea-coast'. A saddle landscape of this kind, with yellow depressions and green elevations, enclosed by blue mountains in their distance, forms the subject of Dürer's last water-colours. In 'Kalchreut' the eye is led by leaps and bounds from house to house, from roof to roof into the distance, and at no point is it invited to rest awhile, not even on the two figures seated on the bench, beneath tree-tops as overwhelming as Edward Munch's ghost trees, which are certainly not calculated to make us think of a village Romeo and Juliet. The unknown valley must, I believe, lie not far from 'Kalchreut', for it is bounded by similar, perhaps by the same chains of hills. It is hardly necessary to stray as far abroad as Brinckmann, who identifies this valley as being in the area between the abbey of Banz and Vierzehnheiligen.

One motive from these Franconian landscapes reappears in one of Dürer's engravings. Kirchehrenbach near Forchheim (L. 824, Haarlem) is combined with Ehrenbürg (Walberla) in Franconia and an imaginary seascape to form the background of the etching on iron of 1518, the 'Great Cannon'.

Dürer's landscapes were seen by him and, as painters put it, 'grasped'; Altdorfer's landscapes, in comparison, seem to have been dreamt and felt. In Dürer's conception there were no fir-trees waving their moss-grown tops in the mountain wind, his mountains obey the laws of geology, their structure is clear. Wolf Huber's mountains, on the other hand, spring up like petrified fountains. If we compare Dürer's water-colour landscapes with the landscape elements in his paintings, we occasionally find him taking from his store of sketches and introducing into the grandiose concerto of the pictorial construction some Tyrolese folksong, but as a general rule Dürer did not consider landscapes as seen by the traveller to be worthy of serving, without modification, as the scene of some sublime event. To his mind, a great subject required a great setting. In his Munich painting of the Nativity, or in the Adoration of the Magi in Florence, for example, he felt constrained to reproduce the traditional setting of the birth of Christ—the dilapidated shed and the ruins. In honour of the Child free rein had to be given to all the tricks of perspective architectural drawing—arches, walls, vistas and rafters open to the sky—only in the far background is there a glimpse of open landscape above the restricted and domesticated foreground of the picture. The immediate surroundings of the Mother and Child, the Holy Family, the Shepherds and the Magi—the tree, the bush, the fence, the iris and the gilliflower, the butterfly and the finch—constitute what may be termed the Holy Family's 'household landscape', in contrast to the 'wild' landscapes amidst which mythological events ('Hercules and the Birds of Stymphalis') or allegorical beings ('Adoration of the Trinity') are depicted. But, however much the landscape backgrounds in Dürer's paintings, woodcuts and engravings are adapted, they do not blend with the figures, which do not move within the landscape, as they do in the works of Giorgione, but remain as if standing before it. This is the fundamental limitation of Dürer's rendering of landscape. When, in a drawing or a water-colour, he has to deal with Nature alone, he is, without knowing it, far ahead of the Italians. But so soon as he unites landscape and figure, the seams are obvious and the human figure—always Dürer's main preoccupation —forces the surrounding landscape into the background.

When Dürer between 1510 and 1518 created the maturest and freest of his landscape sketches and water-colours, he reached his goal and had set out along that high road of Germanic art which leads from Late Gothic to Rembrandt and on to Van Gogh and Munch. As a landscape artist Dürer also took this road, but for him it seemed to be a byway, which he abandoned when he was attracted by other problems—the human figure and the characters of men, and the 'last things'.

When Dürer set out with his wife and her maid for the Netherlands, his head was full of questions which were far removed from pure landscape. If he sketched the world from the ship, the carriage or his inn, it was because he was looking for peculiar features, or because he picked some architectural element out of the landscape and sketched it as if it had been a human figure. In addition to this, until during his return journey to Germany he received in black and white the ratification of his yearly pension from Charles V, he was plagued by financial worries and plunged into a whirl of business and people which left him little time for thought and for quiet drawing from Nature. Nevertheless, it is during this journey that we encounter the word 'landscape-painter', and it is Dürer himself who uses the new term with reference to Joachim Patinir, whose honoured wedding-guest he was. Dürer also made a sketch of the zoological garden in Brussels with its labyrinth and fountains (L. 427, Vienna, Akademie) and notes that it was 'an amusing thing, pleasing to me, like a paradise, such as I had never seen'. But we seek in vain in Dürer's sketch-book for Dutch landscapes. The sketch of Bergen-op-Zoom (L. 317, Chantilly) and the houses of Tiel on the Waal in the portrait of Caspar Sturm (L. 340, Chantilly) are but poor consolation for the loss of the view of Middelburg.

39

The insertion of landscape details in portrait sketches has been described as peculiar to Dürer, but the juxtaposition of large close-ups of heads and distant landscapes was not intended by him to be a new discovery in the field of portrait composition. The heads and the landscapes have no relationship to one another. The landscapes were inserted wherever there was room for them near already existing heads, e.g. the tower of the church of St. Michel in Antwerp beside the head of a man (L. 338, Chantilly). Dürer used the pages of his sketchbooks very sparingly during his journey—we find, for instance, on one and the same page two Rhenish castles: Stolzenfels, opposite Lahnstein, and the Marksburg near Braubach (L. 856, Brunswick). The landscape of Andernach, drawn during his return up the Rhine from Cologne (L. 59, Berlin), had to be content to occupy the vacant space by the side of the portrait of a man from Antwerp.

92

The two sketches of Aachen, showing the Town Hall (L. 339, Chantilly) and the Minster (L. 404, London), must be classified as architectural portraits rather than as landscapes. The condition of these two historical buildings at the time is reproduced with the greatest fidelity, and when they were restored, Dürer's sketches were used as documentary evidence of their former appearance. There is, however, one sketch made by Dürer during this journey which cannot be relegated to the 'topographically correct' class, and that is the drawing of the landing-place outside the Scheldt Gate at Antwerp (L. 556, Vienna). The austerity and economy of its linear construction give this black-and-white sketch a virile grandeur, worthy of comparison with the flaming water-colours of the youthful Dürer. Here, too, Dürer pointed the way to future developments in the representation of landscape. His successor in spirit and truthfulness was Van Gogh.

93

94

By the time he returned from the Netherlands, Dürer was already carrying the germ of the illness which ultimately caused his death and had only a few more years to live, but his head was full of plans, enough to have kept a master busy until he was seventy. Landscape had given way to the representation of the human form. Behind the heads of Pirckheimer and Melanchthon, of Frederick the Wise and Albrecht of Brandenburg, behind the patricians Muffel and Holzschuher, no window allows us to catch a glimpse of distant landscapes; stern and solid, the neutral grounds stand behind these studies of character. In the engravings of the Apostles Philip, Bartholomew and Simon, there is barely an indication of space—

a bare slope, the lower part of the stem of a tree, a little piece of ground, and nothing more! Only on the table at which Erasmus of Rotterdam is working (engraving of 1526) is there a vase full of wild flowers, as if to reconcile us with this withered old scholar.

51

Perhaps, while Dürer was transforming his 1520 sketch of Erasmus into a model for the engraving, he looked through some of his old folders in his Nuremberg atelier and found there some of his old flower-sketches, or the 'Large Tuft of Grass' (L. 472, Vienna). How long ago it must have all seemed! Twenty-three years had passed since he lay in the grassy meadows, listening, watching, feeling, smelling, as reverent in his attitude towards Nature as Goethe, who has left us a description of a similar experience: 'When . . . I lie in the long grass . . . and perceive the thousands of multifarious little blades of grass close to the earth, when I feel close to my heart the teeming of the little world among the stalks, the countless unfathomable forms of the little worms and insects, and feel the presence of the Almighty who created us in His image, the spirit of Universal Love which bears us aloft and keeps us in eternal bliss, then I often yearn and think: Ah, if thou couldst but express this again, if thou couldst but breathe it on to paper, that which lives so fully and so warmly within thee that it would become the mirror of thy soul, as thy soul is the mirror of Infinite God . . .'

*Feeling for
Nature*

Those who wish to weave a garland of fame for the landscape-painter Dürer—and who would not?—may find in the garden of his art an abundance of flowers, buds and leaves. From his own garden in Nuremberg Dürer must often have carried great bunches of flowers into his atelier—the great lilies, those proud attributes of saintly women (L. 637, Bremen), a bunch of violets (L. 470, Vienna), and all the little folk from the roadside, the hedges in the meadows and the gardens of the peasants—Turk's head, heartsease (wrongly identified as viper's bugloss, L. 840, Bremen), celandine (L. 586, Vienna), columbine (L. 585, Vienna), and their modest neighbours of the 'Little Tuft of Grass'—hornwort, clover and yarrow (L. 471, Vienna). In Dürer's eyes they were all equal.

*Love of
Flowers*

118-121

LANDSCAPE. DETAIL FROM 'ST. MICHAEL FIGHTING AGAINST THE DRAGON'
(Apocalypse, 1498)

CHAPTER NINE

PEASANTS · BURGHERS AND SOLDIERS

*Genre
Painting*

THE cradle of the 'genre', or 'popular', element in painting was the Church. Into the art of the Middle Ages, with its strict regard for rank and station, there gradually penetrated all kinds of figures from the realm of the 'man in the street'—first in the modest rôle of subordinate figures in religious pictures, and then more openly and confidently. With the increasingly realistic tendencies of Late Gothic, the protagonists of biblical episodes came to resemble more and more the ordinary burgher. Devotional art turned to scenes from everyday life. There was a growing demand for secular narrative, and as there was no branch of art which catered for secular subjects alone, the artists turned naïvely to the Scriptures and filled them with the warmth and vivacity of life. Period costumes, period figures and atmosphere brought a popular element into religious drama and religious art, while preserving all the droll and fearsome, naïve and visionary traits that are the essence of Old German art. Tumblers from the country fairs were transplanted into pictures of the Dance of Salome, the Centurion of Capernaum became a lansquenet and St. George a mediaeval knight. Every child could recognize in St. Peter a real fisherman and in Joseph a real carpenter.

All this existed in German and Flemish art before Dürer's time. The 'Master of the Amsterdam Cabinet', the 'Master E.S.', Schongauer and others—and also the pupils in Wolgemut's workshop in the backgrounds of their great altarpieces—introduced figures taken from everyday life into the story of the Passion—soldiers, peasants and artisans—or turned some individual figure of a popular kind into a print which would appeal to popular taste and achieve a ready sale. The soldiers whom the 'Hausbuchmeister' shows throwing dice for the clothing of Christ, are soldiers such as could be seen every day on the high roads, and Schongauer's little peasant, leaning on his sword as if it were a stick, was a familiar figure. It was because people could not see enough of such burlesque figures that Dürer adopted them in his own works.

*Dürer's
Attitude to
Genre-painting*

We cannot, therefore, claim for Dürer the honour of having introduced peasants, burghers and soldiers into art, but his attitude to the genre element differed from that of his predecessors. The broadening of his outlook is a very significant expression of his whole conception of life and an unmistakable sign of the transformation which was taking place in the minds of German men on the eve of the Reformation and the great peasants' war.

*Peasants in
German Poetry*

The German peasants of the Middle Ages were not a clearly defined class, living under the same conditions and filled with the same feelings; they were a sociological medley of categories which could not easily be distinguished one from the other and included such types as gardeners, wine-growers and farming townsmen. Their economic history had been full of changes and they suffered from that hereditary ill of all Germans—difference of opinions. There could be no greater contrast than that between the well-to-do peasants of the farms in the

Frisian marshes or on the hereditary farms of Westphalia, who were as free as the air, and the little tenant-farmers of Franconia, who were the serfs of secular and ecclesiastical landowners. There was a vast difference between the world as seen through the eyes of the proud countryfolk of Switzerland and the views of the oppressed peasantry of Central Germany. And in addition to this, the economic condition of the peasantry in West and South Germany varied in the course of the centuries, just as the position of the knights had its ups-and-downs.

In poetry these changes can be followed more clearly than in the formative arts. Neidhart von Reuental, who introduced peasants into German thirteenth-century literature, was a minor Bavarian nobleman who left his little estate near Landshut to become a singer, dancer and fiddler at the various courts, where he poured forth all the sarcasm of an impoverished nobleman on the stupid peasants who tried in every way to ape the knights. Scorn for the 'villagers' is the keynote of his 'Sommer- und Winterlieder'—'they wear tight coats and tight collars, red hats, black hose and buckles on their shoes'. These are by no means the obtuse and oppressed peasants who first made their appearance in poetry, but self-conscious, prosperous men fond of indulging in eating, drinking and dancing. The peasant types created by Neidhart survived until well on into the sixteenth century. A 'village' lyric poetry thus developed in reaction to the somewhat mawkish and over-refined court lyric, and the solemn epics of chivalry were parodied by the 'peasant epics' such as Wittenweiler's 'Ring'.

Towards the end of the Middle Ages the central power of the Emperor began to decline and the power of the secular and ecclesiastical landowners increased, which brought about a corresponding decline in the prosperity of the peasants both in the open country and in the small towns. The transition from a natural to a financial economy and the application in Germany of Roman law in matters concerning the peasantry led to much oppression and reduced the peasantry to misery. Tradition, old customs and the whole conception of right were despised or destroyed. Life in the country was subjected to unnatural regulations, to the benefit of the princes, the towns and the Church, and to the detriment of the peasants, who fell more and more heavily into debt. The countryside was ravaged by pestilences and the crops failed. The fields were damaged by the landowners when out hunting and by the game which the peasants were forbidden to kill, while the embargo on fishing, the restrictions on timber-felling and the high rents further enraged the peasants and offended their natural conception of right and wrong. The peasants who revolted at Brunswick in 1488, at Worms in 1513 and at Nördlingen in 1525 demanded the dismissal of the 'Roman' jurists from councils and tribunals; among the twelve 'peasant articles' there was one which read: 'God gave men dominion over all things that live on the land, in the air and in the waters.' The peasants were appalled at the injustice of the world, which seemed to them irreconcilable with Divine Justice. The Abbot of Trittenheim relates that the peasants carried a flag, showing on the one side the Crucified Christ and the 'Bundschuh', and on the other a picture of a kneeling peasant and the slogan: 'Naught but the Justice of God.'

Economic Position of the Peasants

There were thus many complicated motives which led up to the peasant revolts at Niklashausen in 1476 and at Untergrambach in 1502, to the 'Poor Conrad' rebellion in Württemberg and Baden in 1514 and finally to the tragic Peasants' War of 1525. Though economic distress may have been the dominant factor, there was also a demand for sweeping reforms, which attempted to justify themselves on religious grounds, but were politically of the most radical nature. When the peasants of Trittenheim were asked to formulate their demands, they said that they wanted to be as free as the Swiss Confederates, to abolish all ownership and rule of the land. The flags of the rebellious peasants, bearing the symbolic peasant's shoe which indefatigably treads the native soil, were brandished throughout Southern, Western and Central Germany. But these scythe-wielders and flail-swingers and their auxiliaries, the lansquenets and vagabonds who flocked to join them, had no unity and no leadership. Neither the political fanaticism of a knightly peasant-leader like Florian Geyer, nor the religious fanaticism of the 'Rebel in Christ' Thomas Münzer, could, in the long run, replace discipline and faith. The hunger march of the peasants shattered itself against the military might of the Princes and the Swabian League and against the walls of the Marienberg at Würzburg. One of the greatest German movements was drowned in the blood of German peasants.

That is the historical background against which Dürer's peasants must be seen. The Franconian peasants were among the poorest of Southern Germany. Ulrich von Hutten wrote of them from the standpoint of a knight: 'Those who produce our food are quite poor peasants, to whom we hire out our fields, our vineyards, our meadows and our woods. The yield which comes from them is, for the work done, poor and scanty, but they work with great labour and diligence so that it may become rich and profitable, for we must be careful housekeepers.'

Of the age-old struggle between peasants and knights there is no trace in Dürer's prints. The creator of the 'Apocalypse' has left no drawings of the peasants' struggle to gain their rights as men. Only once does Dürer abandon the attitude of a genre artist and give us a glimpse of human suffering—in the drawing and

engraving of the Prodigal Son (1498?). This Prodigal Son from the Bible, crying aloud to Heaven from the midst of the crumbling stables of a Franconian farm, is at the same time a symbol of the German peasant, that prodigal son of the German nation.

Dürer's clients in the cities wanted to see, and eagerly purchased, pictorial representations of the figures familiar to them from carnival plays and farces. With all the arrogance of the petit bourgeois, the carnival poets of Nuremberg poured out their scorn on the stupid, boorish, dirty peasants. These satires are in reality sad proofs of the lack of class-solidarity in Germany and of the gulf between town and country. Even the nicknames given to these figures of peasants reveal the sentiments of the poets, readers and spectators, e.g. Ackertritt (Clodhopper), Molkenfrass (Milk-swiller), Weinschlund (Wine-guzzler) and others even less polite. Hans Sachs' anecdotes are good-humoured, but even he looks upon peasants as blockheads and their wives as hoydens. It is, however, true that priests and knights, merchants and soldiers were treated in the same summary way on the stage.

German Sarcasm

Ridicule is common to all nations, because it is one of the oldest forms of converse among simple and young people. But the Middle Ages transformed the German form of ridicule from playful teasing into biting sarcasm, from fatherly humour into annihilating satire, sparing neither station nor age, neither profession nor human weaknesses. Folksongs, proverbs, books of anecdotes and school-books are full, too full, of witty criticism of society. To popular humour in the fifteenth and sixteenth centuries came a new recruit—the popular picture, which made fun of the foremost figures in national life. The need for laughter and ridicule was a necessary counterpart to the deadly earnestness and harsh sentiments of the time, when humanistic learning could combine in one and the same head with belief in witches, and gentle adoration of the Virgin Mary could be found in the same mind which took pleasure in bawdiness.

In Dürer's work, however, we find neither religious satire nor sarcasm at the expense of the peasants. Dürer was too chivalrous to indulge in a campaign of hate against the Papacy and the Church, too good-humoured to participate in the coarse jokes about the countryfolk. His pencil never drew Bartschi Dripnose, the peasant hero of the comic epic, nor Mützi Rumpwagger, his beloved. He left it to the poets to describe the brawling, boozing and guzzling which were the rule at peasant weddings. Characteristic of Dürer's good-tempered, almost *Dürer's* affectionate way of making fun of the peasants is that remarkable woodcut of *Bonhomie* 1525, a design for a 'monument', which Dürer himself describes in the third book of his 'Art of Mensuration'. Round the pedestal of this 'Victory Monument' are cows, sheep and pigs. In the midst of four baskets containing cheese, butter, eggs, onions and cabbages is an oat-bin, with a cauldron upside-down on top of it. From a cheese-bowl on the bottom of the cauldron rises the actual column, consisting of a butter-churn, then a milk-jug, from which emerge four dung-forks swathed in sheaves, on which hang spades, mattocks, flails and forks. The capital consists of a hen-coop and the whole is surmounted by the figure of a peasant, seated on an earthenware vessel and transfixed by a sword. Such a monument satirizes the victor rather than the vanquished. That Dürer meant this design to be a harmless piece of fun is confirmed by the fact that immediately afterwards he gives us the design for a monument to a drunkard, made up out of beer-barrels, mugs and dishes of food. Dürer would hardly have been a despiser of the peasants, for he always had a silent liking for the 'little people', which emerges throughout his work. Perhaps he still felt in his veins the blood of his ancestors, who had been small farmers and had driven their horses across the Hungarian steppes.

Dürer's fantasy was in its essence a plastic, rather than an epic imagination—it *Peasant Figures* preferred human figures to events. We have by Dürer's hand no drawing of a ploughman, to whom Holbein the Younger gave such imperishable form in his pictures of Death. Nor did Dürer, like the elder Breughel, paint the return of the peasants from the fields; he merely produced individual genre-figures of peasants in the form of prints. From about 1498 date the two engravings, equal in

132, 134 format, of 'Three Peasants Talking' and 'The Peasant and his Wife', which were perhaps to form part of a series he had planned. Instead of the German village landscape which we find in Holbein's woodcut about twenty-eight years later, Dürer makes use of an old-fashioned bare fold in the ground, on which the figures stand without any background. The three peasants engaged in conversation must therefore be considered as costume studies rather than as genre-figures. Their clothing is a mixture of rustic and knightly dress. One of them is wearing boots and spurs and is carrying a basket of eggs to market; another, in belted tunic and hose, supports his weak knees by leaning on a knight's sword, the blade of which is sticking out of the battered scabbard—an eyesore for the military-minded.

That peasants should go about armed outside their farms was looked upon as natural in those disturbed and boisterous times, and Hutten has described vividly how the knights reckoned on being attacked as soon as they left the solid walls of their castles. This engraving of the three peasants has been interpreted by some as a kind of illustration to some scene from a book and the bearded peasant has been identified as a trouble-maker, the 'Hebestreit' who occurs in Neidhart's poems. It is likewise possible that the peasant quarrelling with his wife is an allusion to some episode which would be familiar to contemporary readers from anecdotes and proverbs. The woman looks as if she had been cut out of a costume study; she imitates the poise of a grand lady of the town and her face, prematurely aged and sullen, is indifferent to her husband's hysterical scolding. Is he reproaching her for trying to play the lady, or is he Neidhart's 'Clodhopper' and she his shrewish wife Fridauna?

Folk-dances and Dancers

These somewhat sorry peasant figures soon disappear from Dürer's pictorial stage. When he returns to similar themes about 1514 he introduces us to a very 131 different type of peasant—a man and wife, round-headed and short-legged, prancing around with gusto. The woman is holding in her free hand a knife, a purse and a bundle of keys, which strike against her hip with every bound. Hubert Schrade would like us to believe that this picture of a dancing couple is the symbol of the spirit of late mediaeval times—'the effect is that of a dance on the edge of the world, over and above the world'. According to Allihn, this ursine capering is a peasant reel, the 'Hoppedei', which peasants were allowed to dance, whereas they were forbidden to indulge in the courtly 'Hovetanz', which was reserved for noble couples. But Dürer, because he always wanted to depict the humorous side of country life from the viewpoint of the city merchants, was probably thinking of another dance, the 'Ruppelrai', which by all accounts must have been a lively affair, for Albert Achilles of Brandenburg's statesman, Ludwig von Eyb the Elder, a native of Franconia, writes in 1473: 'When the "Ruppelrai" starts, happy is he who stays at home.'

The engraving Dürer made in 1514 represents a folk-dance. Fifty years earlier, a great German sculptor, Erasmus Grasser, had erected a lasting memorial to *Morris-dancers* Late Gothic dancing with his sixteen figures, of which ten have been preserved, of morris-dancers (Munich, Stadtgeschichtliches Museum), which prove that dancing was not merely the rough-and-tumble business of carnival nights, but that it had a highly refined, artistic form of its own, as well as surviving in the form of the rustic reel. Body and costume (from the cap to the pointed shoes), face and carriage (from artful smile to supple, whimsical fingers), are converted into rhythm and caprice. In the fifty years separating Dürer's dancers from Grasser's, lies the Renaissance, which brought with it a feeling for the heavy and the massive. Grasser's morris-dancers are children of the Gothic period. Dürer's 'Ruppelrai' dancers belong to the Renaissance—notwithstanding that the sculptor depicted tumblers and the engraver peasants.

Dürer's peasants are the hardy children of the German soil, loud and unabashed in the expression of their sentiments and unrestrained both in their sorrow and their joy. In the marginal drawings for the Emperor Maximilian's prayer-book, *136–139* we find Dürer making fun of the peasants for imitating the 'Hovetanz'; while attempting to pirouette like the 'fine' people, the peasant balances a glass on his head (illustration to the 99th Psalm). The village cock crows the 'Jubilate', accompanied on the shawm by the village musician. Another peasant instrument is the bagpipe; the piper in the engraving of 1514 leans against a tree while he *133* plays. Angels, on the other hand, prefer the lute or the harp (e.g. in the Life of the Virgin, in the print of the Adoration of the Virgin). When the Bethlehem shepherds visit the manger, they bring their bagpipes with them (e.g. in the 'Little' woodcut Passion). A charming angel musician at the feet of the enthroned Virgin accompanies on the lute the distribution of the rose-garlands in the painting of 1506. The peasant couple in the engraving of 1519 belong to the hardy race of *128* dancing peasants. Here, too, is a scene familiar to everyone who crossed the market-place in front of the town hall—two modest little peasants offering their eggs and hens for sale. In later years H. J. Beham depicted peasant couples of this type, with pithy and appropriate inscriptions, e.g. 'It's cold . . . but it doesn't matter' or 'If we could only manage to sell . . . we'd have a drink'. But the most moving figures of peasants in German art were created by a wood-carver—the peasant with a cock and the peasant with a sucking pig on Nikolaus Hagenauer's altar of St. Anthony from Isenheim (Munich, Böhler Collection).

Dürer was content to depict single figures, couples, or at the most groups of *Portraits of Peasants* three. He never made engravings of a market-place or a kermis, Bavarian brawls or village weddings. We have, however, two portraits of peasants by his hand— the head of a bearded peasant in a cap, executed in water and opaque colour (L. 227, London), and the peasant-woman from South Tyrol ('Una vilana windisch'; *24* L. 408, London). These are two human studies of great power—on the one hand, the well-to-do, honest and devout Franconian peasant, with small, bright eyes in his leathery face, and on the other, the hearty, almost animal face of the smiling girl from South Tyrol, of Wend origin, whom Dürer drew during his journey to Venice in 1505.

When Dürer assembled the representatives of classes and professions in his 'Adoration of the Trinity', he did not confine himself to Emperors and Kings, *69–71* Pope and Cardinals, monks and nuns, knights and noble ladies; he also depicted peasants as they come from the fields, their flails over their shoulders. This great masterpiece thus becomes the expression of a new humanity and of a new piety as well. Kneeling on benches of clouds, they form a real congregation—'Man and woman, young and old, lord and serf, mother, maid, parents, children, as God brings us all together' (Luther). The theory advanced by Else Ziekursch, that this painting does not represent the Adoration of the Trinity by the whole of Christendom, but the Kingdom of God in Heaven and upon Earth—the Augustinian 'Civitas Dei', with Pope and Emperor as deputies of Christ—tends to confuse rather than to interpret.

Townspeople We can include under the generic term 'burgher' the many types of townspeople who appear in Dürer's pictures, from the cooks to the patricians, from the carpenters to the scholars, and to the same category belong also those few scenes of burgher daily life such as the 'Men's Bath' and the 'Women's Bath'. Dürer lived in one of the largest, busiest, proudest and richest cities of Germany, as a townsman among townspeople. Beneath the glittering surface of the imperial city of Nuremberg, which could offer a worthy reception to princes, lay the shadow of violent contrasts between rich and poor. The peaceful atmosphere of the city of the Minnesingers was often disturbed by town riots and class struggles, which were due to economic conditions (burden of taxes, accumulation of wealth in a few hands), or else were of a religious or political nature (the struggle against the nepotism of the patricians or the demand for a share in local government). The social structure of a town of the size and European importance of Nuremberg was very complicated, but it explains the eternal unrest which prevailed not only in the open country, but also behind the city walls. At the top of the social ladder were the great merchants, who might also be industrialists, like the mineowner Landauer, or big landowners, like Pirckheimer, and the whole of the financial and political power was in their hands. Then came the artisans who had become wealthy, some of them to the extent of becoming owners of large firms, like the publisher Koberger. On an equal footing with them were those members of the clergy who owned land or engaged in commerce. Then came the multitude of medium and small craftsmen, between whom and the artists there was no sharply-defined social boundary, though the artists had freed themselves of the restrictions of the guilds and were considered as being, both socially and intellectually, members of the upper bourgeoisie. Still lower in social degree were the wage-earners in commercial and agricultural undertakings—the gardeners and vineyard workers. And lastly came the proletariat, the 'pöbel', who swarmed in the suburbs and were the staunch supporters of every rebellion. The age of Dürer classified these beings of a lower order under the term 'Hans hinter der Mauer' ('Hans behind the wall') and they included potboys, taverners, jesters, gallows-birds, beggars, rogues and vagabonds.

Rioting in German Towns Between 1509 and 1514 there were several risings in Nuremberg, just as there were in the neighbouring towns of Schweinfurt, Nördlingen, Speyer, Worms, Ratisbon and elsewhere. Of these 'Hans behind the wall' was not the only instigator—the workshop labourers also rose against the patricians. The marked economic differences, the preponderance of those who possessed either little or

VIEW OF TRENTO. Water-colour, about 1495. Bremen, Kunsthalle

nothing at all, compelled the Nuremberg Council in 1525 to modify its taxation policy. A regulation was introduced, whereby those who owned 100 guilders or less were to be exempt from all taxes. The number of small incomes was so great that the Council had to make concessions, at least as far as the direct taxes were concerned. But the real source of revenue was indirect taxation levied on beer, wine, fish, meat and salt, and this naturally weighed most heavily on the lower classes of the population. A bitter wind was blowing through the picturesque lanes of Old Nuremberg and rendered men, too, bitter and defiant, but also determined to survive. Life had no use for the stay-at-homes who, like Dürer's 'Doctor', crouched in front of their stoves and found temptation and reward only in their dreams.

106

The pictures which we draw for ourselves of German towns during the Late Middle Ages are still far too highly coloured by romantic poetry and art history. The towns did not consist merely of churches and town halls, towers and bridges, patrician mansions and fortresses. There were also the houses of the burghers, most of which were half-timbered or built entirely of wood, and streets which were rarely paved, full of rubbish-heaps and cattle. Within the circle of the walls there lay gardens, monasteries, farms and open spaces. In short, a town was like an overgrown, fortified village, rustic not only in appearance, but also in its mode of life. We must not let ourselves be deceived by that Italian politeness which induced the Venetian Ambassador, Alvise Mocenigo, to describe Nuremberg as the 'Venice of Germany'.

The Mediaeval City

We are familiar with the appearance of the inhabitants of Nuremberg at that time. Dürer, too, drew with documentary fidelity costume sketches, and in doing so was merely following a custom of the age; examples are the Nuremberg lady in house-dress (L. 463, Vienna); in churchgoing dress (L. 464, Vienna) and in ball-dress (L. 465, Vienna). He took the same artist's interest in the dress of Venetian women (L. 187, Frankfurt; L. 629, Basle; L. 459 Vienna) and of Flemish women (L. 385, Paris). Dürer made a portrait of his wife wearing a coif which he had bought in Zeeland, and brought back with him from Riga three drawings which until recently were believed to be costume studies of Icelandic women, because the word 'eiffland' (Livonia) was misread as 'eysland' (Iceland) (L. 373, 374, 375, Paris). Dürer's journey to Livonia was not such an adventure as might seem, when we remember that many German artists went to Eastern Europe, e.g. Veit Stoss, Hans von Kulmbach and Dürer's own brother, Hans Dürer.

Costumes

135.

At the beginning of the sixteenth century there was already a lively interest in folklore and national costumes. Matthäus Schwarz of Augsburg, chief book-keeper to the Fuggers, had himself portrayed in every new suit of clothing he acquired from 1520 on, and his son continued this custom after 1560. In East Friesland costume pictures were made by order of Unico Manniga, 'because I perceive that the old Frisian adornment and costume is falling into disuse and our successors will not know how their forefathers were clad, therefore I have ordered that they be all "counterfeited".' The costumes in Dürer's engravings, woodcuts and paintings also merit attention. Among the early engravings, for example, is

THE MEN'S BATH (About 1497–8)

the so-called 'Love Offer' (about 1496). The motive is undoubtedly of popular origin, for it illustrates the melancholy truth that so many things on this earth, even the love of a young woman, can be bought. The girl is wearing her best dress and her finest coif, while the old debauchee has donned his fur-edged cloak and wears those wooden overshoes which were the only means of emerging dryshod from the mud of a mediaeval village street. The engraving of the 'Cook and his Wife' (1500?) is a costume study and an illustration at the same time. The riddle of *127* this picture has been solved by Konrad Lange—in depicting this comic couple, Dürer was illustrating the anecdote from the 'Knight in the Tower', in which the magpie chatters about the eel; the woman has eaten the beautiful eel which the man had already seen cooking in the pan, and the magpie is whispering this secret into the ear of the fat cook, who is almost bursting with rage.

Dürer thus made good-humoured fun of the peasants, but he did not spare the burghers either. In that treasury of Dürer's humour, the Emperor Maximilian's prayer-book, in the margin of the verso of folio 51 we find a stout Nuremberg housewife—Goethe calls her an innkeeper's wife—who has just returned from market with a large cheese and a basket of eggs, while on top of her headgear— a really 'speaking' heraldic animal—perches a cackling goose (or is it, as Ernst Ehlers believes, a swan as attribute of a peasant woman singing the praises of her wares?). With the same smile in his eyes Dürer drew the old woman beneath the text of a psalm (folio 48, verso), who has fallen asleep over her distaff, while the beer-mug beneath explains the reason of her sleepiness.

Dürer's only real genre-pictures of city life are the bathing scenes—the pen- *Bathing Scenes* drawings of women bathing (L. 101, Bremen, 1496, and L. 398, Chatsworth, 1516) *117* and the woodcut of the 'Men's Bath' (1497-98). In German towns at the end of *Ill. p. 154* the fifteenth century there were numerous public bath-houses, mostly let by the towns to lessees, e.g. in Vienna, about 1480, there were twenty-nine, in Berlin twelve and in Frankfurt am Main fifteen. The purpose of these bath-houses was not only hygienic; they were also public resorts and meeting-places. People went there to bathe, but not for that purpose alone—eating and drinking formed part of the programme and in Nuremberg the Meistersingers held singing classes in the bath-houses and there were even special 'bathing songs'. The clients also indulged in bath-house politics—'they sit there,' says a contemporary writer, 'and talk heresy against God and Emperor.' When Dürer drafted his plan for an ideal town in his treatise on fortifications, he did not forget to draw in a men's bath and a women's bath—opposite each other—in one of the main streets. A fifteenth-century saying bears testimony to the popularity of these resorts—'Wine inside and water out, then will we right merry be.'

If Dürer had wanted to imitate one of Hans Sachs' epigrammatic poems, he would not have let this opportunity slip of indulging in pornographic humour of the grossest kind, but he drew the women and their bathing procedure with the most scrupulous objectivity. Here, too, he preserved a measure of artistic dignity. Dürer was no prude, but he eschewed vulgarity. R. Wustmann has attempted to identify the men bathers as members of the artistic fraternity of Nuremberg spending the evening together—Wolgemut, Pleydenwurff and their apprentices, among them the young Dürer, who, in cap and gown, watches the joyous sporting of his elders, but the fact remains that any small tradesman would have looked the same, and these tough and leathery gentlemen might just as well be some of the butchers, bakers, tanners, smiths, tailors, clothmakers, furriers and brewers who sent their representatives to the 'Little Council'. When we consider these bathing scenes, we feel that we would gladly have dispensed with the 1497 engraving of the 'Four Nude Women', the bodily forms and attitudes of which are in part a remodelling of the figures from the 'Women's Bath' in the Italian manner, if Dürer had left us a few more of these vivid scenes from popular life. Michelangelo created his cartoon of bathing soldiers in order to demonstrate the standing, sitting and bending attitudes of nude figures, and Dürer used his 'Men's Bath' for the same purpose. Bathing scenes gave Italian artists a welcome opportunity of displaying their mastery of the nude. In Franciabigio's 'Uriah's Letter' (1523, Dresden), we see an elegant women's bath, and Girolamo Macchietti made use of the Thermae of Pozzuoli in order to paint a masterly version of a men's bath (Florence, Palazzo Vecchio).

Burgher Elements in Religious Pictures

Dürer's religious pictures are also interspersed with burgher elements. On the occasion of her marriage to Joseph, Mary is dressed according to the latest Nuremberg fashion, as if she were walking through the portal of St. Sebaldus. The wife of the unhappy Job, pouring manure over her husband as he sits on the dunghill (wing of the Jabach altar, about 1500, Frankfurt am Main), is a portly burgher's wife, emptying her dishwater in the yard, and the two musicians who accompany the scene on drum and fife are so lifelike, that attempts have been made to identify *9* the drummer as a self-portrait of Dürer. Among the representatives of the various classes in the 'Adoration of the Trinity', both peasants and artisans appear, the latter wearing felt hats.

75

Dürer's finest rendering of the homely atmosphere of burgher life is St. Jerome's study. The learned Cardinal occupies a typical burgher room, complete with what was then the latest modern convenience—large windows of bull's-eye glass. That a workroom can be more than a 'den' or a bookworm's retreat and that it is often the battlefield in which the mind achieves its victories and suffers its defeats, was well known to Dürer from the hours he spent at his table in his house by the Tiergärtnertor, battling with words in his efforts to put his thoughts on paper or struggling with problems of form as he tried to wrest beauty from Nature.

Soldiers

129, 130, 124

There remains one category which we have yet to consider among the many and varied types which populate Dürer's pictures—the soldiers. They include the soldiers in his renderings of the Crucifixion; St. George (engraving of 1505–08), dismounting from his horse; St. Eustace (engraving of 1500–03), the huntsman, rising from his knees; the 'Ensign' (engraving of 1500–05), rolling up his standard; the 'Rider' (engraving of 1514), leaping from the saddle with a jingling of metal; the Turk (etching of 1518), leaving the Nuremberg cannon; and innumerable lancers, falconers, bowmen, camp-followers, standard-bearers, etc. The patricians Stephan *53, 54* and Lukas Paumgärtner forget that they are supposed to be St. George and

THE LARGE PIECE OF TURF. Water-colour, 1503. Vienna, Albertina

St. Eustace (Munich, Paumgärtner altar-piece) and become Nuremberg militiamen. In addition to German soldiers, we also have the Irishmen whom Dürer saw in Flanders (L. 62, Berlin), when Calais was still in English hands, and strange-looking Turks. In 1523 he sketched one of the English longbowmen who accompanied the ambassador, Lord Morley, to Nuremberg (L. 365, Bayonne).

The age in which Dürer lived was filled with war and rumours of war, not only in distant lands, but also on German soil. Soldiers were familiar figures everywhere and military service, for knights, burghers and peasants alike, was taken for granted. According to the imperial register of 1521, Nuremberg could be called upon to supply forty men on horseback and 250 infantrymen. The free imperial city of Nuremberg had no standing army of its own, but it had a well-trained and well-armed militia recruited from among the burghers and artisans. Young men volunteered to go to the wars at any time, if called upon to do so, and on Sundays they practised shooting with muskets and crossbows. Dürer's father, the glass-painter Hans Wolgemut, the card-painter Winterberger and many other artists and artisans all served in the town militia. And this was no mere pastime, for Nuremberg, like other German cities, was continually involved in feuds with neighbouring princes. In 1450 Nuremberg, in league with twenty-seven other towns, had defeated the Burgrave Albrecht Achilles of Hohenzollern and twenty-two other princes. In 1502 the Margrave Kasimir of Anhalt, in league with Franconian knights, declared a feud against the city and it came to a battle in the Nuremberg Forest, during which the Nuremberg leader, Ulmann Stromer, was hard pressed by Götz von Berlichingen. At the Frauentor the guilds were standing to under the command of Willibald Pirckheimer, with the artists Peter Vischer, Hans Böham, Sebastian Lindenast etc. in their ranks. Stromer succeeded in drawing his adversary under the fire of the cannon on the Frauentor and compelling him to retreat. A Nuremberg contingent under Pirckheimer took part in the Emperor Maximilian's campaign against the Swiss. In 1523 Nuremberg took the field as a member of the Swabian League, contributing a thousand foot-soldiers, a hundred cavalrymen and twenty-two large cannon. During this campaign forty knights' castles were burned to the ground and Franz von Sickingen fell in his beleaguered castle of Landstuhl. The troops of the victorious league, under the Steward of Waldburg, entered Nuremberg. Dürer himself took a keen interest in military matters, especially in those concerning artillery and fortifications, and he was himself present as a spectator at the siege of Hohenasperg, by troops under Georg von Frundsberg, in 1519. Dürer afterwards made from memory a sketch of the beleaguered fortress (L. 52, Berlin). All artists at that time had an expert knowledge of weapons and the making of weapons. The Swiss painters Urs Graf, Nikolaus Manuel called Deutsch, and Hans Leu were both artists and soldiers, who derived their living and their style of painting from the Swiss wars and their service as lansquenets. Hans Leu was killed in battle in 1531.

Even when there was no war in progress, life was dangerous. One had always to reckon with attacks by highwaymen on the main roads, and even on hunting and fishing expeditions a passage of arms with the neighbours was not uncommon.

Military Service in Dürer's Time

Siege of Hohenasperg

In the inns itinerant scholars, fugitives, couriers etc. were only too ready to draw the knife. Ulrich von Hutten, who nevertheless found it 'a pleasure to live', has given us a clear idea of the gulf which separates the age of the Renaissance and the Reformation from what Jacob Burckhardt calls our age of security. The knight of that time was not only the shining hero of the tournaments, a noble castellan and a brave officer; he had also to combine in himself many other talents—he was a farmer and a warrior, a landlord and a magistrate, a vassal of the Emperor or of some prince or ecclesiastical chapter; life in his castle was neither picturesque nor comfortable. In a letter to Pirckheimer, Hutten writes: 'Whether our dwelling be in the mountains or in the plain, it is never built for comfort, but for defence, surrounded with wall and moat, and inside crowded with stables for cattle and horses, and dark sheds full of cannon, pitch and sulphur and what else belongs to warlike equipment in arms and machines. Everywhere is the stink of powder, and what with the ordure of the dogs, it is a charming and pleasant smell! Horsemen come and go, and gangs of robbers, thieves and highwaymen, for generally our houses stand open and our people seldom know or ask who a man is. You hear the bleating of sheep and the bellowing of oxen, the barking of dogs and the shouting of the labourers, the rumbling and creaking of carts and waggons, and even, in our neighbourhood, where the woods are close, the howling of wolves. The whole day is filled with fear and anxiety for the morrow, with endless movement and lasting tumult.'

Soldiers as Artists' Models   The soldiers interested the artists primarily as genre and costume figures. The fantastically attired lansquenets, and in particular the mounted men, were eagerly studied by the 'Hausbuchmeister', by Martin Schongauer, by the 'Master of the Amsterdam Cabinet' and by the 'Master P. P. W.'. The great picture of the 'Swabian War', painted in 1499, increased the popularity of the soldier motive. Dürer, too, in his younger days, was interested in soldiers as costume figures. In his engraving of 1495–96, we find slender, restless figures of the type dear to the 'Hausbuchmeister', swathed in the theatrical trappings of the lansquenets, standing like men of a picquet on the watch. In a drawing in Berlin (L. 2, 1498) three armed men, leaning on their long lances, are holding a council of war; some critics have given this drawing the pompous title of 'The Oath on the Rütli', but that is ridiculous—the Swiss Confederates did not look like that. In the woodcut of 1497–98, a knight rides down from his castle, with a man-at-arms running behind him. Such scenes were also the subjects of poems, and Wustmann has found a literary parallel to this woodcut—the 'Lied vom Schüttensamen' (about 1500) relates how a faithless man-at-arms lured his robber lord down from his castle into the forest and betrayed him into the hands of a troop of horsemen from Nuremberg.

Turks   In the midst of all these German and Swiss warriors, we find occasional Turks (e.g. the engraving of the 'Turkish Family', 1494). Both Flemish and Northern Italian artists had found the picturesque aspect of these foreigners irresistible, and in Germany the 'Hausbuchmeister' and Schongauer depicted Turks before Dürer. The 'Turkish Family' is an adaptation from a print by the 'Hausbuchmeister', which has been militarized by transforming the whip into a crossbow and the woman's headgear into a turban, while the drawing of 'Two Distinguished Turks with Servant' (L. 93, London) is a repetition of a peaceful group in Gentile Bellini's 'Procession of the Holy Cross', painted in 1496, though Dürer transforms the white servant into a negro and deprives the Turks of their beards. In Dürer's marginal drawings for the Emperor Maximilian's Prayer-book we find yet another Oriental, this time leading a camel (Folio 42, verso). *136*

Dürer's studies of soldiers change in character after the end of the century and we suddenly find the warrior in all his earnestness, dignity and beauty standing out amidst the costume figures. The standard-bearer proudly flourishes his ensign *130* (engraving of 1500–05); St. George sits his horse like a real soldier (engraving of 1505), ignoring the dead dragon at his feet and looking straight to his front, as if awaiting the arrival of the next monster. Quiet, restrained strength, rigid attitude, calm assurance of victory without the need of bombastic gestures, all the essential characteristics of the soldier are clearly emphasized, culminating in the engraving of the Christian Knight who fears neither Death nor Devil. *125* In the engraving of 1513 Dürer's 'Knight' is the worthy descendant of the heroes of the Nordic sagas. In Maximilian's time the knights belonged to a military caste which was rapidly dying out. The Romantic conception of the knight, clinging to antiquated forms of costume, behaviour, thinking and fighting, surrounded the last of the knights with a lingering touch of glamour—like the last glow of a dying fire.

DETAIL FROM THE FOOT OF A MONUMENT OF THE PEASANTS' WAR
(1525, Woodcut)

CHAPTER TEN

DÜRER AND LUTHER

THE two greatest Germans of their time never met face to face, but in the intellectual field their paths crossed. In a letter written to Georg Spalatin in 1520, Dürer asks him to thank the Elector of Saxony for sending him some of Luther's writings and goes on to say: 'And if, with God's help, I come to Martin Luther, I will counterfeit him with diligence and engrave him on copper, as a lasting memorial of that Christian man who has helped me to overcome great fears.'

Portraits of Luther

Dürer's hope was never fulfilled, and we can only try to imagine what the creator of the portraits of Melanchthon and Maximilian would have made of the head of the great Reformer. The well-known portraits of Luther by Lucas Cranach the Younger, and the less well-known, but more realistic pen-drawings by Luther's pupil and constant companion, Wilhelm Reifenstein (1545–46), are but poor consolation for the absence of a portrait by Dürer. A Doctor Luther, drawn by Dürer's hand, would have been very different from the prevailing conception of Luther which is the unfortunate result of inferior portraiture—a pastor in his gown, with the Bible under his arm and his eyes raised to Heaven. Dürer knew what this aggressive Reformer really looked like—the 'Junker Jörg' whom Lucas Cranach sketched, the mysterious horseman, on his way from the Wartburg to Wittenberg, whom the Swiss student Johannes Kessler met in an inn in 1522. 'We found there a man, sitting alone at a table with a little book before him . . . We deemed him to be naught else than a horseman sitting there after the custom of the country, in a red leather cape, doublet and hose, without armour, a sword at his side, his right hand on the hilt of the sword, the other grasping the book. His eyes were black and deep, sparkling and flashing like a star, so that they could not easily be met.'

Luther's Opinion of Dürer

It is difficult to say what Luther thought of Dürer. He knew Dürer's graphic work, for in 1518 Dürer sent him as a gift some woodcuts or engravings by his hand. We do not know what these were, but from the letter of thanks which Luther sent to Dürer by the hand of Scheurl, one is tempted to think that among them was 'The Knight, Death and the Devil', for it reminds us of Luther's own words: 'It is pleasing to God that we fear neither man nor devil . . . for He alone will be feared.' In any case, Luther knew of Dürer's European fame and had the greatest regard for him. When thanking Eobanus Hesse for sending him a funeral ode on Dürer, Luther wrote: 'Concerning Dürer, it seems to us fitting that we should mourn this very pious man, but you may deem him fortunate that Christ has illuminated him and taken him at so good an hour out of these stormy times which will soon become more stormy, so that he, who was worthy to see only the best, may not be compelled to witness the worst. May he rest in peace with his fathers. Amen.'

Luther's Attitude to Art

That Luther, when he wrote these words, was thinking only of Dürer as a man, and not of his art, is obvious. Luther had a deep feeling for music, but not for the formative arts. Luther's sensitiveness and power of imagination found their outlet in the impetuous torrent of the language of the people. He was interested in the formative arts only in so far as he could use them as political weapons in his struggle against Rome. Luther was the first great German politician who—following the example of the Wyclifites and Hussites in Bohemia—deliberately, with a full realization of their power to influence the masses, made unscrupulous use of polemical pictures. He was well aware of the propaganda value of woodcut prints, which could speak to all in a language comprehensible to all, and he did not shun either the coarsest similes or the bitterest scorn, if they could serve him in his struggle against the Holy See. Luther's propaganda pictures exploited every possibility which graphic art could offer.

But Dürer was not one of Luther's draughtsmen; he was not the Reformer's chief adviser on propaganda by means of art. He never allowed his pencil to serve the purposes of religious disputes. This was not for lack of conviction or enthusiasm, but rather on account of his innate idealism and his aloofness, both as an artist and as a man, which also made him reluctant to depict the extremes of physical pain. Dürer, for example, never 'humanized' sacred figures or episodes in the manner of Grünewald's powerful renderings of the Passion; he always endowed them with a certain aloofness and dignity. The polemical requirements of the Reformation were thus far better satisfied by the more drastic methods of the Cranach workshop, which in 1521 produced the 'Passional of Christ and Antichrist', one of Luther's most celebrated propaganda publications. In Dürer's circle, Luther could find artists better suited to his purpose, e.g. Hans Sebald Beham, to whom the print of the 'Fall of the Papacy' is attributed, and Peter Vischer the Younger, who in 1524 produced that famous drawing, which hung on the walls of Goethe's home in Frankfurt, showing Luther as a nude hero of ancient times.

Dürer and Ecclesiastical Politics

It is, therefore, wrong to imagine that Dürer used his art to help Luther's political aims, but it is, on the other hand, correct to say that Luther and Dürer held the same fundamental views on life. The source from which both of them drew their inspiration was a new depth of religious feeling, experienced as a rebirth and a transformation of the noblest heritage of German mysticism. Luther left the eternal Christian truths untouched, but he and his followers allowed themselves full freedom in their appropriation of the figure of Christ and their interpretation of the essence of Christianity. The revolution of Christian conscience, which Luther proclaimed, made a profound appeal to Dürer, because his piety was manifested in meditative earnestness and in a constant struggle for peace of conscience. Dürer was torn by feelings of responsibility, he thirsted for truth and clarity concerning the ultimate purpose of life, just as he desired to solve the ultimate problems of art. It was this kind of personal religious feeling which was at the root of Dürer's admiration for the person of Luther and his acceptance of the doctrines of the Reformation.

Revolution of Christian Conscience

In their profession of aloofness from reality and at the same time of closeness to life, in their characteristically German enthusiasm for the spiritual and the life to come, coupled with joyous materialism and unreserved acceptance of this earthly life, Dürer and Luther were men of the same blood. They did not flee this earthly life with its lawful obligations, its joys and its sorrows; they did not avoid it or find fault with it; they accepted it and drained it to the dregs. Manly earnestness went hand in hand with an almost boyish cheerfulness. This fidelity to life combined with keen observation of men and animals, this respect for what was small and unpretentious, this knowledge of the heights and depths of the journey through life, assured both Luther and Dürer a ready response from the hearts of their fellow-men.

Love of Animals

122, 123, 126, 139

Dürer and Luther were thus alike in their human warmth and in their superhuman heroism, in the intimacy of their daily lives and in their sublime aspiration to the transcendental. Two little examples will at least give an idea of this inner relationship. In 1530 Luther writes from Koburg to his colleagues in Wittenberg: 'There is a little wood in front of our window, where the jackdaws and crows hold their parliament.' On another occasion Luther composed a solemn complaint of the thrushes, blackbirds, finches, linnets, goldfinches, 'and other pious and honourable birds who will fly over Wittenberg in the autumn', against his old servant, Wolfgang Sieberger, who is accused of bird-snaring, 'given in our heavenly dwelling beneath the trees and under the common seal of our feathers'. Reading these words of Luther, we are inevitably reminded of the amusing scenes in Dürer's marginal drawings for Emperor Maximilian's Prayer-book. The story of the hare fleeing before the hounds which took refuge in Luther's wide sleeve, breathes the same kindly conception of Nature as Dürer's watercolour of a hare, as his renderings of dogs, birds, squirrels and monkeys (e.g. the

126

'Dance of Monkeys', L. 864, Basle, 1523). Dürer was always surrounded by household pets and his fantasy never tired of playing with them; there is hardly one of his important works in which some animal does not appear.

In one other respect Dürer and Luther are akin—each of them in his own way a pioneer and a revolutionary—in their attitude towards the German language.

The German Language

Throughout the Middle Ages Latin was the international language of the Church—of its liturgies, hymns, sermons and biblical commentaries. But Latin was also the language of secular scholars and of itinerant minstrels. Dürer's 'Apocalypse' was first published with both German and Latin text, the second edition with Latin text only. The Latin verses which accompany the 'Life of the Virgin', the 'Great Passion' and the 'Little Passion', were written, as we have already mentioned, by Dürer's learned friend, Benedict Schwalber (Chelidonius). Intellectual works of monumental size were generally published only in Latin.

The one great exception to the rule—the debate between the 'Husbandman' and Death in German prose, published in Bohemia soon after 1400, had no imitators. German prose, which in this work by Johannes de Tepla of Saaz became the expression of personal experience and suffering, lost its noble function and was used merely for household purposes and commercial intercourse. Anyone who could not or would not speak Latin, and wished to appeal to the public at large, used German verse, for most people felt themselves more at home in verse than in colloquial speech. There thus arose an epigrammatic and dogmatic form of German verse with traditional forms, which Dürer, too, adopted on occasion, e.g. on the three single prints of 1510, 'Christ on the Cross', the 'Schoolmaster' and the 'Lansquenet and Death'. In writing these explanatory verses, Dürer was certainly not trying to ape the poets; he wanted to express the thoughts which he had at heart in a form which would be easily understood by all.

Luther's philological achievement was that he transformed 'vulgar German' into German prose and used it as a weapon in the battle for the souls of his fellow-countrymen. There had been German Bibles (both manuscript and printed) before Luther's time, but it was his translation of the Bible, his hymns and his pamphlets, which gave added power of expression to colloquial German prose and thus made it an instrument for influencing the masses. Luther's first four pamphlets appeared in 1520, and about the same time Ulrich von Hutten—modelling himself on Luther and at his instigation—began to produce works in German prose. In 1520 he published his 'Complaint in German' against the decay and corruption of the Church. One year later, when Charles V was elected Emperor, Hutten published another pamphlet entitled: 'How the Popes have been against the German Emperors.' German thus became a political language. *Luther's Philological Achievement*

Dürer, following in the footsteps of Notker Teutonicus and Lucidarius, turned German prose into a scientific language. His phrasing is often uncouth, he had a hard struggle with meanings and the moulding and rendering of thought, but he nevertheless contrived to turn the German of his time into a vehicle which would convey a theory of art to his fellow-countrymen. With infinite trouble and touching seriousness, he transformed himself from a writer of letters and diaries into a writer on matters of art, and he was the first to use German for this purpose. Compared with the huge volume of Luther's intellectual writings, Dürer's production was modest, but the intention and the achievement were equally important and equally bold. *Dürer's Scientific German*

Even before 1520 Dürer had belonged to a circle of men of high intellectual gifts and social position, which had formed itself around the Vicar General of the Augustin Eremite monastery in the Weinmarkt, Johann von Staupitz. This circle was deeply impressed by the early writings of Luther. Staupitz, Holzschuher, Ebner, Nützel, Scheurl, Spengler and Dürer were in favour of a return to the original sources of Christianity and of personal participation in religious questions. Doubts as to the propriety of ecclesiastical institutions were less important to these men than the question of the 'justification' of the soul in the eyes of God. Lazarus Spengler was clerk to the Council of Nuremberg and had been a friend of Dürer's since their early days; he was an upright and active man, and one of the most gifted orators and writers in council circles. He met Luther personally when the latter passed through Nuremberg in 1518 on his way to Augsburg. Luther called Spengler, whose 'Defence' of the Wittenberg monk was printed in German, the real Reformer of Nuremberg. We know that Dürer and Spengler exchanged witty verses, but they must certainly have discussed more earnest subjects together. *Supporters of Luther in Nuremberg*

From the Dutch painter Jan van Scorel, who was Dürer's pupil in Nuremberg before 1519, we know that even at that time Dürer supported the teaching of Luther, which, to use the Dutchman's own words, was already beginning to *Dürer and the old Church* 'move' the German world. Like his Nuremberg friends, Dürer believed in the possibility of Reform within the old Church, from which he never seceded. Before their journey to the Netherlands, Dürer and his wife went on a pilgrimage to Vierzehnheiligen near Bamberg. During their stay abroad, Frau Agnes went regularly to confession—and Dürer made a note of the 'stivers' which she gave to the monk. Dürer never left the Church, either openly or privately, but his

Supporters of Luther in Antwerp

mind wrestled with the problem of his attitude towards religion. In Antwerp he was able to continue the religious discussions he had begun in Nuremberg, for Luther's writings had been circulating in Antwerp since 1518 and had been reprinted there. The Augustin convents (Luther himself had been an Augustin friar) were one of the chief centres of the movement for religious reform. Dürer went often to the Observant monastery of St. André in Antwerp and made a sketch of its Prior in token of gratitude. With the Vicar General Link, a native of Nuremberg, he was on such close terms of friendship that he asked the 'Vicarius' to take some of the more bulky items of his baggage home with him, namely the large turtle's shell, the fisherman's shield, the long pipe, the long gun and the fishes' fins, and two small casks of lemons and capers. He also frequented another, very different circle, in which the Luther movement was eagerly discussed with a view to its political possibilities—that of the wealthy and cultured Portuguese merchants, the 'factors' of the King of Portugal, among whom he found his first patrons and from whom he received much hospitality. Dürer thus spent the critical years of the German Reform movement in a foreign country, and more-over, in the territory of its bitterest opponent, Charles V. In Antwerp every item of news concerning the religious controversy in Germany was eagerly received and discussed by friend and foe. In Antwerp there lived, like an ambassador of Humanism, the 'arch-heretic' Erasmus of Rotterdam, but in Antwerp, too, there worked the clever and energetic Papal Legate Aleander, who demanded 'half a dozen Lutherans, to be burned alive'.

False Report of Luther's Arrest

Into this atmosphere of acute tension there fell like a bomb the news that Luther had been kidnapped during his return from the Diet of Worms. Dürer was in Antwerp; he had 'counterfeited cleanly and diligently' in oil colours 'Jobsten' (his host Plankvelt) and the latter's wife, when the rumour reached the city that Luther had been 'treacherously' arrested. A wave of indignation swept over the city. Dürer, usually so sparing and careful in his choice of words, suddenly became eloquent. The arid pages of his little account-book are covered with lamentations—indignation at what he supposed was a violation of the imperial safe-conduct, grief at the loss of this man illuminated with the Holy Ghost, dismay of the flock deprived of its shepherd, wild searching for a successor—all these emotions are jumbled together in their search for expression and, strangely enough, find it, which in a man like Dürer can only be attributed to the effect of violent emotion. Dürer writes: 'Whether he lives or whether they have murdered him, I do not know, but he has suffered in the cause of Christian truth . . . Ah, God in Heaven! have pity upon us; pray for us, Lord Jesus Christ; save us when our time shall come, preserve in us the true Christian faith, summon with Thy voice

ST. PAUL AND ST. MARK. Detail from the 'Four Apostles'. 1526. Munich, Aeltere Pinakothek

Thy scattered sheep . . . Call together once more the sheep of Thy fold, many of whom are still to be found in the Roman church, together with Indians, Muscovites, Russians and Greeks, who have been scattered by the covetousness of the Popes and by the false odour of sanctity . . . And if we lose this man, who has written more clearly than any man in these past 140 years, to whom Thou hast granted the evangelical spirit, then do we pray Thee, O Heavenly Father, that Thou will grant Thy divine spirit to another, who may bring together again all Thy Holy Christian Church, that we may again live a pure and Christian life, and that through our good work, all infidels, Turks, heathens and 'Calicutians', may turn to us and accept the Christian faith . . . O God, if Luther is dead, who will henceforth expound to us so clearly the Holy Gospel? What might he not have written in twenty or thirty years! O all ye pious Christian men! Help me diligently to mourn this man inspired of God and pray to Him that He may send us another enlightened man!'

It was high time for Dürer to leave the Netherlands. On 13th July 1521, shortly after his departure, Luther's writings were publicly burned in Antwerp as a sequel to Aleander's enforcement of the Edict of Worms. Then came one blow after another. Cornelius Grapheus, who had presented Dürer with a copy of Luther's writings, was arrested, together with the Prior of the Augustin convent. In October Erasmus deemed it wiser to vanish from the scene of battle. In 1523 two young Augustin monks were burned at the stake in Brussels.

During the years which followed his return to Germany Dürer developed *Heroic* that state of mind which inspired him to create the great works of his late period— *Sentiments* the Nuremberg portraits and the 'Four Apostles' (actually, three Apostles and one Evangelist). These masterly works, to which Dürer dedicated himself with all the gravity befitting a 'last will and testament', were influenced by local episodes in the great spiritual battle of the Reformation, but in them he also expresses to a greater degree than in any other work the heroic sentiments of the age.

Dürer found in Luther's achievements and words in the religious field exactly what he had so earnestly sought in the field of art—certainty, final clarification and liberation. It was for this that he had gone to Italy, had searched through books and questioned men, for this that he had meditated and racked his brains until he stood on the borders of the dark realms of melancholy. Dürer's sympathy with Luther's spiritual experience and his ready acceptance of the triumphant spirit of the Reformation are already manifested in the 'Knight, Death and the Devil'. His 'Four Apostles' are his formal confession and courageous defence of the new ideals. Such an interpretation of the engraving can be easily proved; the painting speaks for itself. Dürer's 'Knight, Death and the Devil' is an allegory of *125* the combatant ethical spirit of Luther's time; the 'Four Apostles' is a 'political *82-4* hymn', a direct contribution to the social and religious controversy. Neither of these works should be viewed from a purely aesthetic standpoint. Each must be considered in the light of Dürer's whole personality and the spirit of the age.

Like the 'Apocalypse'—Dürer's first major achievement—the 'Four Apostles' was painted on the artist's own initiative, and not in fulfilment of a patron's commission. In the autumn of 1526 Dürer offered to present to the Nuremberg Council 'a panel to which he had dedicated more diligence than to other paintings', in order that this work might be 'preserved as a memory of him'. This was the painting of the 'Four Apostles'. The Council accepted the gift—but also paid Dürer a fee for it. The older scholars, e.g. Thausing and Zucker, saw in the 'Four Apostles' Dürer's 'monument' to the Reformation, or even went further than this and described it as a monumental propaganda picture directed against the Roman church. A more thorough knowledge of the history of the Reform movement in Nuremberg, and in particular the studies of Merz, Heidrich, Neumann, von Schubert and others, have revealed how very much more complicated were the personal, artistic, religious and political circumstances surrounding the genesis of Dürer's last great work.

Warning to 'Worldly Regents'

Undoubtedly we can read on the foreheads of these four figures what Thausing has called the boldest achievement of the German race—the Reformation. But the moral warning which they convey is a warning against the enemies in the Reformation's own camp. The biblical references inscribed on the pictures (II Peter, 2. 1 and 2; I John, 4. 1–3; II Timothy, 3. 1–7; Mark, 12. 38–40) are intended as an appeal to the consciences of all 'worldly regents' and to remind them of one of the hardest tasks which confront the rulers of mankind—the eradication of noxious and misleading elements from the ranks of their own party. The term 'regents' is a reference to the Nuremberg form of local government, which consisted, according to a statement by Christoph Scheurl dating from 1516, of the 'Little Council' (42 members) and the 'Grand Council' (over 200 members). Among the members of the 'Little Council' were the thirteen 'old' and thirteen 'young' burgomasters. From the thirteen 'old' burgomasters were elected the seven supreme 'Regenten' and from these again the three 'Hauptmänner', of whom two were treasurers or 'Losunger', while the third was the leading representative of the craftsmen.

Position in Nuremberg

But was the position in Nuremberg really so serious as to warrant this warning from Dürer and to make him feel that it was incumbent upon him to nail his theses to his pictorial confession and deposit a political testament in the hands of the Council? At the time of the Nuremberg Diet in 1524, there were two opposing factions in the city—a section of the populace which was led, but also misled, by ecclesiastical elements sympathetic to Luther, and a Council which was conscious of its responsibilities, but was politically by no means united. The 'worldly regents' saw their position threatened by very powerful adversaries—by the Emperor, by the Southern German Catholic princes, and by the Bishop of Bamberg, to whose diocese Nuremberg belonged. In the convents of the Dominicans, Franciscans and Carmelites, the papal party still possessed strongholds, but the new church service after the Wittenberg pattern had already been introduced into the two parish churches. The supporters of Luther, however, were lacking in determination and in uniform leadership.

General Feeling of Insecurity

There was social, as well as religious unrest and this added to the confusion. A paralysing sensation of insecurity lay over the town. It was from the midst of such a situation that Dürer wrote in December 1524 to Nikolaus Kratzer, court astronomer to Henry VIII of England: 'Of new rumours it is not good to write at this time, but there are many evil things afoot.' The spring of 1525 brought a clarification of the position in so far as the Council 'gave the Pope and the Papacy their congee'. After the decisive religious discussion between the mendicant friars and the evangelical pastors, most of the convents were suppressed and recalcitrant priests were either warned or banished from the city. There was now no longer any reason to regard the Catholic Church as a serious danger, and in 1526 Dürer would hardly have thought it necessary to accompany his pictures by a warning to the Council against an enemy who had already been vanquished. But another peril had arisen. The contrast between high and low, rich and poor, which had led to the first political and social movements among the populace during the fifteenth century, became acute at the time of the Reformation, when socialistic tendencies were combined with anti-clerical.

The great social movement which swept over Central and Southern Germany in 1525 is known rather loosely as the 'Peasant War', but it was really a 'Burgher War' also, and was fought in the towns as well as in the open country. The cities had to defend their dual position as powerful landowners and town administrators. The instigators of this unrest had a mixture of anticlerical, reformatory and radical-communistic aims. In Nuremberg in 1524 an innkeeper from Wöhrd and a clothmaker's journeyman were executed for inciting the peasants and burghers to free themselves from their oppressive burdens. In 1525 unrest among the peasants spread from Eastern Franconia to the environs of Nuremberg. The burghers thought the time had come to pay no more taxes and to rebel against all forms of imposts. All the 'rebels', however, invoked the Holy Gospels and the Word of God. The Bible was considered to be not only the source of faith, but also a code of social law according to which Germany must be reformed. The 'twelve articles of the peasants', which still met with Luther's full approval, were also a mixture of economic demands and religious arguments. The popular preachers who inveighed against tithe and rents, gave force and effect to their arguments by quoting passages from the Bible. It was for this reason that the Nuremberg Council caused sermons to be preached explaining the real significance of the 'Freedom of a Christian Man'—to the great dissatisfaction of the 'man in the street'. 'When they see,' writes Pirckheimer, 'that things will not be divided and made common property, as they had hoped, then they curse Luther and all his adherents.' Thomas Münzer issued a pamphlet entitled: 'Against Martin Luther, the spiritless, soft-living Flesh in Wittenberg.' Not only iconoclasts and ana-baptists, but also unruly Augustin friars threatened to appropriate the Lutheran movement for their own purposes and to ruin it with their excesses. Free will asserted itself against the authority of the law, while the individual boasted of his rights as opposed to those of the community. The intellectuals, to whom Dürer had been drawn and whom he was bound to support, were concerned with the preservation of the authority of the Council in secular and ecclesiastical matters and with the combating of wild sectarianism and destructive individual action on the side of the Lutherans.

Peasant War and Burgher War

Iconoclasts and Anabaptists

The external impulse which drove Dürer to abandon his atelier and enter the
arena of conflicting opinions, was the trial of Denck, the Rector of the school of
St. Sebaldus, and the three 'godless painters', Hans Sebald Beham, Barthel Beham
and Georg Pencz, in January 1525. Denck believed that the Scriptures should—to
use Luther's expression—'be thrust under the bench' and replaced by his own
mystic doctrine of the achievement of Godhead through the Love of God. The
three pupils of Dürer who had fallen under the influence of this strange man,
went even further. With all the radical-mindedness of young artists, they denied
the fundamentals of Christianity—the Bible, Baptism, Communion and even the
person of Christ and God. The judges were men with a knowledge of the world
and of their fellow-men and they did not take the exuberant utterances of the
young painters too seriously. It is true that all the accused were banished, but
when the peasant uprising had been suppressed, and the city authorities felt that
their position was once more assured, the young artists were allowed to return
to Nuremberg. Dürer, however, felt it incumbent upon him to uphold the in-
violable authority of the Word of God both privately and publicly, as a friend
and ardent supporter of Luther and as the acknowledged leader of the artistic
fraternity. It was not only the case of the godless painters that worried both Dürer
and the Council; there were other artists in Nuremberg as well who tended
towards apocalyptic fanaticism, sectarianism, anabaptistry and Communistic
ideas, e.g. the painters Hans Greiffenberger and Hans Platner, the form-cutter
Hieronymus Andreae, and the painter Paul Lautensack the Elder. To defend the
pure doctrine of Luther against such 'false prophets', Dürer entered into the fray,
with pictures and the written word, on the side of authority, thereby defending
not only his own reputation and the honour of his station, but also art itself, for
anabaptistry went hand in hand with iconoclastic tendencies. In the dedication
(to Pirckheimer) of his 'Art of Mensuration' (1525) Dürer complains that 'now
with us and in our times the art of painting is held by some in ill repute and it is
said that it serves idolatry'.

Dürer was aware that his unequivocal attitude to these things would have met
with the approval of Luther, who had rejected in the sharpest terms the invocation
of the Gospel by the 'mad, raving populace'—'He who dies for the princely
cause, will become a holy martyr; he who dies for the other will go to the devil;
therefore they should be overthrown, stifled and killed by all those who can,
secretly and publicly, for it must be remembered that there is none more poisonous,
more harmful and more devilish than a rebellious man.' Dürer's support of
authority was not only the expression of his political views as a member of the
city bourgeoisie, it was also a proof of his clear sense of realism. Once the struggle
in Nuremberg had gone in favour of the Lutherans, all constructive elements had
to combine to protect the real ideals of the movement against internal party
dissension and to give to the Reformation that permanent form which would
transform it from the religious-political movement of the revolutionary years
into the Evangelical Church. Dürer's 'Four Apostles' stand at this parting of the
ways like watchmen of the olden days.

The positive content of the inscriptions also breathes the spirit of Lutheranism. Firstly, the emphasis on Christ as God Incarnate, Dürer's belief in the Lord 'who has achieved our salvation'. Secondly, his unshakable attitude towards the Holy Scriptures, the 'holy pure Gospel'. Thirdly, Dürer's profession of his support of higher authority even in religious questions, which in those days were not private matters, but crucial problems of policy and statesmanship. It was on such a conception that Dürer based his theory of the rights and duties of the State in matters concerning religion, which in this case include the suppression of the Lutheran 'street-corner preachers'.

The course of events after Dürer's death justified his attitude. From a letter written by Pirckheimer in 1530 to the mathematician Tscherte, we learn that both Dürer and Pirckheimer were deeply disappointed in their hope that 'Roman knavishness and the roguery of monks and priests would be corrected', for 'when one looks at it, it would seem that things have changed for the worse and the Lutheran knaves make the other knaves seem pious'. The ideals of the Reform movement were gravely compromised by the materialism of certain of its supporters and by the decline of morals within the Lutheran party, and the opposition to this decline came from that sound category of burghers to which Dürer, Hans Sachs and others belonged. Luther himself condemned far more vigorously than Erasmus, far more clearly than Pirckheimer and far more passionately than Dürer, the moral laxity of the new Evangelical Church. In 1532, for example, he wrote: 'Peasants, burghers and nobles, notwithstanding the light of the Gospels, are now more avaricious, more haughty and more arrogant and show more wantonness and pride than they did under the darkness of the Papacy . . . and they are ten times more wicked than they were under the Papacy.'

Events after Dürer's Death

Why did Dürer choose the 'Four Apostles' as the motive of the work which was to represent his confession of faith? Since the beginnings of monumental Christian art, the Apostles had been regarded not only as heroes, but also as preachers and heralds of things to come. Dürer was thus remaining in the old tradition by making these heroes of Christianity speak once more, by making them the mouthpieces of eternal truth. The 'Four Apostles' of 1526 have a whole series of forerunners in Dürer's studies of great religious personalities. In the 'Jesus among the Doctors' he surrounds the Saviour with figures of thinkers, holding books, searching in them and emphasizing the text with word, glance or gesture. Two years later (1508) the scribes have become Apostles, standing by the tomb of the Virgin as she ascends to Heaven. Dürer's Jewish scribes show traces of the grotesqueness with which Nordic art depicted witches and sorcerers, but southern monumentality surrounds the Christian heroes with dignity and stature in the Heller altar-piece. The study for St. Paul (L. 19, Berlin) has a 'heroic garb'. The head of an Apostle with upturned eyes in a drawing in Vienna no longer shows the hairsplitting spirit of the scribes, but is an expression of the purest piety of a believing heart. Later, Dürer's Apostles cease to be subsidiary figures in pictures of events and become independent 'personalities'—first of all, the figures of St. Paul and St. Thomas in the engravings of 1514, who are men moved

Forerunners of the 'Four Apostles'

60

M

by both inner and external emotion, grave messengers of Christ, whose ardent spirit shines in the haloes around their heads. These 'reminders' of the Gospel are transformed in the engravings of the Apostles Bartholomew, Simon (1523) and Philip (1526) into 'rocks of the Church', defying all opposition, and at the same time the source of the living spring of faith.

We thus arrive at the threshold of Dürer's last version of the theme—his painting of the 'Four Apostles'. Between the two groups of engravings of Apostles, there lies, as Meder has shown, a series of painted heads of Apostles, of which those of St. James and St. Philip (1516) have been preserved (in Florence). That Dürer was concerned with the formation of ideal types of spiritual warriors, of men obsessed by their mission, and not with depicting characters from the history of religion, is proved by the fact that he used the head of St. Paul from the engraving of 1514 for the countenance of the St. James in Florence (Uffizi). Dürer used this kind of transference from one person to another on one other occasion—the study for the robe of St. Philip (engraving of 1526, L. 580, Vienna) was used for the St. Paul in the 'Four Apostles'. Large-scale designs for the heads of St. Mark, St. Paul and St. Peter—now authenticated beyond all reasonable doubt—may be seen in the Kupferstichkabinett in Berlin (L. 72, 89, 369). The moving figure of the weeping St. John (L. 29, Bremen) also belongs in the broader sense to this community of saints—it was intended for a Crucifixion which was never painted.

Portrait Heads   There is also a link between the 'Four Apostles' and another side of Dürer's work—the late portraits. From portraits of men of strong character (the Electors of Mainz and Saxony, Pirckheimer, Melanchthon and Varnbüler), Dürer passed to the expressive heads of the Apostles. The portraits of his great living contemporaries were Dürer's preparation for those mighty figures, in which the essence of the German Reformation is embodied for all time.

An examination of the 'Four Apostles' shows that two of them are conceived and executed as the chief figures, the 'leading' heads, while the other two are but secondary figures. St. John and St. Paul dominate the stage, while St. Peter and St. Mark are added and inserted wherever room can be found for them. This is a method of composition which Dürer had had in mind since his Venetian days, since he first saw Giovanni Bellini's 'Madonna enthroned with four Saints', painted in 1488 (Venice, Frari). The youthful Dürer was impressed by the way Bellini inserted his mighty figures in the narrow panels—two in the forefront and two in the 'gaps' of the background. The impression remained dormant in his mind and twenty-five years later became the germ of the construction of the 'Four Apostles'. Bellini's painting is a triptych, and it is probable that this was also Dürer's original intention, i.e. that a centre panel—Pauli suggests a Madonna Enthroned in the style of Dürer's sketch in Bayonne (L. 363)—would have been flanked by the two panels with the figures of the four Apostles. Did Dürer abandon this idea because he no longer wished to present a 'santa conversazione' of 'free and beautiful characters' (which is Jacob Burckhardt's description of Bellini's great painting), but a sermon by desperately earnest men of God, in which no woman, not even the holiest and most venerable of all women, might participate? Or did Dürer limit himself to two panels of Apostles, simply because, in the course of his work, he decided that the work should hang in the Rathaus and not in a church, and thus abandoned the idea of a purely devotional picture? Those are questions which it is impossible to answer. The external arrangement of the four Apostles is in accord with the inner grouping. The texts which accompany the foremost Apostles, St. John and St. Paul, contain the whole substance of the sermon.

The relationship is different when we come to consider the action of the picture. St. John and St. Peter are absorbed in the Word; St. Paul and St. Mark stand before us with the Bible closed, but the sword drawn. The old mediaeval contrast between the 'vita contemplativa' and the 'vita activa' is embodied in these two pairs of Apostles, of which one is concerned with the study of the divine truths as manifested in the Word, and the other with the defence of these truths against disbelievers, scoffers and those who would lead us astray. Reading and the fortification of belief through reading are no less strongly emphasized than the threat of the sword. These men were not to be trifled with—no more than Luther himself, who did not hesitate to advocate resort to the sword, when the Word was not enough.

What gives to these four figures of Apostles a visible and intellectual unity is, first of all, their mission—to profess, to warn and to threaten. But there is also the fact that they belong to the race of religious heroes, the racial characteristics of which are imprinted on each of these four heads. There is a quadruple variation of the heroic type, and similarly, a quadruple division of the spiritual mood and of the message they convey, for the inscription contains quotations from the writings of all four. It is characteristic of Dürer's scientific processes of thought that, in order to achieve the individualization of the four figures, he did not select at random four impressive heads from among his studies, but, after deep reflection, made each one of the four represent a fundamental attitude of the human soul. For this reason we would be wrong to ignore the assertion of the writing-master Neudörfer, who was closely associated with Dürer during the years in which he created the 'Four Apostles' and who executed the inscriptions for him. Neudörfer states that Dürer conceived the four figures as representing the four complexions or temperaments. This may be true to the extent that in Dürer's conception the wealth of individual spirituality could be reduced to the basic formulae of the melancholic, choleric, sanguine and phlegmatic temperaments. St. John has the features of a melancholic plunged in meditation—he is a brother to Dürer's mighty 'Melancolia'. St. Peter's rôle is one of phlegmatic composure. St. Mark—in the chalk drawing of 1526 even more clearly than in the painting—has the wide-open eyes and dishevelled hair of the choleric—his next-of-kin in Dürer's profane work is Holzschuher, whom Dürer painted in the same year. St. Paul is firmly grasping the hilt of his sword—the energy of the sanguine temperament is on the point of breaking forth.

The deeper conception—at all events for modern eyes—is that of the St. John and St. Peter. Here the heroic element is all character, heroic strength has become the spirit of heroism. How typical of Dürer that he should have given to the

Variations of the Heroic Type

50
head of St. John the features of Melanchthon, the man of peace, the scholar and educationalist whose portrait he engraved in 1526! One could even say that in the four Apostles we have four Luthers—the man of the Bible, the thinker, the leader and the fighter. The four expressive heads are like crowns to the monumental treatment of the draperies, which, in relation to the spiritual content of the whole picture, give an impression of simplicity, almost of monumental bleakness. The resolute figures rise before our eyes like statues. The chilling spirit of Italian classicism created the forms of these draperies, from which the expressive power of Gothic folds has vanished. Dürer made a sketch for the robe of St. Paul as early as 1523 (L. 580, Vienna), which he also used for the St. Philip in the engraving of 1526.

The typically German mixture of spiritual tension and grandiose form, of idealism and earthliness, of pulpit eloquence and expediency, of ethical absolutism and an artist's absorption in his problems, tends to alienate the foreign observer, as does the essence of the German character in general. 'Confessional' pictures are remote from the modern man, because he no longer understands the mission they fulfilled in public life and tends to judge, from the purely aesthetic standpoint, something that has developed on very much broader lines. Dürer's 'Four Apostles' was intended for the low-ceilinged room in the Rathaus of Nuremberg in which the city treasurers worked, that is to say for a room in which decisions vital to the future of the city were taken. Against their dark background, in frames so narrow that their physical power and intellectual significance seem to overflow the edges, these four figures must have had an almost frightening, or at all events deeply impressive effect. The 'worldly Regents' were compelled to come quite close to them, for in addition to the figures, there was the inscription—those lines of text which were the mediaeval method of heightening the eloquence of the figures, like the scrolls in the hands of saints in earlier times.

The Inscription

Carl Neumann, who has made the most thorough investigation of the inscription of the 'Four Apostles', draws attention to the curious lack of harmony between the monumental attitude of the figures and the calligraphic flourishes of the inscription. This text for a sermon is not inserted in the form of an ornament within the area of the painting, as is the case with Dürer's portrait engravings of the Elector of Saxony or of his friend Varnbüler; disproportionately small and confused, it appears beneath the feet of the mighty Apostles. Dürer did not attempt to suit it to the style of the draperies by choosing monumental roman letters, but preferred to use this small 'Fraktur' or Gothic script. Johann Neudörfer, as he himself tells us in 1547, wrote this text in Dürer's work-room. The so-called Nuremberg 'Fraktur', designed by Neudörfer and Andräes, was used in 1522 for the Triumphal Car of the Emperor Maximilian and for the printed editions of Dürer's theoretical works. The fate of this inscription is curious. In 1627, when the Elector Maximilian of Bavaria wished to acquire Dürer's 'Four Apostles' for Munich, the Nuremberg Council, in an endeavour to save the painting for Dürer's native city, drew attention to the disapproval which the wording of the inscription might arouse among the Jesuits of Munich. Maximilian, however, found a solution for

Ill. p. 124

YOUNG VENETIAN WOMAN. 1505. Vienna, Kunsthistorisches Museum

the problem. He had the inscription sawn off and sent it back to Nuremberg together with Gärtner's copy of the original.

By adopting this combination of picture and text, which to us seems so strange, Dürer was, at the height of his development as a painter, returning to a tradition of his work as an illustrator. The 'Apocalypse', the two woodcut 'Passions', the 'Life of the Virgin' and the 'Triumphal Car of the Emperor Maximilian' were accompanied by printed texts. When Dürer had to create a picture designed to appeal not only to the senses, but also to the intellect, he provided this documentary picture with a written commentary, thereby emphasizing once again the popular illustrative character of his art.

Picture and Text

Art did not give the age of Luther and Dürer a new imprint. On the contrary, the arts acquired new forms and subjects because life now had a new meaning. The fear of the approaching end of the world, which had dominated the end of the fifteenth century, gradually gave way to the dawn of a heightened sense of existence. This new Germany, upon which the eyes of Europe were focused, was not, like Italy, primarily concerned with questions of artistic culture, but was dominated by political and religious movements. This upheaval in the life of the nation let loose long-dormant forces, the violence of which terrified timid minds, while the leaders strove to master them. The full import of these forces was not appreciated by those who were living at the time. In Germany there was no 'Renaissance' in the sense implied when we speak of the Italian Renaissance.

New Meaning of Life

Although the so-called great intellectual movement had a certain aspect of universality, nevertheless the Renaissance was in its origins and until the end of the thirteenth and the fourteenth centuries, fundamentally a national, Italian phenomenon. As an ideal of a patriotic revival, the Renaissance idea first germinated in the minds of the exiled Dante, Petrarch and Rienzi, but the ideal they had in mind was an intellectual, and above all an artistic ideal. The domain in which the Renaissance gained a firm footing, in which it acquired a more than national significance and, on account of its power over men, became dangerous for all who were not Italians, was the domain of fantasy. The cultural idea of the Renaissance —there was also the secondary phenomenon of a political Renaissance idea— drew its strength from the instinctive aversion of the Italian mind for everything foreign—and in Italy 'foreign' at that time meant everything to do with France, the Netherlands and Germany. The Italian Renaissance was able to bring about a rebirth of antique Roman art, because there was a blood-relationship between the Italian mind and that of the Antique. The Italians of the Renaissance were inspired by the traditions of their own soil and of their own blood. Patriotic feeling, national pride and consciousness of race surrounded the cradle of the Italian Renaissance, the ultimate aim of which was the achievement of a national style of life and art. But for this very reason, the Renaissance could not possibly become an 'article for export'.

National Character of the Italian Renaissance

What art historians call the 'German Renaissance' was an adaptation, an elaboration, and also an incorporation and 'Germanization' of foreign intellectual matter—but unfortunately it was rarely accompanied by a rebirth or restoration of the creative powers of the German people. It is, however, possible to discern the beginnings of a German Renaissance in the sense of a regeneration (Dürer) of the past glories of German art. We know of Peter Vischer the Elder, for example, that he was an ardent collector of old Franconian wood-carvings, and Adolf Feulner has pointed out that the classicism of the Apostles on the tomb of St. Sebaldus was transmitted through works, such as the synagogue of the sculptures in Bamberg Cathedral, which were considered to be 'antique'. In other words, inspiration was drawn from old German, not foreign models. Peter Vischer had never been to Italy.

Rebirth of the Moral Ideal in Germany

In one field, however, Germany's leadership was undisputed—in the field of religion. For the Germans the Renaissance period meant an intensification and deepening of the feeling of piety. And in Germany, too, we see a rebirth—the revival of the demand for a moral ideal. For Germany, too, the Renaissance period was, in the words of Jacob Burckhardt, 'the period of the Discovery of Man'. But it was the discovery not of the artistic or scientific man, but of the man who is responsible to God and his conscience alone—a type of man which was rediscovered and liberated by the Lutheran Reformation.

Form and Word

This intellectual revolution, this Renaissance of the spirit, could not be reflected —as it was in Italy—in architecture, in sculpture or in painting, but it found an even clearer and more decisive mode of expression in books, pamphlets and illustrations. In the beginning of the Italian Renaissance was form, in the beginning of the German Reformation was the Word. The two essentials of the Lutheran Reformation—the demand for a standard of morals and the determination to 'let the Word be'—are clearly expressed in Dürer's 'Four Apostles', in the figures and in the inscriptions beneath them.

THE FIRST KNOT
(About 1507)

CHAPTER ELEVEN

SERVICE AND FREEDOM

THAT art is 'free' and that it is freedom which distinguishes 'fine' from 'applied' art, is a dogma which originated in the earliest academies and gradually passed into the general conception of art. By freedom was meant the exemption of art from prejudice and material aims, the independence of the artist vis-à-vis patrons and their wishes, the absence of set programmes and precepts. Dependence of the artist on corporate bodies or communities, on clients and commissions, was held to constitute subjection. But this aesthetic liberalism, which sang the praises of the freedom of artists, forgot that such a blessing might be purchased at far too high a price, since it exonerates the artist from the normal conditions of life, and that the spiritual loneliness and rootlessness of the modern artist, working exclusively according to his own ideas, is one of the consequences of individual freedom. It also forgot that 'service', for an artist, does not necessarily mean loss of liberty, but represents a beneficial constraint, freedom from petty worries, order and security. It may be a good thing for an artist if the age in which he lives offers him an outlet for the products of his genius. Those who complain of lack of freedom are the little artists; great artists have known how to preserve their freedom while carrying out definite, circumscribed tasks, and, conversely, when undertaking independent work, have imposed obligations on themselves.

Aesthetic Liberalism

We should be misreading history, and misunderstanding Dürer, if we were to pity him because, during the best years of his career as an artist, he employed so much of his strength and fantasy in the service of the Emperor Maximilian. It will be more relevant if we consider how Dürer preserved his freedom in the course of his 'service' and how he imposed 'service' upon himself within his 'freedom'. Dürer did not look upon service as an imposition, because for him it was a natural thing that art should be in the service of that for which it was created —'the art of painting is used in the service of the Churches'. It was also used in the service of the courts, of the burghers and of the scholars—in other words in the service of life.

Art in the Service of Life

Viewed from another standpoint, from within, the antithesis 'Service and Freedom' has a special meaning of its own. It is not merely a question of Dürer's relationship to his employers, it is not limited to his work in the service of religious and literary ideas and the degree of freedom he was granted in the composition of his pictures—it is manifested in his own relationship to the subject of each of his works. In everything to do with his subjects Dürer imposed rigid conditions upon himself, and profound respect for the smallest details guided his hand. By paying such minute attention to subordinate details, Dürer did not endanger the effect which the subject produced on himself and his contemporaries; on the contrary he gave it that impressiveness, lifelikeness and living warmth which to him were inseparable from art. The significance of the subject-matter for Dürer was not a question of 'picturesqueness'; he never painted a 'still life', because for

Importance of the Subject

'EX-LIBRIS' OF WILLIBALD PIRCKHEIMER
(Woodcut, attributed to Dürer)

him even dead things were alive. If he had to draw all sorts of chattels, he did not consider that this implied a loss of freedom; he looked upon it as a self-imposed task and as a service not worth mentioning which he, as an artist, was rendering to life. In this he was helped by his origin and upbringing, by his habit and philosophy of life.

Dürer was not born in a painter's atelier; he sprang from a goldsmith's workshop and the family traditions of goldsmiths. Love for the individual subject was in him the starting-point of his artistic attitude to the world. His love for it was not subordinated to the pleasures of thought. He never abandoned this faithfulness to, and joy in, his subject; the link which bound him to his craftsman's background was never broken. Throughout his life he remained a goldsmith constantly engaged on other, more important tasks. His profoundest works are the very ones in which we find the greatest attention to details, which were meant to be taken seriously—the furnishings of St. Jerome's study, the instruments in the 'Melancolia', the seven lamps of fire around the kneeling St. John, the goblet and the reins of the 'Great Fortune', the turtle's shell in the 'Sea-monster', the bed-curtain in the woodcut of the death of the Virgin (Life of the Virgin), the table of Herodias (woodcut of 1511), the candlesticks and the shrine on the altar before which the penitent is scourging himself (woodcut of 1510), which reminds us of the shrine containing the imperial relics (Nuremberg, Germanisches Nationalmuseum). It is not merely the realism, the accuracy of rendering, which are important in Dürer's case, but the fact that all these objects exist of their own right and have not been sacrificed on the altar of the representation of ideas. A man of this way of thinking would see in the drawing of a coat of arms far more than the mere execution of a commission; for him it would be a free artistic creation ranking on the same level as other work. Dürer's heraldic and ornamental works are often considered as the stepchildren of his art and are therefore neglected, but they are important if we wish to understand Dürer, and they contributed towards the reputation which he gained for himself in the world.

75
103
102, 97

Dürer's age loved emblems, devices, crests, book-plates and armorial devices of all kinds, in the first place because it loved everything symbolical. For the title-pages of Pirckheimer's books Dürer designed a beautiful border (1513). Heraldry was a widespread branch of learning; the painting of coats of arms was all part of the day's work. In every device people detected a meaning, every coat of arms 'spoke'. The popularity of hieroglyphics in Humanistic circles at the time of Maximilian deserves mention at this point. The hieroglyphics complex embraced a field of knowledge different from that of astrology, but had nevertheless many points in common with the latter. Giehlow's exhaustive studies have shown that Horapollon's 'Hieroglyphics', translated by Pirckheimer from Greek into Latin and illustrated by Dürer, was one of the chief sources of the symbolism on the Triumphal Arch of Maximilian. Egyptian hieroglyphics had not yet been deciphered, but were looked upon as evidence of profound wisdom. Horapollon, for example, constructed a mystical zoology on the basis of hieroglyphs taken from the animal world.

The Science of Hieroglyphics

THE ARMS OF THE REICH AND OF NUREMBERG
(1521, Woodcut)

*Heraldic
Ornament*

Apart from its symbolical significance, heraldic ornament in Dürer's time had an importance of its own from the purely formal point of view. Heraldic foliage developed as an independent growth on the somewhat overladen tree of Late Gothic ornamentation. This art found ample scope in tracery, reticulated and groined vaulting, hood-mouldings, finials, crockets, brackets, corbels etc. Dürer's 'Life of the Virgin' contains numerous examples of such craftsman's work, sometimes reminding us of the work of a turner or carpenter, at other times of a goldsmith's (e.g. the rich ornamentation of the archway in the woodcut of the Betrothal, or the foliage above the rounded doorway in the Circumcision). When Dürer draws coats of arms, we seem to detect in the foliation of the helmets the joy of a goldsmith's or armourer's hand. Despite his pleasure in the decorative aspect of armorial art, however, Dürer did not forget the strictly heraldic elements. When Michel Beheim, because he did not like it, returned a design by Dürer for his coat of arms, Dürer, in his reply, asked him to leave the mantle as he had drawn it, so that it should not cover up the torse, i.e. the twisted sendal strips, crowning the helmet. Heraldically speaking, Dürer was right; Beheim was adopting the subjective standpoint of a layman (woodcut, about 1507–10).

*Coats of Arms
Ill. pp. 13, 178*

We possess paintings and prints of coats of arms by Dürer. It was a custom of the time to combine coats of arms with the portraits of their bearers. Shutters, sliding or opening on hinges, for portraits have been preserved, e.g. the sliding shutters in Berlin (Deutsches Museum) bearing the arms of Hieronymus Holzschuher and Dorothea Münzer; in Nuremberg (Germanisches Nationalmuseum) with the arms of Oswolt Krell and Agathe von Essendorf, with 'wild men' as supporters; the arms of the Tuchers and Rieters in Weimar, borne by Hans and Felicitas Tucher; and in the Uffizi the combined arms of the Dürers and Holpers, which once belonged to the portrait of Dürer's father. Dürer, who was proud of these armorial bearings of his family, drew them for the woodcut of 1523. They show: on a field gules, a white door, with open wings or, beneath a penthouse roof, upon a triple mount vert, in a shield indented sinister. The helmet bears upon a torse the bust of a negro guardant sinister, with pointed cap and earrings, between a pair of mighty eagle's wings. The title-page of his 'Instructions on Fortification', which Dürer dedicated in 1527 to the then King and later Emperor Ferdinand, is adorned with the royal arms surrounded by the chain of the Golden Fleece. The third edition of the Nuremberg codex, 'Reformation der Stadt Nürnberg', has on the title-page the arms of the Reich and of the city of Nuremberg beneath a tablet inscribed 'Sancta Justitia 1521', supported by angels. Above we see the arms of the German Empire, denoting that the supreme imperial jurisdiction was in the hands of the city; below, on the left, is the shield with the Virgin Eagle, denoting (as Heinrich Brockhaus has established) the 'universitas' of the burghers, the corporation and community of the city; on the right is Nuremberg's second coat of arms, the parted shield, in which the colours, three bands of red and two of white, are taken from the 'blood banner', i.e. the enfeoffment banner of the old empire, while the demi-eagle denotes the city's share in

17

the imperial power. Among the private coats of arms which Dürer designed for friends, acquaintances or patrons, the arms of the brothers von Rogendorff are noteworthy for their decorative beauty and inspiration; according to his diary, Dürer sketched them in 1520 during his journey to the Netherlands, for execution as a woodcut.

Heraldic Ornamentation
140

A transition to semi-heraldic free ornamentation and embellishment is seen in the two imaginary coats of arms engraved on copper—Death (1503) and the Lion with a Cock (1503?). The 'wild man' with a cleft stick, through which the band of the shield runs, is Death, who is clasping a Nuremberg bride—a coat of arms which might well have served as frontispiece to a Dance of Death. A crowing cock, most unheraldic in its realism, surmounts the helmet of the escutcheon with the lion. This helmet must have formed part of the stock-in-trade of Dürer's atelier, for it appears on several other occasions, once even in a sketch alone (L. 327, Bayonne).

This heraldic bent, freed from the restraint of pure heraldry, is found constantly in Dürer's work as a characteristic of his ornamentation. With its mingling of the clear with the intricate—the rational and the romantic, the significant as well as the characteristic—heraldry was particularly suited to Dürer's conception of form. Horses' tails and birds' feathers, the hide of a rhinoceros and the fluttering lambrequin of a helmet, are heraldically rhythmicized and embellished. Such is the inspiration of the lightbearer known as the 'Leuchterweibchen' (L. 413, Vienna), drawn by Dürer for Pirckheimer, the meaning of which is: Wisdom as bringer of light, with the eloquent birch-tree crest of the Pirckheimers and the birch-bough bearing light. The celebrated engraving of the 'Sudarium of St. Veronica' with two angels (1513) is also quite heraldic in its conception, for the angels holding the Sudarium resemble the supporters of an armorial shield.

146

Portraits of Emperors

One of the few official commissions which Dürer received from the City of Nuremberg had a heraldic, historiographic character, and imposed upon him a close cohesion between content and form. In 1510 he was commissioned to paint the portraits of the Emperors Charlemagne and Sigismund in the coronation regalia of the Emperors of the Holy Roman Empire. Dürer made a series of careful studies of the imperial crown, orb and sword (L. 166, 167, 168, Nuremberg) and of the rest of the regalia—'this is the robe of the Holy Great Emperor Charles 1510' (L. 519, Vienna). In order to make the portrait of the Franconian emperor as lifelike as possible, Dürer loaned to him the fine, virile countenance of the court historian, Johannes Stabius.

In 1424 the Emperor Sigismund—after causing Huss to be burned at the stake—had handed over to a Nuremberg delegation in Prague the insignia and relics of the empire, which had subsequently peregrinated from city to city, from castle to castle. It is said that this precious collection was packed like a consignment of fish and that even the driver had no idea that he was conveying the holy symbols of the empire, until he saw a procession emerging from the gates of Nuremberg to receive them. The insignia and relics were housed in the church of the Hospital of the Holy Ghost, and every year until 1523, on the second Friday after Easter,

EMPEROR MAXIMILIAN. Water-colour, 1518. Vienna, Albertina

they were shown to the people on the 'holy stool' in front of the Frauenkirche in the market-place, the ceremony being known as the 'Heiltumsweisung'. Among them were the imperial crown, sceptre, orb and sword, made for the Emperor Conrad II (1024–1039), and sacred relics such as parts of the manger, pieces of the tablecloth used at the Last Supper, thorns from the Crown of Thorns. During the night before the 'Heiltumsweisung' the relics were placed in the chamber of relics of the Schopper Haus on the market-place, and Dürer's portraits were destined for this chamber—the Emperor Charlemagne as being supposedly the first wearer of the regalia, and Sigismund as the benefactor of Nuremberg who had entrusted the imperial treasures to the city for safe-keeping. (The shrine which contained the relics is now in the Germanisches Museum and the insignia themselves have been returned to Nuremberg.) As a boy and as a man, Dürer must often have seen and admired these most venerable products of the goldsmith's art. An echo of the excitement which overcame the populace on beholding the insignia is to be found in Goethe's 'Poetry and Truth'; as a boy, Goethe watched the entry of the insignia into Frankfurt am Main in 1764.

On the entrance wall of the Rathaus in Nuremberg are three large allegorical frescoes—the 'Harmony of Civic Government' (the word 'harmony' being, as Heinrich Brockhaus points out, used in the same figurative sense as 'concert' in the expression 'Concert of Europe'), the 'Administration of Justice', symbolized in the customary way by the story of the Calumny of Apelles, and the 'Triumphal Car of the Emperor'. The designs, at least for the two last-named pictures, were made by Dürer (L. 577, Vienna, Calumny of Apelles). Wölfflin and other writers are of the opinion that we also possess a decorative design by Dürer—the fine water-colour (1521, L. 407, London) of foliage and flowers with mythological episodes—for a wall pierced by Gothic windows. Three medallions contain stories of feminine triumphs—Bathsheba bathing, Samson and Delilah, Phyllis riding on the back of Aristotle; beneath, are a pelican in its nest, Pan and his pipes and a pelican feeding its young. The subject-matter, in my opinion, invalidates the supposition that these beautiful decorations were intended for the great hall of the austere town hall, but it is possible that they are the design mentioned in Dürer's diary of his journey to the Netherlands, where he writes that he has made a sketch for 'Tomasin' (Tomaso Bombelli) 'after which his house will be painted'. These antique heathen subjects would have appealed to a wealthy and cultured Italian, and it would seem as if Dürer were referring to the painting of a façade.

Pictures in the Rathaus

From 1512 onwards the Emperor Maximilian I made use of Dürer's artistic skill for the fulfilment of his vainglorious projects. The Emperor was filled with a consciousness of the grandeur of his house and with an urge to imitate the Roman Emperors. Caesar, Titus and Constantine had had their triumphal processions and triumphal arches—and Maximilian wanted to have them, too. In 1501 he founded the 'Collegium Mathematicorum et Poetarum' in the University of Vienna and imagined that, by so doing, he was behaving like a Roman Emperor. His plans knew no bounds, but his means were, and remained, limited. Even in that respect Maximilian's projects differed from those of his classical predecessors,

Maximilian's Vainglorious Projects

but the psychological background was also different. This Habsburg prince combined with his megalomania a desire to be close to his people. With all his arrogance, he remained the genial Austrian cavalier, and in the minds of his subjects he was not the wearer of the imperial crown, but the man who went hunting on the Martinswand. For the execution of his projects he needed a 'university of arts and sciences'—scholars like Stabius, Pirckheimer, Pfinzing, Treitzsauerwein, to draw up programmes, edit the imperial writings, find artists and examine their designs. He employed poets and musicians, philosophers and historians, together with painters of court scenes, military exploits and tournaments, such as Hans Burgkmair. Skilled and trusted counsellors like Peutinger acted as negotiators between the Emperor and the various offices and workshops.

Three Illustrated Books and Three Works of Art

Out of all the manifold mass of projects of triumph and glory, only a few were executed and many of the Emperor's pet ideas were never realized, or at least only in part. Three illustrated books deal with the Emperor's life—that life so rich in political and amorous adventures, in victories in the lists and on the battlefield, in bridal and martial processions, in festivals and hunting-parties. These books are the 'Freydal', the 'Theuerdank' and the 'Weisskunig'. The formative arts were to preserve the Emperor's fame for all time by means of three works—his tomb, the triumphal arch and the triumphal procession. 'Freydal' was intended as a kind of prelude to 'Theuerdank'. Freydal is the young Emperor Maximilian himself, who journeys to the courts of sixty-four princesses to gain victories in the various forms of knightly prowess—running, tilting and combat on foot. By 1515, 255 miniatures had been prepared for this book, of which five exist in the form of woodcuts. The four tournament scenes and the 'Torch-dance at Augsburg'—more important for the history of civilization than for that of art—are nowadays generally supposed to have been cut from sketches by Dürer.

'Freydal'

The Book of Wrestling and Fencing

Dürer must have made a thorough study of the theory of combat on foot. The 'Book of Wrestling and Fencing' (Vienna, Nationalbibliothek), with its two hundred illustrations of wrestlers and fencers, probably dates from shortly after the year 1500. Dörnhöffer, and after him Flechsig, support Dürer's authorship, but with the qualification that Dürer's participation consisted only in a kind of revision of already existing textual and illustrative material. It is, therefore, not, like his treatise on fortification, an original production or theory of Dürer's and none of the coloured illustrations are drawn from life. The book, to the transcription of which, in Flechsig's opinion, Pirckheimer contributed as well as Dürer, is more important for the idea it gives of the scope of his interests than as an example of his artistic ability.

'Theuerdank'

'Theuerdank'—the word means 'one who thinks of adventure'—is likewise a camouflaged biography of Maximilian. He himself and other historical persons appear in it under fictitious names and mingle with allegorical figures. For the text of this late imitation of the courtly epic two men were responsible—the Nuremberg Prior and Imperial Counsellor Melchior Pfinzing and the notary Max Treitzsauerwein—their task consisting of giving literary form to the drafts dictated by the imperial author himself. S. Schäuffelein made 118 woodcuts for the 1517 edition of the book, in which Maximilian glorifies himself and his deeds and describes his adventurous journey to bring back his bride, Mary of Burgundy (Princess Ehrenreich). Theuerdank's adversaries are Fürtwittig, Unfalo and Nydelhardt, who in the end are shamefully defeated and put to death. Many are the dangers which Theuerdank-Maximilian encounters, whilst hunting chamois, wild boars and bears, on the battlefield and in the lists.

The third book, 'Weisskunig', is a fantastic prose romance. It is based on a *'Weisskunig'* Latin autobiography of Maximilian's, recast by Max Treitzsauerwein, and adorned with 257 woodcuts by Hans Burgkmair, which give us charming little pictures of the young Maximilian at school, at play and indulging in chivalrous exercises. Most of the book, however, is dedicated to the life of Frederick III, the old 'Weisskunig', from the time of his betrothal in 1450. The life of his son Max, the young 'Weisskunig', is described by author and illustrator until 1513. The work was left unfinished.

These books of travel and adventure give an inkling of the Emperor's restlessness. *Restlessness of* He was a 'flying' Emperor, always travelling about his wide domains, never really *the Emperor* at home anywhere, always a self-invited guest. His favourite town was Augsburg, which was the scene of his manifold undertakings, but this 'last of the knights' never had a permanent 'residency'. The old emperors had 'no home but the stirrup, no residence but the saddle' (Thausing). Where, then, could Maximilian have frescoes painted, where could he erect statues, since his person was not permanently connected with any town? The equestrian statue of the Emperor, which Burgkmair designed after Italian models for Gregor Erhart and which was destined for Augsburg, remained a roughly hewn block of stone. Maximilian was everywhere—and art, the herald of his fame, had to proclaim him everywhere. The only branch of art which could do this, which, like the Emperor himself, could travel from city to city and from country to country, was graphic art, the printing of illustrations. The printing of books and pictures was the new great *Printing* power, with which the ruler of a Western Empire entered into an alliance. That was the real reason of Maximilian's projects for books and woodcuts, a contributory factor being also the realization that to print a triumphal arch would cost far less than to build it. In 1514 Maximilian commissioned the Salzburg sculptor *Plans for* Hans Valkenauer to make statues of the eight Emperors and four Empresses who *Statues* were buried in Speyer Cathedral, where the statues were to stand before twelve pillars. Owing to the death of the Emperor in 1519, this grandiose plan was never executed. The only plastic monument which owes its origin to Maximilian is his tomb in Innsbruck, modelled on the funeral processions to be seen on the tombs of French, Flemish and Burgundian princes. Twenty-eight ancestors in blood or spirit, wrought in bronze, were to surround the imperial sarcophagus. Among these ancestors were representatives of the countries which Maximilian ruled— King Arthur, Theodoric, Caesar, Clovis and Charlemagne. But even this monumental tomb was not destined to become the last resting-place of the restless Emperor. Maximilian died in 1519 at Wels in Upper Austria, his coffin is in the Schlosskapelle at Neustadt and only his sarcophagus is in the Hofkirche at

DETAIL FROM THE TRIUMPHAL PROCESSION OF EMPEROR MAXIMILIAN
(The Burgundian Wedding. About 1515)

Innsbruck. The figure of Henry the Lion is immortalized in our minds by the bronze lion in Brunswick; the figure of Maximilian of Habsburg triumphs on the printed page.

The Triumphal Arch and Triumphal Procession of Maximilian are the largest woodcuts in existence. The Triumphal Arch is over 9 feet 10 inches high and almost 9 feet 10 inches wide. Maximilian must certainly have been familiar with 'triumphs' as represented by Italian art, e.g. Mantegna's, which he may have got to know through the Gonzagas. Descriptions of antique triumphal processions and buildings could be found in a book known to Maximilian, Valturio's 'De Re Militari', while Jacobus Argentoratensis' woodcuts of the 'Triumph of Caesar' provided graphic models. But there was also a German building which provided inspiration for the form and decoration of the Triumphal Arch—the Wappenturm, or armorial tower, erected at Innsbruck in 1496 by the architect and painter Jörg Kölderer, whose coat of arms (an important discovery by Fischmaler) can be seen at the foot of Maximilian's Triumphal Arch, next to those of Stabius and Dürer. Stabius was responsible for the intellectual design, Kölderer reduced the whole to miniature painting, and Dürer sketched the most important parts for the woodcutter. In addition, Wolf Traut, Hans Springinklee and perhaps Hans Dürer were also employed as designers. The commission was given to Albrecht Dürer in 1512, the formula, as laid down by Stabius, being that the 'Arch of Triumph of the Emperor Maximilian shall be erected after the manner of the "arcus triumphales" of the Roman Emperors in the City of Rome, of which some have been destroyed and some can still be seen'. Work on the project lasted until 1519.

The Arch was built up out of ninety-two woodcuts. It is, in reality, a Hall of Fame, for we can see the floor of a fairly spacious room inside. Four great pillars on plinths higher than a man, without entablatures, flank the three narrow passages —so narrow that they seem little more than slits. The whole effect is that of a tower rather than of an arch. The narrowness of the actual arches and the steps leading up to them—in contrast to the antique triumphal arches—would make it impossible for a coach and horses to pass through them. The question, what material would have to be used for the arch, never entered the minds of the designers. This world of flowers and musicians, of censers and griffins, is a paper world. The idea of a real arch was completely obscured by the conception of this gigantic pictorial arch with its sham architecture. All that mattered were the pictures and the texts printed beneath them. The central arch, higher in proportion than the others, is the 'Gate of Honours and Power'; the left side-arch is the 'Gate of Nobility', and the right, the 'Gate of Praise'. In a kind of tabernacle on the front of the cupola crowning the whole, sits the Emperor in coronation robes, surrounded by symbolical animals—lion, bull, crane, serpent, dog and cock. Giehlow's researches into the craze for allegory in Humanistic circles at Maximilian's time have shown that these animals, which are also found in Dürer's marginal drawings to the Emperor's prayer-book, formed part of the hieroglyphic 'mysteries'. Countless mysterious elements of this kind were doubtless inserted into the decoration of

The Triumph
141

The Triumphal Arch
141

Ill. p. 186

N

THE TRIUMPHAL ARCH OF EMPEROR MAXIMILIAN
(Detail. 1515)

the Arch and Procession of Triumph and the prayer-book. Solving heraldic and hieroglyphic picture-puzzles must have been an intellectual pastime for those learned members of the Emperor's entourage who were schooled in this movement, and may have consoled them for the lack of ocular enjoyment which this woodcut monster offered. In the central compartment above the main arch we again find the Emperor in his coronation robes, beneath him his genealogical tree and on either side 102 coats of arms of countries over which his sceptre held sway. Above the two lateral arches are twenty-four representations of the Emperor's deeds and campaigns. On the arrow-like strips on the extreme right and left are the members of the imperial family. The flanking pillars are divided into twelve compartments, three of which are empty, the remainder depicting Maximilian's many virtues, deeds, undertakings and interests. Amidst all this, a multitude of human, animal and vegetable forms is creeping, fleeing and moving. On the corners stand musicians, apes squat on the steps, dragons stick out their tongues, cranes hop, men contort themselves in coils of lilies, watchmen stand half concealed behind double pillars, figures of Pan dance on the cupola. An unrestrained joy in adornment has taken possession of the whole structure and covered it with ornaments which belong to no category of aesthetics or style. North and South, Late Gothic and Renaissance, lifelike movement and rigid stylization, tectonic feeling and atectonic treatment—every kind of motive is there, and over and above all these discords of detail resound the drums and trumpets of the glorification of Maximilian.

Where was Dürer? What was his share in all this? His are the middle arch, the *Dürer's Share* floral festoons, the cranes, the crown and insignia, the great pillars crowned with griffins and the animals on the capitals. When, amidst the raucous tones of streetminstrels proclaiming the glory of Maximilian, we seem to hear the song of a bird, when, out of the must of dusty hieroglyphics, there rises the scent of fresh lilies, then do we know that this is Dürer's work. Then the acanthus of the corinthian capital is transformed into oak-leaves or ivy, then the griffin grasping the scroll with Maximilian's motto, which was Dürer's too—'Keep measure'— *Ill. p. 28* ceases to be a tame animal of architectural ornamentation and becomes a savage bird of prey, looking as if he would do anything but 'keep measure'. If anyone had drawn Dürer's attention to the 'irrational' quality of the architecture of this Triumphal Arch, he would probably have been told to remember the German temperament. 'The German temperament must be borne in mind,' writes Dürer in his treatise on mensuration, 'for all those who want to build something new, wish to have a new fashion for it, which has never been seen before.'

It was Maximilian's intention that the Triumphal Arch of 1515 should be supple- *The Triumphal* mented by the Triumphal Procession, with its pièce de résistance, the imperial *Procession* coach. The Arch consists of a series of woodcuts placed one on top of the other, the *142-3* Procession of woodcuts placed one after the other, eight of them depicting the *Ill. p. 184* imperial coach, these latter being published separately in 1522, after Maximilian's death. This so-called 'Great Triumphal Car' and the smaller car known as the 'Burgundian Wedding' are by Dürer, who also had a share in the other parts of the

Procession, though these in the main are the work of Hans Burgkmair and Hans Springinklee. That Dürer had a share, is proved by his designs for court costumes and for the bearers of standards and trophies, e.g. the elegant trot of the horse carrying the bearer of the French trophy (L. 551, Vienna).

144

Literary programmes drawn up by Stabius for the whole Procession and by Pirckheimer for the great Triumphal Car, cramped the style of the artists. The festive spirit of the Italian Renaissance, taking the triumphs of Roman Emperors as its models, had contrived to turn secular 'trionfi' into pageants with an allegorical meaning. Among the allegorical groups the car of the Virtues invariably played a leading rôle. These 'trionfi' survived in the form of paintings, the most outstanding examples being Cossa's frescoes in the Palazzo Schifanoia at Ferrara, Piero della Francesca's 'Trionfo di Federigo di Urbino' in Florence (Uffizi), and Mantegna's 'Triumph of Caesar' at Hampton Court. Inspiration of this kind, together with personal impressions received from witnessing ceremonial entries of emperors, processions, meetings of princes etc., helped Maximilian's artists. In front of Dürer's home in Nuremberg, 'Unter der Vesten', triumphal arches were erected on the occasion of imperial visits. In 1471, 1485 and 1487 Emperor Frederick III had entered the city. In 1512 Dürer had witnessed the solemn reception of Maximilian in Nuremberg and shortly before the completion of the Triumphal Car the entry of Charles V into Antwerp, on which occasion the city's beautiful girls did not, as one might imagine from Makart's huge picture in Hamburg, walk about naked among the crowd, but posed as 'living statues' on pedestals forming part of the structures erected for the pageant, just as Dürer poses his 'Virtues' on brackets of the Triumphal Car.

The Triumphal Car 142

Two preliminary stages of Dürer's Triumphal Car have been preserved. About 1512–13 he made a sketch (L. 528, Vienna) of a dainty ceremonial coach, drawn by nimble horses. In it are seated the Emperor Maximilian, with Mary of Burgundy in front of him, in front of her King Philip the Handsome, his sister Margaret and his wife Joanna the Mad, in front of this trio the emperors-to-be Charles and Ferdinand, with their four sisters in the front seat of all. Dürer made another version of this imperial coach, with its occupants sitting in strict accordance with the rules of precedence, in 1518, this time in the form of a large, coloured sketch (L. 555, Vienna). For the woodcut version of the Car, the imperial relatives were removed and replaced by Virtues, and it was in this form that the Car was transferred to the fresco on the wall of the Nuremberg Rathaus.

The Idea of the Triumphal Car

The team of twelve horses is driven by 'Ratio', seated on the box. Heinrich Brockhaus has discovered with the aid of original sources the allusions contained in this allegorical representation. The foreword to Justinian's 'Institutes' begins by saying that the emperor must be adorned with weapons and armed with laws, so that he may rule justly and be victorious in both war and peace. The idea of the Triumphal Car is based on this conception of the 'Corpus Juris'. The Emperor Maximilian, the crown on his head, sceptre and palm-branch in his hands, the imperial orb and sword ready to his hand, in front of him, is riding in triumph, crowned with victory and accompanied by all the virtues of ruling princes.

Around him are the 'Angel Virtues'—Justice, Fortitude, Prudence and Temperance holding the garlands of Truth, Clemency and Goodness. Security and Confidence escort the Emperor, Reason holds the reins, Experience and Caution check the pace of the horses, Audacity and Magnanimity make them prance. Pirckheimer's text gives precise explanations, e.g. 'In order that Audacity and Magnanimity may not lead the car astray, two other horses are harnessed in front of them, led by Experience and Caution. For where there is no experience and harmony, audacity and magnanimity may well cause harm.' These 'Virtues', as Brockhaus has shown, are probably derived from old prayers used in Nuremberg (e.g. from the Sensenschmid Missal of 1517), one of which includes a prayer that the Emperor may enjoy his triumph in the consciousness of divine virtue.

Among the vehicles in the procession are a few 'mechanical waggons', bearing pictures or allegorical groups representing the Emperor's campaigns and victories. In these the Nuremberg passion for making mechanical figures finds full scope. Some of them are self-propelled, forerunners of the old velocipedes, working on a system of smaller wheels turning larger wheels by means of cogs or worms. Men-at-arms keep the machinery going by turning cranks, adjusting connecting-rods, or pushing the wheels with bars and gripping the spokes as they stride alongside, while others are working a large tread-wheel. Everything which played a rôle in Maximilian's life passes before our eyes in the course of this triumphal march-past—the Burgundian wedding, battles, various forms of hunting such as hawking or the pursuit of chamois, deer, wild boars and bears; music and all the festive mummery of dances and costumes; fencing-matches, races and jousting. The recently discovered New World is not without its representatives, for we see 'Calicutians' who are 'all naked after the Indian fashion'. This graphic dream of Maximilian and Dürer did on one occasion, years later, come to life—in the famous masquerade organized by Munich artists in 1840, for which Eugen Neureuther designed the figurines. Gottfried Keller has left us a magnificent description of this festival in his 'Grüne Heinrich'.

Mechanical Waggons

One can, of course, deplore the fact that a great artist like Dürer should have undertaken to carry out a task of so little inner meaning, that he should so obediently have transformed all this pedantic allegorical rubbish into the clear language of his graphic art. Dürer, however, probably took a different view of the whole matter. The creator of the 'Great Fortune', the 'Sea-monster', the 'Melancolia' and other allegories was familiar with the personification of ideas, and this part of the programme elaborated by Pirckheimer and Stabius would not have caused Dürer any worry. But even the problems of form, such as the architecture and ornamentation of a triumphal arch or the construction and decoration of a ceremonial coach, must have attracted Dürer rather than repelled him. His subjective fantasy sometimes took a delight in those problems of form which occupied the metal-workers and turners, the lacemakers and watchmakers. The Triumphal Car is a gigantic achievement of the goldsmith's art. The canopy above the Emperor's head looks like an inverted spoon, the brackets on which the Virtues stand are like fruit-dishes. Many of the decorative elements betray their

Dürer's Fantasy

Italian origin, e.g. the lion's head on a capital of the Triumphal Arch, which comes from St. Mark's in Venice. Nevertheless, the whole formal conception, for instance that of the great car, is unmistakably German. The harbingers of the 'clear' Italian Renaissance have not succeeded in ousting the Late Gothic 'flourishes'.

Maximilian's Prayer-book

In the service of the Emperor Maximilian Dürer created the most servile of his works—the Triumphal Car; but at the same time he also produced the freest— the drawings for the prayer-book. This is not a manuscript, but a beautiful prayer-book printed on vellum, worthy to rank with the finest manuscripts. The 'court-hand' type was designed by Vincenz Rockner. Five copies of the book are known to exist; it was printed by Schönsperger at Augsburg in 1513 and contains psalms, excerpts from the Gospels, hymns and prayers. One copy, the margins of which are adorned with drawings in colours, has been preserved in two parts, one part being now in Munich and the other in Besançon. The text appears to have been printed rather hastily, some of the work having been left unfinished, probably because Maximilian died on 12th January 1519, before the completion of the printing, stitching and binding.

Purpose of the Prayer-book

The purpose of this prayer-book has not yet been satisfactorily explained. Giehlow has advanced the theory that it was a private edition made by order of the Emperor, the few copies printed being intended for the knights of the Order of St. George, founded in 1469 by Maximilian's father, Frederick III, and Pope Paul II; its religious texts were to inspire the members of the order with enthusiasm for the struggle against the Turks. The marginal drawings in the Munich-Besançon copy were—still according to Giehlow—preliminary sketches for woodcuts, which, however, were never made. A more plausible explanation is that put forward by Georg Leidinger and now almost universally accepted, namely, that only the copy intended for the Emperor was embellished with drawings, which thus constitute an end in themselves. Points which seem to disprove the theory of a projected edition illustrated with woodcuts are firstly the choice for the printing of such an expensive material as vellum; secondly, the system of lines enframing the text and separating the lines of text in the manner of a manuscript; thirdly, the colouring of the drawings and their style, which is not that of preliminary sketches, but has all the characteristics of a definite work. For rich booklovers to have certain copies of a book adorned with drawings or miniatures was in accordance with the custom of the time. For Pirckheimer Dürer embellished title-pages with miniatures, and he had a correspondence with Cardinal Albrecht of Brandenburg concerning a missal which he and Nikolaus Glockendon were to illustrate with drawings. In addition to the marginal drawings by Dürer's hand, the Munich portion of the prayer-book contains others by Lucas Cranach. Hans Baldung Grien, Hans Burgkmair, Jörg Breu, and perhaps also Hans Dürer and Albrecht Altdorfer, contributed to the decoration of the pages now preserved in Besançon.

The Drawings in the Prayer-book

The pictorial decorations of the prayer-book were intended for the eyes of Maximilian, that 'saturnian' man prone to fits of melancholy. The aim was to gladden his heart, to captivate his desultory mind, to provide food for his always

136–9

lively fancy. Dürer's marginal drawings are full of caprice, they are a performance in themselves, and one might almost call them the noblest artistic form of the tumbler's art performed in front of a royal audience. Free from all restraint and distortion, these drawings are not intended to be translated into the language of book-printing, and thereby coarsened; their function is to retain their light and frolicsome form. It is true, however, that Dürer did not devote equal zeal to every page. Together with pages the margins of which are completely filled with drawings, we find others which are illustrated only at the top or bottom or on one side, while on others again there are only a few flourishes. Dürer's contributions are of every species, ranging from calligraphic pen-decorations to visionary pictorial conceptions. In this respect, too, these drawings bear witness to the scope of Dürer's genius. They were signed by another hand in 1515.

Illustrations and Text

The relationship between illustration and text in the prayer-book is the freest imaginable. Only rarely is the subject-matter of the prayers, hymns or Gospel extracts represented in pictorial form; more often the meanings of text and picture run parallel, or else are in direct contrast with one another. Dürer's drawings deviate from the text, play around it and return to it again, like a dog out for a walk with its master. The rhythm of reading, e.g. the resumption of interest at the beginning of a new chapter, or the lowering of the pitch at the end, are reproduced to a certain extent by the accentuation which Dürer's drawings give to the beginnings and ends of portions of the text. In contrast to an illustrator, who must subordinate himself strictly to the text, like Hans Burgkmair did with his illustrations for the 'Weisskunig', Dürer felt himself free to paraphrase, to alter and even to criticize the text, this freedom, however, being a matter of form and of sentiment. Nobody appears to have disturbed Dürer at his work and care was absent from his elbow. 'Here his glorious nature is displayed in all its gaiety and humour' (Goethe).

Dürer's Humour

Dürer's humour, with its mixture of realism and paternal benevolence, is of the same type as Gottfried Keller's and is also akin to that of Luther, though he never achieves the latter's boisterous bluntness. Dürer occasionally indulged in little jokes; for instance, one page of the prayer-book contains the words 'Pater Noster' and 'temptationes,' which at once suggest to Dürer's imagination: 'Lead us not into temptation'—even though this may not be the actual burden of the prayer; he thereupon illustrates it by drawing a picture of a fox playing a shawn and luring away a flock of stupid, hysterically cackling hens (Folio 34, verso). How could Dürer resist such a temptation? The consciousness of human frailty (prayer on Folio 9, verso) inspires him to represent that helper in all our needs, the physician, who, while critically examining a specimen of urine held in his right hand, grasps with his left a rosary, thus making sure of divine assistance. The prayer for benefactors, 'Pro benefactoribus interpellatio' (Folio 15, recto) really refers to more generous men than the burgher in his fur-lined mantle who drops a little coin into the starving beggar's bowl, but Dürer's drawing tells us what a 'benefactor' looks like. That favourite subject, the Temptation of St. Anthony, is transformed from the magical heroic atmosphere of Schongauer's representation

139

of the Saint tortured by demons into a burgher idyll (Folio 24, verso). An article published by the 'Weimarer Kunstfreunde' in 1809 contains the following description of this drawing: 'A nice little woman enters, offering the Saint a bowl, while the Devil, from behind, blows words of evil advice into his ear through a pair of bellows. Greater naivety, simplicity and truth, and in a certain sense more charming figures, than the Saint and the little woman, are to be found nowhere. The woman comes to tempt him; he sits there, sunk in meditation, rigid with an almost grotesque indifference; there is not a touch of brazenness about her, on the contrary she has an appearance of shyness and delicate coquettishness which stands her in good stead and even makes her charming.'

All the categories of human beings are represented: Knights, burghers, beggars, a hermit and a physician, musicians and lansquenets, Turks and Indians, some awake, some asleep, some sober, others drunk; angels and saints descend from Heaven, fauns and satyrs come down from Olympus, little devils come up out of Hell. Dürer's love of animals is given free play. In his water-colour of the 'Virgin with Animals' he had gathered together all manner of beasts round the Madonna's throne and from the earliest times the study of animals had been a feature of his art. On the coasts of the Adriatic Dürer sketched lobsters and crabs, he made an excursion to the North Sea in the vain hope of sketching a whale; in the great ports of Italy he saw lions, apes, camels, elks and bisons; at home he kept Pomeranians, poodles and pointers; in the Franconian forests he came across squirrels, foxes and deer; in the fields, hares, badgers and rabbits. During his journeys through the Tyrol, Dürer's sharp eyes detected ibexes and chamois perched high up among the rocks—and in the background of the engraving of Adam and Eve (1504) he inserted a memory of these mountain animals. In 1523 he sketched the dancing apes (L. 864, Basle), which has a place of its own among Dürer's sketches of animals, for it leads us from reality to fantasy, from the zoological to the psychological sphere, and is, as Kurt Gerstenberg has pointed out, a forerunner of the seventeenth-century pictures of animals at play, painted by Netherlands artists such as Teniers and Ostade. The first known picture of a rhinoceros, from Lisbon (1515, Pen-drawing and woodcut, London), is by Dürer's hand, shown with a smaller horn on the back of its neck, in addition to the normal horn on its snout, which is not a mistake on Dürer's part, but is a characteristic of the Indian rhinoceros. Dürer's source was a sketch enclosed in a letter written from Lisbon by Valentin Ferdinand to Nuremberg friends.

Animals have always been popular in the art of Northern Europe. We have only to think of old German animal ornaments and Gothic choir-stalls and gargoyles, and, apart from the fabulous beasts such as dragons, unicorns and griffins, many animals became popular characters in fairy-tales and fables, e.g. the hedgehog, the wolf and the fox. In 1498 there was published in Lübeck the most celebrated of all animal epics, 'Reynke de Vos', with woodcut illustrations. Humorous parodies such as the cunning fox or the wolf disguised in a monk's cowl, preaching to hens, ducks and geese, appeared everywhere and were reproduced by every form of technique—on choir-stalls and tapestries, in drawings and woodcuts.

Dürer as a Depictor of Animals

56

122–4

110

126

Love of Animals

Dürer's love of animals and German tradition were not, however, the only
reasons for the appearance of such large numbers of animals in the drawings for
the prayer-book—there was also the character of the man for whom the book
was intended. Maximilian I, often disappointed by his fellow-men, was fond of
animals. Because he was an ardent and intelligent hunter, he introduced severe
laws to protect ibexes from extermination; he loved to have his room full of
birds, whose song was more agreeable to the imperial ear than the mournful
utterances of his chancellors. In Dürer's and Cranach's marginal drawings Maximilian could feast his eyes on every species of game to be found in his forests,
while birds fluttered, hopped and twittered on every side—cocks, hens and
pheasants; swans, ducks and geese; eagles, goshawks and falcons; screech-owls,
barn-owls and great horned owls; storks, kingfishers, spoonbills and cranes. And
to this aviary was added a terrarium—lizards and serpents, turtles and frogs.

Maximilian and Hunting

Every perusal of the prayer-book tempts us to some new grouping of the
drawings, on account of the endless variations in the relationship between illustration and text. Side by side with very free renderings, or even distortion of the
serious import by some humorous marginal sketch, we find cases of strict subordination of the illustration to the wording of the text. St. Sebastian, St. Barbara
and St. Apollonia form part of the prayers addressed to them, just as the little
angel's head belongs to the 'angelica voce'. Before the eyes of the devout worshipper praying after the elevation of the Host, appears the image of Christ with
the Stigmata and the Instruments of His Passion. King David plays the harp while
his lips sing the 129th Psalm. The warrior who, before entering into battle, reads
the 91st Psalm—'quando bellum adeundum est'—finds in the margin not only an
angel reading his psalter, but a scene of battle between knights and peasants (Folio
28, recto). 'O sing unto the Lord a new song!' is the first line of the 98th Psalm,
and seven musicians with drums and trumpets illustrate the 'jubilate'. 'The earth is
the Lord's, and all that there in is' (Psalm 24)—and in Dürer's fantasy this includes
the newly discovered world of India and the 'Calicutian' man whom he sketches
in the margin.

Subordination of Illustration to Text

Dürer's drawings for Maximilian's prayer-book are like a great reservoir of
reminiscences of ideas which occur elsewhere in his work. Everywhere we find
familiar figures and motives. The motive of St. John the Evangelist with book and
eagle, to whom the Mother of God appears in an aureole, known to us from the
title-page of the 1511 edition of the 'Apocalypse', is found once more in the
prayer-book at the beginning of the Gospel of St. John (Folio 14, verso). In
delicacy and animation the marginal drawing is far superior to the woodcut. The
theme of the 'Knight and Death' occurs twice in the prayer-book. The recto of
folio 12 contains the prayer for the dying, and Dürer symbolizes the inexorable
law of Death which prevails throughout Nature by showing us, in the right
margin, a battle high up in the skies between a falcon and a heron, while far
below, beneath the clouds, Death holds up the hour-glass before the terrified eyes
of a knight, whose right hand instinctively reaches for the pommel of his sword.
But the sand is running out and the bony hand of Death grips his lower arm as if

Reminiscences of Other Works

to say 'It is too late!'. Dürer returns again to the theme of the inevitability of
Death—which is in contrast to the moral victory of the knight over Death and

137   the Devil in the engraving of 1513—in the lower margin of the verso of folio 37.
This time, however, there is no connection between the text and the illustration,
which shows us a knight mounted on an exhausted horse whose forelegs are
already knocking together; the horseman turns, as if to utter a despairing oath,
towards Death who has overtaken him with the long stride of the reaper. The
next sweep of the scythe will sever the horse's fetlocks.

Very often one of these marginal drawings is the maturest solution of a motive
often treated by Dürer before. Take, for example, the subject of 'Hercules and
the Birds of Stymphalis', already represented in the Nuremberg picture and in a
sketch (L. 207, Darmstadt). The Hercules of the prayer-book drawing battles
with the birds like an Alpine hunter warding off an eagle (Folio 39, verso).
Dürer must have been thinking of his Venetian days when he drew the playful
little angel pressing his left foot on the shell of a snail (Folio 51, recto). The
sudarium of St. Veronica, here (Folio 56, recto) borne by child angels, reminds us
of the engraving of 1513, insuperable in the heraldic beauty and grandeur of the
conception of Christ. We have already mentioned, as masterpieces of genre
representation, the old woman fallen asleep by her distaff (Folio 48, verso) and the
'innkeeper's wife returning from market' (Folio 51, verso), that woman with the
basket of eggs and cheese whom Goethe described as 'Albrecht Dürer's insuperable
masterpiece'. But what about the burgher sitting in the right margin of the recto
of folio 45? The worthy man has fallen asleep over his book, his tall hat has fallen
from his head which is resting on his hand. Was Dürer with a silent smile parody-
ing his own figures of thinkers and readers—his St. Anthony sitting outside a
mountain town and his 'Melancolia'?

Styles and   In the world of these marginal drawings, moods, styles and effects are all
Effects   intermingled. Goethe very aptly remarked that Dürer utilizes the narrow, high
spaces of the margins in the same way as Italian painters used the surfaces of
pilasters, and it may well be that he was influenced by the engravings of Mantegna's pupil, Zoan Andrea. On some folios Dürer arranges his decorations
around a central axis, e.g. the recto of folio 19, in which little angels are uprooting
an ornamental column from its base, or on folio 56 (recto). Here the construction
is built up on strictly symmetrical lines—the socle, the angel, the laurel-wreath,
the festoon with the mask. The drawing of the souls in purgatory (folio 16,
recto) made a particularly deep impression on the classicists of Weimar because
it is so Italian in conception—'as admirably conceived in relation to the space, or
rather as admirably at one with it and as directly resulting from it, as those
famous Fates on a pilaster of the Vatican loggias'.

Late Gothic foliage is combined with Renaissance festoons of fruit, and similarly the effects are intermingled. Dürer's draughtsmanship blends the decorative
with the natural, the letter with the flourish, and vice versa. The line of his pen,
after drawing a drum, runs into a cartridge-like ornament, frees itself from this
entanglement by means of a few twists and runs on, first outlining the profile of a

Pan-like mask and then, with an elegant bound passes from the left to the upper margin, where with one stroke it delineates the figure of a pacing lion. The line glides from the abstraction of calligraphic compass-work into the realism of an animal's body or of a plant, and then—without, so to speak, pausing for more than a second in the natural world—emerges from it again and returns once more to its favourite element of exquisite flourishes. The mesh of lines surges around the rigid block of characters, at one point throwing out a wave into the type area, at another flowing in a slow trickle back into the open space of the margin.

In his work for this truly imperial prayer-book, Dürer's fantasy covers a multitude of fields, traversing heaven and earth, reality and fairyland, and many periods of his own life, while his line frees itself from the restraint of the exclusively realistic and of the exclusively allegorical. At one moment it is intent on reproducing with Düreresque fidelity an object; in the next, it frees itself from all objectivity and moves as an independent force in the midst of arabesques and flourishes. The pen obeys every movement of the hand and it is impossible to distinguish what has been drawn from what has been written. The art of calligraphy and the art of painting combine to form a delicate and entertaining branch of graphic art.

Dürer was also a master of calligraphy. Endowed with an unfailing steadiness of hand—we are told that he could draw a perfect circle with his free hand—trained in a goldsmith's workshop and accustomed to engraving the thinnest lines firmly and cleanly upon a tough surface, he took a lively interest in all problems of form relating to calligraphy or type. This is proved by his designs for Gothic and Latin letters. Italian influences can be discerned, e.g. the roman alphabet, inspired by Luca Pacioli's 'Constructions', and the curious woodcuts of the 'Six Knots', which are derived from the intricate linear designs (the so-called 'Academia Leonardi Vinci') introduced by Leonardo and disseminated by Italian engravings. But Dürer's interest in line was also derived from another, old German source. There was a revival—modified by Late Gothic influences—of the old Nordic delight in the intertwining and interlacing of forms, in the play of labyrinthine curves and in the endless harmonies of freely moving lines. Because the drawings for this prayer-book, destined for the eyes of one man alone, are derived from a perennially flowing source, they have retained their interest down to our own days.

Only once has German art achieved world-wide recognition—in the days of Dürer. His genius was more generally acknowledged abroad than that of Hans Holbein the Younger. Whereas Dürer had no followers of his own rank in Germany—and that was the one great tragedy of his life—his art became the common property of all the civilized countries of Europe even during his lifetime. Was it not indeed a compliment to the German master that Raphael in 1517 for his 'Bearing of the Cross' ('Lo spasimo di Sicilia', Madrid, Prado) should have borrowed the figure of Christ from the woodcut of the same theme in Dürer's 'Little Passion'? The influence of Dürer was reflected in almost every branch and technique of art—in graphic art, in painting and sculpture, in glass-enamelling

Recognition of German Art

and in Gobelin tapestries. The history of Dürer's influence—a field of art history which has not yet been thoroughly explored—begins with the appropriation, borrowing and imitation of his technical processes and pictorial motives by Italian and German artists, leads us to the solution of problems, known to Dürer, in the representation of space and landscape by the painters of the Netherlands, can be traced throughout French and Spanish art and culminates in the 'Old German' tendency of the German Romantics.

A decisive factor in the appreciation of Dürer at the beginning of the nineteenth century was the publication of his drawings for Maximilian's prayer-book. In 1808–1809 Nepomuk Strixner's reproductions of 'Albrecht Dürer's Christian-mythological Drawings' were published with the aid of what was then the new technique of lithography—that is to say, redrawn and without the text of the prayer-book, which is so indispensable to their comprehension. On seeing these

Goethe and the Marginal Drawings

drawings, Goethe, whose admiration for Dürer had blown alternately hot and cold, whose youthful enthusiasm had been subsequently damped by the 'hard, adventurous, affected' aspect of his work, was once more deeply moved. Under the influential imprint of the 'W.K.F.' (Weimarer Kunstfreunde), he had two appreciations by Heinrich Meyer of Strixner's lithographic reproductions published in the 'Jenaische Allgemeine Literaturzeitung' and from the heights of the Weimar Olympus caused it be made known that Dürer's drawings were like 'the peace of God which passeth all understanding'.

The impulse provided by the rebirth of this work of Dürer's had far-reaching effects. For three hundred years this treasure had lain virtually hidden, and now it was suddenly brought into the light of day, to exercise its magic charm. Strixner's lithographic reproductions of Dürer's drawings are a milestone in the history of the influence of reproduction processes on art. They were the source of a stream of production. This priceless heritage was passed from hand to hand and gave

Influence of Dürer in the 19th Century

rise to a new stylistic movement in German graphic art. Goethe viewed with a benevolent eye Cornelius' illustrations for 'Faust', because they were Düreresque in conception, and Neureuther's commentary on Goethe's ballads pleased the poet because it was inspired with the spirit of the Munich prayer-book. From Neureuther's illustrations for Schiller's 'Song of the Bell' and Robert Reinick's 'Songs of a Painter with Marginal Drawings by his Friends' down to the illustrations of Schwind and Ludwig Richter and Adolf von Menzel's series of lithographs, 'A Painter's Pilgrimage', right on into the popular illustrations of the Late Romantic period, we can follow the impulses which the publication of the prayer-book drawings imparted to the art of illustration.

An appropriate motto for Dürer's life would be 'Ich dien'. Dürer knew that he was the leader of German art; in the growing fame of his reputation he could see the confirmation of his own conviction of his artistic merit. But it was with him as it was with his favourite Saint—St. Christopher. He bore the spirit of German art upon his sturdy shoulders through the roaring waters of his time. But the further he went, the heavier the burden became, and the greater the responsibility of the task he had undertaken.

CHAPTER TWELVE

PLASTIC SENSE

THE lists of Dürer's works compiled by scholars include many more works than we have been able to discuss here. We have merely shaken the golden bough of Dürer's art and gathered up the ripest fruits. But if we search among the branches, we shall still come across many that have remained hidden.

The link between 'liberal' and applied art in Dürer's work is provided by the frame of his 'Adoration of the Trinity', the figures on which were designed by Dürer himself. Dürer's activity in many branches of craftsmanship was probably much more extensive than is dreamt of in our scholastic widsom. The versatility of his talent and technique lends colour to this supposition, as does also his whole temperament. Dürer, who was a master in all things, was the recipient of innumerable requests. He was asked to supply designs for reliefs and medallions, for decorative paintings, for book-decorations and paintings on glass. Two of the reliefs in the Fugger Chapel in the church of St. Anna at Augsburg were executed after designs by Dürer. Many works of this kind must have been lost, especially those executed in fragile materials, such as glass. Others, such as silver goblets, may have been preserved, but are unknown because the name of Dürer has never been connected with them. It is, therefore, a matter of pure chance if here and there we come across authenticated examples of Dürer's skill as a craftsman.

For the 'Twelve-man House' in Nuremberg, Landauer, its founder, commissioned not only the altar-piece—Dürer's 'Adoration of the Trinity'—but also a set of glass windows. These were completed in 1508, two years before the delivery of the painting. The designs and cartoons for them were made by Dürer, but we do not know to what extent Dürer collaborated in the execution on glass in Veit Hirsvogel the Elder's workshop (the paintings on glass are in the Schloss Museum, Berlin). The middle window represents the Sacrifice of Isaac, and on either side are the Fall of the Angels, the Queen of Heaven, the Wise and Foolish Virgins, Evangelists, Apostles and members of the donor's family. Robert Schmidt has pointed out that the figures of animals in the corners and the foliage show traces of Dürer's style at the time of his 'Apocalypse', whereas the deep colouring reveals the influence of Venetian painting.

Dürer had been in a goldsmith's workshop and had therefore been schooled in the execution of small plastic works. It is true that after he had learned to work 'cleanly', his 'pleasure' drew him away from goldsmith's work to painting, but the plastic sense remained in his blood and his fingertips retained their feeling for tangible form. That Dürer made a design for a work in metal for one of his colleagues in the goldsmiths' guild, has been proved beyond all doubt. As a wandering apprentice he was cordially received by Caspar and Paul in Colmar and by Georg Schongauer in Basle. Two brothers of Martin Schongauer, who died in 1489, were goldsmiths and their father had also been a goldsmith. Wherever Dürer went on his travels, he visited the goldsmiths, drew their portraits and was

Dürer as Craftsman

Plastic Sense

LAMPS
(Detail from the Woodcut, 'St. John Beholds the Seven
Lamps of Fire' (Apocalypse) 1498)

received as an honoured guest. In Antwerp he designed fillets for the local gold-smiths; in Brussels he made a sketch of a seal for the master-goldsmith Jan. Among Dürer's sketches we find designs for pendants, spoon-handles, buckles, goblets and scabbards, in fact for everything which normally came from a gold- *149* smith's workshop. On the borderline between small and large plastic works, are Dürer's sketches for tableware, table-fountains and two ordinary fountains. One of the latter was to be surmounted by a lansquenet flourishing a banner, the other by a rustic figure with a goose (L. 414 and 421, Vienna). Dürer was a native of a *147-8* city which delighted in fountains. On the market-place in Nuremberg stood Heinrich Behaim the Elder's 'beautiful fountain'; in 1557 Labenwolf's exquisite fountain, surmounted by a boy carrying a banner, was erected in the courtyard of the Rathaus. Heinrich Brockhaus has pointed out that Dürer's design, made in 1527, for a fountain surmounted by a standard-bearer is, in its construction, closely related to the Labenwolf fountain.

We find reminiscences of sculptural works, and especially of Venetian decorative *Sculpture in* sculpture, in all kinds of unexpected places in Dürer's prints. In the background of *Dürer's* the first woodcut of the 'Apocalypse', representing the martyrdom of St. John, *Graphic Art* we find the column surmounted by the Lion of St. Mark from the Piazzetta. The edge of the plate in the engraving of the 'Great Horse' intersects a column crowned by a standing figure. Three times in the woodcuts of the 'Life of the Virgin' (1506), plastic works appear as decorations of imaginary buildings. On an archway, through which the Virgin passes on her way to her Presentation in the Temple, above spandrels adorned with reliefs, is the figure of a mythological hunter with a pitch-pan. In the hollow of a wall in the Annunciation, there appears, like a high relief, the half-figure of an angel. The recumbent figure of Moses with the Tablets of the Law appears as decoration of a tympanum in the Adoration of the Virgin. But the greatest work of sculpture which Dürer saw on his travels, Michelangelo's Madonna in Bruges, has left no direct trace in his work.

Did Dürer himself ever create works of sculpture? We know, at all events, *Medallions* that, like Lucas Cranach the Elder, Burgkmair and other artists, he made designs for medallions. We have already mentioned the portraits of Frederick II of the Palatinate and of Ulrich Starck, and the sketch for a medallion of himself. Dürer must undoubtedly have had a great influence on the carvers of small sculptural works in his own time, either directly, by making designs for medals and plaques, or indirectly, because his graphic art is a treasury of figures, into which one had only to plunge one's hand—and many were the artists who actually did so!—in order to find a model for a medal or a small relief in the style of Dürer. Among the items which Habich maintains are independent works of Dürer, but which Winkler and Bange consider very doubtful attributions, are the following: the relief of a nude in silver (New York, Metropolitan Museum), of which there are bronze and lead casts and replicas in soapstone, the medallions of Pirckheimer, Wolgemut, Stabius and Charles V, the so-called Agnes Dürer, the so-called Dürer the Elder, and a female portrait. Dürer's design for the medallion of Charles V is *151* authenticated. As for the others, one is inclined to agree with Wölfflin, that the medallists worked from sketches by Dürer. For instance, the position of the legs of the female nude reminds us of Dürer's study for the Eve of 1510 (L. 518, Vienna). The actual authors of the works, however, were probably some of those skilful fabricators of 'cabinet pieces' who existed at the beginning of the seventeenth century. A drawing in Dessau is an illuminating example of the genesis of a small work of sculpture 'after Dürer'. It shows the same female nude as the silver relief in New York, but combines this domestic Venus with a 'wild man', which in turn is derived from Dürer's engraving of 1503 for the 'Coat of Arms with Skull'. One is tempted to believe that the female figure is likewise derived from a sketch, and it looks very much as if the Dessau drawing was executed before the New York relief.

The regulations concerning the use of noble metals which were enforced in Nuremberg also give rise to doubts as to whether he himself produced works in these metals. Dürer held that he was not, or at all events that he was no longer an expert in the technique of metals. When Frederick the Wise asked for his advice in connection with the casting of a medal of which Dürer had sent him the design, the latter replied that he had no experience in such matters and was therefore unable to give the required information. As Dürer did not cut his own woodcuts on the block, it is unlikely that—apart from the period of his apprenticeship in the goldsmith's workshop—he ever cast works in precious metals after his own sketches and models. He was, however, in both cases so familiar with the materials, tools and processes employed, that he could conceive and draw works for reproduction on wood or metal or for casting in silver.

The metal appliqués after designs by Dürer and his own designs for other types of craftsman's work, e.g. for paintings on glass, etchings on scabbards, helmets and armour, are interesting because they bear witness to the universality of Dürer's creative genius, but the fact that we know of such minor works does not add anything essential to our general picture of Dürer. Whether we possess or know of drawings by Dürer for such purposes or not, the fact remains that by the grace of God he was endowed with the plastic sense. The proof of Dürer's

Plastic Feeling in the Drawings plastic sense does not lie in this silver relief and a handful of medallions, it is to be found in the wealth of plastic feeling in his drawings. It is all there for everyone to see—the pleasure in the round, the joy in the firmness of the body, the delight with which Dürer's line describes the curves of a form, the poise and counterpoise of arm and leg, the play of light and shade on the undulations of a back, the tubular intricacies of folds. Every drawing by Dürer is an invitation to the eye to comprehend the construction of a form by means of the sense of touch.

It was his pleasure in reality, that sure instinct of genius, which persuaded Dürer to devote himself to the art of projection. He became a draughtsman and a painter, and as such he accomplished his historical function and achieved his place in history. But as a painter and draughtsman he also carried on the great traditions of German sculpture. In Dürer's woodcuts there lives on, as we have already pointed out, far more of the heritage of German wood-carving between 1480 and 1500, than of the traditions of a provincial school of painting such as

DÜRER'S STUDY. Nuremberg, Dürerhaus.

VENICE. Detail from a woodcut by Jacopo de' Barbari. 1500.

Wolgemut's. If we must insist on naming some great artist as the 'model' whom Dürer was following when he created the stalwart figures of the four Apostles, then our choice must fall on the unknown master who carved the great figures of founders in Naumburg cathedral. The classic sculptural style of the German Middle Ages found a distant echo in a painting of the age of the German Reformation.

The Heritage of German Sculpture

The fundamentally plastic conception of Dürer's figures facilitates their translation into terms of reality, thus giving rise to artistic impressions which are curiously full of contradictions. A figure like the 'Great Fortune', so earth-born and tangibly real, cannot, despite its allegorical significance, be relegated to the ideality of the realm of fantasy. On the other hand, for a whole series of 'ideal' figures, it has not yet been possible to find any interpretation from the world of the living. In a drawing dating from 1516 (L. 194, Frankfurt am Main) one male and four female figures, all nude, are inserting a candlestick into a socket. In a pen-drawing of 1515 (L. 195, Frankfurt am Main), in style closely related to the sketch just mentioned, we again find five nudes; two men are binding a third to a tree, like one of Michelangelo's fettered captives, while two women look on. There is also a third mysterious group of five—the five nude men in a drawing of 1526 (L. 875, Berlin). It is tempting to try to follow the train of thought which inspired these three drawings. For the last-named it has been suggested that it is a study for a Transfiguration or for a scene from the Last Judgement, and it has even been christened 'The Resurrected', although there is no trace of tombs. Or would it be more correct to call it 'The Rescued', that is to say, five men thanking God for their salvation? Erica Tietze-Conrat has drawn attention to the affinity between this group of five nudes and a group of men on a raft in an Italian engraving representing the Flood. The allegorical meaning of this group must remain doubtful, but from the point of view of form the interpretation seems clear. These nudes look like sketched 'bozzetti', like the experiments of a sculptor modelling with his pen the attitudes of standing and kneeling, bending and rising. This drawing from Dürer's last years might well be called his 'homage to Michelangelo', for it pays homage to the pure spirit of sculpture.

Plastic Fantasies

o

CHAPTER THIRTEEN

LIMITS OF ADMIRATION

WE cannot, and do not want to approve of every work by Dürer. We are separated from him by more than four hundred years. It is useless to detract from the value of the legitimate admiration which all feel for Dürer's masterpieces, by demanding that the same admiration should be felt for every engraving he made—after all, the real Dürer is not visible in every engraving. It is no disparagement of Dürer's greatness if we rely upon the divining rod of our feelings to tell us whether we are approaching a vein of gold, or whether we are passing over what, to us nowadays, is barren ground. True love is not blind.

It is not the frequent juxtaposition of the tranquil and the shrill, the clear and the glaring, the harsh and the uncouth, which imposes limits upon our admiration for Dürer; that, after all, is but an expression of vigour and closeness to life, an assertion of diligence, fidelity and sincerity, even though it may be expressed in the unwieldy language of an old Franconian workshop. We reach the limit when this bubbling vitality seems to be in danger of being suffocated by the blight of scholasticism, the dusty book-learning of abstractions, the fossilization of ornamentality.

What then, we must now ask, lies in the depressions between the lofty peaks of Dürer's greatest works? What did he produce in those dull hours which followed upon periods of high tension? Where were the reefs in the ocean of his creative activity? What forms—among so many which make so deep an appeal—are now meaningless? In which works is the fire of Dürer's conception extinguished by the cold wind of laborious invention and pure reason? It is not a question of forming, with meticulous or arrogant censoriousness, a museum of those works by Dürer which we do not like, but we must certainly endeavour to show, with the aid of a few examples, what it is that no longer appeals to us. Suppose, for example, that a document were to be found proving that the so-called Basle group of woodcuts—the illustrations for Terence, the 'Ritter vom Turn' (1493) and the 'Narrenschiff'—were really cut from drawings made by Dürer in his youthful days. Very well, this group would thereby be brought out of the twilight of stylistic criticism into the full light of historical theory. The controversy as to the name of the artist—or artists—would not, as Wölfflin feared it might, continue in saecula saeculorum, and we would have to fit these woodcuts in among Dürer's youthful works and assign them their place in the history of art. In actual fact, however, no such document has been found, and even if it were to be found, the legitimate place which these woodcuts would occupy in the history of Dürer's art would not entitle them to an equal place in our estimation. These woodcuts, around which a rampart of literature has been erected, would remain what they were before—questionable works of art, no matter how many proofs of their authenticity were available. They would add nothing essential to the picture of Dürer which we carry in our minds and which he himself planted there. Let us also leave it to those connoisseurs who can hear the grass of stylistic criticism growing, to settle among themselves whether Dürer collaborated or not in the execution of the group of pictures for the Darmstadt altar-piece (about 1493), or to what extent the scenes from the Passion in the Dresden altar-piece are the work of pupils following designs by Dürer. Even the centre panel of the Dresden altar-piece, the authenticity of which is somewhat unjustly doubted, is for some the most interesting picture of Dürer's youthful period and for others an indigestible fragment, a misunderstood Mantegna. Leaving aside the background, which has suffered damage, we have in this picture an excessively harsh Virgin adoring a rigid, doll-like Child, with tiny little angels swarming around her like buzzing wasps. The violent contrast between the tiny dimensions of the Child and angels and the frigid, towering figure of the Virgin makes it impossible to appreciate this painting, however much we would like to do so. 'Micromegaic' was the term which Goethe coined to denote this combination of the dwarfish and the gigantic.

Even among those works of Dürer the authenticity of which has never been doubted there are some which we must set aside, unless—which God Forbid!— only professional art historians are to be allowed to pass judgement on his pictures. There are examples of emptiness and mawkishness, while repugnant or slightly comic elements are not lacking. How little the St. John on the title-page of the 'Apocalipsis cum Figuris' (1511), who looks as if he were suffering from the morbid pessimism of a modern writer, has in common with the fiery young St. John of the following prints. The Gothic decorativeness of the attitude is often in contradiction with the spiritual situation or the bodily sufferings of the figure. The 'Man of Sorrow' (engraving of 1509), who opens the 'Little Passion', is holding the scourge with two fingers, the movement producing an effect of shivering rather than of pain. The 'Man of Sorrow' with outstretched arms (engraving of 1498–1500) depends for its vitality on the gesture, but the gesture does not live. The 'Salvator Mundi' (New York, Metropolitan Museum) is insupportably mawkish and the long-legged Lucretia (1518, Munich) is painfully tedious. Dürer's interest in freaks is understandable, it is a by-product of the passion for collecting and delight in the study of Nature; nevertheless we cannot help feeling repugnance when we see the head of a child with an old man's beard (Paris 1527).

Here, once again, we must be careful to avoid a misunderstanding. Availing himself of the right of an artist anxious to explore every aspect of life, Dürer in his Treatise on Proportion set out to show 'how one must depict beautiful and ugly things'. It is not the existence of ugliness in itself which arouses repugnance; ugliness can be the concomitant phenomenon assigned by God to the devilish and the sub-human, and there is also a form of ugliness which is allied with depth of character. Only eyes spoiled by the contemplation of smooth plaster casts of classical sculptures can be blind to the rugged formal harmonies of a naked woman's body such as that of the 'Great Fortune'. What is outside the scope of our admiration is what one might call the unnecessarily abnormal, the sheer abortion.

102

Meaningless Forms

110

In Dürer's work we find numerous forms which meant something only to him and to the men of his time, or which are so vociferous that they drown the gentle melodies of a pictorial subject. To the first group of forms which have lost their meaning belong the 'ideal' nudes. To understand the engraving of Adam and Eve (1504) in its full significance for Dürer's theoretical knowledge and practical ability, the spectator must be armed with a mass of knowledge of art history. And what is left of the large engraving of Hercules (1500), if we do not possess a thorough knowledge of the subject-matter and the previous ways in which it has been treated? The ordinary spectator shakes his head when he sees this nude giant gripping his cudgel as if it were a horizontal bar in a gymnasium. To the second category of over-vociferous forms belong the Late Gothic draperies. The surge of folds around the feet of the silent 'Virgin with the Pear' (engraving of 1511) seems, to our eyes, excessive, but to the eyes of Dürer's contemporaries it was impressive. In the 'Life of the Virgin', so dear to the German heart, the scene of the Presentation in the Temple is laid amidst a forest of pillars. In the left foreground one of the spectators is embracing one of the columns, as if, like Samson, he wanted to bring down the roof. One cannot explain to everyone who contemplates with amazement this print, his eye fluttering like a trapped bird from ceiling to floor and back again, what are the reasons underlying this spatial construction or why Dürer set his heart upon buildings such as these, which would make any architect shudder. Even if it were possible to expound the whole genesis of this woodcut, would that open the door to artistic appreciation, or, in other words, would it provide the link between picture and spectator?

Dürer's Meticulousness

We honour Dürer for his self-dissatisfaction, that keynote in his moral character, but we cannot ignore the fine lines of peevishness in his kindly countenance. His meticulous methods, which were an expression of this condition of soul, involve us in a labyrinth of lines, at the very moment when we want to travel far and wide on the wings of Dürer's fantasy. That this meticulousness and pedantic exactitude, this distortion and complication of form, have some of their roots in the goldsmith's workshop from which Dürer sprang, is something which we feel and know, but the impression it makes on us is that it is tinged with obstinacy amounting almost to faddishness. Figures can be found in Dürer's work which seem to have been drawn from jointed dolls hung around with clothes. That Dürer did actually use wooden puppets, is revealed by his Dresden sketch-book, as Weixlgärtner has convincingly proved.

German Renaissance Ornaments

And now for the world of pure form! Dürer's candlesticks and goblets, helmets and greaves, his bridles and coaches, his chairs! The debasement of the formal language of the German Renaissance by its degenerate successors in the nineteenth century has filled us with such aversion, that we are inclined to lay the blame on the innocent forefathers of these misshapen great-grandchildren of the Renaissance style. From the historical point of view that is wrong, but the instinct is right. No power of learned persuasion can induce the men of today to show enthusiasm for ornaments which met with general approval in Dürer's time. We heave a sigh of relief when Dürer abandons his imitations of Gothic or Italian ornaments, in order to devote himself, in godlike freedom and with delight in his Nordic heritage, to the play of line. After all, nobody expects us to admire the literary parallel to Renaissance ornamentation—sixteenth-century poetry—except perhaps for some hymn of Luther's which strikes a chord in our hearts.

We find not only extinct forms, but also extinct subjects—humanistic allegories, Renaissance heraldry and hieroglyphics are for us but empty shells. Even if we are attracted by something in Dürer's rendering of these materials, it is because his magic power could give a hint of animation to numbness, a spark of warmth to frigidity. Even his heraldic animals are temperamental. As a story, the 'Penance of St. Chrysostom' (engraving, about 1496–97) is a remote, almost grotesque episode; as an artistic phenomenon it is comprehensible to all. St. Mary Magdalen, the beautiful sinner, ascending naked to Heaven, a cloak of little angels round her shoulders (woodcut, about 1507–10), drawn on by heavenly harmonies, forms a euphonious whole which, because its beauty speaks for itself, needs no explanation of the iconographical and theological theme, despite the fact that it is a very unusual one. The subject is dead, but the form lives.

Meaningless Subjects

Evaluations of this kind are subjective and cannot be supported by proofs, but they have their justification, for behind them is that ultimate source of all artistic impressions—instinct. If the fantasy of the artist and the instinct of the art-lover did not form part of the realm of knowledge, it would be a bad thing for knowledge. These irrational forces are an integral part of the attitude of the German nation towards Dürer's art; it is this attitude which is important and all our considerations must be based upon it. We do not accept Dürer in the form in which timid and often mistaken scientific methods would like to present him to us; we create for ourselves the Dürer who is of use to us in our own lives. That is the man whom Robert Vischer compared to an eagle, when he spoke of the 'flaming eyes and rustling wings in his art'.

Instinct as Ultimate Source of Impressions

CHAPTER FOURTEEN

WITH COMPASS AND RULER

Importance of Dürer's Writings

IN the biography of an artist, the importance given to the various aspects of his work is really a difficult matter. A biographer wishing to compile a 'Goethe' after Goethe's own heart, would have to give pride of place to his treatise on optics, his osteological studies and the second part of 'Faust'. To write of Dürer from Dürer's own standpoint, would mean attaching the greatest importance to his scientific writings. Dürer took the greatest pains with his theoretical works; he devoted years to the study of perspective, proportion and an art of mensuration applicable to various fields, but did not succeed in presenting his thoughts in a conclusive and systematic form. Death plucked the pen from his hand, but the scientific writings which appeared during his lifetime and after his death aroused the admiration of his contemporaries. That a great artist should not be content with his supreme gift, but should try to get an insight into the scientific aspect of his activities, was something new for Northern Europe and worthy of the highest commendation! The numerous editions in various languages bear witness to the rapid dissemination of Dürer's writings throughout Europe. The Treatise on Proportion, for example, appeared in German in 1528; the Latin translation by Camerarius, which spread the fame of the book abroad, was published in 1532–34 and several times reprinted; in 1557 the Treatise appeared in French, in 1591 in Italian, in 1599 in Portuguese, in 1622 in Dutch and in 1660 in English. In his 'Art of Painting', published in 1649, the Spanish writer Francisco Pacheco quotes Dürer as an authority.

It would, however, be wrong to consider Dürer's writings through the eyes of the men of the sixteenth and seventeenth centuries. Every age has the right, or even the duty, to concentrate on those aspects of a great artistic personality which are of the greatest interest to it. But in Dürer's case, these are certainly not the scientific sides of his character. Dürer's writings are still important even for us, not on account of their often disputed and for Dürer himself not always clear conclusions, but because of what they reveal to us of Dürer's character. Through-

The Seeker after Truth

out his life Dürer was an ardent seeker after truth, a striver for knowledge. In 1512 he wrote: 'It has been instilled into us by Nature that we should wish to know much, that we may thereby perceive the real truth of all things.' Research was innate in Dürer. For him it was more than a noble occupation, more than a sublime pleasure; he looked upon it as a moral duty. That is the real point, and for the proper understanding of Dürer, what he eventually found is less important than the fact that he looked for it. His refusal to be satisfied, his eternal dissatisfaction with his own efforts, is part of Dürer's greatness. To him we could apply the words of Kleist: 'I love the man who strives to achieve the impossible.'

The importance of Dürer's writings is not affected by the fact that his doctrines cannot be reduced to conclusive and lasting formulae, expressing the substance of his theoretical system; this would, in any case, be impossible, simply because

Dürer thought differently about the same problems at different stages of his life. After all his meditation on the laws of art and Nature he came to the negative, but honourable conclusion that 'Such things I hold to be unfathomable'. Which is what Goethe felt when he spoke of 'silent veneration of the inscrutable'.

Theory and Practice

We cannot understand, or at all events we can only partially understand Dürer's books, if we see in him a philosopher or even an 'aesthete', instead of an artist. Dürer's theory and Dürer's practice acted and reacted on one another; his practical work influenced his thought, and his thought has a part in the variations of his modes of expression, of his 'style'. The stronger element, fed from deeper sources, was Dürer's creative power; theory came second. Apart from one or two attempts to transfer theory directly into his work, Dürer never subjected his art to any aesthetic dictates—not even to those of his own invention. He did not wish to set up a canon of beauty or to write a codex of art; he wanted only to be the interpreter of his own art. By using the empiricism of his life as a celebrated artist in order to obtain an insight into the principles underlying his work, he wanted to do something which had never been done in Germany before—'to our German young men I appeal alone'. All the knowledge acquired with such pains was to have been concentrated in one last great work—the 'Food for Young Painters'—and handed down as Dürer's legacy to those 'able young men who love such art more than silver and gold'. Jacopo de' Barbari never revealed the secrets of his atelier to Dürer, who craved to know them and valued them more highly than a kingdom. Jacopo kept his theory to himself, but Dürer considered it to be a moral obligation to bequeath his spiritual capital to the generations of artists who were to follow him.

Creative Genius and Passion for Knowledge

The premise of any evaluation of Dürer's importance as a theoretician is that we leave all prejudices at home, such as the romantic idea of an artist who, in order to create, has only to draw something out of the 'depths of his soul', or the belief that the old masters did not share the knowledge common to their time, or the error of thinking that creative genius and a passion for knowledge are incompatible in the same breast. One admission, however, must be made: anyone who peruses one of Dürer's books for the first time without being himself a theoretician, is bound to be deeply disappointed. He finds mathematics where he expected to find art; he sees a shadowy assembly of puppets, when he had hoped to peep into Dürer's sketchbooks. Heads and figures are inserted into intricate systems of lines, compass-strokes become constructional points, rectangles and circles are drawn in. At one point it seems as if an architect had been drawing projections and elevations of human bodies; at another, as if a sculptor had constructed a truly 'cubic' figure out of so many cubes. Everywhere we look, we find Dürer approaching exuberant life 'with compass and ruler'.

116

Spiritual Urges

Every unprejudiced man will at once ask how these books originated, from what spiritual urges and as a result of what external impulses; how much of what at first seems to be a confusion of subjects is Dürer's own and how much he derived from elsewhere; and, finally, what is the spiritual link between all this effort and Dürer's art. We continually hear non-artists expressing astonishment because Dürer was not satisfied with being able to say anything he wanted in the language of art and to reproduce anything he saw, but was continually racking his brains in an effort to 'get behind' laws which he was already following by instinct. In short, we are continually faced with the question: Why was it the ambition of this great practician to become an equally great theoretician? To which Dürer, shaking his head, would have answered, that such a question was to him just as incomprehensible as if he were to be asked why he was religious. Because as a man and an artist he saw and thought beyond himself, because he was always seeking after the 'lasting thoughts' and endeavoured to preserve in concrete form what existed only as a transient apparition.

Genesis of the Books

Nowhere has Dürer left us any detailed account of the manner in which his books originated, but from time to time he lets drop a few hints from which we are able to reconstruct the history of his theoretical conceptions. In the course of frequent discussions on art with Pirckheimer, Dürer asked: 'Whether there are books still extant which instruct us on the construction of human limbs', and was told in reply that there had been such books, but 'they are no longer available— they have, alas!, been lost'. Whereupon Dürer set to work to discover for himself the secrets of measurements and numbers in Nature and art. He brought the results of his reflections and projections on the drawing-board to Pirckheimer, for the latter's consideration and suggestions, and Pirckheimer then advised him to publish his theory. Dürer hesitated to produce 'such a book of wonders', because he did not feel himself to be competent, and he looked around for learned men who might be able to advise him. 'But I found none who had described such things except a man called Jacobus, a good and amiable painter, born in Venice, who showed me a man and woman whom he had drawn from measurements.' But Jacopo de' Barbari would not explain his 'theory' to the German artist in detail. Owing to the 'lack of teachers' north of the Alps, the only course left open to Dürer was to study Vitruvius, 'who writes a little on the limbs of men', to read Pliny and to act on his own initiative. Dürer himself thus refers us to three sources—books, teachers, and his own atelier experience. To Dürer, godson of the publisher Koberger, books had been familiar since his childhood days and he had friends among the writers, printers, readers and collectors of books. Filled with an insatiable thirst for knowledge—and in that respect he was a true son of the Renaissance period—Dürer abandoned the habits of the book-shy craftsmen and adopted those of the book-worshipping scholars. Euclid and Vitruvius are the two classical writers whose authority Dürer repeatedly invokes. In 1505 Dürer purchased a Euclid in Venice and during his stay in Italy he must have studied it and discussed it with others. In October 1507 he writes to Pirckheimer that he is riding to Bologna 'concerning the art of secret perspective, which a man would fain teach me'. Geometrical problems in their application to painting tormented Dürer, who eagerly followed anybody who promised to give him a deeper insight into those atelier secrets so well known to the Italian artists. In 1524, when he was drafting his first books, Dürer again made enquiries concerning a German edition of Euclid. The demand for this mathematical bible of antiquity

Dürer's Sources

was then general; for instance, the parish priest of St. Johannis in Nuremberg, Johannes Werner, made a German translation of the elements of Euclid (the manuscript of which has been lost) for the edification of Sebald Beheim, the founder of bells and cannon. A halo of mystery also surrounded the name of Vitruvius, whose books were translated into German by Johann Petrejus of Nuremberg. When Dürer was in Aachen on his way to Flanders, he saw the ancient columns in the Minster, and noted in his diary with great satisfaction that they were strictly in accord with the precepts of Vitruvius. What Dürer owed, as regards book-knowledge, to the library of his friend Pirckheimer, cannot be established in detail, but it must certainly have been a great deal. He was acquainted with the theory of Pomponius Gauricus, of which Pirckheimer possessed a copy. It was more than an act of friendship when in 1507 Pirckheimer dedicated his translation of Theophrastus' 'Characteres Ethici' to Dürer, who borrowed from this book the idea of 'complexions', that is to say the relationship between temperament and external appearance (character and constitution). 'It is possible to make a portrait, from which Saturn or Venus looks out.'

Dürer had a rooted conviction that the Ancients held the key to the riddle of the formative laws of Nature and art and that the Italians had more or less mastered the problem, but kept their solution a jealous secret from the eyes of foreigners. One had, therefore, not only to read the writings of classical authors, but also to take advantage of every opportunity for learning more from Italians and in Italy. His link with the intellectual world beyond the Alps was to be the Italian painter Jacopo de' Barbari, also known as 'Jacob Walch' (= 'the foreigner'). Trained in the Venetian school of Vivarini, Jacopo was a versatile, but only second-rate artist. *Jacopo de' Barbari* His best, and best-known, picture is the signed still-life in the Ältere Pinakothek at Munich, painted in 1504 and showing a partridge, a pair of iron gauntlets and a crossbow bolt. When Dürer went to Venice in 1495, he found Jacopo there, already well known as an artist to other Italian artists in the city and also frequenting the society of the South German merchants. 'When I was still young and had never heard of these things' (the theory of proportion), writes Dürer, describing how Master Jacopo gave him certain mysterious hints. The acquaintanceship must have been resumed about 1500, when Jacopo, who in the meantime, probably thanks to the German colony in Venice, had been appointed the Emperor Maximilian's 'Conterfeter and Illuminist', was in Nuremberg. The clever and cultured Italian was passed on with recommendations from one princely court to another. Frederick the Wise entrusted him with works for Wittenberg, Torgau, Naumburg, Lochau and Weimar; Joachim of Brandenburg took him with him to Frankfurt an der Oder in 1507. One year later Jacopo accompanied Philip of Burgundy to the Netherlands, where he finally became court painter to the Regent Margaret. By the time Dürer visited Flanders, Jacopo was already dead. Dürer made one last attempt to get hold of his secret theory of measurements and numbers in the human body, when in 1521 he asked the Regent in Malines to present him with 'Master Jacob's little book'. But the Princess, as she explained to Dürer, had already promised the coveted sketchbook to her court artist, Barend van Orley.

Jacopo de' Barbari not only influenced Dürer's theoretical ideas, but also left traces of his influence in some of Dürer's practical work. One of the least pleasing of Dürer's works, the 'Salvator Mundi' in New York, reminds us of Jacopo's 'Christ Blessing' in Dresden, painted about the same time. Reciprocal influences are recognizable in the graphic art of the two artists, but it is not always clear who gave and who received. (Compare, for example, Jacopo's engraving of 'Fame and Victory' with Dürer's engraving of the 'Three Witches'; Jacopo's engraving of 'Apollo and Diana' with Dürer's engraving of the same subject, etc.).

Italian Literature

A number of books provided Dürer with a vague idea of what was going on in the artistic circles of the Italian Quattrocento, especially in the Academy of Florence, in the fields of aesthetics, the doctrine of art, astrology, medicine and philosophy. Marsilius Ficinus' correspondence with Giovanni Cavalcanti, Pico della Mirandola etc., was published by Dürer's godfather Koberger in 1497, and Ficinus' three books on healthy living were also known in Germany through translations. That the Florentine conception of melancholy and Saturn influenced Dürer's engraving of 'Melancolia' has already been mentioned, and Ficinus' macrobiotic theories also provided Dürer with ideas for his projected 'Food for Young Painters', in which he intended to deal not only with the education of the mind, but also with the hygienic aspect of an artist's life. If Dürer continually speaks of the 'arts and secrets' of Nature about which the ancient philosophers knew so much, he is thinking of that conception of Nature as the supreme artist which was discussed by Florentine scholars and artists, and was also known to Leonardo and to Leon Battista Alberti. A link between Italian and German Humanism was provided by a friend of Dürer, Pirckheimer and Melanchthon— I. Reuchlin, whose book, 'De Arte Cabbalistica', was published in 1517. Dürer's contact with the ideas of Alberti and Leonardo must have been indirect, perhaps through Luca Pacioli, for none of Alberti's works had been printed at that time. Some of his lesser works appeared in Basle after Dürer's death and Leonardo's brilliant conceptions in the fields of art and natural science lay hidden in his manuscripts. That copies of the treatise came into Dürer's hands is quite possible, for otherwise it would be difficult to explain certain similarities of wording in the works of Dürer and Leonardo. Drawings by Leonardo must certainly have been seen by Dürer in Italy, but it is curious that he mentions him by name as seldom as he does the greatest master of perspective of the time, Piero della Francesca. From all this material Dürer was able to form for himself an idea of the Italian doctrine of art—one aspect of which was the theory of proportion— based on the aesthetic conceptions of Antiquity and on the precise methods of natural science. He realized that here was a conception of 'art' far more comprehensive than the usage and practice of craftsmen, for it demanded a knowledge and representation of the visible world based on scientific foundations. It was Dürer's lofty ambition to do the same for Northern Europe by adopting the same means—humanistic scholarship (writings of classical authors), the exact sciences (compass and ruler) and his own experience of art and life.

The modern reader is naturally inclined to ask why Dürer chose to clothe his *Significance of Dimensions and Numbers* investigations in the thorny garb of mathematical textbooks. Dürer's age was the adolescence of mathematics in the North, the golden age of the exact sciences in the West. The idea that all secrets could be solved by means of numbers and the conviction that all things are subordinated to dimension and weight, had been part of the intellectual heritage of Europe since the days of Aristotle. The arts and crafts were also based on measurements. The 'Meistergesang' shows us to what extremes the worship of dimensions and numbers can lead. The astronomers and cosmographers relied on numbers and only the so-called 'divine arts'— theology and its worldly sister, metaphysics—were free from the tyranny of mensuration. But mathematics meant primarily theoretical and applied geometry. 'Through geometry thou canst prove much of thy work,' wrote Dürer in his book on human proportions, immediately after the famous sentence about wresting art from Nature. And it was in Nuremberg that the study of applied mathematics celebrated its greatest triumphs, with the creation of marvellous instruments for measuring time and space, such as the astronomical tables, quadrants, astrolabes, terrestrial and celestial charts. It was within the walls of Nuremberg that Martin Beheim in 1490 invented his 'orb', i.e. the first globe. Dürer's own house was a former home of astronomical science, for he purchased it from the astronomer Bernhard Walther, a pupil of the great Johann Müller Regiomontanus. Dürer associated with mathematically trained and inventive minds such as Celtis, Stabius, Heinfogel and Kratzer, who to him was 'in many things almost necessary and useful'. In 1515 he drew for Johann Stabius, from notes given to him by the astronomer Heinfogel, the northern and southern celestial spheres. The 'Stabian map of the world' (about 1515) is the first perspective *Ill. pp. 212–213* representation of the globe, and the drawing for it was made by Dürer. To Pirckheimer's edition of Ptolemy, published in 1525, Dürer contributed the folio with the armillary sphere. The expressive heads of the winds transform these scientific woodcuts into fanciful decorations in Dürer's best manner. The best example of the saturation even of philosophical meditations with mathematical symbols is the work of Nicolaus Cusanus, who wrote about the rotation of the earth and interspersed his descriptions of gyroscopic phenomena with profound philosophical observations. Before 1490 there appeared the 'Geometria Deutsch', a mathematical handbook, which provided Dürer with hints, e.g. for the construction of his profile heads by means of vertical and horizontal lines within a rectangle.

To the impulses which Dürer received from the Renaissance culture of the *Secrets of the Masons* Italians, was added the spiritual heritage of the secrets of the German masons and the methods employed in Nuremberg workshops. Dürer grew up in the spirit of Gothic draughtsmanship. In the goldsmiths' workshops and the masons' yards processes of drawing and calculating were handed down, for example, the principle of parallel projection, i.e. the obtaining of a ground-plan from two elevations, a process probably invented and developed in the masons' yards, which Dürer, as he himself says, borrowed from the practice of stonemasons. B. M. Roriczer's

STABIUS'S MAP OF THE WORLD (About 1515)

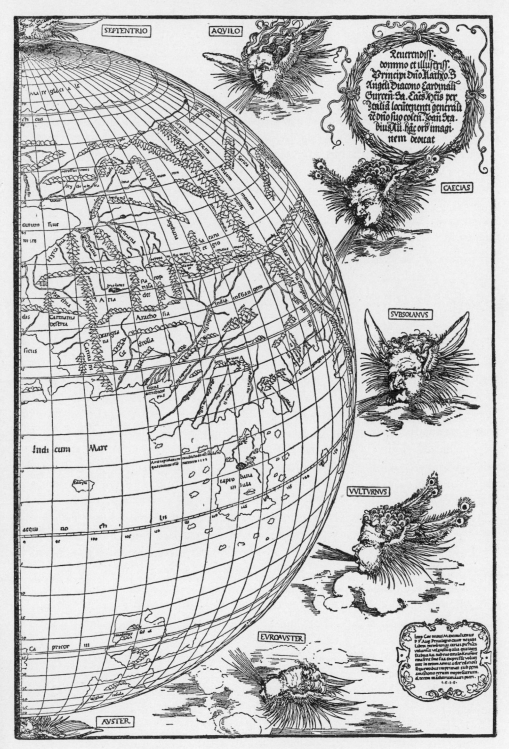

STABIUS'S MAP OF THE WORLD (About 1515)

'Büchlein von der Fialen Gerechtigkeit' (1486) handed on the draughtsman's technique of obtaining a plan by the combination of elevations. Italian and German ideas are mingled in Dürer's theoretical writings; the traditions of German masons and metal-workers are combined with the most modern methods of Renaissance painters and engineers.

Linguistic Expression

This intricate material, doubly complicated by the fusion of old with new, of his own ideas with those of others, was a severe test of Dürer's ability as a thinker. But the greatness of his achievement lies in the fact that he not only wrestled with ideas and moulded them, but gave them linguistic expression by coining German terms. The Italians had a much easier task, for they wrote in a highly-developed, pliant language and employed a terminology which had its roots in ancient tradition. They could also rely on their aesthetic ideas finding an echo among a wide circle of connoisseurs, artists, scholars, art-lovers and cultured dilettanti. But the situation was quite different in Germany and for Dürer. There was no public for books dealing with the theory of art; Dürer had to create his own public, and hoped to find it among the succeeding generations of artists for whom his works were primarily intended. There was virtually no language capable of conveying aesthetic ideas; this, too, had to be created, laboriously and after much struggling with words. For the Southern German in which Dürer had to express himself was a language still in process of formation—unwieldy, uncouth, intended and suited for quite different purposes. German was used for sermons, religious tracts and the formulation of laws, but the literary language, for secular purposes, was still in its infancy. The only classes who were masters of the written language were the clergy, the scholars and the functionaries of the chancelleries, joined, very gradually, by some burgher anxious to participate in the intellectual life of the nation. Dürer was the first German artist who—at a time when artistic form was at its zenith—endeavoured to liberate the form of the language from its mediaeval shackles. Here again, the important point is that he wanted and longed to do this.

During the years between his journey to the Netherlands and his death, Dürer tried to put into his scientific writings everything that he had been carrying in his head since his first journey to Italy. Three books were evolved, two of which were published in his lifetime. The first book bore the title: 'Treatise on Mensuration with the Compasses and Ruler in lines, planes and whole bodies, compiled by Albrecht Dürer and printed for the use of all lovers of art with appropriate figures in the year 1525.' This book, dedicated to his friend and counsellor Willibald Pirckheimer, was intended not only for painters, but also for goldsmiths, cabinet-makers, sculptors, stonemasons and other lovers of art. It deals mainly with the theoretical and practical problems of perspective in art.

Usage and Art

It need hardly be said that, even before his second journey to Italy and before he had read books on perspective, Dürer was capable of representing spatial depth according to the ordinary rules of drawing. As a pupil of Wolgemut, and by dint of constant practice, he had mastered the 'usage' of craftsmanship, but what he aspired to achieve was 'art', in the sense of theoretical knowledge of the customary methods of representing space. In the 'Life of the Virgin' there are prints which reveal pride in his 'perspective' ability and pleasure in its application—sometimes to the detriment of the narrative. The hall of the Temple in which Dürer places the scene of the 'Presentation' is one of these products of a journeyman's virtuosity. The linear construction of space and the spatial distribution in the 'Martyrdom of the 10,000 Christians' (1508) are quoted as exemplary models in the second edition (1509; first published in 1505) of the textbook written by Jean Pélerin (Viator), who explained how figures should be drawn on a surface receding into depth according to the visual theory of Democritus. Dürer, therefore, was not a follower of Viator, but vice versa.

68

For the scientific theory of perspective in art Dürer was indebted to other writers. First of all to Euclid, and secondly to Piero della Francesca, whose treatise, 'De Prospectiva Pingendi' was written between 1470 and 1490. Some of the statements of Euclid and Piero are reproduced by Dürer word for word. It has never been established whom Dürer meant when he spoke of going to Bologna to receive instruction in the 'secrets of perspective'. It is generally assumed that he meant Luca Pacioli, a pupil of Piero della Francesca, despite the fact that in 1506 Pacioli was not in Bologna, but in Florence. In any case Dürer brought home with him the mathematical explanation of what he had already learned by practice—the perspective system of representation, based on the idea of a cone of sight intersected by a transparent plane. It is characteristic of Dürer that he did not rest content with proofs based on numbers and diagrams, but, in order to illustrate the method and facilitate the transfer of the perspective image to paper, constructed instruments and showed the working of these by means of illustrations inserted in the text. Once again Dürer's Nuremberg ingenuity and delight in craftsmanship were asserting themselves.

Perspective in Art

The first woodcut shows the 'Draughtsman and the Seated Man'. Between the model—the seated man—and the artist's eye as it peers through an adjustable sight-vane, is a glass plate (the transparent plane intersecting the cone of vision). The artist draws the seen image with black chalk on the glass plate, whence it is subsequently transferred to paper. The second woodcut shows the 'Draughtsman and the Lute', and the apparatus has already become more complicated. The focusing eye is replaced by a ring let into the wall of the atelier, while the line of vision is represented by a thread running to a point on the lute which is being drawn. To keep the thread taut, a weight is attached to the extremity which passes through the ring on the wall, and at the other end the thread is fastened to a needle, which an assistant can move from one point of the model to another. On its way from the eye (the ring) to the object (the lute), the line of vision (the thread) passes through a frame, strung with threads to form a system of co-ordinates. The point at which the thread intersects the frame—indicated by the co-ordinates—is the position which the point the artist has just focused has to occupy in the pictorial plane. One point after another is thus transferred on to the sheet of drawing-paper hinged to the frame. The third instrument was, according to Dürer's own statement, invented by Jakob Keser. The 'Draughtsman and the

Dürer's Aids to Drawing

Ill. p. 226

Jug' shows the artist focusing the object through a sight-vane at the end of a thread, which is fastened at its other extremity to a ring in the wall, the point focused being marked on the glass plate. The fourth process is an improvement on the first. The draughtsman focuses the recumbent woman through a frame strung with threads, and the drawing-paper lying in front of him is also divided into squares, so that every point seen on the model can be marked on the paper in its proper square. These methods are not original inventions of Dürer's; the use of a frame strung with threads is mentioned by Alberti and glass plates were used in Lombardy about 1500. Both methods are described by Leonardo. On the other hand, the practical idea of substituting the ring in the wall for the eye and the taut thread for the line of sight, is Dürer's.

The Anatomical Problem
Representation of space signified the problem of perspective; representation of the nude was the 'anatomical problem', the second question to which Dürer devoted much time and trouble. Anatomy, like perspective, was part of the Italian theory of art. By means of dissection and the study of models, artists like Pollaiuolo and, in particular, Leonardo had laid the foundations of a systematic treatment of anatomical questions. In Germany it was not possible to learn anatomy by dissecting corpses and even the use of models for the study of the nude was hampered by strict regulations. Dürer's only recourse, therefore, was to train himself by copying Italian works. After Mantegna he drew the Bacchanal with Silenus (L. 454, Vienna, 1494) and the 'Battle of Tritons' (L. 455, Vienna); in 1495 he produced the fine drawing after Pollaiuolo (L. 347, Bayonne), which, as already mentioned, played a leading rôle in the history of the 'Hercules' engraving. Dürer must also have seen somewhere—perhaps in Jacopo de' Barbari's atelier— a sketch of the Belvedere Apollo, which was discovered during the papacy of Alexander VI.

Studies in Proportion
It is easy to understand how Dürer was intrigued by Jacopo de' Barbari's obscure hints, and perhaps also by some of his studies in proportion. They seemed to open the way to a purely constructive representation of the nude, by means of measurements and numbers, without the necessity of performing dissections or working with models. But Dürer soon realized that Jacopo's mysterious allusions were not leading him anywhere, and he turned to Vitruvius, who had laid down a canon for the representation of male figures. Following Vitruvius' directions as to measurements, Dürer produced drawings such as the recumbent woman (L. 466, Vienna), which some writers have tried to connect with the 'Sea-monster', the so-called Apollo or 'Sol' with the solar disk (L. 233, London), the nude man with serpent and glass (L. 181, Berlin), all between 1500 and 1501. These drawings are thus merely studies in proportion, which for no reason whatsoever have been given high-sounding archaeological titles (Aesculapius, Apollo, Sol). For twenty-seven years Dürer wrestled with these problems of form, before he was able to formulate the results of his studies in his great work. He probably read part of the proofs of his book, but did not live to see it published. 'Herein are comprised four Books of Human Proportion, devised by Albrecht Dürer of Nuremberg and described for the use of all those who bear love to this art.'

DÜRER'S HOUSE AT THE TIERGÄRTNERTOR, NUREMBERG.

DÜRER'S GRAVE IN THE ST. JOHANNIS CEMETERY, NUREMBERG.

Dürer starts from Vitruvian measurements and formulates his own theories of proportion; he begins with geometrical figures and goes on to arithmetical measurements. Both these methods, however, serve to determine only the chief points of the body, between which the outlines of the body can be freely drawn. On the basis of constructional sketches, Dürer presumably made actual drawings. His preparatory studies for the 1504 engraving of 'Adam and Eve', for example, are made up of a series of drawings, which in their turn are based on constructional sketches. To this 'Adam and Eve' group belong the prints of 'Eve' (L. 235, London, and L. 393, Oxford), the 'Man with a Club' (L. 351, Bayonne) and the 'Adam and Eve' (L. 173, New York). Between 1504 and 1513 Dürer made a whole series of studies in proportion, of which some are to be found in the Dresden sketchbook and all were preparatory studies for the great publication. The studies in male and female proportions (e.g. L. 475, Adam, Vienna; L. 476, Eve, Vienna) can also be grouped around the theme of 'Adam and Eve'. On the other hand, in 1506–07 he executed the two paintings of Adam and Eve (Madrid), which are undoubtedly 'ideal' figures and were undoubtedly painted under Venetian influence, but which, nevertheless, like the self-portrait in Munich, were created without the help of constructional sketches. Harmonious figures like those of Dürer, or of any other artist, can be made to fit in with constructional schemes, for no other reason than that their proportions are harmonious, but that does not prove that they were based on constructional sketches. A canon is an aid, but is not an indispensable premise for the creation of normal figures. 'When, through long counterfeiting, one knows all things by heart', one no longer needs compasses and ruler in order to construct a symmetrical body. However many years Dürer may have wrestled with problems of proportion, however much he may have meditated, written, calculated and drawn, there is not a single work by him, except the 1504 engraving of Adam and Eve, of which we can say with certainty that it was 'constructed'.

Let us turn now to the 'Treatise on Proportion'. It is a widespread notion among art critics that Dürer constructed 'ideal' figures, the principle, or rather the principles, of such constructions being developed in Dürer's treatise. All of which is true, but the error already lies in assuming that because Dürer in his treatise deals only with 'ideal' figures and their construction, we must conclude that these 'constructed' figures of normal human beings were the only figures which he considered 'beautiful'. Dürer's 'Treatise on Proportion' does not deal exclusively with 'ideal' figures; it deals with human proportions in general; it does not contain one obligatory standard, it contains a number of schemes of proportion. The assumption that the central problem, and therefore the essence of the book, is beauty, is false. The question of beauty is not the nucleus of the whole book; it is only a special instance which forms part of a far deeper problem, namely Nature's law of form—the organism as a work of art. Dürer—as Hans Kauffmann has noted with particular emphasis—was not an aesthete, he was a student of Nature; his aim was not stylistic, it was morphological. And lastly, it is also a misapprehension to believe that Dürer, with the help of his canon founded on mathematics,

Methods of Mensuration

107–10

108–9

111–2

110

The Laws of Nature

P

wanted to show how Nature ought to be. What Dürer wanted to show was what Nature is and how she creates, so that the artist may emulate Nature by working as Nature works; the artist must extract from Nature the law of form concealed within her; if he does that, then he has mastered art and his work of art will be an organism. 'I therefore hold that the more exactly a picture is made to resemble men, the better that work will be . . . But many are of another opinion and would tell us how men should be. I would not quarrel with them for that. But in this matter I hold that Nature is our teacher and that the fancies of men are foolishness. The Creator made men as they should be and I hold that the comely form and fairness are found in the multitude of all men. He who can draw that out rightly, him will I rather follow than one who would make a measurement of his own finding which some men have had.' Those who start from the false premise that Dürer, under the influence of the theoreticians of the Italian Renaissance, wanted to rationalize art, will find themselves confronted with an insuperable mass of contradictions in his book. Different methods run parallel or are intermingled; idealistic and naturalistic systems of thought intersect each other; there is no clear dividing line between calculation and free invention. If, on the other hand, we endeavour to consider his textbook from the standpoint of Dürer's reverence for Nature and his experience of life, then everything can be fitted together without undue effort, and apparent contradictions are reconciled into the uniformity of a profound conception of Nature.

Individual and Species   What Dürer asked himself was: How does Nature work? She creates an infinity of forms. No egg is exactly like another, and yet one egg is like another, in so far as it is also an egg. On the one hand we have an overwhelming multiplicity of individuals ('differentiable things'), on the other the relative similarity of species, by which the dissimilarity of individuals is limited, since the variable element here encounters a constant. These general laws of Nature are also applicable to human individuals and human types. Types can be differentiated, for example, according to age—old and young; according to sex—man and woman; according to race—white and black; according to station—peasant and nobleman; or according to temperament—melancholy and sanguine, and so on. Dürer starts from the basic truth that every form of existence, every human being, is a thing in itself, differing from all other beings, but that every individual has certain traits in common with others of its own kind—characteristics of sex, age, race, station or temperament. That which an individual has in common with other members of its species enables us to compare it with the rest of the species (comparison of the dissimilar), but that which belongs to the individual alone and makes it a 'differentiable thing', is the 'inversion' of similarity. This inversion, or deviation from the form of the species, can have varying degrees and can even reach the extremes of abnormality. Every living being is thus a variant of its species and therefore has a place, assigned to it by God, in the infinite succession of phenomena.

Comparableness and Inversion   Such were the two concepts which Dürer formulated in order to explain the formative law of Nature—the concept of 'comparableness' and the concept of 'inversion'. The 'comparableness' of the dissimilar is the constant, the 'inversion' of the similar is the variable element in the dual nature of every being. With the aid of comparableness, I can form individuals into pairs and groups, which, despite dissimilarities of their members, have a common element of similarity which makes them a uniform group. With the help of inversion, I can produce within a species the individual richness of life. There are, however, limits both to comparableness and to inversion. If, for example, the artist carries comparableness too far, his figures will resemble each other too closely; the characteristics of the species will be too strongly marked and the individual element will disappear. If, on the other hand, the artist exaggerates inversion, his group formation (composition) will be lost amidst inconsistencies and variations, or his figures will exceed the limits of the species, in which case he will create something which in Nature is impossible, a 'monstrosity' or a 'vision'. 'Let every man beware lest he make something impossible, which Nature cannot permit; unless he wish to create a vision, in which he may mingle all kinds of creatures (mingle the species). All things must rhyme alike.' That applies both to the great world of a species and to the little world of a human organism. There are many cubes, great and small, but each cube must have the characteristics of a cube, they must all 'rhyme'. There are many sorts of men—fat and thin, large and small—but they must all have the normal constructional characteristics of a man. Any 'lack of rhyme', e.g. a limp, 'is not beautiful'.

'All things must rhyme alike', including the proportions of the human body. *Constitution and Character* That is the only law of proportion which Dürer formulated—and followed. It is the law of Nature, which—expressed in modern language—makes constitution conform with character and does not place the head of a weakling on a robust body, or vice versa. The artist must therefore be careful not to make 'one part fat, the other lean, as if he were to make fat legs and thin arms . . . or fat before and lean behind . . . or the head of a youth, the breast of an old man, the hands and feet of a man of middle age'.

The constructional principles of Nature also serve as rules for artists. By using *Rules for Artists* 'inversion', i.e. variation, the artist ensures variety of life; by using comparableness, i.e. a constant, he achieves regularization amidst an immense variety of forms. The aim is always that everything should 'rhyme', which is also Nature's aim. For Dürer the approach imposed by the age in which he lived was through mathematics, first through geometry and then through arithmetic.

It is now clear why Dürer does not shrink from changing his methods in the *Choice of Types* course of his book. He does not lay down one standard type of 'ideal' human being, but inserts, for instance, five different types between the extremes of fat and thin men, finally leaving it to the artist to choose between types calculated according to the precepts of Vitruvius and those constructed according to Alberti. The important thing is that among the types chosen everything should 'rhyme', in other words should be in harmony. The various measurements which Dürer gives are possible, but not obligatory. The importance of mensuration lies in the fact that, without humanly possible measurements, an artist cannot create humanly possible men. A man who has the formative law of Nature in his blood, can derive from given figures new forms which are in accord with Nature. The question as to why Nature constructs forms according to the laws of variation and constancy, cannot be answered; it is one of God's secrets, one of those things which Dürer held to be 'unfathomable'. God put art (the law of construction) into Nature, but God also gave men of artistic talent the power to 'wrest' the hidden secrets of form from Nature. That is the meaning of Dürer's most frequently quoted saying: 'For in truth art lies hidden in Nature—he who can wrest it from her, possesses art.' Fr. Ottmann has drawn attention to a quotation from Paracelsus which is similar in metaphor and meaning: 'The divine lies hidden in man, like ore in a mountain, like the drug in a plant.'

*The Law of Beauty*Dürer's scientific thinking thus terminates on a note of deep piety, but of a piety which was of a virile and active kind. Dürer does not raise his hands in supplication to Heaven, begging for the gift of beauty; pious, but at the same time bold, he sets to work and wrests the law of beauty out of the depths of Nature.

*The 'Instruction on Fortification'*The 'Art of Mensuration' and the 'Treatise on Proportion' are linked by a whole series of similar points of view with the second of Dürer's books which appeared in his lifetime: the 'Instruction on the Fortification of Cities, Castles and Towns' (1527). In the first place, this work, devoted to questions of military technique and the building of towns, also endeavours to raise 'usage' to the level of 'art', by formulating a scientific theory of the art of fortification based on the practice of military engineers in Germany and Italy and on the crude methods of soldiers. Secondly, it, too, consists of a mixture of Dürer's own ideas and those he borrowed from others, while the limitations of Dürer's time are interspersed with brilliant anticipation of the future; like the other books it is a combination of German mediaeval tradition and the spiritual movement of the Italian Renaissance. In other words it is a synthesis of all available knowledge, supplemented by Dürer's own genius. Thirdly, in this work it was Dürer's aim to do for his own country what the Italians had done for theirs. In dealing with the theory of proportion, he modelled himself upon Alberti; his theory of fortification is inspired by Filarete, though the inventive head of Leonardo appears here and there in the background. In my book (1917) on Dürer's 'Instruction on Fortification' I traced the relationship between Dürer and his Italian predecessors and contemporaries. Fourthly, the 'Instruction on Fortification' is another child of Dürer's fantasy, subjected to the rules of mathematics and dealing with things which can be measured with compasses and ruler. In his other books Dürer meditated on the construction of 'ideal' men and animals; here he deals with the planning of ideal fortifications and ideal towns.

The Turkish Peril

*90*That a burgher of Nuremberg should think of fortifications, was only natural. Dürer grew up in a fortified city, dominated by a castle, surrounded by walls and moats. One of his best-known landscape water-colours (L. 103, Bremen) shows part of the mediaeval walls on the west side of the town. Outside the walls lay fortified villages (e.g. Heroldsberg and Kraftshof). With the development of firearms, the city walls began to lose some of their effectiveness. Greater protection against the fire of a besieging army became necessary and emplacements had to be constructed for the cannon of the defending forces, special attention being paid to the possibility of close-range fire and the enfilading of moats.

Such considerations were timely, for since the fall of Otranto in 1490, fear of the Turks had once more cast its shadow over Western Europe. Many Nuremberg families could still remember the eleven hundred Nurembergers who had gone to take part in the liberation of Belgrade by Janos Hunyadi, of whom only a fraction had returned to their Franconian homeland. It was doubtless the Turkish peril which induced Dürer to publish his book and to dedicate it to the grandson of Maximilian, King Ferdinand of Hungary and Bohemia, 'not only that a Christian may protect us from the others, but that the lands on the Turkish borders may be saved from their violence and bombardment'. Dürer was a good prophet—two years after his death Vienna was besieged by the Turks.

Contents of the Treatise on Fortification

Dürer's treatise on fortification covers four subjects. Firstly, three different technical methods of building a bastion ('Schütte'); secondly, the project of a blockhouse ('Klause'); thirdly, the planning of an ideal capital city; fourthly, suggestions for the strengthening of already existing fortifications. Within the framework of the fortification of a town and castle, Dürer develops his plans for the design of an ideal town, with exact instructions for its layout. In the investigation of each of these four questions Dürer, as usual, mixes reality with fancy, sober observation of facts with Utopian dreams. His designs for bastions are on a gigantic scale, without any consideration for the finances of cities or princes— 'for it is better that a ruler should spend much money and remain, than that in one year he should be overrun by his enemy and driven from his country'. The woodcuts in the book, which are in perfect harmony with the Gothic type, give

Bastions and Blockhouses

a very clear idea of the masonry of the bastions and their internal arrangements, e.g. access to the battlements, shafts for ventilation and for carrying away smoke, staircases and emplacements. Dürer's blockhouses are designed for the defence of mountain passes or positions between the sea and the mountains. One such blockhouse for coastal defence can be seen in the drawing in Milan (L. 876). The military interest of these lies in their circular plan, and Dürer speaks of them as 'round houses' or 'round castles'. These 'ideal' casemates are distinguished from the real strongholds (e.g. the 'Venedier Clause' at Arco, L. 303, Berlin) which Dürer saw on his first journey to Italy, by the more practical design for defence purposes and the greater attention paid to their internal layout.

Dürer's fortified town and castle is the first example of a German 'polygonal front', which he substitutes for the circular plan of his blockhouse. A defence regulation forbids the construction, within a radius of one (German) mile, of houses or any other form of cover which might interfere with the field of fire. The town is protected by a double ring of ramparts with a main ditch and secondary ditches. Battlements covering the main ditch, and defensive casemates covering the secondary ditches, provide for close-range defence. Dürer has thought of all the military exigencies—drill-grounds, stabling on the perimeter of the town, covered galleries in the bastions, city gates disposed in echelon, 'so that, if one should be lost in an assault, the others may remain secure'. Provision is also made for offensive action by preparing the terrain in front of the main ditch for sorties and break-throughs.

By far the most interesting and most original item in Dürer's book is, however, his scheme for the development of a town. The eastern corner ('A' in the illustration) of Dürer's ground-plan is the spiritual corner, accommodating the church, the sacristy, the vicarage with its courtyard and little garden—not forgetting even the pear-trees. The southern corner ('C') is occupied by four foundries—'they must lie here on account of the winds, for the most prevalent winds throughout the year, the North and West winds, and also the East wind, will drive the poisonous fumes (from the foundries) away from the castle and only the rare South wind will blow them towards it'. Dwellings for the coppersmiths, moulders, turners and other artisans were also to be in the vicinity of the foundries. Before one of the gates of the castle—on the East side—is the communal centre of the city, the market-place, the town hall with its courtyard and fountain—but without shops on the ground-floor! Dürer's father once sold his gold and silver ware in a shop on the ground-floor of the Nuremberg Rathaus. The blocks of houses abutting on the town hall are 'tenements' with courtyards. The south-west quarter of the town contains the great arsenals, with fireproof cellars, the granaries, timber-warehouses and houses for artisans. A men's bathing establishment lies opposite a bathing-place for women in one of the working-class quarters. The distribution of the various trades in certain quarters and streets is most carefully arranged; for example, the cartwrights live near the ramparts, 'so that they may lay their stakes and timber against the inner scarp'. The need to provide for the defence of the city in wartime dominates the whole plan. The northern corner ('D') is occupied by the emergency food depot—'in this building fats, salt, dried meats and other foodstuffs will be stored, and on floors beneath the roof, corn, oats, barley, wheat, millet, peas, linseed and other such things will be stowed'. These words remind us of the Nuremberg corn warehouse (the so-called 'Kaiser-stallung') built in 1499 within the castle walls and of the warehouses for meat and cereals in the town itself. The food industry is accommodated in the north-east corner of Dürer's 'ideal' town—butchers, bakers and brewers, close to the walls, 'so that they may have their cellars and taverns there'. The 'ideal' town thus bears a strong resemblance to a typical old Bavarian city! As for the artists—'the King's goldsmiths, painters, sculptors, silk-embroiderers and stonemasons' do not inhabit a colony of their own, but live among the rest of the craftsmen. According to the dimensions given by Dürer, the size of this 'ideal' city is slightly smaller than that of old Nuremberg, but in appearance it was to be very different from Dürer's native town.

As in his theory of art, so in his treatise on fortification, especially in that portion of it which deals with town-planning, there is a mingling of German-Gothic tradition and Italian neo-classical ideas. The regular layout is derived from the Roman 'castrum', and the hygienic conception also goes back to Antiquity, similar notions having been resuscitated by men of the Italian Renaissance, e.g. Alberti. Mediaeval, on the other hand, are the assignation of the trades to certain quarters and the creation of streets entirely reserved for craftsmen. Nuremberg is a picturesque labyrinth of winding lanes, but Dürer's ideal city has straight, broad roads, intersecting each other at right angles. Dürer's plan is his ideal, but he does not pretend that it is the only solution of the problem. He puts forward his ideas on military, hygienic and economic questions, but admits that other ideas on town-planning have an equal claim to recognition, just as, beside the 'ideal' men (Adam and Apollo) and 'ideal' women (Diana and Eve), other human beings of different proportions (e.g. the 'peasant' and 'nobleman' types) have an equal right to existence.

If we seek a parallel to Dürer's ideal town in the Germany of his time, our only possible choice is the celebrated 'Fuggerei' in Augsburg. In 1519 the sons of 'Jacob the Rich' began the building of fifty houses containing more than a hundred small dwellings. Today this settlement still looks like a fragment of Dürer's ideal town, and even the little fountains at the crossroads are not lacking. Dürer had close connections with the Fugger family. Before his second journey to Italy he negotiated with the Fuggers and may have been commissioned by them to paint the 'Festival of the Rose-garlands'. In 1518 he was in Augsburg again, and it is quite possible that, during the session of the Diet, the plan for the 'Fuggerei' was discussed between the artist and the great merchants. We know nothing of buildings erected by Dürer himself, but from a note in the diary of his journey to the Netherlands we learn that he once acted as architectural designer. For the Regent Margaret's physician, writes Dürer, he had to 'make a sketch of a house, after which he desired to build one'. When Dürer was asked to give an opinion on building projects at the monastery of Gnadenberg near Altdorf, he, a son of Nuremberg, that city of steep sloping roofs, advocated, for economic reasons, a flat roof (W. Funk).

The 'Fuggerei' in Augsburg

A number of prints and sketches may be grouped together with Dürer's treatise on fortification. Two siege scenes may be compared with each other—the drawing of the actual siege of Hohenasperg (L. 52, Berlin) and the large woodcut of the siege of an imaginary town (dating from 1527). Although he was present at the siege of Hohenasperg (May 1519), Dürer did not make his drawing until later, but his infallible memory enabled him to draw the fortress and the positions of the besieging army and artillery with historical exactitude. The woodcut of 1527, on the other hand, might well have served as an illustration to the treatise on fortification. It shows the siege of a mediaeval town, similar to Nuremberg, with towers, walls and gates. From these old-fashioned fortifications a bastion projects, corresponding to Dürer's designs and of fantastic dimensions. In front of the bastion is a deep and wide ditch, in which are little casemates, round and open at the top. The battery on the platform of the bastion is firing at the guns of the besieging army, which, partly in closed and partly in open formation, occupies the whole of the landscape as far as the baggage park and the herds of cattle, behind which villages are seen in flames. We read in one of the draft versions of the treatise on fortification—and the passage would seem to indicate that Dürer was thinking of his woodcut—the following words: 'Item, during the time in

Pictures of Sieges

which the bastion is offering violent resistance, the others should sally forth from the city from two sides, with firearms and good men and in good order, and should manfully endeavour to break through the enemy, or at least to hinder him in his assault.'

The etching of the 'Great Cannon' (1518), which has already been mentioned in connection with Dürer's landscapes, may likewise be classified among his military works. A Turk—copied by Dürer from figures of Gentile Bellini—probably conceived here as a prisoner of war, is standing in front of a Nuremberg culverin. Behind the Turk is a hussar carrying a satchel slung on his left hip, a forerunner of the modern hussar's sabretache. Nuremberg was famous for its cannon-founders, such as Sebald Beheim and Andreas Pegnitzer; the latter and his son produced cannon-royal, culverins, mortars etc. In 1516 Andreas Pegnitzer supplied Wladislaus von Sternberg, chancellor of Bohemia, with a great gun known as 'the Lion'. Lorenz Beheim was chief master of ordnance to Cardinal Rodrigo Borgia, who later became Pope Alexander VI. Since childhood Dürer had been familiar with all kinds of work in metal. During his travels, he visited not only goldsmiths—his artistic next-of-kin—but also gun-makers and cannon-founders. In the workshop of Hans Poppenreuter, gun-maker to Charles V in Malines, he saw 'wonderful things'; on the back of a sketch of a woman, he drew a mortar (L. 123, Bremen), which may possibly have been one of these 'wonderful things'. He includes a sketch of a cannon and its carriage in his treatise on fortification. 'Portraits' of cannon were no novelty in Italy and Germany. The Nuremberg painter Albrecht Glockendon, for example, made several for the 'arsenal books' compiled by order of the Emperor Maximilian. In the 'Triumphal Arch', the Emperor is seen sitting among his beloved cannon, for which learned scholars like Peutinger had to find names. There was a cannon-royal named 'Wake up'; field-guns were christened 'Leopard', 'Nightingale', 'Tickler' etc.

Art historians do wrong when they look down with a mixture of pity and contempt on the 'amateur' efforts of artists in the military field and consequently dismiss Dürer's treatise on fortification as a thing of scant importance. In writing this book and in taking an interest in the things with which it deals, Dürer was in very distinguished company—he was rivalling Leonardo and Michelangelo. Francisco de Holanda informs us that in 1530 Michelangelo said to him: 'When Pope Clement and the Spaniards laid siege to Florence, the enemy was held up for a long time by the machines which I had caused to be erected on the towers . . . which shows how painting can be used. It can be used for giving the proper form to engines and instruments of war, to bombards and arquebuses, it can be used for building bridges and fashioning scaling-ladders, and above all it can be used for the plans and proportions of fortifications, for ramparts, ditches, mines and counter-mines.' With those words Dürer would have heartily agreed. And there is also another point which should be remembered. Dürer's study of the theory of military architecture is a presage of a new development which was to appear in the period of German Baroque—military engineering as a basis of monumental architecture, with military engineers and artillery officers as masters of sacred and profane architecture (Speckle, Dientzenhofer, Balthasar Neumann, Knobelsdorff).

It is difficult to say to what degree Dürer's treatise on fortification had a direct influence on practice. Truth and fiction are here inextricably mingled. To Dürer's influence are ascribed the renovation of the Nuremberg fortifications near the castle, the Laufer Tor and the Schwabenberg, the reconstruction of the Spittlertor and the widening of the Wiener Graben. The author of a memorandum on the defences of Halle in the sixteenth century, the chief councillor Caspar Querhammer, was a follower of Dürer's doctrines and wanted to put them into practice, especially as regards the elimination of dead ground at points liable to be stormed, by means of Dürer's 'little casemates'. The new fortifications of Ingolstadt, built in 1539 by Reinhardt Graf zu Solms, with their earthworks and masonry bastions, were almost certainly influenced by Dürer's theories. In Schaffhausen between 1564 and 1582 the 'Unnot' was built, a two-storey circular erection on a hexagonal base, which looks like a realization of one of Dürer's 'round castles'. What Dürer had only dreamed of, was realized at the end of the sixteenth century by the great Strasbourg engineer, Daniel Speckle. In his 'Architecture of Fortifications', published in 1589, Speckle endeavours to free himself from the Italian theoreticians: 'Let them know that I will be bound by no rule, if I find and know something better.' And he did find something better.

Influence of Dürer's Treatise on Fortification

Three centuries after Dürer had written his treatise on fortification, modern writers on technical military subjects recognized its importance. The 'neo-Prussian' school, which began with the erection of fortifications on a large scale after the Napoleonic wars, returned to the ideas of Dürer. In 1867 Colmar von der Goltz, with all the authority of an expert, proclaimed that it was 'not until our own times that his fame was made known; he was too far in advance of his own times'.

The factual contents of Dürer's books and of his manuscript drafts for them (in London, Nuremberg and Dresden) are now out-of-date and of interest only to experts. But the personal element in his writings still remains as a living force. Dürer's legacy to the nation was the liberation of art from the shackles of 'usage' and the ennoblement of the artistic profession by giving it a share in the responsibility for cultural and political life. Dürer dragged the German artist out of the cosy atmosphere of his workshop into the bitter wind of contemporary events and into the rushing tide of the life of his time. To use Dürer's own words, he printed his books 'for the benefit of the common weal'.

Dürer's writings are textbooks in their form, but in their spirit they are personal manifestations. In the grandiose conception of these works and in their thoroughness, bordering almost upon meticulosity, we see the conscientious, tirelessly seeking man. Dürer was a modest man and a proud artist, a plain burgher, but conscious of being a German. His heart was in his homeland, but his spirit roved far afield. To understand the factual contents of his writings, we need much book-learning; to understand their inner meaning, we need only to know the character of Dürer. To this aspect of his work, too, we may apply the words which Goethe wrote in his 'Art and Antiquity on the Rhine and the Main': 'This admirable man can be explained from himself alone.'

Concerning his technical writings, Dürer once expressed the bold hope that, from what he had kindled, 'in the course of time a fire will arise which will shine throughout the world'. These words are not the expression of personal arrogance, but are inspired by the same feeling of patriotism which led Dürer to write at the end of the inscription on his 'Festival of the Rose-garlands' those three words— 'Albertus Dürer Germanus'.

THE DRAUGHTSMAN AND THE LUTE
(1525)

CHAPTER FIFTEEN

THE HERITAGE OF DÜRER

ALBRECHT DÜRER died, but German art did not die with him. It lived on, and assumed the heritage of Dürer. He bequeathed to it a wealth of pictorial motives, technical processes and theoretical ideas, but he also left something greater and far more important. His legacy was primarily of a moral kind. Thanks to Dürer, German painting and German graphic art once more became living ideas. The Nuremberg master raised German art to a high level in the eyes of the world. The social position of artists improved during his lifetime *Position of Art* and their efforts within the framework of national life achieved a new significance. *and Artists* Artists no longer sought protection beneath the mantle of the Church. Spiritually free and socially exalted, they allied themselves with a society which was breaking away from the old Church and with the powers of civilization. Painting, in particular, was raised by Dürer to a new level. He was always proud to describe himself as a painter. His 'Food for Young Painters' was conceived as a manual of instruction, and it was in a work of painting that he made the deepest confession of his ideals.

Dürer might well feel that he was the 'Praeceptor Germaniae'. But foreigners, *Dürer and* as well as Germans, benefited from his teaching, or covertly imitated him. The *Posterity* Mannheim exhibition of 1928, 'Dürer and Posterity', displayed the works of numerous imitators of Dürer, both German and foreign. Of those who were not in the real sense heirs of Dürer, but merely exploiters, parasites and plagiarists, we do not intend to speak here.

During the short space of a generation, in the thirty years which elapsed between Dürer's 'Apocalypse' and his death, there were many changes in the life and art of Europe. On the threshold of the century the Italian Renaissance had bestowed *The Italian* its gifts upon all. To the architects, and in an even greater degree to the stone- *Renaissance* masons, it gave the decorative forms of the 'antique' style; to sculptors it gave the ideal proportions of the human body, harmonious lines and tranquil gestures; to painters it gave a wealth of new subjects, deep harmony of colour, proved schemes of pictorial construction, and an all-pervading aroma of secularity.

Dürer paid two visits to Italy. In the home of the Renaissance—and probably in Germany as well—he saw and heard more of foreign methods than is generally supposed. Leonardo's scientific and artistic experiments made a deep impression on him and he was very close to Giovanni Bellini—his 'Festival of the Rose-garlands', his 'Virgin with the Goldfinch' and his 'Virgin and Child' (Collection *61* of Baron von Thyssen-Bornemisza) are proofs of this; as a portrait-painter he learned much from Giorgione and he understood Raphael—as witness his 'Adoration of the Trinity'. But the firmer the foothold the Renaissance gained in Germany, the more Dürer regained his freedom. He was still what Goethe called the 'wood-carved Dürer', his art was still full of German intricacies, of Gothic angularity and Nordic reverie. Dürer's 'Four Apostles' is one of his latest, *82-4*

and also one of his most German works. The fundamental questions which busied
Dürer were not questions of form, but questions of character. And he found the
answers to these questions not in the works of Renaissance artists, but in himself.

*Rôle of
Painting*

By the time Dürer closed his eyes, painting and graphic art had assumed in
Germany the leading position which had been held by sculpture before the
beginning of the century. It is symptomatic of the ascendancy of painting that the
creators of religious pictures no longer had to rely on the collaboration of wood-
carvers. The only carved frame which forms an integral part of an altar-piece by
Dürer, the frame of the 'Adoration of the Trinity', was designed by Dürer
himself (the architectural features are derived from memories of Padua; the 'Last
Judgement' reminds us of the portal of the church of St. Lorenz in Nuremberg).
In the 'Four Apostles' inscriptions take the place of a plastically expressive frame.
Grünewald's Isenheim altar-piece, on the other hand, with its symbiosis of
painting and wood-carving, still belongs to the Middle Ages. The powerful
impulses were given by painting, and primarily by Dürer himself.

*Nuremberg
Sculpture*

All around him, however, Dürer saw created a number of sculptural works
which remained as permanent features of Nuremberg and which are like mile-
stones on the path which the Renaissance took through Germany. Adam Krafft
had died in 1508. His tabernacle in St. Lorenz, begun in 1493 and finished in 1496,
is a work of architecture rather than a work of sculpture, a dream in stone rather
than an obelisk, and, intricate and German, belongs to the fifteenth century.
How often must Dürer have walked from the Tiergärtnertor to the cemetery of
St. Johannis, past the 'Seven Falls of Christ', which Adam Krafft graved on stone
plaques between 1505 and 1508 as Stations of the Cross. Krafft had the Renaissance
feeling for form in his blood; he did not deliberately acquire the spirit of the new
age—it was born in him.

In 1513, the same year in which Dürer made his engraving of 'The Knight,
Death and the Devil', there was created the most knightly of the heroic figures
for the tomb of the Emperor Maximilian in the Hofkirche at Innsbruck: Peter
Vischer the Elder's King Arthur. This master, with his family workshop, forsook
the sign of Late Gothic for that of the Renaissance. The transition can be traced
from the tomb of Archbishop Ernst in Magdeburg to the tomb of St. Sebaldus in
Nuremberg (1508–1519). That which, in Dürer's case, took place in the breast
of one man—the encounter between North and South—is found, in Peter Vischer's
case, in one work. The tomb of St. Sebaldus is one of the most remarkable
examples of the historical problem of 'Fathers and Sons'. In St. Lorenz, that hall
of fame of Nuremberg art, there had hung since 1517 the 'Annunciation' by Veit
Stoss. This carving in wood is an overgrown ornament, a gigantic toy of heraldic
decoration, similar to Dürer's coats of arms and ex-libris.

*Düreresque
Motives in
Sculpture*

Closer to Dürer's workshop are those works of sculpture of his own time which
blithely draw on his wealth of ideas. Hans Brüggemann, for example, for his
great altar-piece in Schleswig Cathedral, used motives from Dürer's 'Little
Passion'. For his epitaph in Eichstätt, Loy Hering adapted the 'Adoration of the
Magi' from Dürer's 'Life of the Virgin'. The little stone relief known as 'The

Garden of Love' (Berlin, Deutsches Museum) is full of reminiscences of Dürer; in it we find again the Eve of the 1504 engraving, the woman from the 'Sea-monster' and the 'Voluptas' from the engraving of Hercules. In a relief by Peter Vischer the Younger (Berlin, Deutsches Museum), we likewise find Dürer's Adam and Eve transformed, as regards both form and subject, into Orpheus and Eurydice.

Dürer never maintained a large workshop on the scale of those of Wolgemut and Cranach. Wolgemut lived until 1519, and Dürer painted him three years before his death. Although Dürer had at heart the education of his artistic successors, and although he felt himself to be the leader of a generation, he did not, and did not want to, produce a whole series of little Dürers. Nevertheless he had both a small and a larger circle of followers. Of Hans Dürer, about whom we know so little, one thing at least is certain—that he was taught by his brother. Dürer's contemporary, Hans von Kulmbach, is described by Neudörfer as an 'apprentice' of Dürer, and we can well believe this when we see Hans Süss von Kulmbach's pictures, and the design for the Tucher altar-piece in St. Sebaldus was made by Dürer. Wolf Traut's relationship to Dürer must have been similar (Artelshofen altar-piece of 1514, Munich, Bayrisches Nationalmuseum). *Dürer's Pupils*

The heirs to Dürer's art are to be found in a wider circle around his workshop. They worked further afield in Augsburg, Ulm, Ratisbon, Nördlingen, Strasbourg, etc., and Dürer's sphere of influence even extended beyond Southern Germany to Switzerland.

That Hans Leonhard Schäuffelein worked in Dürer's atelier is certain. His altar-piece in Ober-St. Veit (Vienna), dating from 1505–08, was probably painted from designs by Dürer and under the latter's supervision. In his mature works, however, he was influenced by the sculpture of Augsburg more than by the painting of Nuremberg (altar-piece of St. Sebastian, 1521, Nördlingen, Museum). Hans Burgkmair also worked in Augsburg, that gateway through which the Italian Renaissance penetrated into Germany. But the Italy which this generation of artists revered, was no longer Dürer's Italy. Neither Burgkmair, nor Jörg Breu, nor Christoph Amberger would have echoed Dürer's description of Giovanni Bellini as 'the best in painting'. For them, Venice was the city of Titian, Palma and Veronese. In Nuremberg they were beginning to know of Florentine painters such as Bronzino, as is revealed in the portraits of Georg Pencz. As an illustrator, painter and graphic artist, Burgkmair was one of Germany's greatest masters of ornament and splendour. He could do anything he chose, and he chose what his generation liked—decorative beauty after the Italian model. After Burgkmair, with his southern clarity, Dürer seems like a 'Magus of the North'. In the service of Maximilian, Dürer, Burgkmair, Schäuffelein and Cranach worked side by side. *Hans Burgkmair*

In 1531 Melanchthon named 'Dürer, Cranach and Matthias' (Grünewald?) as the foremost painters in Germany. Lucas Cranach the Elder was one year younger than Dürer and came from the Franconian-Saxon borderland. His contemporaries overrated him and posterity has underrated him, because the real Cranach was obscured by the mass of alleged Cranach pictures. The investigations of modern *Lucas Cranach the Elder* scholars have rescued the early pictures from the mass of workshop productions. In them, Cranach, with his sincerity and profundity, his independence and freshness, is a worthy rival of Dürer, i.e. of the Dürer of the 'Apocalypse', the 'Great Passion' and the 'Life of the Virgin'. In tune with the spiritual atmosphere of these works of Dürer's are Cranach's 'Rest on the Flight into Egypt' (Berlin, Deutsches Museum), painted in 1504, and the 'Crucifixion' of 1503 (Munich, Ältere Pinakothek). The naturalness and originality of these works soon disappeared amidst the large-scale production of pictures which followed upon Lucas Cranach's successes, after he was called to the court of Wittenberg. The early Cranach is charming, the later Cranach disappointing, except for his portraits—after all, it was he who painted Martin Luther!—and a group of small mythological allegories. In his 'Apollo and Diana' (1530, Berlin, Deutsches Museum) and his 'Judgement of Paris' (1530, Karlsruhe, Museum) and in other pictures, commonplace provincial whimsicality is combined with an almost refined eroticism, echoes of Late Gothic decorativeness with a classical tendency translated into contemporary Saxon terms. Whereas Dürer's genius soared higher and higher with every work and probed deeper and deeper, Cranach's brilliant talent declined after his early successes. He was inspired by Dürer, especially in his graphic art, and they worked together on the same important commissions, but of Dürer's heritage nothing was transmitted to Cranach.

What points of contact could Cranach and those others who were accustomed to living in the temperate zone of the soul, have with Dürer? For instance, with his 'Four Apostles' or his 'Melancolia'? It was easy to follow Dürer, but no one could be his successor. One man, Hans Baldung Grien, did try to keep close to the glowing and severe Dürer. Born, like Grünewald, on the classic soil of Alsace, he, too, knew the Isenheim altar-piece, and he may even have worked in Dürer's atelier. On his journey to the Netherlands Dürer took with him some prints by 'Grünhansen', in order to sell them, like his own, abroad. And after Dürer's death, Grien inherited a lock of the master's hair. Frau Agnes would hardly have entrusted this relic to one who was alien to the house and the heart of the dead master. Grien, the Böcklin of the sixteenth century, brought with him from Strasbourg fantasy, energy and vivacity. How close he was to Dürer, and also how far away from him, is shown if we compare, for example, his head of an old man (Berlin, Deutsches Museum; formerly attributed to Dürer) with Dürer's head of St. James, painted in 1516 (Florence, Uffizi). Grien painted a 'character-head', Dürer the head of a man full of character. Dürer depicted Death under many aspects and made his witches ride through the air. Hans Baldung Grien also experimented with these subjects. But Death as depicted by Dürer is more of a spectre than Grien's figures of Death; when we see Dürer's witches, we are prepared to believe that they could fly to the Brocken, but Grien's witches merely look as if they might be able to act as witches. The spirit of the age is certainly visible in both cases, but with what differences! Grien followed the spirit of his age, while Dürer rose above it. Behind his Knight we see the Devil, but there are no ghostly figures behind his Four Apostles. The powers of darkness

Hans Baldung Grien

dwell in the bosom of man; that is where they are to be found and to be over-come! It was the same path which Luther trod, who actually saw the Devil in the flesh and then fought against the Anti-Christ which every man carries in his breast.

In one field, however, which Dürer, the Christopher Columbus of German painting, discovered as a new world for art, in landscape, one of his followers took an independent path. We are not thinking of the landscape prints of Hirsch-vogel or Lautensack, but of Albrecht Altdorfer's landscape paintings. In his *Albrecht Altdorfer* 'Alexander's Battle' (1529, Munich, Ältere Pinakothek) Altdorfer contrives to express the heroic by means of the landscape. Dürer never saw this picture. In an Italian representation of a kindred theme, Piero della Francesca's 'Battle of Constantine' (Arezzo), it is a gesture which decides the outcome of the day; Constantine defies the armies of Maxentius with the sacred emblem of the Cross, and this gesture releases the magical powers which, like death-rays, compel the enemy to flee. Altdorfer—and in that, too, he is a man of the North—symbolizes the battle of nations by means of a conflict in the firmament. Above the Greek lines we see the rising sun, symbol of victory; above the Persian host, the moon's sickle, presage of defeat, is fading. To the groundwork of the Northern conception of Nature are added reminiscences of the 'unborn terrors' (Stefan George), of man's struggles against storms and mists, of the heart-rending loneliness of the sea and the mountains, and of the relief which the gentle dawning of the day brings with it.

But the dividing line, here so clearly marked, between German and Southern art does not coincide—and herein lies the tragedy of the artists who followed Dürer—with the geographical barrier of the Alps. On the contrary, it runs through the very heart of German art, one might almost say through the heart of every German artist of the sixteenth century.

On the boundary of the realm of colour Dürer called a halt. His colouring— *Dürer's Colour* much admired by the Italians and much criticized by the Germans—was that of the Late Gothic period, enriched by that of the Venetian school. For Dürer, colour was the bright garb of real things and he used colouring primarily to heighten the modelling of bodies. Only in some of his water-colours did Dürer go beyond the objective function of colour and cautiously open to it the gateway to the soul. Goethe has spoken of the 'sensual-moral effects' of colour, by which he meant the emphasis which colour can give to feeling. Colour, thus conceived and thus applied, can express something which line can neither add nor express at all. It engenders an urge towards the fanciful and a propensity to reverie; it is the magic means with which one of the greatest of German magicians, Matthias Grünewald, *Matthias Grünewald* dominated and inflamed the souls of men, but also corrupted them and led them astray.

We do not know what Dürer thought of his rival Grünewald. The inner conflict of the period, between the Middle Ages and the new era, between the Roman Catholic Church and the German Reformation, between an old order in process of dissolution and a new order in process of formation, is also visible in these two opposite poles of German painting—Dürer and Grünewald. At one point their paths seem to meet. Jakob Heller, who commissioned Dürer to paint the altar-piece of the Assumption of the Virgin, after the completion of this work about 1510, had two wing-panels added to it, on which Grünewald painted the figures of St. Cyriacus and St. Lawrence, grey on grey. Dürer's panel was destroyed by fire, as if Fate did not approve of this association between the two greatest geniuses of German painting.

Grünewald was incapable of being a fellow-traveller or a follower, he was the pupil of no one and was neither a predecessor nor an heir. He stands alone, without visible links with the past or with that which came after him. We can speak of 'Dürer and his times', but 'Grünewald and his times' would be a contradiction in terms. Fate did not withhold from this great solitary genius the laurels of fame, but it did deny him a place in the hearts of his fellow-countrymen.

Hans Holbein the Younger

Between Dürer and Hans Holbein the Younger lies the space of a generation. But in this short space of time the face of the German world had changed. The fervent piety, the life-blood of the Reformation, had been turned into frigid theology. The age of 'God-minded' men was past, and worldly spirits were now at the helm. The spirit of logic and the 'Ratio' of the Italian Renaissance entered into the spiritual domain no longer filled with sentiment and intuition. Holbein the Younger was not, like Dürer, a man after the pattern of Luther; he was of the type of Erasmus, cool, deliberate and neutral. From the very start he had mastered completely the new international language of art, but it must also be stressed that he spoke the idiom of the Renaissance with an unmistakable German accent. His coolness was not Italian, his sensitiveness to line was not a gift of the South. And is not Holbein's objectivity, on which so much of his fame rests, a truly German inheritance?

Holbein was homeless and yet at home wherever the highest achievements of art were esteemed. By birth a Swabian, he became an Aleman; born a German, he died in the service of England. Dürer remained to the end of his life a burgher of Nuremberg, but Holbein was a cosmopolitan. How characteristic it is of this impenetrable man that his most moving picture should be a picture of a dead man —the Body of Christ in the Tomb (1521, Basle). And at no time, either before or after, did Holbein ever surpass the poetical profundity of his 'Noli me tangere' (Hampton Court), in which he shows such perfect understanding for the repelling gesture of Christ—that 'touch me not' which was spoken from the very depths of his heart.

Imitators of Dürer

Even after the death of Holbein the Younger there was an abundance of artistic talent in Germany. Dürer's pupils, Hans Sebald Beham and Georg Pencz, lived until 1550. We must also remember H. Rottenhammer, Ch. Schwarz, J. Heintz the Elder, etc. All these were Germans who went on painting, but they were no longer German painters. Dürer's wish—'Would to God that I might live to see the works and art of the future great masters, of those yet to come!'—was not fulfilled. However long he had lived, his desire would not have been granted, for there were no great masters left in Germany.

The imitation of Dürer had its first renaissance about the end of the sixteenth and the beginning of the seventeenth centuries, in the works of the painter Hans Hoffmann and the goldsmith Hans Petzolt. But the spirit of Dürer was not born again. It seems like a gruesome allegory that Dürer's grave should have been *Dürer's Grave* 'cleared' after the extinction of the Frey family. In the earth which had received the mortal remains of Dürer, the Hospital of the Holy Ghost interred five prebendaries between 1653 and 1663. When, after thirty years of destruction of the nation's cultural and economic foundations, the conscience of Germany awoke again, the painter Joachim von Sandrardt, who was also the first art historian to write in German, acquired the site of Dürer's desecrated grave and bequeathed it to the Academy of Nuremberg. Germany was once more mindful of her 'great heroes and noble spirits'.

Q

THE HOLY TRINITY
(Woodcut, 1511)

THE PLATES

I
PORTRAITS

1. SELF-PORTRAIT OF DÜRER AS A 13-YEAR-OLD BOY. 1484. Silverpoint drawing. Vienna, Albertina.

2. THE ARTIST'S FATHER. 1497. London, National Gallery.

3. SELF-PORTRAIT. About 1492/93. Pen-drawing. Erlangen, University Library.

4. SELF-PORTRAIT. About 1493. Pen-drawing. Lwów, Ossolinski National Institute.

5. SELF-PORTRAIT. 1493. Paris, Louvre.

6. DÜRER'S WIFE AGNES. About 1495. Pen-drawing. Vienna, Albertina.

7. AGNES (?). About 1497. Silverpoint drawing on toned paper, heightened with white. Bremen, Kunsthalle.

8. SELF-PORTRAIT. 1498. Madrid, Prado.

9. TWO MUSICIANS (Self-portrait of Dürer as drummer?). Wing-panel of the Jabach Altar-piece.
About 1500. Cologne, Wallraf-Richartz Museum.

10. DÜRER AS A SICK MAN. About 1510. Pen-drawing and watercolours. Bremen, Kunsthalle.

11. SELF-PORTRAIT. 1500 (?). Munich, Ältere Pinakothek.

12. SELF-PORTRAIT OF DÜRER AND PORTRAIT OF WILLIBALD PIRCKHEIMER.
Detail from the Martyrdom of the ten thousand Christians. 1508. Vienna, Kunsthistorisches Museum.

13. DÜRER'S MOTHER. 1514. Charcoal drawing. Berlin, Kupferstichkabinett.

Das hat albrecht durer noch seiner hawssfrawen Contrafet zw antorff Jn der nidelend
kleidung Jm Jar 1521 do sy ameinander zw der e gehabt hettñ XXVIÿ Jor

14. AGNES DÜRER. 1521. Silverpoint drawing. Berlin, Kupferstichkabinett.

15. STUDY OF A NUDE (Self-portrait of Dürer). About 1507 (?). Pen and brush drawing.
Weimar, Schlossmuseum.

6. THE MAN OF SORROW (Self-portrait of Dürer?). 1522. Metal-pencil drawing on green paper. Bremen, Kunsthalle.

19. FELICITAS TUCHER. 1499. Weimar, Schlossmuseum.

18. HANS TUCHER. 1499. Weimar, Schlossmuseum.

20. ELSBETH TUCHER. 1499. Kassel, Gemäldegalerie.

21. YOUNG VENETIAN WOMAN. 1505. Vienna, Kunsthistorisches Museum.

22. PORTRAIT OF AN UNKNOWN MAN (the tailor Hans Dürer?). 1500. Munich, Ältere Pinakothek.

23. PORTRAIT OF A MAN (supposed self-portrait). 1505. Kremsier, Archiepiscopal Palace.

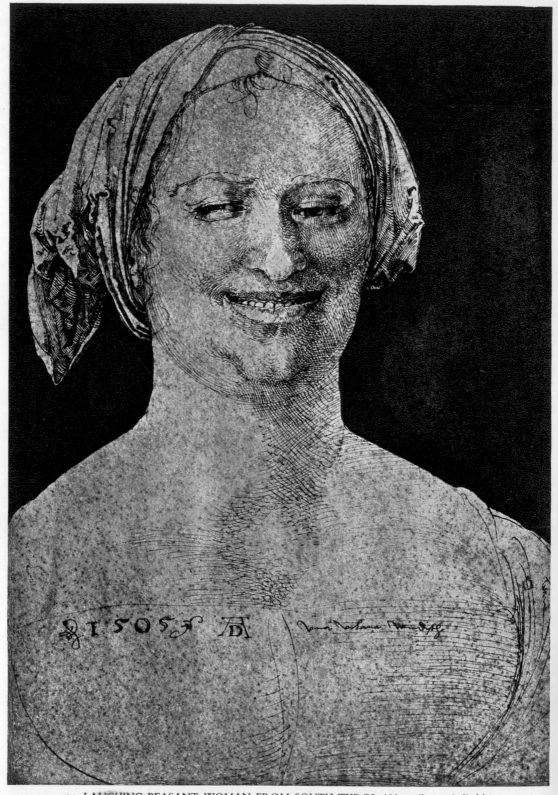

24. LAUGHING PEASANT WOMAN FROM SOUTH TYROL ('Una vilana windisch').
1505. Pen-drawing. London, British Museum.

25. PORTRAIT OF AN UNKNOWN WOMAN (Agnes Dürer?). Between 1500 and 1506 (?).
Water-colour on canvas. Paris, Bibliothèque Nationale.

BILIBALDI·PIRKEYMHERI·EFFIGIES
·AETATIS·SVAE·ANNO·L·III·
VIVITVR·INGENIO·CAETERA·MORTIS·
·ERVNT·
·M·D·XX·IV·

26. WILLIBALD PIRCKHEIMER. 1524. Copperplate engraving.

1503·

27. WILLIBALD PIRCKHEIMER. 1503. Charcoal drawing. Berlin, Kupferstichkabinett.

28. PORTRAIT OF A MAN. 1507. Vienna, Kunsthistorisches Museum.

29. PORTRAIT OF A GERMAN WOMAN FROM VENICE (Anna Dorssin?). About 1507. Oil colours on parchment. Berlin, Deutsches Museum.

30. LUCAS VAN LEYDEN. 1521(?). Silverpoint drawing. Lille, Musée Wicar.

31. PORTRAIT OF A MAN (Lucas van Leyden?). 1521 (?). Charcoal drawing. London, British Museum.

32. DÜRER'S BROTHER ANDREAS. 1514. Pen-drawing. Vienna, Albertina.

33. PORTRAIT OF A GIRL. 1515. Charcoal drawing. Berlin, Kupferstichkabinett.

34. DÜRER'S TEACHER, MICHAEL WOLGEMUT. 1516 (inscription 1519). Nuremberg, Germanisches Museum.

POTENTISSIMVS MAXIMVS ET INVICTISSIMVS CÆSAR MAXIMILIANVS
QVI CVNCTOS SVI TEMPORIS REGES ET PRINCIPES IVSTICIA PRVDENCIA
MAGNANIMITATE LIBERALITATE PRÆCIPVE VERO BELLICA LAVDE ET
ANIMI FORTIDVDINE SVPERAVIT NATVS EST ANNO SALVTIS HVMANÆ
M CCCC LIX DIE MARCII IX VIXIT ANNOS LIX MENSES IX DIES XXV
DECESSIT VERO ANNO M D XIX MENSIS IANVARII DIE XII QVEM DEVS
OPT MAX IN NVMERVM VIVENCIVM REFERRE VELIT

35. THE EMPEROR MAXIMILIAN. 1519. Vienna, Kunsthistorisches Museum.

36. MATTHÄUS LANG VON WELLENBURG, Archbishop of Salzburg. 1522. Pen-drawing. Vienna, Albertina.

1520

Erasmus von Rotterdam

37. ERASMUS OF ROTTERDAM. 1520. Charcoal drawing. Paris, Louvre.

38. AGNES DÜRER AND A GIRL FROM COLOGNE (from the Sketchbook of the Journey to the Netherlands). 1520. Silverpoint drawing. Vienna, Albertina.

39. CASPAR STURM (from the Sketchbook of the Journey to the Netherlands). 1520. Silverpoint drawing. Chantilly, Musée Condé.

40. HEAD OF A NEGRO. 1508. Charcoal drawing. Vienna, Albertina.

41. THE NEGRESS KATHARINA. 1521. Silverpoint drawing. Florence, Uffizi.

42. ALBRECHT OF BRANDENBURG, Archbishop of Mainz (The Great Cardinal)
1523. Copperplate engraving. Berlin, Kupferstichkabinett.

43. CARDINAL ALBRECHT OF BRANDENBURG. About 1518. Charcoal drawing. Vienna, Albertina.

44. THE ELECTOR FREDERICK THE WISE. 1522/23. Silverpoint drawing. Paris, École des Beaux-Arts.

· CHRISTO · SACRVM ·

ILLe·DEI·VERBO·MAGNA·PIETATE·FAVEBAT·
·PERPETVA·DIGNVS·POSTERITATE·COLI·

D·FRIDR·DVCI·SAXON·S·R·IMP·
ARCHIM·ELECTORI·
·ALBERTVS·DVRER·NVR·FACIEBAT·
·B·M·F·V·V·
·M·D·XXIIII·

45. FREDERICK THE WISE. 1524. Copperplate engraving.

46. BERNHARD VON RESTEN (?). 1521. Dresden, Gemäldegalerie.

47. PORTRAIT OF AN UNKNOWN MAN. 1524. Madrid, Prado.

48. EOBANUS HESSE. 1526. Silverpoint drawing. London, British Museum (Inscription not by Dürer).

49. JACOB MUFFEL. 1526. Berlin, Deutsches Museum.

50. PHILIPP MELANCHTHON. 1526. Copperplate engraving. Berlin, Kupferstichkabinett.

IMAGO · ERASMI · ROTERODA
MI · AB · ALBERTO · DVRERO · AD
VIVAM · EFFIGIEM · DELINIATA ·

ΤΗΝ · ΚΡΕΙΤΤΩ · ΤΑ · ΣΥΓΓΡΑΜ
ΜΑΤΑ · ΔΕΙΞΕΙ

· M D X X V I ·

51. ERASMUS OF ROTTERDAM. 1526. Copperplate engraving. Berlin, Kupferstichkabinett.

52. ULRICH STARCK. 1527. Chalk drawing. London, British Museum.

II
THE RELIGIOUS ASPECT

53. STEFAN PAUMGÄRTNER AS ST. GEORGE.
Wing panel of the so-called Paumgärtner Altar-piece.
About 1500. Munich, Ältere Pinakothek.

54. LUCAS PAUMGÄRTNER AS ST. EUSTACE.
Wing-panel of the so-called Paumgärtner Altar-piece.
About 1500. Munich, Ältere Pinakothek.

55. THE NATIVITY. Centre panel of the so-called Paumgärtner Altar-piece. About 1500. Munich, Ältere Pinakothek.

56. THE VIRGIN AND CHILD WITH ANIMALS. About 1505. Water-colour. Vienna, Albertina.

57. THE PRODIGAL SON. About 1498. Copperplate engraving.

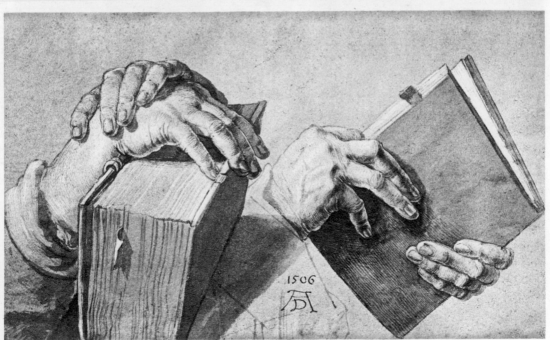

58–59. HAND STUDIES for the painting: The Young Jesus with the Doctors. 1506. Brush drawings.
Above: Vienna, Albertina. Below: Brunswick, Hausmann Collection.

60. THE YOUNG JESUS WITH THE DOCTORS. 1506. Rome, Galleria Barberini.

61. THE FESTIVAL OF THE ROSE-GARLANDS. 1506. Prague, Museum.

62. WORSHIPPER. Detail from the Festival of the Rose-garlands. 1506. Prague, Museum.

1506

63. THE ARCHITECT HIERONYMUS OF AUGSBURG. (?)   Study for the Festival of the Rose-garlands. 1506.
Brush drawing. Berlin, Kupferstichkabinett.

64. THE ASSUMPTION OF THE VIRGIN. Centre panel of the Heller Altar-piece. 1509. Copy of the burned original
Frankfurt am Main, Städtisches Museum.

65. HANDS OF AN APOSTLE. Study for the Heller Altar-piece. 1508. Brush drawing. Vienna, Albertina.

66. APOSTLE. Study for the Heller Altar-piece. 1508. Brush drawing. Vienna, Albertina.

67. APOSTLE. Study for the Heller Altar-piece. 1508. Brush drawing. Vienna, Albertina.

68. THE MARTYRDOM OF THE TEN THOUSAND CHRISTIANS BY ORDER OF KING SHAPUR OF PERSIA
1508. Vienna, Kunsthistorisches Museum.

69. ADORATION OF THE TRINITY. 1511. Vienna, Kunsthistorisches Museum.

70. DETAIL FROM THE ADORATION OF THE TRINITY: Moses and David.
1511. Vienna, Kunsthistorisches Museum.

71. DETAIL FROM THE ADORATION OF THE TRINITY. 1511. Vienna, Kunsthistorisches Museum.

72. THE VIRGIN SITTING BENEATH A TREE. About 1511. Pen-drawing. Berlin, Kupferstichkabinett.

73. VIRGIN AND CHILD. 1512. Vienna, Kunsthistorisches Museum.

74. CHRIST IN LIMBO. 1512. Copperplate engraving from the 'Little Passion'.

75. ST. JEROME IN HIS STUDY. 1514. Copperplate engraving.

76. ST. JEROME. 1521. Lisbon, National Museum.

77. HEAD OF AN OLD MAN. Study for 'St. Jerome'. 1521. Brush drawing. Vienna, Albertina.

78. STUDY FOR THE 'ST. JEROME'. 1521. Brush drawing. Vienna, Albertina.

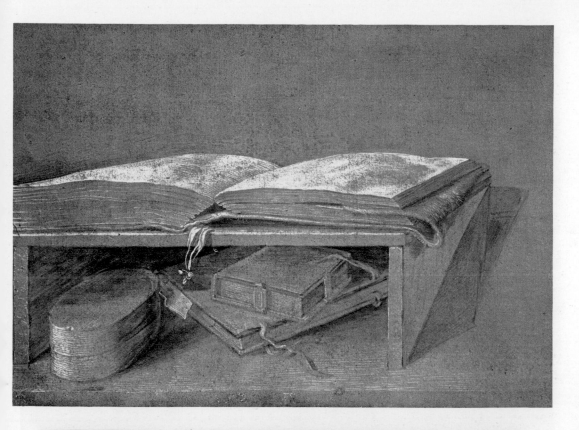

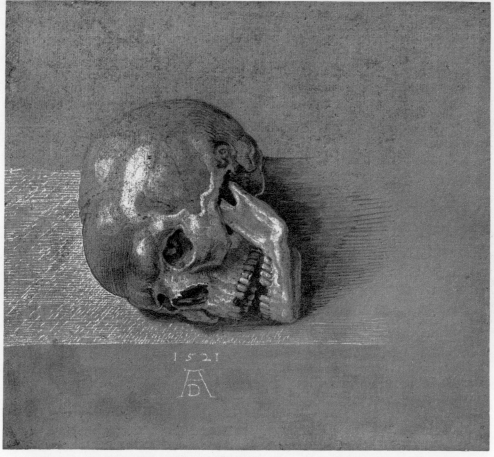

79 and 80. STUDIES FOR THE 'ST. JEROME'. 1521. Brush drawings. Vienna, Albertina.

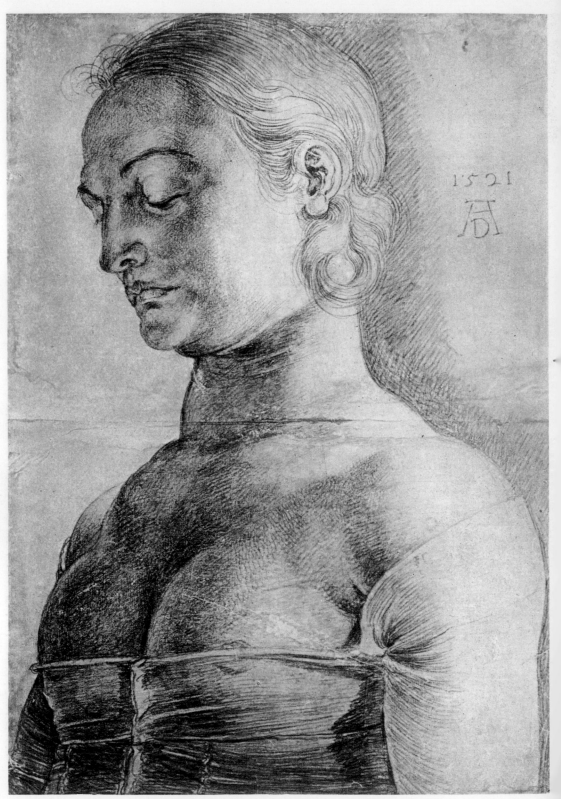

81. ST. APOLLONIA. 1521. Chalk drawing. Berlin, Kupferstichkabinett.

82 and 83. THE 'FOUR APOSTLES'. 1526. Munich, Ältere Pinakothek.

84. ST. PAUL AND ST. MARK. Detail of the 'Four Apostles'. 1526. Munich, Ältere Pinakothek.

III
LANDSCAPE

85. THE HOUSE BY THE POND. Between 1495 and 1497. Water-colour. London, British Museum.

86. THE VIRGIN WITH THE MONKEY. About 1497. Copperplate engraving. (In the background the House by the Pond.)

87. INNSBRUCK. 1494. Water-colour. Vienna, Albertina.

88. THE WIREDRAWING-MILL. About 1494. Water-colour. Berlin, Kupferstichkabinett.

NUREMBERG, WITH THE LITTLE CHURCH OF ST. JOHN. About 1494. Water-colour. Bremen. Kunsthalle.

90. NUREMBERG SEEN FROM THE WEST. About 1496. Water-colour. Bremen, Kunsthalle.

91. CASTLE ON A ROCK BY THE WATERSIDE. About 1501. Water-colour. Bremen, Kunsthalle.

92. PORTRAIT OF A MAN AND RHINE LANDSCAPE NEAR ANDERNACH (from the sketchbook of the Journey to the Netherlands). 1521. Silverpoint drawing, Berlin, Kupferstichkabinett.

93. THE MINSTER AT AACHEN (from the sketchbook of the Journey to the Netherlands). October 1520. Silverpoint drawing. London, British Museum.

94. THE SCHELDT GATE AT ANTWERP. 1520. Pen-drawing. Vienna, Albertina.

95. MOUNTAINOUS LANDSCAPE. Detail from the Self-Portrait in Madrid (plate 8). 1498.

IV
FANTASY

96. PUPILA AUGUSTA (from the Myth of Venus?). About 1496. Pen-drawing. Windsor Castle Library.

97. THE SEA-MONSTER. About 1500. Copperplate engraving.

99. THE WITCH. About 1500-1505.
Copperplate engraving.

98. 'DEATH' (The Incubus?). About 1493-1494.
Copperplate engraving.

100. 'KING DEATH ON HORSEBACK'. 1505. Charcoal drawing. London, British Museum.

101. HORSEMAN ASSAILED BY DEATH. 1497. Pen-drawing. Frankfurt am Main, Städelsches Kunstinstitut.

102. 'NEMESIS' (THE 'GREAT FORTUNE'). About 1500–1503. Copperplate engraving.

103. MELANCOLIA. 1514. Copperplate engraving.

104. DESPAIR. About 1516. Etching on iron.

105. DÜRER'S VISION. 1525. Watercolour with manuscript text. Vienna, Kunsthistorisches Museum.

V

THE HUMAN FORM

106. 'THE DOCTOR'S DREAM'. About 1497-1499. Copperplate engraving.

107. ADAM AND EVE. 1504. Pen-drawing. New York, Pierpont Morgan Library.

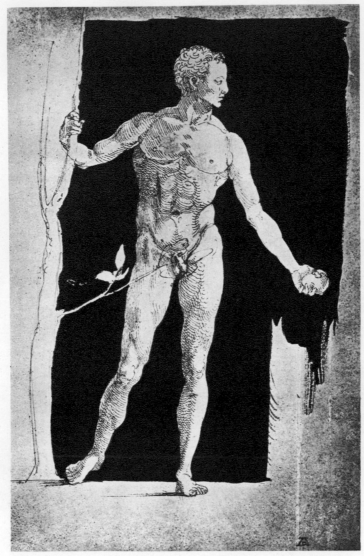

108. ADAM. 1506. Constructed figure. Pen-drawing. Vienna, Albertina.

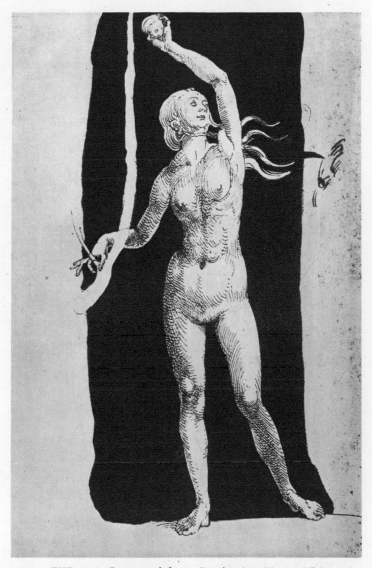

109. EVE. 1506. Constructed figure. Pen-drawing. Vienna, Albertina.

110. ADAM AND EVE. 1504. Copperplate engraving.

111 and 112. ADAM AND EVE. 1507. Madrid, Prado.

113. STUDY FOR THE ARM OF EVE (painting of 1507) Brush drawing.
Formerly Vienna, Albertina.

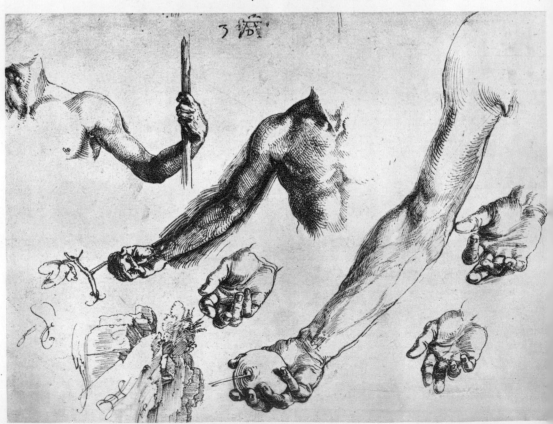

114. ARM STUDIES FOR ADAM (engraving of 1504.) Pen-drawing. London, British Museum.

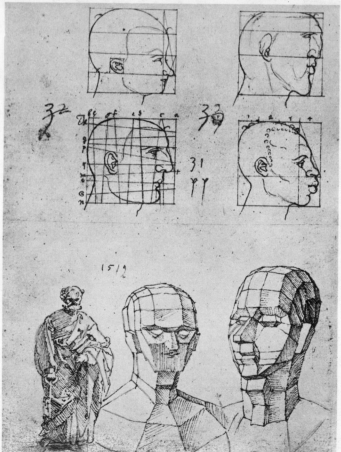

115 and 116. Above: STUDIES IN PHYSIOGNOMY. 1513. Pen-drawing.
Berlin, Kupferstichkabinett. Below: STUDY IN PROPORTION (from the
Dresden Sketchbook). Dresden, Sächsische Landesbibliothek.

117. THE WOMEN'S BATH. 1496. Pen-drawing. Bremen, Kunsthalle.

VI

PLANTS AND ANIMALS

118. THE LITTLE PIECE OF TURF. About 1502. Water-colour. Vienna, Albertina.

119. BUNCH OF VIOLETS. About 1502. Water-colour. Vienna, Albertina.

120. COLUMBINE. About 1502. Water-colour. Vienna, Albertina.

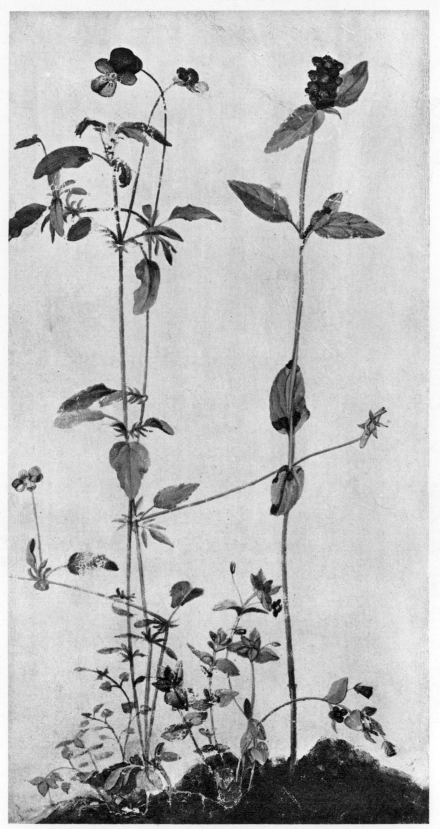

121. PLANT STUDY (VIPER'S BUGLOSS). 1496. Pen-drawing and water-colour.
Vienna, Albertina.

122. YOUNG HARE. 1502. Water-colour. Vienna, Albertina.

123. SQUIRRELS (by Dürer?). 1512. Painted in opaque colours. Berne, Mr. Ludwig Rosenthal.

124. ST. EUSTACE. About 1500–1503. Copperplate engraving.

125. THE KNIGHT, DEATH AND THE DEVIL. 1513. Copperplate engraving.

126. DANCE OF MONKEYS. 1523. Pen-drawing. Basle, Public Gallery.

VII
PEASANTS, BURGHERS AND SOLDIERS

127–130. Above, left: THE COOK AND HIS WIFE. 1497–1500. Copperplate engraving. — Above, right: PEASANTS AT THE MARKET. 1519. Copperplate engraving.—Below, left: GIRL ON HORSEBACK AND A LANSQUENET. About 1497–1500. Copperplate engraving. — Below, right: THE STANDARD-BEARER. About 1500–5. Copperplate engraving.

131–134. Above, left: PEASANTS DANCING. 1514. Copperplate engraving.–Above, right: THREE PEASANTS TALKING.
About 1497–1500. Copperplate engraving. — Below, left: THE PIPER. 1514. Copperplate engraving. — Below, right:
THE PEASANT AND HIS WIFE. About 1497–1500. Copperplate engraving.

135. VENETIAN LADY. 1495. Pen-drawing. Vienna, Albertina.

VIII

SERVICE AND FREEDOM

tia in labijs tuis. Responsori.
Propterea bñdirit te deus in
eternum. Pater noster. Et ne
nos. Benedictio. Precibus et
meritis:vt sequitur post.
Iste psalmus et alij duo se
quentes cum suis antiphonis
dicuntur diebus martis et ve
neris:antiphona Specie tua:
et pulchritudine. Psalmus.
Euctauit cor meũ ver
bum bonum:dico ego
opera mea regi.Lingua mea
calamus scribe: velociter scri

136. MARGINAL DRAWING FROM THE PRAYER-BOOK OF THE EMPEROR MAXIMILIAN.
Pen-drawing. 1515. Munich, Staatsbibliothek.

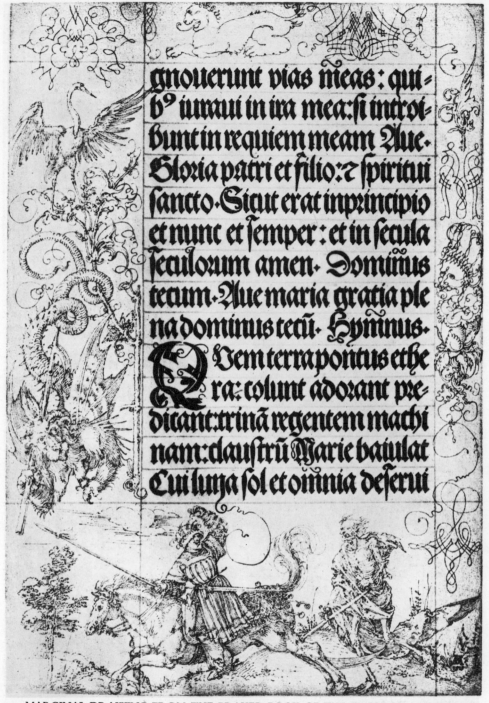

gnouerunt vias meas: qui
b⁹ iuraui in ira mea: si introi
bunt in requiem meam Aue.
Gloria patri et filio: z spiritui
sancto. Sicut erat inprincipio
et nunc et semper: et in secula
seculorum amen. Dominus
tecum. Aue maria gratia ple
na dominus tecu. Hymnus.
Quem terra pontus ethe
ra: colunt adorant pre
dicant: trina regentem machi
nam: claustru Marie baiulat
Cui luna sol et omnia deserui

137. MARGINAL DRAWING FROM THE PRAYER-BOOK OF THE EMPEROR MAXIMILIAN.
Pen-drawing. 1515. Munich, Staatsbibliothek.

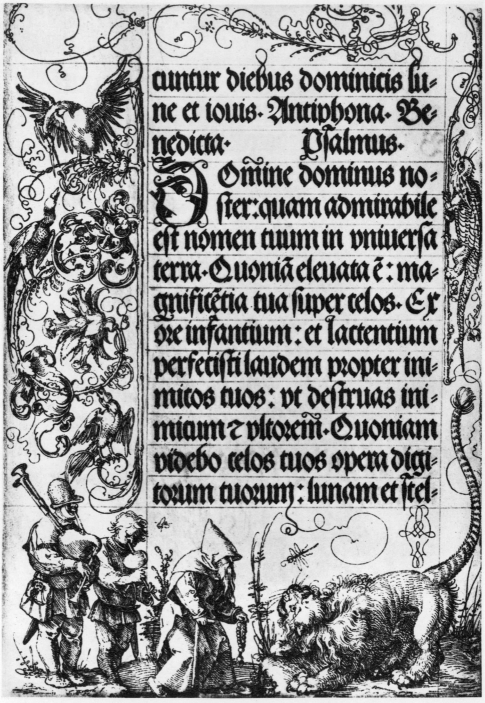

cuntur diebus dominicis lu-
ne et iouis. Antiphona. Be-
nedicta. Psalmus.
Omine dominus no-
ster:quam admirabile
est nomen tuum in vniuersa
terra. Quoniã eleuata ẽ: ma-
gnificẽtia tua super celos. Ex
ore infantium: et lactentium
perfecisti laudem propter ini-
micos tuos: vt destruas ini-
miaum ꝣ vltorem. Quoniam
videbo celos tuos opera digi-
torum tuorum: lunam et stel-

138. MARGINAL DRAWING FROM THE PRAYER-BOOK OF THE EMPEROR MAXIMILIAN.
Pen-drawing. 1515. Munich, Staatsbibliothek.

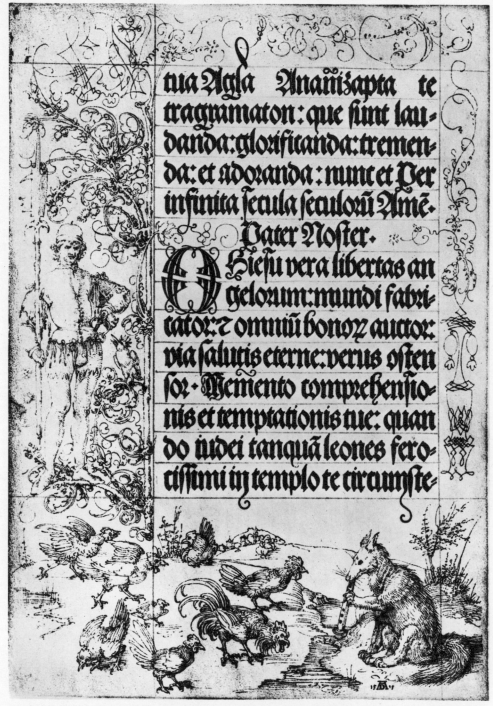

tua Agla Anani3apta te
tragramaton: que sint lau-
danda: glorificanda: tremen-
da: et adoranda: nunc et Per
infinita secula seculorū Amē.
Pater Noster.
O Iesu vera libertas an
gelorum: mundi fabri
cator: z omniū bonoz auctor:
via salutis eterne: verus osten
sor. Memento comprehensio
nis et temptationis tue: quan
do iudei tanquā leones fero
cissimi in templo te circumste

139. MARGINAL DRAWING FROM THE PRAYER-BOOK OF THE EMPEROR MAXIMILIAN.
Pen-drawing. 1515. Munich, Staatsbibliothek.

140. COAT OF ARMS WITH LION AND COCK. About 1503. Copperplate engraving.

141. THE TRIUMPHAL ARCH OF EMPEROR MAXIMILIAN. 1515. Woodcut.

142. THE SMALL TRIUMPHAL CAR. 1518. Pen-drawing. Vienna, Albertina.

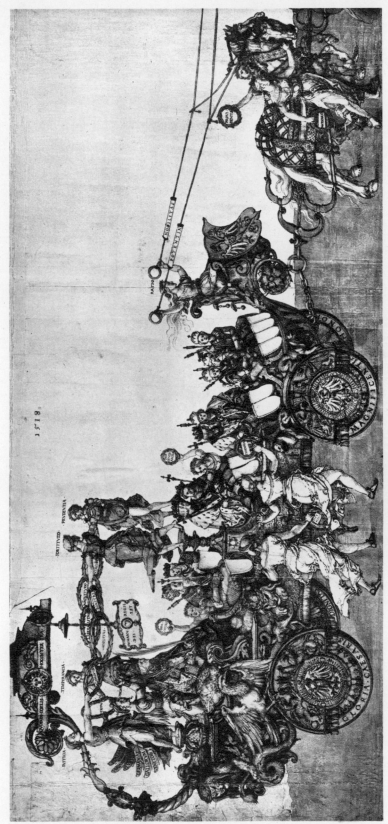

143. THE GREAT TRIUMPHAL CAR OF EMPEROR MAXIMILIAN (Left half). 1518. Pen-drawing and water-colour. Vienna, Albertina.

144. HORSEMAN WITH BOHEMIAN TROPHY. 1518. Pen-drawing. Vienna, Albertina.

IX
HANDICRAFT AND PLASTIC ART

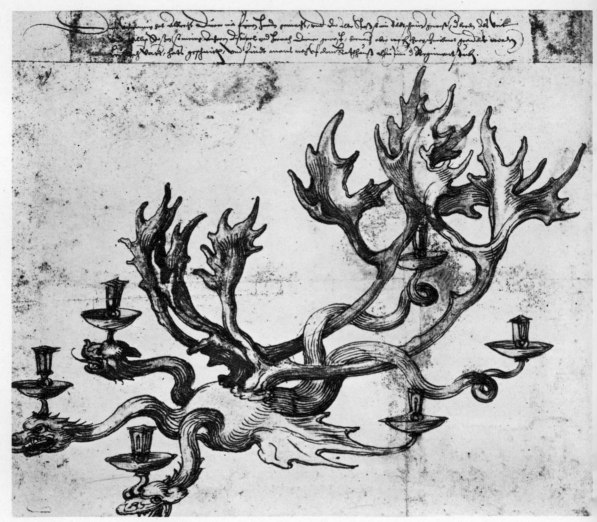

145. DESIGN FOR A CHANDELIER OF ANTLERS. About 1500. Pen-drawing. Constance, Wessenberg Gallery.

146. DESIGN FOR A CHANDELIER OF ANTLERS AND A NYMPH ('Leuchterweibchen'). 1513.
Water-colour drawing. Vienna, Kunsthistorisches Museum.

147–149. Above: DESIGNS FOR FOUNTAINS. 1527. Pen-drawing. Vienna, Kunsthistorisches Museum.
Below: DESIGNS FOR SIX GOBLETS. Pen-drawing. Dresden, Sächsische Landesbibliothek.

150. SHAFT OF A COLUMN WITH VINES. From the right centre column of the Triumphal Arch. Woodcut.

151. MEDALLIONS (supposedly designs by Dürer). So-called Pirckheimer, Agnes and Wolgemut. Berlin, Münzkabinett.

LIST OF TEXT ILLUSTRATIONS
LIST OF PLATES
LIST OF COLLECTIONS
INDEX

LIST OF WOODCUTS REPRODUCED
IN THE TEXT

LIST OF PLATES

1. *Self-portrait of Dürer as a 13-year-old Boy.* 1484. Silverpoint drawing. $10\frac{7}{8} \times 11\frac{5}{8}$ inches. Vienna, Albertina.
2. *Portrait of the Artist's Father.* 1497. On wood. 20×16 inches. London, National Gallery.
3. *Self-portrait.* About 1492–3. Pen–drawing. $11\frac{1}{2} \times 7\frac{7}{8}$ inches. Erlangen, University Library.
4. *Self-portrait.* About 1493. Pen–drawing. $10\frac{7}{8} \times 8\frac{5}{16}$ inches. Lwów, Ossolinski National Institute.
5. *Self-portrait.* 1493. On canvas, transferred from vellum. $22\frac{1}{4} \times 17\frac{1}{2}$ inches. Paris, Louvre.
6. *Dürer's Wife, Agnes.* About 1495. Pen–drawing. $6\frac{1}{8} \times 3\frac{7}{8}$ inches. Vienna, Albertina.
7. *Agnes* (?). About 1497. Silverpoint drawing on yellowish-grey paper, heightened with white brushwork. $8\frac{1}{2} \times 6\frac{1}{2}$ inches. Bremen, Kunsthalle.
8. *Self-portrait.* 1498. On wood. $20\frac{1}{2} \times 16\frac{1}{8}$ inches. Madrid, Prado.
9. *Two Musicians.* (Self-portrait of Dürer as drummer?) Wing-panel of the Jabach Altar-piece. About 1500. On wood. $37 \times 20\frac{1}{2}$ inches. Cologne, Wallraf-Richartz Museum.
10. *Dürer as a Sick Man.* About 1509. Pen–drawing, slightly heightened with water-colour. $5 \times 4\frac{5}{8}$ inches. Bremen, Kunsthalle.
11. *Self-portrait.* 1500(?). On wood. $25\frac{9}{16} \times 18\frac{7}{8}$ inches. Munich, Ältere Pinakothek.
12. *Self-portrait of Dürer and Portrait of Willibald Pirckheimer.* Detail from the Martyrdom of the 10,000 Christians. 1508. Vienna, Kunsthistorisches Museum.
13. *Dürer's Mother.* 1514. Charcoal drawing. $16\frac{9}{16} \times 11\frac{15}{16}$ inches. Berlin, Kupferstichkabinett.
14. *Agnes Dürer.* 1521. Grey metal pencil drawing on dark violet paper. $15\frac{7}{8} \times 10\frac{5}{8}$ inches. Berlin, Kupferstichkabinett.
15. *Study of a Nude* (Self-portrait of Dürer?). About 1507(?). Pen and brush drawing on green paper. $11\frac{1}{2} \times 6\frac{1}{16}$ inches. Weimar, Schlossmuseum.
16. *The Man of Sorrow* (Self-portrait?). 1522. Metal-pencil drawing on green paper. $16\frac{1}{16} \times 11\frac{7}{16}$ inches. Bremen, Kunsthalle.
17. *Oswalt Krell.* 1499. On wood. Centre panel $18\frac{7}{8} \times 15$ inches; width of the wing-panels $6\frac{5}{16}$ inches. Munich, Ältere Pinakothek. (With wing-panels, formerly in Germanisches Museum, Nuremberg.)
18. *Hans Tucher.* 1499. On wood. $11 \times 9\frac{7}{16}$ inches. Weimar, Schlossmuseum.
19. *Felicitas Tucher.* 1499. On wood. $11 \times 9\frac{7}{16}$ inches. Weimar, Schlossmuseum.
20. *Elsbeth Tucher.* 1499. On wood. $11 \times 8\frac{5}{8}$ inches. Kassel, Gemäldegalerie.
21. *Young Venetian Woman.* 1505. On wood. $13\frac{3}{4} \times 10\frac{1}{4}$ inches. Vienna, Kunsthistorisches Museum.
22. *Portrait of an Unknown Man* (the tailor, Hans Dürer?). 1500. On wood. $11\frac{7}{16} \times 10\frac{1}{4}$ inches. Munich, Ältere Pinakothek.
23. *Portrait of a Man* (by Dürer? Supposed self-portrait). 1505. Kremsier, Archiepiscopal Palace.
24. *Laughing Peasant Woman from South Tyrol* ('*Una Vilana Windisch*'). 1505. Pen-drawing and wash. London, British Museum.
25. *Portrait of an Unknown Woman* (Agnes Dürer?). Water-colour on canvas. $10\frac{1}{16} \times 8\frac{1}{2}$ inches. Paris, Bibliothèque Nationale. (Here shown correctly; in earlier reproductions, reversed.)
26. *Willibald Pirckheimer.* 1524. Copperplate engraving. $7\frac{1}{8} \times 4\frac{1}{2}$ inches.
27. *Willibald Pirckheimer.* 1503. Charcoal drawing. $11\frac{1}{8} \times 8\frac{3}{16}$ inches. Berlin, Kupferstichkabinett.
28. *Portrait of a Man.* 1507. On wood. $13\frac{3}{4} \times 11\frac{7}{16}$ inches. Vienna, Kunsthistorisches Museum.
29. *Portrait of a German Woman from Venice* (Anna Dorssin?). About 1507. Oil colours on parchment. $11\frac{3}{4} \times 7\frac{7}{8}$ inches. Berlin, Deutsches Museum.
30. *Lucas van Leyden.* 1521(?). Silverpoint drawing. $9\frac{3}{8} \times 6\frac{3}{4}$ inches. Lille, Musée Wicar.
31. *Portrait of a Man* (Lucas van Leyden?). About 1521(?). Charcoal drawing. $14\frac{7}{16} \times 10\frac{1}{8}$ inches. London, British Museum.

383

32. *Dürer's Brother, Andreas.* 1514. Pen-drawing, bistre. $11 \times 8\frac{9}{16}$ inches. Vienna, Albertina.

33. *Portrait of a Girl.* 1515. Charcoal drawing. $16\frac{5}{8} \times 11\frac{7}{16}$ inches. Berlin, Kupferstichkabinett.

34. *Dürer's Teacher, Michael Wolgemut.* 1516 (inscription 1519). On wood. $11\frac{7}{16} \times 10\frac{5}{8}$ inches. Nuremberg, Germanisches Museum.

35. *The Emperor Maximilian I.* 1519. On wood. $28\frac{3}{4} \times 24\frac{1}{4}$ inches. Vienna, Kunsthistorisches Museum.

36. *Cardinal Lang von Wellenburg.* 1522. Pen-drawing. $15\frac{1}{8} \times 10\frac{11}{16}$ inches. Vienna, Albertina.

37. *Erasmus of Rotterdam.* 1520. Charcoal drawing. $14\frac{11}{16} \times 10\frac{11}{16}$ inches. Paris, Louvre.

38. *Agnes Dürer and a Girl from Cologne* (from the Sketchbook of the Journey to the Netherlands). 1520. Silverpoint drawing. $5\frac{1}{16} \times 7\frac{1}{2}$ inches. Vienna, Albertina.

39. *Caspar Sturm* (from the Sketchbook of the Journey to the Netherlands). Silverpoint drawing. $5 \times 7\frac{7}{16}$ inches. Chantilly, Musée Condé.

40. *Head of a Negro.* 1508. Charcoal drawing. $12\frac{5}{8} \times 8\frac{9}{16}$ inches. Vienna, Albertina.

41. *The Negress Katharina.* 1521. Silverpoint drawing. $7\frac{7}{8} \times 5\frac{1}{2}$ inches. Florence, Uffizi.

42. *Albrecht of Brandenburg, Archbishop of Mainz* (the Great Cardinal). 1523. Copperplate engraving. $6\frac{7}{8} \times 4\frac{15}{16}$ inches.

43. *Cardinal Albrecht of Brandenburg.* About 1518. Charcoal drawing. $16\frac{13}{16} \times 9\frac{1}{8}$ inches. Vienna, Albertina.

44. *The Elector Frederick the Wise.* 1522-23. Silverpoint drawing. $7 \times 5\frac{7}{16}$ inches. Paris, École des Beaux-Arts.

45. *Frederick the Wise.* 1524. Copperplate engraving. $7\frac{3}{8} \times 4\frac{13}{16}$ inches.

46. *Bernhard von Resten* (?). 1521. $17\frac{15}{16} \times 12\frac{7}{16}$ inches. Dresden, Gemäldegalerie.

47. *Portrait of an Unknown Man.* 1524. On wood. $22\frac{1}{16} \times 14\frac{3}{16}$ inches. Madrid, Prado.

48. *Eobanus Hesse.* 1526. Silverpoint drawing on yellowish-white paper. $6\frac{5}{8} \times 4\frac{5}{8}$ inches. London, British Museum. (The inscription is not by Dürer.)

49. *Jacob Muffel.* 1526. On canvas, transferred from wood. $18\frac{7}{8} \times 14\frac{3}{16}$ inches. Berlin, Deutsches Museum.

50. *Philipp Melanchthon.* 1526. Copperplate engraving. $6\frac{7}{8} \times 5$ inches.

51. *Erasmus of Rotterdam.* 1526. Copperplate engraving. $9\frac{13}{16} \times 7\frac{5}{8}$ inches.

52. *Ulrich Starck.* 1527. Chalk drawing. $16\frac{1}{8} \times 11\frac{5}{8}$ inches. London, British Museum.

53. *The Paumgärtner Altar-piece.* Wing-panel: Stefan Paumgärtner as St. George. About 1500. On wood. $61\frac{13}{16} \times 24$ inches. Munich, Ältere Pinakothek.

54. *The Paumgärtner Altar-piece.* Wing-panel: Lucas Paumgärtner as St. Eustace. About 1500. On wood. $61\frac{13}{16} \times 24$ inches. Munich, Ältere Pinakothek.

55. *The Nativity.* Centre-panel of the so-called Paumgärtner Altar-piece. On wood. $61 \times 49\frac{5}{8}$ inches. About 1500. Munich, Ältere Pinakothek.

56. *The Virgin and Child with Animals.* 1505. Pen-drawing and water-colour. $12\frac{5}{8} \times 9\frac{9}{16}$ inches. Vienna, Albertina.

57. *The Prodigal Son.* About 1498. Copperplate engraving. $9\frac{3}{4} \times 7\frac{1}{2}$ inches.

58. *Hand Study* for the painting: The Young Jesus with the Doctors. 1506. Brush drawing in Indian ink, heightened with white, on blue paper. $7\frac{1}{2} \times 9\frac{7}{8}$ inches. Vienna, Albertina.

59. *Hand Studies* for the painting: The Young Jesus with the Doctors. 1506. Brush drawing in Indian ink, heightened with white, on blue paper. $9\frac{15}{16} \times 16\frac{7}{16}$ inches. Brunswick, Hausmann Collection.

60. *The Young Jesus with the Doctors.* 1506. On wood. $25\frac{1}{8} \times 31\frac{1}{2}$ inches. Rome, Galleria Barberini.

61. *The Festival of the Rose-garlands.* 1506. On wood. $63\frac{3}{4} \times 76\frac{9}{16}$ inches. Prague, Museum.

62. *Worshipper.* Detail from the Festival of the Rose-garlands. 1506. Prague, Museum.

63. *The Architect Hieronymus of Augsburg* (?). Study for the Festival of the Rose-garlands. 1506. Brush drawing on blue paper. $15\frac{1}{4} \times 10\frac{5}{16}$ inches. Berlin, Kupferstichkabinett.

64. *The Assumption of the Virgin.* Centre panel of the Heller Altar-piece. 1509. Copy of the original, destroyed by fire. $72\frac{7}{8} \times 53\frac{5}{16}$ inches. Frankfurt-am-Main, Städtisches Museum.

65. *Hands of an Apostle*. Study for the Heller Altar-piece. 1508. Brush drawing with white lights on dark ground. $11\frac{7}{16} \times 7\frac{3}{4}$ inches. Vienna, Albertina.

66. *Apostle*. Study for the Heller Altar-piece. 1508. Brush drawing in Indian ink, with white lights, on dark ground. $12\frac{7}{16} \times 9$ inches. Vienna, Albertina.

67. *Apostle*. Study for the Heller Altar-piece. 1508. Brush drawing in Indian ink, on green and pink paper, heightened with white. $12\frac{1}{2} \times 8\frac{5}{16}$ inches. Vienna, Albertina.

68. *Martyrdom of the 10,000 Christians by order of King Shapur of Persia*. 1508. On canvas, transferred from wood. $39 \times 34\frac{1}{4}$ inches. Vienna, Kunsthistorisches Museum.

69. *The Adoration of the Trinity* (All Saints). 1511. On wood. $56\frac{11}{16} \times 51\frac{9}{16}$ inches. Vienna, Kunsthistorisches Museum.

70–71. *Details from the 'Adoration of the Trinity'*. 1511. Vienna, Kunsthistorisches Museum.

72. *The Virgin sitting beneath a Tree*. About 1511. Pen-drawing in brown ink. $10\frac{7}{8} \times 8\frac{1}{8}$ inches. Berlin, Kupferstichkabinett.

73. *Virgin and Child*. 1512. On wood. $19\frac{5}{16} \times 14\frac{9}{16}$ inches. Vienna, Kunsthistorisches Museum.

74. *Christ in Limbo*. 1512. Copperplate engraving from the 'Little Passion'. $4\frac{9}{16} \times 2\frac{15}{16}$ inches.

75. *St. Jerome in his Study*. 1514. Copperplate engraving. $9\frac{3}{4} \times 7\frac{3}{8}$ inches.

76. *St. Jerome*. 1521. On wood. $23\frac{5}{8} \times 18\frac{7}{8}$ inches. Lisbon, National Museum.

77. *Head of an Old Man*. Study for the 'St. Jerome' of 1521. Brush drawing in Indian ink, with white lights, on dark paper. $19 \times 16\frac{1}{2}$ inches. Vienna, Albertina.

78. *Study for 'St. Jerome'*. 1521. Brush drawing in Indian ink, with white lights, on greyish-violet paper. $15\frac{9}{16} \times 11\frac{1}{2}$ inches. Vienna, Albertina.

79–80. *Studies for 'St. Jerome'*. 1521. Brush drawings in Indian ink, heightened with white, on greyish-violet paper. No. 79: $7\frac{13}{16} \times 11$ inches; No. 80: $7\frac{1}{8} \times 7\frac{9}{16}$ inches. Vienna, Albertina.

81. *St. Apollonia*. 1521. Chalk drawing on green paper. $16\frac{1}{4} \times 11\frac{7}{16}$ inches. Berlin, Kupferstich-kabinett.

82–83. *The 'Four Apostles'*. 1526. On wood. Each panel $80\frac{5}{16} \times 29\frac{1}{8}$ inches. Munich, Ältere Pinakothek.

84. *St. Paul and St. Mark*. Detail of the 'Four Apostles'. 1526. Munich, Ältere Pinakothek.

85. *The House by the Pond*. Between 1495 and 1497. Water- and opaque colour. $8\frac{3}{8} \times 8\frac{3}{4}$ inches. London, British Museum.

86. *The Virgin with the Monkey*. About 1497. Copperplate engraving. $7\frac{1}{2} \times 4\frac{7}{8}$ inches.

87. *Innsbruck*. 1494. Water-colour. $5 \times 7\frac{3}{8}$ inches. Vienna, Albertina.

88. *The Wiredrawing Mill*. About 1494. Water- and opaque colour. $11\frac{1}{4} \times 16\frac{3}{4}$ inches. Berlin, Kupferstichkabinett.

89. *Nuremberg with the little Church of St. John*. About 1494. Opaque colour. $11\frac{7}{16} \times 16\frac{5}{8}$ inches. Bremen, Kunsthalle.

90. *Nuremberg seen from the West*. About 1496. Water- and opaque colour. $6\frac{7}{16} \times 13\frac{9}{16}$ inches. Bremen, Kunsthalle.

91. *Castle on a Rock by the Waterside*. About 1501. Opaque colour. $6 \times 9\frac{13}{16}$ inches. Bremen, Kunsthalle.

92. *Portrait of a Man and Rhine Landscape near Andernach* (from the Sketchbook of the Journey to the Netherlands). 1521. Silverpoint drawing. $4\frac{3}{4} \times 6\frac{13}{16}$ inches. Berlin, Kupferstichkabinett.

93. *The Minster at Aachen* (from the Sketchbook of the Journey to the Netherlands). October, 1520. Silverpoint drawing. $4\frac{3}{4} \times 7$ inches. London, British Museum.

94. *The Scheldt Gate at Antwerp*. 1520. Pen-drawing. $8\frac{3}{8} \times 11\frac{1}{8}$ inches. Vienna, Albertina.

95. *Mountainous Landscape*. 1498. On wood. (Detail from the Self-portrait, Plate 8.) Madrid, Prado.

96. *'Pupila Augusta'* (from the Myth of Venus?). About 1496. Pen-drawing in ink. $9\frac{5}{8} \times 7\frac{5}{8}$ inches. Windsor Castle Library.

97. *The Sea-Monster*. About 1501. Copperplate engraving. $9\frac{11}{16} \times 7\frac{3}{16}$ inches.

98. *'Death'* (The Incubus?). About 1493–94. Copperplate engraving. $4\frac{4}{8} \times 4\frac{1}{8}$ inches.

99. *The Witch*. About 1500–05. Copperplate engraving. $4\frac{5}{8} \times 7\frac{1}{8}$ inches.

100. *King Death on Horseback*. 1505. Charcoal drawing. $8\frac{1}{4} \times 10\frac{1}{2}$ inches. London, British Museum.

101. *Horseman assailed by Death*. 1497. Pen-drawing. $9\frac{1}{2} \times 6\frac{5}{16}$ inches. Frankfurt-am-Main, Städelsches Kunstinstitut.

102. *'Nemesis'* (*The 'Great Fortune'*). About 1500–03. Copperplate engraving. $12\frac{15}{16} \times 8\frac{13}{16}$ inches.

103. *Melancolia*. 1514. Copperplate engraving. $9\frac{7}{16} \times 6\frac{5}{8}$ inches.

104. *Despair*. About 1516. Etching on iron. $7\frac{1}{4} \times 5\frac{5}{16}$ inches.

105. *Dürer's Vision*. 1525. Water-colour and manuscript. $11\frac{13}{16} \times 16\frac{3}{4}$ inches. Vienna, Kunsthistorisches Museum.

106. *'The Doctor's Dream.'* About 1497–99. Copperplate engraving. $7\frac{3}{8} \times 4\frac{11}{16}$ inches.

107. *Adam and Eve*. 1504. Pen-drawing and sepia, ground covered with brush colour. $9\frac{1}{2} \times 7\frac{7}{8}$ inches. New York, Pierpont Morgan Library.

108–109. *Adam and Eve*. 1506. Constructed figures. Pen-drawings, sepia, ground covered with brush colour. No. 108: $10\frac{7}{16} \times 6\frac{9}{16}$ inches; No. 109: $10\frac{5}{16} \times 6\frac{1}{2}$ inches. Vienna, Albertina.

110. *Adam and Eve*. 1504. Copperplate engraving. $9\frac{15}{16} \times 7\frac{5}{8}$ inches.

111–112. *Adam and Eve*. 1507. On wood. No. 111: $82\frac{1}{4} \times 31\frac{15}{16}$ inches; No. 112: $82\frac{1}{4} \times 32\frac{11}{16}$ inches. Madrid, Prado.

113. *Study for the Arm of Eve* (1507 painting). 1507. Brush drawing and wash, on blue paper. $13\frac{1}{4} \times 10\frac{9}{16}$ inches. Formerly Vienna, Albertina.

114. *Arm Studies for Adam* (engraving of 1504). Pen-drawing, two kinds of ink. $8\frac{1}{2} \times 10\frac{3}{4}$ inches. London, British Museum.

115. *Study in Physiognomy*. 1513. Pen-drawing. $40\frac{9}{16} \times 51\frac{9}{16}$ inches. Berlin, Kupferstichkabinett.

116. *Study in Proportion*. From the Dresden Sketchbook. Dresden, Sächsische Landesbibliothek.

117. *The Women's Bath*. 1496. Pen-drawing. $9\frac{1}{8} \times 8\frac{7}{8}$ inches. Bremen, Kunsthalle.

118. *The Little Piece of Turf*. About 1502. Water-colour on vellum. $4\frac{1}{2} \times 5\frac{3}{4}$ inches. Vienna, Albertina.

119. *Bunch of Violets*. About 1502. Water-colour on vellum. $4\frac{11}{16} \times 4\frac{1}{8}$ inches. Vienna, Albertina.

120. *Columbine*. About 1502. Painting in opaque colour. $14\frac{5}{8} \times 11\frac{1}{2}$ inches. Vienna, Albertina.

121. *Plant Study* (*Viper's Bugloss*). 1496. Painting in opaque colour on vellum. $11\frac{1}{2} \times 5\frac{7}{8}$ inches. Vienna, Albertina.

122. *Young Hare*. 1502. Water-colour and white opaque colour. $9\frac{7}{8} \times 8\frac{7}{8}$ inches. Vienna, Albertina.

123. *Squirrels*. (Supposedly by Dürer.) 1512. Painting in opaque colours. $8\frac{1}{2} \times 8\frac{5}{8}$? inches. Berne, Collection Ludwig Rosenthal.

124. *St. Eustace*. About 1500–03. Copperplate engraving. $14 \times 10\frac{3}{16}$ inches.

125. *The Knight, Death and the Devil*. 1513. Copperplate engraving. $9\frac{7}{8} \times 7\frac{1}{2}$ inches.

126. *Dance of Monkeys*. 1523. Pen-drawing. $11\frac{3}{4} \times 8\frac{7}{8}$ inches. Basle, Public Gallery.

127. *The Cook and his Wife*. 1497–1500. Copperplate engraving. $4\frac{3}{8} \times 2\frac{15}{16}$ inches.

128. *Peasants at the Market*. 1519. Copperplate engraving. $4\frac{9}{16} \times 2\frac{7}{8}$ inches.

129. *Girl on Horseback and a Lansquenet*. About 1497–1500. Copperplate engraving. $4\frac{1}{4} \times 3$ inches.

130. *The Standard-Bearer*. About 1500–05. Copperplate engraving. $4\frac{9}{16} \times 2\frac{13}{16}$ inches.

131. *Peasants Dancing*. 1514. Copperplate engraving. $4\frac{5}{8} \times 2\frac{15}{16}$ inches.

132. *Three Peasants Talking*. About 1497–1500. Copperplate engraving. $4\frac{5}{16} \times 3$ inches.

133. *The Piper*. 1514. Copperplate engraving. $4\frac{1}{8} \times 2\frac{15}{16}$ inches.

134. *The Peasant and his Wife*. About 1497–1500. Copperplate engraving. $4\frac{5}{16} \times 3$ inches.

135. *Venetian Lady*. 1495. Coloured pen-drawing and wash. $11\frac{7}{16} \times 6\frac{13}{16}$ inches. Vienna, Albertina.

136–139. *Marginal Drawings from the Prayer-book of the Emperor Maximilian*. 1515. Each page $10\frac{7}{8} \times 7\frac{3}{8}$ inches. Munich, Staatsbibliothek.

140. *Coat-of-Arms with Lion and Cock*. About 1503. Copperplate engraving. $7\frac{3}{8} \times 4\frac{13}{16}$ inches.

141. *The Triumphal Arch of the Emperor Maximilian*. 1515. Woodcut. $134\frac{1}{4} \times 115$ inches.

142. *The Small Triumphal Car*. 1518. Pen-drawing in brown ink. $6\frac{3}{8} \times 18\frac{3}{4}$ inches. Vienna, Albertina.

143. *The Great Triumphal Car of the Emperor Maximilian*. Left half. Pen-drawing and water-colour. 10 inches high; length of the whole drawing 181 inches. Vienna, Albertina.

144. *Horseman with Bohemian Trophy*. 1518. Pen-drawing and wash. $17\frac{1}{16} \times 12$ inches. Vienna, Albertina.

The painting reproduced on Plate 23 was first published by Otto Benesch, who suggested that it might be a self-portrait of Dürer. F. Winkler rejects this attribution and considers the painting a possible work of Hans von Kulmbach. The original has been damaged by fire. As it is very difficult to find reproductions of this interesting attribution, and as the original has now become inaccessible, the publishers have inserted a reproduction in order that this painting, which certainly merits discussion, may not fall into oblivion.

PHAIDON PRESS

LIST OF COLOUR PLATES

LIST OF COLLECTIONS

(The numbers refer to the Plates)

INDEX

THE SIXTH KNOT
(About 1507)